Resources for Teaching

THE STORY
AND ITS WRITER

An Introduction to Short Fiction

Fifth Edition

PREPARED BY

Ann Charters
University of Connecticut

Sam Charters

William E. Sheidley
University of Southern Colorado

D1403319

BEDFORD/ST. MARTIN'S   Boston   New York

Contents

Contents

STORIES

ABE AKIRA

Peaches (p. 9)

Abe (pronounced *Ah-bay*) presents the reader with the theme of his story in his second sentence: "... I am constantly being shocked anew at how outrageously deceptive memory is." Within a few more sentences, however, he seems to be so certain of the facts that he is relating and the story itself is so interesting that most readers will find they quickly forget that he has already told them not to trust memory at all. As he tells us about something that he isn't certain he remembers, he manages to tell us about many things that he does remember. He seems to "remember" everything else about his life. We learn about his father's career in the navy, his brother's mood when studying for a naval examination, conversations his mother had with a neighbor, stories that his mother told him, and the garden the family kept during the war.

"Peaches" is a story that examines memory. The author begins with something he has remembered all of his life, then he slowly deconstructs this memory, turning it inside out as he unravels its threads, only to find that they lead him into more uncertainty. Something happened, and it might have been something important, but he is never able to formulate clearly what it might have been. The heart of the story is the enigma of the last lines — a vision of himself as a boy, wheeling a baby carriage that holds himself as a baby. What he seems to be saying with this image is that by letting our lives be guided by our faulty memories, we become the creators of our selves, since our memories are within us. He is also perhaps suggesting, in the words of a well-known phrase, that "the child is father to the man."

The student will know from the headnote that Abe's father was a naval officer in World War II who never recovered from the shame of Japan's defeat. Most of the detail in the story, written in the tradition of the literary genre that the Japanese refer to as the I-novel, is autobiographical. As Abe looks closely at his memories of childhood, he encounters possibilities that suggest darker events. Perhaps his mother was bringing home black market goods, or perhaps the conversation he overheard between his mother and the landlord wasn't entirely innocent. There is also the terrifying memory of the night his father refused to forgive his mother for something that the author doesn't remember clearly. As Abe blunders into the dark side of his memory, he is reminding his reader that often there are moments we choose not to remember. He has created his story around something he remembered that might not have been true at all.

Questions for Discussion

1. Why might readers not automatically question the presence of peaches and frogs in the winter?
2. When the author decides that they couldn't possibly have been wheeling a load of peaches on a winter night, he says, "Nowadays, perhaps. But back then? Unthinkable." What does he mean?
3. What does he decide to change about his memory of the night in order to make his memory "consistent"?
4. Does this change achieve his object? How can the reader accept the idea of a "memory" that can be changed to suit a new idea?
5. Although the story is set in Japan, could it have just as well been set anywhere else? Why or why not?

Topics for Writing

1. A student could test the validity of a personal memory as Abe did with his memory, deciding whether he or she would agree with the author's opening statement that there is nothing more unreliable than memory.
2. CONNECTIONS   A student could compare Abe's "Peaches" with Borges's "The Garden of Forking Paths," which also has the uncertainty of memory as its subject.

Suggested Reading

Suzuki, Tomi. *Narrating the Self: Fictions of Japanese Modernity.* Stanford, CA: Stanford UP, 1996. Chapter "The Furor over the I-Novel: The Question of Authenticity." 48–65.

CHINUA ACHEBE

Civil Peace (p. 19)

Achebe narrates this story about the "civil peace" prevailing in war-torn Nigeria after the Biafran war with an ironic control that provides a strong contrast to the human suffering portrayed in the story. When the story opens, we learn that the protagonist, Jonathan Iwegbu, considers himself lucky to have survived the war with his wife and three of their four children. The terms of his survival, and the price he continues to pay for his own and his family's safekeeping despite the official end to the civil war, are dramatized in the events of the story.

Jonathan Iwegbu is an excellent example of what the critic Frank O'Connor called "the little Man" in short story literature, a figure projecting a distinctive aura of human dignity despite his all-too-apparent vulnerability and isolation. Like the clerk in Gogol's story "The Overcoat," Jonathan Iwegbu is tormented by the people around him (the soldiers who threaten to shoot up his house and force him to give up his money), yet his fundamental decency speaks so directly to us that we seem to hear him say, as in Gogol's story, "Why do you [bother] me? . . . I am your brother."

Questions for Discussion

1. Is "Civil Peace" a fully developed short story or an anecdote? What qualities in the narrative — characterization, setting, plot — lead you to your answer?
2. Explain the irony in the title of the story.
3. Jonathan Iwegbu acts as a self-reliant head of his family throughout the narrative. Why then does Achebe emphasize the "miracle" of his family's survival and the "monumental blessing" of his house's survival, and why does he repeat the phrase "nothing puzzles God" at the end of the story?

Topic for Writing

1. Translate into conventional English the words of the leader of the group who knocks on the door of Jonathan's house and demands money from him in the middle of the night. Analyze the dramatic effect of this dialogue as the climax of the story.

Related Commentary

Chinua Achebe, An Image of Africa: Conrad's "Heart of Darkness," p. 1411.

Suggested Readings

Achebe, Chinua. *Girls at War and Other Stories*. New York: Ballantine, 1973.
Chargois, J. A. *Two Views of Black Alienation: A Comparative Study of Chinua Achebe and Ralph Ellison*. Bloomington: Indiana UP, 1973.
Wren, R. W. *Achebe's World*. Washington, D.C.: Three Continents, 1980.

SHERMAN ALEXIE

The Lone Ranger and Tonto Fistfight in Heaven (p. 23)

Although students will have little difficulty understanding the content of Alexie's story, they may be unfamiliar with the reference of the story's title, which seems to have no immediate connection to the story itself. In the story there is no specific mention of the Lone Ranger or Tonto, and nothing about a fistfight, in heaven or on earth. Some students will be familiar with the fictional characters in the title, but there may be students who are not, since it has been many years since they were a ubiquitous presence in American popular culture.

The Lone Ranger was a member of the Texas Rangers, a law enforcement group that was instituted in the nineteenth century to bring justice to the wild Texas frontier. In the fictional story, a group of rangers riding in a deserted area were ambushed by bandits, and all but one of them was killed. The survivor, severely wounded, was found by an "Indian," Tonto, who nursed him back to health. Together they set out to find the killers, and then rode on together through a long career, bringing justice to the West in Saturday matinee film serials, books, comic books, radio programs, and television. The Lone Ranger wore a mask to protect his identity and fought his enemies with silver bullets. When they had accomplished their mission, he and Tonto would move on, always leaving behind one of the silver bullets as a sign to the people he had helped.

The characters have obvious connections to other figures of myth and legend, such as Robin Hood, who also reinforced the belief in the power of the lone individual to effect change in society. The role of the "Indian," who was usually played by a white actor in dark make-up, was secondary, even though Tonto saved the Lone Ranger's life again in several episodes. There was also a suggestion of the fictional characters Don Quixote and Sancho Panza in the Lone Ranger's idealism and in Tonto's dependent role. Despite their years together, Tonto never learned English, expressing himself in a kind of pidgin English dialect. With the title of the story Alexie seems to be telling the reader that the myth is dead, and with the death of the myth the natural antagonism between the white man and the Indian can now be openly expressed. Native Americans had long complained about Tonto's role as a virtual servant to the white ranger, and in the years when the figures became fixtures of popular culture there were already cynical jokes questioning the relationship.

As students read the story more closely, they will realize that on another level Alexie is suggesting that the fistfight between the Lone Ranger, who represents white society, and Tonto, who represents Indian society, reflects a deep conflict within himself. There is almost no plot to the story. The only thing that happens — and we don't learn about it until close to the end — is that the narrator receives a phone call from the white woman whom he once lived with, abused emotionally, and finally left in the middle of the night. The story is a series of remembered incidents through which he is made conscious of the conflict he feels between his Indian background and the white culture he has chosen to enter. By presenting the story as memory, he is able to introduce other elements that his memory dredges up — from failed treaties between the Indians and the whites, to memories of old basketball games, to his self-conscious description of his attempt to frighten the clerk of an all-night store. The reader is aware that Alexie himself was a good basketball player, and that he consciously participated in white culture on many levels, so the story has a strong element of autobiography.

Questions for Discussion

1. Is the title of the story meant seriously or ironically?
2. Why does the protagonist purposefully frighten the clerk of the 7-Eleven?
3. When he describes the clerk swallowing hard "like a white man does," is he suggesting that someone else — an African American or an Asian American — would not be frightened in the same situation?
4. In the italicized sentence beginning "We'll take Washington and Oregon," to what is the author referring? Is it a specific or a general reference?

5. When he describes three white soldiers playing polo with a dead Indian woman's head and compares this to the U.S. policy in Central America, what is he saying about America's treatment of other races and peoples?
6. When he says that his failure to do anything with his life is normal "for almost any other Indian in the country," is he speaking cynically or out of genuine despair?

Topics for Writing

1. Some critics have suggested that Alexie is making a career by manipulating white Americans' guilt over the destruction of the Native American peoples. Discuss this idea in terms of the actions of the protagonist in the story.
2. In the story, there are two examples of police mistrust of minority peoples. Have students discuss whether these are, or are not, valid descriptions of police attitudes.

Suggested Reading

Alexie, Sherman. *The Lone Ranger and Tonto Fistfight in Heaven.* New York: HarperCollins, 1994.

WOODY ALLEN

The Kugelmass Episode (p. 30)

Like most works of fiction based on impossible or unlikely suppositions, "The Kugelmass Episode" entertains us with the device on which it is grounded. Rather than developing the intellectual puzzles of science fiction, however, Allen mainly offers gently satiric jokes made possible by the incongruities arising from his donnée. When her class notices that on page 100 "a bald Jew is kissing Madame Bovary," the teacher in South Dakota, without consulting her desk copy, blames the problem on a mass-media stereotype, drug-crazed students; a professor at Stanford sees in the incredible instability of the text a confirmation of a mindless academic cliché: "Well, I guess the mark of a classic is that you can re-read it a thousand times and always find something new." Thus we transform what is unfamiliar into bricks for the wall of presupposition that barricades us from the truth. Meanwhile, Allen delights in collapsing the distance between "good literature" and everyday banality. Emma admires Kugelmass's leisure suit; he thrills her with black panties and designer slacks; and, like every other good-looking girl who goes to New York, she dreams of a career on the stage.

But the fantasy on which Allen bases his tale has deeper roots. Like Faust, Kugelmass dreams of transcending human limitations, of living for a while free from the constraints of time and ordinary causation. He abandons human science and philosophy, here represented by his shrink, and turns to magic. Although Persky resembles an auto mechanic more than Mephistopheles, he offers an equally dangerous and meaningful temptation to Kugelmass. If the professor lacks the poetry and grandeur of his Faustian predecessors, he is motivated by parallel

5

desires. Bored with his life and unable to love the people he shares it with (who can blame him?), he bargains for something he expects will be better. Appropriately, given the diminished scale of modern heroism, he signs away not his soul but merely a "double sawbuck." As happens especially with Marlowe's Dr. Faustus, for his reward Kugelmass gets only what he is capable of imagining. Emma Bovary as he experiences her talks and acts like any woman he could have picked up at Elaine's — exactly what he wanted, and what he turns her into by bringing her out of the novel and into the Plaza Hotel.

After the near-disaster of his affair with Emma, Kugelmass swears off philandering, but of course he has not learned his lesson. When he asks Persky to use the wondrous machine to send him for a date with "The Monkey" of *Portnoy's Complaint*, Kugelmass reveals the utter emptiness of spirit that hides behind his glib pop-culture romanticism, and it is fitting that he ends up scrambling through a desert inhabited by predatory words without meaning.

The intellectual and moral universe that Kugelmass inhabits even before his final translation is no less devoid of meaning. Allen's fantasy shows how the sophistication of modern life can drain the spirit out of human language, desires, and relationships. Kugelmass claims to have "soul," but his needs are quoted from advertisements in *The New Yorker*. The language of commercial psychology debases even his dreams, whose imagery is third hand and probably phony: "I was skipping through a meadow holding a picnic basket and the basket was marked 'Options.'" Kugelmass picks his mistress as from a menu; he decides to plunge into the supernatural (but for exceedingly *natural* reasons) more easily than he chooses between red and white wine (as if those were the only possibilities); significantly, he is most comfortable minimizing the importance of what he is doing: "'Sex and romance,' Kugelmass said from inside the box. 'What we go through for a pretty face.'"

Through the fantastic device of Persky's box, Allen achieves the small dislocation necessary to reveal that remark of Kugelmass's as a pitifully inadequate cliché. The story is full of such instances, and the technique embodies its larger vision. We choose the things we say to describe our lives to ourselves because they have been purged of discomforting truths. Allen shows that these statements are illusions. Kugelmass regards his life as a novel that has turned out badly. Rather than seeking to understand why he has come to a second marital dead end burdened with financial obligations and bored with his family, he tries to escape from the present and reenact the past. He wants only to enter *Madame Bovary* before page 120, and he dreams of starting life over in Europe, selling the (long defunct) *International Herald Tribune* "like those young girls used to."

The story leaves us with an implicit question: What redemption is possible for Kugelmass and the culture — our culture — that he represents? Is there an alternative to the Hobson's choice between desperation and meaninglessness?

WILLIAM E. SHEIDLEY

Questions for Discussion

1. Comment on the situation of Kugelmass as described in the first two paragraphs. Do you think his circumstances are unusual? Where should we lay blame for his predicament?

2. Kugelmass "had soul." What does that term seem to mean in this context?
3. Interpret Kugelmass's dream. Is it profoundly symbolic?
4. How effective is Dr. Mandel? Why does Kugelmass need a magician?
5. Discuss Persky. What might be Allen's basis for this character? How important is Persky to the story?
6. What factors enter into Kugelmass's choice of a mistress? What does this event suggest about his attitude toward literature? toward women?
7. Explore the implications of this quip: "She spoke in the same fine English translation as the paperback."
8. Review the first conversation between Kugelmass and Emma. Has Kugelmass really been transported into *Madame Bovary*? Does it resemble the novel as you read it or as you imagine it to be?
9. What does Allen achieve by noting the effect of the sudden appearance of the Kugelmass episode in the novel on various readers?
10. "By showing up during the correct chapters, I've got the situation knocked," Kugelmass says. Consider the implications of that idea. Would you like to live only certain chapters of your life?
11. Why does Emma want to come to New York? Why does Kugelmass want to take her there? Are the ensuing problems entirely the result of her being a character in a novel?
12. As Persky struggles to repair his box and Emma consumes "Dom Pérignon and black eggs," Kugelmass becomes more and more agitated. Finally, he contemplates suicide ("Too bad this is a low floor") or running away to Europe to sell the *International Herald Tribune*. How serious is he? Explain why those ideas accord with his character.
13. Why does it take Kugelmass only three weeks to break his resolution, "I'll never cheat again"?
14. *Portnoy's Complaint* examines, among other things, masturbation and adolescent sexual fantasies. What does it imply about Kugelmass that he chooses that book for his next adventure?
15. Do you think the ending of the story is appropriate? Why should Allen choose a remedial Spanish grammar for Kugelmass's hell rather than, say, a book in which adulterers are punished or in which none of the characters is a good-looking young woman?

Topics for Writing

1. Analyze how Allen crosses the border between life and art in "The Kugelmass Episode" and in his film *The Purple Rose of Cairo*.
2. Discuss the theme of meaningless language in "The Kugelmass Episode."
3. Study the use of language in Allen's story. List familiar phrases. What are their sources? Examine the conversations between characters. How much communication is taking place?
4. People often wish aloud for something they know to be impossible or speak of what they would do *if only*: "If only I had her looks and his money." "If only I were in charge." Imagine a character — yourself or someone you know, perhaps — whose impossible wish comes true. Then what? Follow Allen's lead by using the device to express the real truth in a surprising new way.

5. **CONNECTIONS** Compare and contrast the responses to marvels in Allen's "The Kugelmass Episode" and García Márquez's "A Very Old Man with Enormous Wings."

Suggested Readings

Gianetti, L. "Ciao, Woody." *Western Humanities Review* 35 (1981): 157–61.
Jacobs, Diane. *Magic of Woody Allen.* London: Robson, 1982.
Reisch, M. S. "Woody Allen: American Prose Humorist." *Journal of Popular Culture* 17 (1983): 68–74.
Rose, L. "Humor and Nothingness." *Atlantic* 255 (1985): 94–96.
Shechner, Mark. "Woody Allen: The Failure of the Therapeutic." *From Hester Street to Hollywood.* Ed. Sarah B. Cohen. Bloomington: Indiana UP, 1983. 231–44.
"Woody Allen on the American Character." *Commentary* 76 (1983): 61–65.

DOROTHY ALLISON

River of Names (p. 40)

Allison explains the title near the end of her story: "I've got a dust river in my head, a river of names endlessly repeating. That dirty water rises in me, all those children screaming out their lives in my memory, and I become someone else, someone I have tried so hard not to be." The conflict in her story is both physical and emotional: the protagonist's memories of the violence endured by the members of her family, dramatized in a series of flashbacks, and the hatred she feels for herself since she is still haunted by what she considers her "dirty" poverty-stricken childhood in the American South. The story is open-ended, since the narrator finds no possibility of resolution for either conflict, except in the act of storytelling itself.

Perhaps students will enhance their reading of Allison's story by comparing and contrasting it with Susan Sontag's AIDS story "The Way We Live Now." The subject of both stories is the often brutal nature of human experience. The authors find no easy solutions, nor do they suggest that misery ennobles humankind. On the contrary. The voice of the narrator in each story is the only calm, stable point in the storm of events conjured up by the act of storytelling. The characters are dehumanized, presented by name only in a passing parade of sentences. Yet the reader senses relationships between the names and anticipates some development or deeper revelation of character. Instead, the fictional relationships merely continue until the end of the stories (as when Allison's narrator tells us about her Aunt Raylene's disastrous attempt to leave her abusive husband after she learns that her son Bo would never be "right"). However, there is no satisfying closure for any of the characters in the stories, including the narrators.

Allison's achievement in "River of Names" is her skillful creation of a form and a voice to handle her difficult subject. Her tone is reminiscent of Tillie Olsen's voice in "I Stand Here Ironing" — the lyrical, strong expression of a woman who has survived emotionally devastating experiences. Here the fictional narrator has found a companion in her lover, Jesse, but her sense of happiness seems fragile.

She is a survivor, but she has not been able to come to terms with the trauma of what she was forced to endure in her brutal childhood.

Questions for Discussion

1. Is this an autobiographical or a fictional story? Who is the narrator?
2. What has happened to the narrator's cousin, Tommy, in the first paragraph of the story? How has Allison underscored the horror of his death by describing "the rope around his neck pulled up into the sunlit heights of the barn, fascinating, horrible"? In this description is she exploiting the sensational aspect of the child's death, or is she presenting it with restraint?
3. Does "River of Names" have a plot? Where is it set? Who are the characters? Why is it considered a short story instead of an essay?
4. What is the effect of the narrator's telling her lover "But I lie" at the end of the story? Does this cast doubt on everything the narrator has said, or is it Allison's attempt to avoid sentimentality?

Topics for Writing

1. CONNECTIONS   Compare and contrast the use of names (instead of fully developed characters) in Allison's and Sontag's stories.
2. CONNECTIONS   Compare and contrast the first-person narration in Allison's and Olsen's stories about family life.

Suggested Reading

Allison, Dorothy. *Skin: Talking about Sex, Class, and Literature.* Ithaca, NY: Firebrand, 1994.

SHERWOOD ANDERSON

Death in the Woods (p. 48)

"Death in the Woods" presents a religious image of the earth mother, the principle of connectedness by which life is fostered and sustained. Anderson's depiction of the woman whose job it is to feed animal life, "in cows, in chickens, in pigs, in horses, in dogs, in men," congeals in the visionary revelation of her death scene. To the men and boys who stand around her, the moonlit glimpse of her naked breast — effectively foreshadowed in the incident in which, as a girl, she had her dress ripped open by the German farmer she was bound to — conveys a sense of wonder: They look upon a marble statue of a beautiful young woman in the snow. Near her, or perhaps around her, lies the oval track left by the dogs, at once a prayer ring and a symbol of the interdependence and endless continuity of the life she has served.

It is appropriate that the basis of Mrs. Grimes's scant economy is eggs, whose various connotations are obvious enough. As the nurse of living things, Mrs.

Grimes establishes bonds and fosters community. The world with which she must deal, however, corrodes those bonds. When we first see her she is struggling alone: "People drive right down a road and never notice an old woman like that." The men she feeds are rapacious and cruel — to her and, as in the fight between Jake and the German farmer, to each other. The town treats them all with cold suspicion. Even the butcher who loads her grain bag out of pity would deny the food to Mrs. Grimes's husband or son: "He'd see him starve first." Not Mrs. Grimes, who tacitly reaffirms her theme: "Starve, eh? Well, things had to be fed. . . . Horses, cows, pigs, dogs, men." When she dies the forces for harmony and union that she embodies achieve a momentary victory, as the townspeople fall into a ragged communal procession to witness her death — a ceremony as instinctive as the ring running of the dogs, if somewhat less orderly and beautiful.

Anderson's story progresses from an apprehension of drab poverty and ugliness to a discovery of wonder and beauty. The agency that distills religious and aesthetic emotion out of the profane world of the story is the inquiring imagination of the narrator, who muses over his recollections, reconstructs his story from fragments, and in doing so explains the process of synthesis that takes place as he writes. In its progress from the ordinary to the mystical, from ugliness and privation to a soul-nourishing beauty, the story records a triumph of the creative imagination, which penetrates the surfaces of things to find within them their inherent mythic truth.

What makes that triumph possible is the narrator's subtly expressed identification with Mrs. Grimes. The fascination that causes him to cling to his recollections and finally to work them through may arise, as William J. Scheick argues, from the shock of his initiation into an awareness "of the relation between feeding, sex, and death" that blocks his sexual development; or it may arise from a sense of the hitherto unexpressed mythic implications of the scene in the woods. In either case, the narrator recognizes that the death of Mrs. Grimes has meaning for him — as one who has worked for a German farmer, who has himself watched dogs run in a ring, and who has kept silent; as one who is fed by women; and as one who must die. The story's circular structure, like the ring of dogs and the ring of men around the corpse, transforms compulsion into worship, just as Anderson's art transforms the report of a frightening death into a celebration of life and of the power of the sympathetic imagination to render its beauty.

WILLIAM E. SHEIDLEY

Questions for Discussion

1. Discuss the style of the opening paragraph. What qualities of the old woman's life are reflected in the syntax and rhythms of the prose?
2. How does Anderson modulate from generalization through recollection to specific narration? What change in narrative mode takes place in section II with the paragraph that begins "One day in Winter"? Does the story ever return to its original mode? Where?
3. "Her name was Grimes" — appropriately?
4. What does the narrator mean when he calls the Grimes men "a tough lot"? Are they alone in this in the story?
5. Describe the woman's life with the German farmer. How important to the story is the farmer's having torn "her dress open clear down the front"?

6. How big a part does love play in the relations between people in this story? What other factors are prominent — exploitation? mistrust? violence?
7. Does the butcher's generosity seem a welcome change? How does the butcher compare with Mrs. Grimes as a nurturer of life?
8. How does Anderson prepare us to accept it as probable that Mrs. Grimes would sit down under a tree and freeze to death?
9. Describe the behavior of the dogs. How does Anderson explain it? How does the narrator know it took place?
10. Comment on the tonal effect of the passage "It had been a big haul for the old woman. It was a big haul for the dogs now."
11. What does the corpse look like in the moonlight? Why does Anderson give a concise description of the corpse near the beginning of section IV rather than saving the whole revelation until the men and boys arrive on the scene at the end of that section?
12. Comment on the implications of this line: "Either mother or our older sister would have to warm our supper."
13. Explain the possible meanings of the word "everything" in the first sentence of section V.
14. Discuss the narrator's remarks about why he has told the story. What is "the real story I am now trying to tell"? To what extent is it a story about the narrator himself? About stories and storytelling?

Topics for Writing

1. In an essay, describe Anderson's circular notion of image and structure in "Death in the Woods."
2. Discuss the narrator's struggle "to tell the simple story over again."
3. Write an essay analyzing the role of the community in "Death in the Woods."
4. Describe Mrs. Grimes and the mythic roles of woman in "Death in the Woods."
5. On a second reading, make notes about the narrator. Rearrange his activities, experiences, and concerns into chronological order. What is the narrator's story? What is his conflict? What does he achieve? What does he learn?
6. Read several myths from Ovid's *Metamorphoses*. Rewrite the story of Mrs. Grimes as an Ovidian myth. What changes of tone are necessary? What important themes have you had to abandon? What have you had to invent?

Related Commentary

Sherwood Anderson, Form, Not Plot, in the Short Story, p. 1420.

Suggested Readings

See page 13.

Sherwood Anderson

Hands (p. 57)

Anderson's story "Hands" might be called a portrait. Like a formal painted portrait, it depicts Wing Biddlebaum not only as he exists at a given moment but also in conjunction with certain props in the background that reveal who he is by recalling his past and defining his circumstances. The focal image of the portrait is Wing's hands, around which the other elements of the picture are organized and to which they lend meaning. Further, the story depends for a portion of its effect upon a series of painterly tableaux, from the sunset landscape with berry pickers with which it begins to the silhouette of Wing as a holy hermit, saying over and over the rosary of his lonely years of penance for a sin he did not commit.

In keeping with this achronological narration (which William L. Phillips has shown may in part result from Anderson's thinking his way through the story as he wrote it), neither Wing nor George Willard experiences any clear revelation or makes any climactic decision. Wing never understands why he was driven out of Pennsylvania, and George is afraid to ask the questions that might lead them both to a liberating understanding of Wing's experience.

The reader, however, is not permitted to remain in the dark. With the clear understanding of how the crudity and narrow-minded suspicion of his neighbors have perverted Wing's selfless, "diffused" love for his students into a source of fear and shame comes a poignant sorrow for what is being wasted. Wing's hands may be the pride of Winesburg for their agility at picking strawberries, but the nurturing love that they betoken is feared by everyone, including George, including even Wing himself, whose loneliness is as great as his capacity to love — from which, by a cruel irony, it arises.

William E. Sheidley

Questions for Discussion

1. Define Wing Biddlebaum's relationship to his community as it is implied in the first paragraph. To what extent is the impression created here borne out?
2. Why does Wing hope George Willard will come to visit? Does George ever arrive?
3. Wing's name, which refers to his hands, was given to him by "some obscure poet of the town," and telling the full story of those hands "is a job for a poet." What connotations of "wings" are appropriate? Why is "Wing" a better name for Biddlebaum than, say, "Claw," or "Hook," or "Picker"?
4. Could Wing himself have been a poet? Why does he tell his dreams only to George?
5. Why did the people of the town in Pennsylvania nearly lynch Adolph Myers? Why was he unable to defend himself?
6. Are the people in Ohio any different from those in Pennsylvania? Explain. What about George Willard? Evaluate his decision not to ask Wing about his hands.

7. What other hands do we see in the story? Compare them with Wing's.
8. Explain the implications of our last view of Wing. What is the pun in the last line?

Topics for Writing

1. Write an essay analyzing the crucifixion of Wing Biddlebaum.
2. Consider Anderson's comments in "Form, Not Plot, in the Short Story" (included in Part Two, p. 1420) as a key to his art in "Hands."
3. After reading the story once, jot down your response, including your feelings about Wing, George, the townspeople, and the narrator. Also write, in one or two sentences, a summation of the story's theme as you understand it. Then reread the paragraphs in the order they would have followed had Anderson told the story in chronological order. Would your responses differ? Would the story have an identical theme? Explain.
4. Anderson claimed to have written this story at a sitting and to have published it without rearrangements or major additions or deletions of material. Imitating his process, write a vignette about a person unknown to you whom you see in a photograph. Start with the scene in the photo and end with the same, interpolating previous incidents and background information as they occur to you.
5. **CONNECTIONS** Compare and contrast Anderson's Wing and Flaubert's Félicité.

Related Commentary

Sherwood Anderson, Form, Not Plot, in the Short Story, p. 1420.

Suggested Readings

Anderson, David, ed. *Critical Essays on Sherwood Anderson.* Boston: G. K. Hall, 1981.
Anderson, Sherwood. *A Story Teller's Story.* Cleveland: The UP of Case Western Reserve, 1968.
———. *The Portable Sherwood Anderson.* New York: Viking, 1972.
———. *The Teller's Tales.* Introduction by Frank Gado. Schenectady, NY: Union College P, 1983.
Burbank, Rex. *Sherwood Anderson.* Twayne's United States Authors Series 65. New York: Twayne, 1964. 64–66.
Crowley, John W., ed. *New Essays on* Winesburg, Ohio. New York: Cambridge UP, 1990.
Joselyn, Sister Mary. "Some Artistic Dimensions of Sherwood Anderson's 'Death in the Woods.'" *Studies in Short Fiction* 4 (1967): 252–59.
Phillips, William L. "How Sherwood Anderson Wrote *Winesburg, Ohio.*" *The Achievement of Sherwood Anderson.* Ed. Ray Lewis White. Chapel Hill: U of North Carolina P, 1966. 62–84, esp. 74–78. Originally published in *American Literature* 23 (1951): 7–30.
Rideout, Walter B., ed. *Sherwood Anderson.* Englewood Cliffs, NJ: Prentice, 1974.

Scheick, William J. "Compulsion toward Repetition: Sherwood Anderson's 'Death in the Woods.'" *Studies in Short Fiction* 11 (1974): 141–46.

Townsend, Kim. *Sherwood Anderson.* Boston: Houghton, 1987.

White, Ray Lewis. Winesburg, Ohio: *An Explanation.* Boston: Twayne, 1990.

Margaret Atwood

Death by Landscape (p. 62)

In her article "An End to Audience?" Margaret Atwood writes, "When you read a book, it matters how old you are and when you read it and whether you are male or female, or from Canada or India. There is no such thing as a truly universal literature, partly because there are no truly universal readers." Her story "Death by Landscape" exemplifies this principle of interpretation. For an American reader, or perhaps for a reader from most Western countries, there would be no difficulty in understanding the central incident of the story, the disappearance of a girl on a canoeing trip, but for an educated Canadian reader the story has more specific resonances.

A Canadian reader familiar with art would immediately recognize the symbolism that colors the story through Atwood's use of the paintings by the "Group of Seven" Canadian painters that hang in Lois's apartment. Atwood describes them perfunctorily: "convoluted tree trunks on an island of pink wave-smoothed stone, with more islands behind; . . . a lake with rough, bright, sparsely wooded cliffs . . . ," but for a Canadian the description is evocative of the famous originals. They are small, many of the best of them only seven inches by nine inches, but they are so intense in their color and brushwork that they seem to lift off the panels on which they are painted. In them the painters, for the first time, tried to capture the essence of the Canadian wilderness in the early twentieth century. A Canadian would also know that many of the panels were painted in canoes on wilderness lakes, as the artists tried to keep away from the clouds of mosquitoes, and that by having a number of them, which she had purchased many years before, Lois has become a very wealthy woman. (The Group of Seven painters disbanded in 1932.)

The paintings also evoke memory of a mysterious death: The greatest of the Group of Seven painters, Tom Thompson, was found drowned in a lake in 1917 at the age of thirty-nine, and the cause of his drowning was never discovered.

That memory presages the mystery of the disappearance and possible drowning of Lois's friend Lucy on a summer camp canoeing trip. Despite the flippant tone in which the summer camp is described in all its tawdry hopelessness, the story is haunted by the tragedy that waits there for Lois. Lucy, the girl who disappeared, is seen only in glimpses, almost a dream for Lois of another, more free-spirited self that she will never become. When Lucy disappears, this adventurous part of Lois disappears with her, and from the first description it is obvious that something has been lost for her: "She is relieved not to have to worry about the lawn. . . ." It is almost as though Lois is not fully living, and at the end of the story she doesn't seem to have lived at all beyond that moment all those years ago. "She can hardly remember, now, having her two boys in the hospital, nursing them as babies; she can hardly remember getting married, or what Rob [her husband] looked like. Even at the time she never felt she was paying full attention."

In the end, Lois goes back to the paintings — and they have confused her as much as the other things in her life that have happened since the accident — but suddenly she sees in them, not the tormented power of the painters wrestling to capture something on their tiny panels in their unsteady canoes, but Lucy.

> Every one of them is a picture of Lucy. You can't see her exactly, but she's there, in behind the pink stone island or the one behind that. . . . In the yellow autumn woods she's behind the tree that cannot be seen because of the other trees, over beside the blue sliver of pond; but if you walked into the picture and found the tree, it would be the wrong one, because the right one would be further on.

The paintings in this moment become the symbol of the life that Lois feels she never had, as she sees it in the person of Lucy, whose life ended in one of the lakes the artists captured with unforgettable power.

Questions for Discussion

1. Does Lois suggest that she might be thinking of ending her own life? What does she say?
2. Why does Lois try to make herself into someone like Lucy? Could she ever be like her?
3. What is there in Lois's adolescence to suggest that her life would become so empty?
4. What is the significance of the Indian rituals that were part of the life of every summer camp in this era?
5. How old do you think Lois is now? Why do you think she feels that her life has been without meaning?

Topics for Writing

1. Explain whether Lois's condition at the end of the story makes sense in the context of her experience. Use specific examples from the story to support your position.
2. Write a personal essay about a friendship you may have had like the one between Lois and Lucy.
3. Analyze Atwood's use of landscape in the story.
4. Atwood describes the usual symptoms of trouble that lead teenagers into emotional difficulty. Discuss how she presents these in the story.

Related Commentary

Margaret Atwood, Reading Blind, p. 1423.

Suggested Readings

See p. 17.

MARGARET ATWOOD

Happy Endings (p. 74)

Atwood's story can be read profitably in conjunction with Grace Paley's "A Conversation with My Father." In both, the authors use humor to suggest a certain impatience with the traditional short-story form. Both stories can be read as "metafictions," fictions that comment on the art of telling stories. Atwood's piece is harsher than Paley's in its insistence that happy endings are impossible in stories; Atwood tells us clearly that death is "the only authentic ending" to everyone's story. Paley, in contrast, clearly values both her relationship with her dying father and her own imagination, allowing (even half-jokingly) her fictional heroine the possibility of rehabilitation after her drug addiction and a valued place in society as a counselor in a center for young addicts.

The first time students read "Happy Endings," they may miss the way Atwood connects the stories from "A" to "F." "B" is the first unhappy ending (as Atwood warns us in the third sentence), with the "worst possible scenario" worked out in John and Mary's love affair. Atwood's vocabulary here is deliberately harsh and unromantic, unlike the sentimental clichés of the "A" scenario.

As Atwood continues her permutations of the couples' possible relationships, her stories get shorter and more perfunctory. Her language becomes more elemental, preparing the reader for her summary dismissal of all plots, since they all end in death. In the final three paragraphs, Atwood drops all pretense that she is telling stories and directly addresses her readers, revealing that her true subject is not the emotional life she is creating for her characters but her awareness of the elements of fiction. She defines plot as "what" or "just one thing after another." Then, like the instructor's manual of a short-story anthology, she leaves the rest up to her reader: "Now try How [character] and Why [theme.]"

Questions for Discussion

1. Atwood's authorial presence is the strongest element in "Happy Endings" — does this make the text closer to an essay than a short story? Explain.
2. How does Atwood elicit your curiosity, so that you continue to read this short story? Would you say that she has proven that plot is the most essential element in a story? Is there also an underlying, coherent theme to "Happy Endings"?
3. Would the story still be effective if Atwood omitted her direct address to the reader ("If you want a happy ending, try A.")? Explain.

Topics for Writing

1. Rewrite the story, inventing additional outcomes for John and Mary's relationship.
2. In "Reading Blind" (p. 1423), Atwood gives her criteria for judging whether a story is "good." Using these criteria, how would you rate "Happy Endings"?

3. Ray Bradbury, in his book *Zen in the Art of Writing: Essays on Creativity* (Capra, 1990), writes, "The writer must let his fingers run out the story of his characters, who, being only human and full of strange dreams and obsessions, are only too glad to run. . . . Remember: *Plot* is no more than footprints left in the snow after your characters have run by on their way to incredible destinations. *Plot* is observed after the fact rather than before. It cannot precede action. It is the chart that remains when an action is through." Apply Bradbury's analysis to "Happy Endings."

Related Commentary

Margaret Atwood, Reading Blind, p. 1423.

Suggested Readings

Atwood, Margaret. *Murder in the Dark.* Toronto: Coach House, 1983.
————. *Second Words.* Toronto: Anansi, 1982.
Grace, Sherrill E., and Lorraine Weir. *Margaret Atwood: Language, Text and System.* Vancouver: U of British Columbia P, 1983.
Rigney, Barbara Hill. *Margaret Atwood.* Totowa, NJ: Barnes & Noble, 1987.
Stouck, David. *Major Canadian Authors.* Lincoln: U of Nebraska P, 1988.

Isaac Babel

My First Goose (p. 79)

The narrator in this story is an outsider, a lonely and hungry intellectual who wins a meal and the acceptance of the Cossacks by killing the old peasant woman's goose. He does it roughly, demonstrating that he will "get on all right" at the front. The act is portrayed partly as a rape, partly as a crucifixion. The quartermaster tells him, "you go and mess up a lady, and a good lady too, and you'll have the boys patting you on the back," and that is what he does, trampling her goose under his boot and plunging his sword into it while she repeats, "I want to go and hang myself," and he says, "Christ!" But the narrator recoils from his self-debasement: The night that enfolds him resembles a prostitute; the moon decorates it "like a cheap earring." Lenin says there is a shortage of everything, and though Surovkov believes that Lenin strikes straight at the truth "like a hen pecking at a grain," the narrator uses the spectacles of his learning to discern "the secret curve of Lenin's straight line," the hidden purpose of the speech. The narrator, too, has taken an apparently bold and forthright step in killing the goose, but the secret curve of his straight line has been to gain acceptance by the Cossacks and a share of *their* dinner, which reminds him of his home. As he sleeps with his new friends he dreams of women, just as he saw female beauty in the long legs of Savitsky. But in taking his first goose he has messed up a good lady and stained his heart with bloodshed, and his conscience is not at peace.

Questions for Discussion

1. Describe Savitsky. What is the narrator's attitude toward him? Why does Babel begin the story with this character, who never reappears?
2. What advice does the quartermaster give? Does the narrator follow it?
3. Why are the narrator's "specs" an object of derision? Who else in the story wears glasses?
4. Why does the Cossack throw the narrator's trunk out at the gate?
5. When the narrator first tries to read Lenin's speech, he cannot concentrate. Why?
6. How does the narrator win the respect of the Cossacks?
7. Discuss the difference between Surovkov's understanding of Lenin's speech and the narrator's.
8. Explain the last sentence. What is the narrator's feeling about himself? about the situation he is in?
9. "Lenin writes that there's a shortage of everything." Of what is there a particular shortage in the story?

Topics for Writing

1. Write an essay analyzing the function of sexual imagery in "My First Goose."
2. Explain why the narrator stains himself in "My First Goose."
3. What is the effect of Babel's extreme brevity in "My First Goose"? Describe the way it is achieved.
4. Before beginning to read "My First Goose," write your prediction of what its subject might be on the basis of its title alone. Write a second guess as well. After reading the story, review your predictions. To what extent were the expectations aroused by the title — even if they were not confirmed — relevant to an understanding of Babel's narrative?

Suggested Readings

Carden, Patricia. *The Art of Isaac Babel.* Ithaca: Cornell UP, 1972. 97, 100, 110, 130–31.

Falen, James E. *Isaac Babel: Russian Master of the Short Story.* Knoxville: U of Tennessee P, 1974. 142–45.

JAMES BALDWIN

Sonny's Blues (p. 83)

The marvel of this story is the way the narrator — Sonny's older brother — narrows the physical and emotional distance between himself and Sonny until Sonny's plight is revealed and illuminated in a remarkable moment of empathy and insight. This story of drug addiction in the inner city's black ghetto is as valid today as it was when it was written. By juxtaposing the two brothers — a straight high school math teacher and a heroin addict blues pianist — Baldwin makes it possible for readers to enter the world of the story regardless of their racial background or their opinions about drugs. The author doesn't judge Sonny's plight. Instead, through the brother, he helps us understand it, sympathize with it, and transcend it in a brief shared experience of Sonny's inspired musical improvisation.

This is a long story, and its plot consists mostly of flashbacks, more "told" than "shown" in the reminiscences of Sonny's older brother. Yet the power of Baldwin's sympathy for his characters and his eloquent style move the reader along. Baldwin captures the African American culture of strong family allegiances in the face of American racism. Both Sonny and his brother are trying to survive, and we respect them for their courage.

One of the ways to discuss the story is through an analysis of the narrator's growing sympathy for Sonny. Baldwin tells us that the narrator thinks, after the death of his little daughter Grace from polio, "My trouble made his real." This realization motivates the first scene with the two brothers in which Baldwin begins to build the bridge between them. Separately they watch three sisters and a brother hold a revival meeting on the sidewalk opposite the narrator's apartment, and after they hear the gospel music, the silence between Sonny and his brother begins to give way to shared sound. The scene leads directly to the two brothers going to the bar where Sonny plays and creates an opportunity for the narrator (and the reader) to enter Sonny's world and satisfy his anguished need to share his music with someone who will listen to it and understand.

Questions for Discussion

1. Analyze the following speech, in which Sonny explains to his brother how he has survived (however tenuously) the experience of racism in America:

    "It's terrible sometimes, inside," he said, "that's what's the trouble. You walk these streets, black and funky and cold, and there's not really a living ass to talk to, and there's nothing shaking, and there's no way of getting it out — that storm inside. You can't talk it and you can't make love with it, and when you finally try to get with it and play it, you realize *nobody's* listening. So *you've* got to listen. You got to find a way to listen."

    How does this explanation make Sonny a sympathetic character?
2. Discuss Baldwin's comment on the blues Sonny plays with Creole and the two other musicians at the end of the story:

    Creole began to tell us what the blues were all about. They were not about anything very new. He and his boys up there were keeping it new, at the risk of ruin, destruction, madness, and death, in order to find new ways to make us listen. For, while the tale of how we suffer, and how we are delighted, and how we may triumph is never new, it always must be heard. There isn't any other tale to tell, it's the only light we've got in all this darkness.

    Baldwin's subject is the music, of course, but he is also talking about other forms of creation. What might they be?

Topics for Writing

1. Chinua Achebe describes Baldwin as having brought "a new sharpness of vision, a new energy of passion, a new perfection of language to battle the incubus of race" in his eulogy titled "Postscript: James Baldwin (1924–1987)" (*Hopes and Impediments*, 1990). How does "Sonny's Blues" embody these qualities?

2. **CONNECTIONS** Baldwin's commentary "Autobiographical Notes" (p. 1426) states that he found it difficult to be a writer because he was forced to become a spokesman for his race: "I have not written about being a Negro at such length because I expect that to be my only subject, but only because it was the gate I had to unlock before I could hope to write about anything else." Yet Baldwin's depiction of the life lived by African Americans is unique and very different from Richard Wright's or Ralph Ellison's, Toni Cade Bambara's or Alice Walker's accounts. Compare and contrast "Sonny's Blues" with a story by one or more of these writers to describe how each finds his or her own way to dramatize what Baldwin calls "the ambiguity and irony of Negro life." Could "Sonny's Blues" be set in an Italian American or Jewish American family?

3. **CONNECTIONS** Compare and contrast "Sonny's Blues" with Willa Cather's "Paul's Case."

Related Commentary

James Baldwin, Autobiographical Notes, p. 1426.

Suggested Readings

Bloom, Harold. *James Baldwin*. New York: Chelsea House, 1986.
Burt, Nancy. *Critical Essays on James Baldwin*. Boston: G. K. Hall, 1986.
Campbell, James. *Talking at the Gates: A Life of James Baldwin*. New York: Viking, 1991.
Chametzky, Jules, ed. *A Tribute to James Baldwin: Black Writers Redefine the Struggle*. Amherst: U of Massachusetts P, 1989.
Kinnamon, Kenneth, ed. *James Baldwin*. Englewood Cliffs, NJ: Prentice, 1974.
Macebuh, Stanley. *James Baldwin: A Critical Study*. New York: Third, 1973.
Pratt, Louis H. *James Baldwin*. Twayne's United States Authors Series 290. Boston: G. K. Hall, 1978.
Standley, F. L., ed. *Conversations with James Baldwin*. Jackson: U of Mississippi P, 1989.

TONI CADE BAMBARA

The Lesson (p. 108)

Relationships are an organizational key to this story. "The Lesson" is narrated by Sylvia, one of a group of eight African American children living in an uptown slum in New York City who are "treated" by their neighborhood guide

Miss Moore to an educational visit to the F.A.O. Schwarz toy store at Fifth Avenue and Fifty-seventh Street. The group consists of four girls (Sylvia and her best friend Sugar, the relatively affluent Mercedes and her friend Rosie Giraffe) and four boys (Big Butt [Ronald] and Junebug, and Little Q.T. and Flyboy).

The "lesson" of the story is learned first by Sugar and then by Sylvia. All along Sylvia has assumed Sugar to be her ally, sharing her hostility to all adults as authority figures and to the idea of education. There's a suggestion of foreshadowing when the girls pay the taxicab driver outside F.A.O. Schwarz and Sugar steps in when Sylvia can't figure out the 10 percent tip on the 85-cent fare — "Give him a dime." (This is a taxi fare from twenty-five years ago, when the story was written.) But Sugar plays dumb as usual in her next appearance in the story, when she asks Miss Moore outside the toy store, "Can we steal?"

After the children learn about the high prices of the luxury toys at F.A.O. Schwarz, they return to their homes uptown. Sugar's remark to Miss Moore before they disperse reveals that the afternoon's lesson in economics hasn't been wasted: "this is not much of a democracy if you ask me. Equal chance to pursue happiness means an equal crack at the dough, don't it?" Bambara doesn't tell us whether Sugar intends to begin studying hard in school or to begin dealing drugs (this is the early 1970s), but the blinders formed by her life in the inner-city ghetto have fallen away, and she's clearly dissatisfied with her customary smart-aleck role. In her first response Sylvia is dumbfounded by her friend's betrayal, but within a few minutes she awakens to a sense of rivalry: "But ain't nobody gonna beat me at nuthin." Again Bambara leaves the lesson unspecified, and the reader must imagine *how* Sylvia intends to win the new game she's playing.

Questions for Discussion

1. What is the effect of the inner-city ghetto language in the story?
2. Is Sylvia a reliable or an unreliable narrator?
3. How does Bambara evoke a sense of sympathy for the people enduring the poverty and filth in Sylvia's neighborhood through her descriptions of the relationship of the winos and the newly arrived families from the South?
4. Describe the eight children and their relationships within the neighborhood group. How dependent is Sylvia on her friend Sugar?
5. Who is Miss Moore? Why does she personify the hostile force of "education" to the ghetto children?
6. Why does Sylvia keep the four dollars' change from the taxi fare? What does she do with the money? Is this a convincing ending to the story?

Topics for Writing

1. Write a story using a special dialect that you have learned from your family or friends.
2. **CONNECTIONS** Compare and contrast the authors' uses of African American speech in this story and in Richard Wright's "The Man Who Was Almost a Man." Analyze the different ways the two writers keep the dialect from distracting readers and causing them to lose interest in the stories.

Suggested Readings

Bambara, Toni Cade. *The Sea Birds Are Still Alive: Stories.* New York: Vintage, 1982.

Bell, Roseann P., Bettye J. Parker, and Beverly Guy-Sheftall, eds. *Sturdy Black Bridges: Visions of Black Women in Literature.* New York: Anchor, 1979.

Butler-Evans, Elliot. *Race, Gender, and Desire: Narrative Strategies in the Fiction of Toni Cade Bambara, Toni Morrison, and Alice Walker.* Philadelphia: Temple UP, 1989.

Cartwright, Jerome. "Bambara's 'The Lesson.'" *Explicator* 47.3 (Spring 1989): 61–63.

Evans, Mari, ed. *Black Women Writers (1950–1980): A Critical Evaluation.* New York: Anchor, 1984. 41–71.

Giddings, P. "Call to Wholeness from a Gifted Storyteller." *Encore* 9 (1980): 48–49.

Lyles, Lois F. "Time, Motion, Sound and Fury in *The Sea Birds Are Still Alive.*" *College Language Association Journal* 36.2 (December 1992): 134–44.

Morrison, Toni. "City Limits, Village Values: Concepts of the Neighborhood in Black Fiction." *Literature and the Urban Experience: Essays on the City and Literature.* Ed. Ann Chalmers Watts and Michael C. Jaye. New Brunswick: Rutgers UP, 1981.

Tate, Claudia, ed. *Black Women Writers at Work.* New York: Continuum, 1983. 12–38.

Vertreace, Martha M. "A Bibliography of Writings about Toni Cade Bambara." *American Women Writing Fiction: Memory, Identity, Family, and Space.* Ed. Mickey Pearlman. Lexington: U of Kentucky P, 1989.

———. "Toni Cade Bambara: The Dance of Character and Community." *American Women Writing Fiction: Memory, Identity, Family, and Space.* Ed. Mickey Pearlman. Lexington: U of Kentucky P, 1989.

JOHN BARTH

On with the Story (p. 114)

Although Barth assures us that we are reading a "story-now-in-progress," it will be obvious to the student who follows Barth's story to its conclusion that it isn't a "story," as we have defined a story in our discussions of the story form. There is, essentially, no plot, and although there are two characters, we know almost nothing about one of them. There is also no resolution to the narrative, since Barth chooses to break it off, rather than lead us to any conclusion. The most useful way to describe this piece is to call it a sketch, and, to further qualify this description, it is a sketch that Barth has designed to call into question the concept of a story itself.

Barth disguises his intentions by creating a plausible situation between two plausible people. A man and a woman are traveling cross-country on a plane where they have a brief conversation. The woman is glancing at a story in an in-flight magazine, but she is reading it only superficially because she is worried about the financial situation she faces because of her recent divorce. The man, by coincidence, is the writer of the story. The story has many obtuse mathematical formulations, but these are only distractions, and Barth does not mean for us to take them any more seriously than his two characters take them. The narrative device that drives the situation Barth has sketched out for us is the possibility that the man and the woman will proceed from this casual meeting to a sexual involvement. Barth chooses not to resolve the question that hangs in the air between them. He simply suggests that they might decide to proceed, or they might not — then he breaks off his narrative and in the penultimate paragraph tells us we should remember that "stories are essentially constructs in time."

This sketch might be considered an example of "modernist" writing, which also denies the validity of a "story," but Barth has cleverly managed to present us with an even deeper contradiction. He uses a story to deny that there can be such a thing as a story, and he leaves it up to the reader to decide which of the two ideas is the one that Barth, as a writer, believes himself.

Questions for Discussion

1. The author is careful to give his characters an identity within a specific American social class. What are some of the distinguishing features of the class that he is describing?
2. He has also placed the situation within a specific time frame. What does he tell us about the lives of his characters in order to do this?
3. Both of the women in the story — the woman reading and the woman she is reading about — face specific problems. Are these problems related to the particular time of the story, or are these problems more closely related to a general human situation?
4. What does Barth mean by the term "Boomer Syndrome"?
5. Can the students explain any of Zeno's paradoxes?
6. What are the "three phenomena" the author wants to interconnect?

Topics for Writing

1. Although Barth considers his story an examination of the nature of a story itself, on a less complicated level he has simply left the story of the encounter between the two people on the plane unfinished. A student could develop an ending to the story and justify the ending with reference to hints and suggestions that the writer has presented in his description of the two characters.
2. **CONNECTIONS** The student could compare this story with a story like Italo Calvino's "If on a winter's night a traveler," in which the writer employs a similar narrative device to achieve a different ending.

Suggested Readings

Barth, John. *On with the Story*. Boston: Little, Brown, 1996.
Morrell, David. *John Barth: An Introduction*. University Park: Pennsylvania State UP, 1976. 87–90.

Donald Barthelme

At the Tolstoy Museum (p. 129)

Barthelme's text parodies the style of a museum guide ostensibly written to assist visitors to the Leningrad museum honoring Count Leo Tolstoy, actually one of several museums in that city dedicated to famous Russian writers. The story is full of information, some of it imagined and some of it real, including Barthelme's skillful summary of one of Tolstoy's famous religious parables, the Three Hermits and the Bishop. Drawings illustrate the text to help the reader "get" the jokes.

"At the Tolstoy Museum" employs both the first-person singular "I" and the plural "we" — or the royal "we" — almost as if Barthelme were trying to ape the moral authority of the aristocratic author, whom most scholars place at the top of the Russian literary pantheon. The tearful response of Tolstoy's faithful readers who are receptive to the museum's phenomenal exhibitions (just imagine, thirty thousand pictures of Count Leo Tolstoy!) opens the narrative; the colossal fatigue of the dutiful narrator closes it. In between, Barthelme describes the structure of the building housing the museum and shows us some of its contents, including the "stacks of clean white pocket handkerchiefs" supplied for the weeping visitors. In Barthelme's story, the experience of meeting Tolstoy's eyes in the various rooms is unnerving, and it is impossible to evade feeling guilty, like "committing a small crime and being discovered at it by your father, who stands in four doorways, looking at you."

So much for Tolstoy's "moral authority." But before you dismiss Barthelme's story as an eccentric flight of his imagination, let me tell you that the feeling he describes is real. Twenty years ago I visited the museum in Leningrad devoted to Fyodor Dostoevsky. It was located in the ancient house he lived in as a boy while his father practiced medicine in a clinic close by. In the outer corridor I was told, like all visitors, to remove my shoes and put on huge one-size-fits-all brown paper slippers. As I shuffled from room to room, looking at the exhibits hung high on the walls, I felt totally reduced in size. The experience didn't reduce me to tears, but it definitely made me feel like a minor character in *Crime and Punishment* or a humble pilgrim visiting a distant, obscurely religious shrine.

Questions for Discussion

1. Who is the narrator in this narrative? Why has Barthelme used both "I" and "we"?
2. What is Barthelme suggesting by furnishing illustrations for his text?
3. How does Barthelme use exaggeration in "At the Tolstoy Museum"?
4. In what way does the author conclude the narrative? In what way does he keep it going?

Topics for Writing

1. Discuss whether "At the Tolstoy Museum" is a sketch or a short story. Which elements of fiction has Barthelme included, and which has he omitted?

2. Write an essay in which you imagine how Tolstoy would explicate
   Barthelme's narrative.

Related Story

Leo Tolstoy, The Death of Ivan Ilych, p. 1279.

Suggested Readings

Barthelme, Donald. "Not-Knowing." *Voicelust.* Ed. Allen Wier and Dan Hendrie,
    Jr. Lincoln: U of Nebraska P, 1985.
Couturier, Maurice, and Regis Durand. *Donald Barthelme.* New York: Methuen,
    1982.
Gitlin, Todd. *The Sixties: Years of Hope, Days of Rage.* New York: Bantam, 1987.
Gordon, Lois. *Donald Barthelme.* Twayne's United States Authors Series 416. Bos-
    ton: G. K. Hall, 1981.
Johnson, Alexandra. *The Hidden Writer: Diaries and the Creative Life.* New York:
    Doubleday, 1997. 51–85.
Klinkowitz, Jerome. *Donald Barthelme: An Exhibition.* Durham, NC: Duke UP, 1991.
Leitch, Thomas M. "Donald Barthelme and the End of the End." *Modern Fiction
    Studies* 28.1 (1982): 129–43.
Molesworth, Charles. *Donald Barthelme's Fiction: The Ironist Saved from Drowning.*
    Columbia: U of Missouri P, 1982.
O'Hara, J. D. "Art of Fiction: Donald Barthelme." *Paris Review* 80 (1981): 181–210.
Stengel, Wayne B. *The Shape of Art in the Short Stories of Donald Barthelme.* Baton
    Rouge: Louisiana State UP, 1985.
Trachtenberg, Stanley. *Understanding Donald Barthelme.* Columbia: U of South Caro-
    lina P, 1990.
Wilde, Alan. *Middle Grounds: Studies in Contemporary American Fiction.* Philadel-
    phia: U of Pennsylvania P, 1987. Contains "Barthelme, His Garden."

ANN BEATTIE

The Burning House (p. 140)

Beattie's narration is so oblique that on first reading students may feel they
have missed the point of this story. They will not, however, escape the numb depression that mutes the narrator's — and the reader's — response to the incidents
to such a degree that the narrative seems disjointed. Of course it is not, and discovering its continuities is a gratification for attentive readers.

Not even a casual first reading can obscure the power of the last scene between Frank and Amy. Amy insists that her husband tell her if he's planning to
stay or go to his mistress, and his answer is brutally explicit — as his name,
"Frank," would lead us to expect. He tells her, ". . . [Y]our whole life you've made
one mistake — you've surrounded yourself with men. . . . I'm going to tell you
something about men. Men think they're Spider-Man and Buck Rogers and

Superman. You know what we all feel inside that you don't feel? That we're going to the stars."

A classroom discussion could revolve around the differences between Amy and the males who live in her house. Even Sam the dog shows himself to be "man's best friend" by his devotion to Freddy. In an age of feminist fiction, Beattie's story is a subtle but unmistakable depiction of the gender battleground, and Amy's vulnerability makes her a fragile heroine in this fictional fight to the finish.

Questions for Discussion

1. How does Amy differ from the men in the story? How do the men differ from each other?
2. Does the ending come as a surprise? Explain why or why not.

Topics for Writing

1. Write a story from the point of view of a narrator who is hiding something from himself or herself about his or her spouse. Show how the unrecognized truth presents itself gradually to the narrator.
2. **CONNECTIONS** Write an essay comparing and contrasting "The Burning House" and Katherine Mansfield's "Bliss." How are the two stories' heroines similar? dissimilar?

Related Commentary

Ann Beattie, Where Characters Come From, p. 1434.

Suggested Readings

Beattie, Ann. *What Was Mine: Stories*. New York: Random, 1991.
———. *Where You'll Find Me and Other Stories*. New York: Simon, 1986.
Montresor, Jaye Berman. *The Critical Responses to Ann Beattie*. Westport, CT: Greenwood, 1993.
Murphy, Christina. *Ann Beattie*. Boston: Twayne, 1986.

SAMUEL BECKETT

Dante and the Lobster (p. 152)

Teaching this early Beckett story from *More Pricks Than Kicks* will challenge an instructor's ability to clarify a text in the classroom. Probably the most auspicious way to begin is to make sure that students understand the context in which you approach the story — whether you have assigned it, for instance, as part of a study of European modernist fiction, or as a brilliant example of the achievement of contemporary writers deconstructing our assumptions about reading texts, or as an illustration of the erudition necessary to understand the different levels of meaning in a humorous tale.

Explication is crucial here, since Beckett assumes that the reader will share his range of knowledge of Dante scholarship and Dublin pub life, to give only two recondite subjects crucial to the first steps toward an understanding of his narrative. Yet Beckett's narrative style seems to be so straightforward that most students will read the story without reaching for a dictionary, so the fun in the classroom can begin with their different explanations of what they have read. Then you can explore Beckett's way of proceeding in his opening paragraph to attempt to account for some of their confusion.

The story begins, "It was morning and Belacqua was stuck in the first of the canti in the moon." "It was morning" is a simple declaration of the time of day in which the narrative starts. But who is "Belacqua," and what is "the first of the canti in the moon"? It will be necessary to explain that Belacqua Shuah is the name Beckett has given to his young Irish protagonist in several of the stories in *More Pricks Than Kicks.* Here he is studying Dante's *Divine Comedy* to prepare for an upcoming Italian examination on the text. He is a college student, about the same age as your students. And like them, he is confused but trying very hard to understand his assignments. "He was so bogged that he could move neither backward nor forward." But Belacqua possesses the essential quality of imagination as a reader, and he does persevere with dogged persistence, containing his boredom and intellectual fatigue, as the remainder of the paragraph makes clear. Dante and Beatrice appear to be "real" people to this student. "Blissful Beatrice was there, Dante also, and she explained the spots on the moon to him."

In these first three sentences Beckett has set many traps for the unwary reader oblivious that he or she has stumbled into a bog much like Belacqua puzzling over Dante. There are deep matters hinted at here for the Beckett scholar, questions about justice and mercy, biblical conundrums, the tug between Christian faith and belief. Nothing is what it seems. Belacqua himself is named after an Italian character in Dante's *Purgatorio* who procrastinates; his surname, Shuah, is given to several women in the Bible. Does this mean that Beckett is suggesting his protagonist is bisexual? Or is he afraid of sex, since he has such an uneasy relationship with both the women and the men in the story? Once the students begin to think about the narrative they will see that the story resembles a circular hall of distorting mirrors in a cunningly designed amusement park.

Like Joyce's *Ulysses*, Beckett's narrative encompasses an ordinary day in the life of an unprepossessing Irishman and is organized in fragments around his meals (precisely at noon Belacqua breaks off studying Dante to prepare his lunch of a toasted bread and Gorgonzola cheese sandwich, which he downs in a pub with two pints of draft stout and another bottle of stout before his afternoon Italian lesson back at the college with the lackadaisical but brilliant Signorina Ottolenghi; then he meets his pragmatic aunt at her house, where she boils a live lobster for his dinner).

But what do these meals have to do with Dante's enigma about the markings on the moon in *The Paradiso* and Beatrice's confusing explanation? Beckett writes, "She had it from God, therefore he [Dante? Belacqua?] could rely on its being accurate in every particular." Unhappy Belacqua feels an affinity with both Dante's banished moon-dwellers and the ill-fated lobster (both have a "spavined gait," and the young man imagines how "in the depths of the sea it had crept into the cruel [lobster] pot"). Clearly Belacqua has more imagination than common sense, so Beckett gives himself the last word, when he breaks into the story in the final sentence to contradict his protagonist's facile acceptance of the lobster's fate. Like the lobster, this short story "hero" is out of his depth in the so-called real world, as his author knows best.

Questions for Discussion

1. Why is it important to know that Beckett has set his story in Dublin? What details about his own life as a student in Dublin enter into the story? How do these details about the setting help Beckett establish the voice of the story?
2. Is Belacqua a sympathetic or unsympathetic protagonist? Give details to support your opinion. What is his social class? How does this affect the way he reacts to the other characters in the story? How do his lunch preparations contribute to your feelings about him?
3. Why does the grocer fling out his arms "in a wild crucified gesture of supplication" after talking to Belacqua? How does your impression of the grocer change after he blows his nose in his apron? Why does Beckett show us this contradictory behavior?
4. How does Belacqua regain control of his "choler" after his argument with the grocer?
5. After drinking three pints of beer with his toasted cheese sandwich, how does Belacqua feel going into his Italian lesson with Ottolenghi? How does she treat him? Why is he so taken with her answer to his question "Where were we?"
6. Why does Belacqua dislike Mlle. Glain?
7. Why does Beckett enter the story as the omniscient narrator in the last section of the narration, when Belacqua "drew near to the house of his aunt"?

Topics for Writing

1. Analyze the function of "poor McCabe" in the story. How does the situation of a convicted murderer parallel Belacqua's role as protagonist?
2. Discuss Beckett's references to Dante and *The Divine Comedy* in the story.
3. How does Beckett use humor in "Dante and the Lobster"?
4. **CONNECTIONS** Compare and contrast Belacqua with the protagonist in Woody Allen's "The Kugelmass Episode," who also has a highly imaginative turn of mind about literature.

Suggested Reading

Farrow, Anthony. *Early Beckett: Art and Allusion in* More Pricks Than Kicks *and* Murphy. Troy, NY: Whitston, 1991. Farrow points out that the title of Beckett's book refers to an event in the life of Saint Paul, who was converted from slaughtering the disciples of Christ when he heard a voice from heaven telling him, "It is hard for thee to kick against the pricks" (to make defiant gestures of self-motivated revolt against reality).

AMBROSE BIERCE

An Occurrence at Owl Creek Bridge (p. 162)

What is the reason for the enduring interest of this contrived and improbable tale? Surprise endings frequently draw groans similar to those that greet bad puns, but Bierce's final twist is more likely to elicit shock and recoil. Perhaps the story's success results more from its realization of an intimate and familiar fear than from its sharp, vivid style or its tense pacing. The idea of continued life is all that the human mind, unable to imagine mere "darkness and silence," can propose in view of impending death. By narrating a fantasy of escape so persuasively that we succumb to it, and then by revealing it with the snap of a neck to have been only a fantasy, Bierce forces us to recognize once again the reality of our mortal situation.

If, out of the desire to evade that recognition, the reader seeks to repudiate the story as a piece of literary chicanery, he or she will not succeed. A clearheaded review of section III reveals that the exciting tale of escape could not have been real. Even before Farquhar enters the nightmare forest with its strange constellations and peculiar, untraveled roadway, he has experienced a preternatural heightening of sensory awareness that happens only when one sees with the eyes of the mind, and he has undergone sensations better explained by reference to a slow-motion expansion of a hanging than to his imagined plunge into Owl Creek. The images of his dream emerge from Farquhar's instinctual desire to live, and Bierce renders them with such clarity that the reader can cherish them as well. The same intensity of sensory awareness marks Bierce's conjecture about what it must be like when the noose jerks tight. We feel the constriction, see the flash of nervous discharge, and hear the cracking vertebrae.

Our close participation in the imaginary and real sensations of dying countervails the doomed man's symbolic isolation, which is the burden of section I. While the executioners enact the formal rituals that establish distance from the victim, who is being expelled from the human community (even the sentinels are turning their backs on him), Bierce leads the reader into an empathic communion with him. The agency of this imaginative projection is the coolly exact observational style, which carries us across the plank — Farquhar's first thought to which we are privy is his approval of this device — and into the psyche of the condemned.

Before launching into Farquhar's dying fantasy, however, Bierce goes back, in section II, to narrate the events leading up to the execution. Besides establishing for Farquhar an identity with which we can sympathize, this passage presents him as active rather than acted upon, and so generates a momentum that continues into the story of his escape. The section ends with one of several stark, one-line revelations that conclude passages of uncertainty, illusion, or false conjecture in the story: "He was a Federal scout"; "What he heard was the ticking of his watch"; "Peyton Farquhar was dead." This device of style expresses Bierce's major theme: Whatever we dream of, life is entrapment by death, and time is running out.

WILLIAM E. SHEIDLEY

Questions for Discussion

1. In what ways does section I suggest a psychological time much slower than actual time?
2. Why is it appropriate that the execution take place on a bridge over a river?
3. What is the function of Farquhar's conjectures about escape at the end of section I?
4. In what ways does Bierce try to gain the reader's sympathy for Farquhar? Why does he need to do this?
5. Which events in section III might be read as dislocations of sensations experienced by a man in the process of being hanged?
6. Contrast the descriptive style of a passage from section III with that of a passage from section I.
7. What would be the result if Farquhar's imagined reunion with his wife took place *after* the snapping of his neck?

Topics for Writing

1. Analyze Bierce's handling of time and chronology in "An Occurrence at Owl Creek Bridge."
2. **CONNECTIONS**   Discuss the fiction of effect as a fiction of despair in the works of Bierce, Gogol, and Poe.

Suggested Readings

Bierce, Ambrose. *The Complete Short Stories of Ambrose Bierce.* Lincoln: U of Nebraska P, 1984.
Davidson, Cathy N. *The Experimental Fictions of Ambrose Bierce.* Lincoln: U of Nebraska P, 1984.
Grenander, Mary E. *Ambrose Bierce.* New York: Twayne, 1971.
Stoicheff, Peter. "'Something Uncanny': The Dream Structure in Ambrose Bierce's 'An Occurrence at Owl Creek Bridge.'" *Studies in Short Fiction* 30.3 (Summer 1993): 349–58.
Wolotkiewicz, Diana. "Ambrose Bierce's Use of the Grotesque Mode: The Pathology of Society." *Journal of the Short Story in English* 16 (Spring 1991): 81–92.

JORGE LUIS BORGES

The Garden of Forking Paths (p. 170)

Most students will find this story very difficult to follow, because few of Borges's tangible clues as to setting or characterization are what they seem to be on first reading. The opening reference to Liddell Hart's *History of World War I*; the statement by Dr. Yu Tsun, with the missing first two pages, that describes the actual plot to follow; and the footnote about Hans Rabener, alias Viktor Runeberg, will mystify many readers. Students should be urged to read the story at least twice before attempting a discussion. In fact, some class time might profitably be given to a guided reading of the story, with students explaining their comprehension as they go along.

The commentary on the story in Part Two should also prove helpful. Borges's explanation of his fascination with the image of the labyrinth as "a symbol of bewilderment, a symbol of being lost in life" (p. 1438) explains the motivation behind Yu Tsun's desperate effort to complete his spy mission before he is killed by Captain Richard Madden. Knowledge of his impending death sharpens his concentration on his last action in life. His dilemma might be compared with Flannery O'Connor's dramatization of the final moments of her fictional characters' lives.

Borges's story is different things to different readers, but some highlights to examine are his skill in pacing the narrative to extract maximum suspense from the confrontation between Yu Tsun and Stephen Albert, Yu Tsun's emotional dilemma in his conflicting loyalties, and the inexorable approach of Richard Madden. Borges's description of the labyrinth, with its "high-pitched, almost syllabic music" audible as Yu Tsun approaches Albert's house, is also a tour de force, not likely to be forgotten if one has read the story carefully.

Questions for Discussion

1. Why does Borges begin this story in such an indirect manner?
2. Who is Yu Tsun? Richard Madden? Stephen Albert?
3. Why is Stephen Albert's last name important?
4. Why is Yu Tsun so loyal to his German chief in Berlin?
5. How does Borges establish this as a war story? How do wartime conditions contribute to the narrative?
6. Are there racist overtones in the statement "I wanted to prove to him [the chief] that a yellow man could save his armies"?
7. Borges describes the meeting between Stephen Albert and Yu Tsun very simply: "We sat down — I on a long, low divan, he with his back to the window and a tall circular clock." Why is this description particularly appropriate?
8. Explain the "ivory labyrinth" in Albert's possession and the "chaotic manuscripts" left by Ts'ui Pên.

Topics for Writing

1. Research the Greek legends about labyrinths and relate them to Borges's story.
2. CONNECTIONS Compare Borges's description of Ts'ui Pên's manuscript with the metafictions of Margaret Atwood and John Barth in this anthology.

Related Commentary

Jorge Luis Borges, The Labyrinth in "The Garden of Forking Paths," p. 1438.

Suggested Readings

Agheana, Ion Tudro. *The Meaning of Experience in the Prose of Jorge Luis Borges.* New York: P. Lang, 1988.

Alazraki, Jaime. *Critical Essays on Jorge Luis Borges.* Boston: Twayne, 1987.

Borges, Jorge Luis. *The Book of Fantasy.* New York: Carroll and Graf, 1990.

———. *The Book of Sand.* New York: NAL-Dutton, 1979.

———. *Dream Tigers.* Austin: U of Texas P, 1984.

———. *A Personal Anthology.* New York: Grove Weidenfeld, 1961.

Christ, Ronald J. *The Narrow Act: Borges's Art of Allusion.* New York: New York UP, 1969.

Lindstrom, Naomi. *Jorge Luis Borges: A Study of Short Fiction.* Boston: Twayne, 1990.

McMurray, George R. *Jorge Luis Borges.* Modern Literature Monographs. New York: Ungar, 1980.

Stabb, Martin S. *Borges Revisited.* Boston: Twayne, 1991.

TADEUSZ BOROWSKI

This Way for the Gas, Ladies and Gentlemen (p. 179)

Borowski's story can be taught with another Holocaust story in this anthology, Cynthia Ozick's "The Shawl." "The Shawl" is told by an omniscient narrator describing the ordeal of a woman victim of the concentration camps. "This Way for the Gas, Ladies and Gentlemen" has a more complex point of view, since the narrator is a Polish political prisoner (indeed, he is the writer), and he voluntarily helps the Nazis unload and brutalize the newly arrived Polish Jews.

The thoughtful comments of the Italian concentration camp survivor Primo Levi are helpful here. In *The Drowned and the Saved* (Summit, 1988), Levi explores the situation of the prisoners of war who, like Borowski, survived to tell their tales. According to Levi, the survivors who wrote about their experiences were often political prisoners like Borowski. The camps held three categories of prisoners — political, criminal, and Jewish — and the political prisoners had "a cultural background which allowed them to interpret the events they saw; and because precisely inasmuch as they were ex-combatants or antifascist combatants even now, they realized that testimony was an act of war against fascism."

Furthermore, according to Levi, "the network of human relationships inside the Lagers [camps] was not simple: it could not be reduced to the two blocs of victims and persecutors." The context of the "prisoner-functionary" (like Borowski) is poorly defined, "where the two camps of masters and servants both diverge and converge. This gray zone possesses an incredibly complicated internal structure and contains within itself enough to confuse our need to judge."

Levi continues,

> The arrival in the Lager was indeed a shock because of the surprise it entailed. The world into which one was precipitated was terrible, yes, but also indecipherable: it did not conform to any model; the enemy was all around but also inside. . . . One entered hoping at least for the solidarity of one's companions in misfortune, but the hoped for allies, except in

special cases, were not there; there were instead a thousand sealed off monads, and between them a desperate covert and continuous struggle. This brusque revelation, which became manifest from the very first hours of imprisonment, often in the instant form of a concentric aggression on the part of those in whom one hoped to find future allies, was so harsh as to cause the immediate collapse of one's capacity to resist. For many it was lethal, indirectly or even directly; it is difficult to defend oneself against a blow for which one is not prepared.

"This Way for the Gas, Ladies and Gentlemen" is one of many stories in this anthology that are based on personal experience, meticulously observed, remembered, and re-created as a "story" or work of autobiographical fiction, or "autofiction." Borowski, the narrator, was interned at Birkenau with Communists and Jews from France, Russia, Poland, and Greece. He survived the camp because he cooperated with his jailers in the persecution of victims less fortunate than himself. How does he present his story so that the reader is forced to sympathize with him, even while realizing that this sympathy is itself a faint mirror image of the prisoner's moral dilemma?

A highly rational structure holds together this totally irrational nightmare. The unities of place, time, and point of view are strictly observed. The passage of time is orderly, paralleling the organization of the transport of human beings from train to trucks to crematoria. The narrator is new to his job, and we learn it as he does. As train follows train through the stifling August afternoon and into the evening, we grow exhausted with him. The only variety is the ever-changing stream of prisoners who leave the train, take their brief walk on the platform, and disappear onto the trucks or are sorted out for the work camps. Occasionally an individual achieves humanity, like the young blonde who is so beautiful that she appears to descend "lightly" from the packed train, or the calm, tall, gray-haired woman who takes the bloated infants' corpses from the narrator, whispering to him, "My poor boy." For the narrator, such moments of grace are withheld: He hangs on to his self-control by concentrating on sheer physical endurance.

Questions for Discussion

1. How did the narrator become a storyteller? (The headnote might be helpful here, but students should be encouraged to talk about the cathartic process in the creation of fiction.)
2. What elements of narrative — plot, character, setting, language, theme — are most striking in this story?
3. Is it necessary to know the historic context of the Nazi atrocities in World War II to understand the story? Explain.

Topics for Writing

1. Report on a documentary film or a book about the Holocaust, such as Primo Levi's *The Drowned and the Saved*.
2. **CONNECTIONS** Compare Borowski's story with another example of Holocaust or prison literature you have read — Cynthia Ozick's "The Shawl," or Anne Frank's diary, or Alexander Solzhenitzyn's *One Day in the Life of Ivan Denisovich*.

3. **CONNECTIONS** Compare the psychology of prisoners in Borowski's story and in Frank O'Connor's "Guests of the Nation."

Suggested Readings

Borowski, Tadeusz. *This Way for the Gas, Ladies and Gentlemen.* Trans. Barbara Vedder. New York: Penguin, 1976.

Kuhiwczak, Piotr. "Beyond Self: A Lesson from the Concentration Camps." *Canadian Review of Comparative Literature* 19.3 (September 1992): 395–405.

Walc, Jan. "When the Earth Is No Longer a Dream and Cannot Be Dreamed Through to the End." *The Polish Review* 32.2 (1987): 181–94.

Paul Bowles

Mejdoub (p. 192)

Even if students do not know that Bowles spent most of his life in the Arab quarter of Tangiers, it is obvious from the style of "Mejdoub" that it comes from a different literary tradition. Unlike a story in the Western tradition, there is no attempt to present the central figure of the narrative as a specific individual. We are simply told that he is a man "who spent his nights sleeping in cafés or under the trees or wherever he happened to be." We are never told anything about his background or his family. We don't even know what he looks like. Since he sleeps under trees he might be a beggar, but he also sleeps some nights in cafés, which means he has enough money to pay for something to eat or drink.

Another difference between this story and a narrative in the Western tradition is that the protagonist does not experience an epiphany in the course of the action. The man doesn't learn anything about himself. He simply learns the consequences of certain specific actions. The undifferentiated central character and the absence of a central moment of self-understanding should tell the student that Bowles's narrative could be thought of as a fable or a parable, instead of a short story. Another difference is that the narrative has a clearly intended lesson, which suggests that the best term to describe it is *parable*, a term that should be familiar to students who have grown up with a religious text such as the Bible. If this were an Arabic text there would probably be an additional sentence, with the heading "Moral." The moral is the lesson to be learned from the simple narrative. What is the lesson of Bowles's parable? The lesson is that we finally become the person we appear to be.

If we follow the events of Bowles's parable with this lesson in our minds, we can see that at various points the protagonist decides to appear as someone else, and he becomes in others' minds what he appears to be. First he changes his appearance to become a beggar, and he is obviously successful. To his friends, he appears to be a man of wealth and leisure, but after several years he has truly become the beggar he appeared to be and he feels compelled to return to the city where he is known as a beggar, despite the dangers. When he is thrown into prison, he appears to be a madman, and finally, "it scarcely mattered to him any more, getting to the officials to tell them who he was." For a religious reader there will also be a subtext — that by taking on the appearance, but not the true piety, of the holy madman, the protagonist deserves God's punishment, however it is finally inflicted.

Questions for Discussion

1. The city life that the author describes is very different from the life in our cities. What are some of the differences?
2. The place of the beggar in this society is different from that of a beggar in our cities. Is there a tradition of this kind of holy begging in the history of Western civilization?
3. In the story the author mentions some of the reasons people give the beggar money. What are they?
4. Based on what we have been told about the man, what are the emotional factors that lead him to return to his life of begging, despite the danger?
5. What does the author mean by saying that the children had to feel that they owned the beggar before they would lose their fear of him?

Topic for Writing

1. Analyze the elements in Bowles's parable that are different from the elements of a conventional story in the Western tradition.

Suggested Readings

Al-Ghalith, Asad. "Paul Bowles's Portrayal of Islam in His Moroccan Short Stories." *International Fiction Review* 19.2 (1992): 103–8.

Bailey, J. "Art of Fiction: Paul Bowles." *Paris Review* 23 (1981): 63–98.

Bowles, Paul. *Collected Stories, 1939–1976.* Ed. Gore Vidal. Santa Barbara: Black Sparrow, 1979.

———. *Too Far from Home: The Selected Writings of Paul Bowles.* Hopewell, NJ: Ecco, 1993.

———. *Without Stopping: An Autobiography.* New York: Ecco, 1985.

Caponi, Gena Dagel, ed. *Conversations with Paul Bowles.* Jackson: UP of Mississippi, 1993.

Dillon, Millicent, ed. *The Portable Paul and Jane Bowles.* New York: Penguin, 1994.

Halpern, D. "Interview with Paul Bowles." *Triquarterly* 33 (1975): 159–77.

Hibbard, Allen E. "Expatriation and Narration in Two Works by Paul Bowles." *West Virginia University Philological Papers* 32 (1986–87): 61–71.

Patteson, R. F. *A World Outside: The Fiction of Paul Bowles.* Austin: U of Texas P, 1987.

Pounds, Wayne. *Paul Bowles: The Inner Geography.* New York: Lang, 1985.

Wolff, T. "A Forgotten Master." *Esquire* 103 (1985): 221–22.

Italo Calvino

If on a winter's night a traveler (p. 198)

In the opening sentence of Italo Calvino's story the reader is presented with the paradox of words described as having physical presence. The narrator is perfectly conscious that he is using descriptive phrases to show a railroad station and a locomotive, but he tells us that the steam from the locomotive "covers the opening of the chapter" and that smoke "hides part of the first paragraph." It is not too much of a stretch for many readers to see, in their imagination, steam and smoke drifting across the text on the page, even if they glimpse it only momentarily.

It is at the meeting place between a literary text as a shared "willingness to believe" (or in Samuel Taylor Coleridge's phrase, a "suspension of disbelief") and a literary text as a verbal construct without fixed textual reference that Calvino has posited his story. At least that is what he suggests to the reader in sentences such as "I am the man who comes and goes between the bar and the telephone booth. Or, rather: that man is called 'I' and you know nothing else about him. . . ." Part of the success of the story is Calvino's successful balancing act between these two conceptions of the text.

In the paragraph beginning "Getting rid of the suitcase," Calvino seems to be saying that his text has no predetermined thrust, that its meaning is indeterminate. Then in the next paragraph, beginning "A man whom I do not know," he shifts ground and we are informed that he is describing a specific moment in a specific situation. The man is a courier, involved in a complex exchange of suitcases in a strange provincial railroad station. Since the local authorities are involved in the exchange it is probably related to the Italian antifascist underground, rather than Italy's mafia.

Once the author has set his reader on solid ground the rest of the story can be read as an allusive description of a moment of danger and confusion. The reader, having absorbed the concept of the indeterminacy of a text that Calvino posited early in his narrative, can follow the text with a "willingness to believe" to its conclusion. As the author says of his method early in the story, "Watch out: it is surely a method of involving you gradually, capturing you in the story before you realize it — a trap."

Questions for Discussion

1. What details in the author's description of the station make it clear that the station is not in the United States?
2. Is the description of the people noticing the protagonist entering the station bar meant to be read as a textual conjecture or a factual description?
3. Why does the author compare espresso machines and locomotives?
4. In the second half of the paragraph beginning "The espresso machines in station cafés," the author describes the different way he must present the protagonist's situation. Is he suggesting that his story could have been set in a different time?

5. What does he mean when he says in the paragraph beginning with "You, reader" that "the result would not change much"?
6. Is the situation in which the protagonist finds himself a dangerous one? Could his sense of danger be an explanation for his eagerness to conceal the "reality" of the situation in ambiguity and uncertainty?

Topic for Writing

1. Discuss the ways in which Calvino presents his text as a construct, and the counter means by which he presents it as an assumed reality.

Related Commentary

Salman Rushdie, On Italo Calvino's "If on a winter's night a traveler," p. 1539.

Suggested Reading

Calvino, Italo. *Fantastic Tales: Visionary and Everyday.* New York: Pantheon, 1997.

ALBERT CAMUS

The Guest (p. 208)

One of the key questions raised by Camus's narrative is, Who is the true guest in the story — the Algerian Arab prisoner or the Algerian French schoolteacher? Daru, the schoolteacher, thinks of the prisoner as his guest, but at the end of the story, after watching the freed Arab choose the path to prison, the schoolteacher returns to his classroom to find he has been judged an enemy by the Arabs — on the blackboard is the message, "You handed over our brother. You will pay for this." Daru, who feels at home in the landscape, learns that he is only a temporary guest there. Its Arab inhabitants have found him lacking.

Daru's fairness and impartiality are never in question; the Arab prisoner doesn't want to leave him and doesn't kill him when he falls deeply asleep. But Daru's sense of isolation and solitude is a false one. Camus tells the story in such a way that there is never a time when the schoolteacher is unaware of the presence of both Arabs and French in his environment, beginning with the opening sentence and continuing to the last sentence, when ironically Daru feels himself truly alone, caught between opposing hostile forces.

Given the history of political strife in Algeria, the reader may well ask if Daru hasn't recognized before the story opens that he cannot remain neutral after war is declared as a result of Algeria's struggle to break free of French rule. The story takes place shortly before the French-Algerian war (1954–1962). The schoolmaster's friend Balducci, the old gendarme, warns, "Things are brewing, it appears. There is talk of a forthcoming revolt. We are mobilized, in a way." Then he goes even further, telling Daru, "If there's an uprising, no one is safe, we're all in the same boat." Daru denies the truth of his friend's words, but they neverthe-less foreshadow the hostile message on the schoolmaster's blackboard the next day. Daru is unable to continue what Balducci refers to as the soothing routine of the "comfortable life" he has enjoyed, caring for the poverty-stricken Islamic schoolchildren and tacitly endorsing the status quo.

To be sure, Daru seems to have earned the right to his peaceful life after his service in World War II. After what he has been through he feels anger toward "all men with their rotten spite, their tireless hates, their blood lust." His love for his Arab charges and for the barren, arid landscape of the country of his birth is what sustains him. Denying the political reality of his situation, carefully drawing maps of the distant rivers of France on the blackboard of his one-room schoolhouse, he has retreated to a dream world, until the advent of his uninvited guest brings him back to the world of bloodshed and civil war.

Questions for Discussion

1. Why does Balducci have a different attitude than Daru toward the Arab prisoner?
2. How does the Arab show that he shares Daru's respect for the ancient rule of hospitality — that a guest is never to be harmed?
3. Why has Daru drawn the four rivers of France on the blackboard of his Algerian schoolroom? Why does his action turn out to have ironic implica-tions at the end of the story?
4. How does the scorched landscape of the story contribute to its theme? What is the story's theme?
5. What crime did the Arab commit? Why doesn't he tell Daru he is sorry for what he has done?
6. Why does Daru let the Arab go free?
7. Why do the Arabs watching Daru leave their message on his blackboard?

Topics for Writing

1. Camus once wrote in an essay titled "The Wager of Our Generation" (1957), "No great work has ever been based on hatred or contempt. On the con-trary, there is not a single true work of art that has not in the end added to the inner freedom of each person who has known and loved it." Write an essay in which you evaluate "The Guest" in light of Camus's statement.
2. Analyze the story to account for the presence of both a limited omniscient narrator and an omniscient narrator in the narrative.

Suggested Readings

Eberhard, Greim. "Albert Camus's 'The Guest': A New Look at the Prisoner." *Studies in Short Fiction* 30.1 (Winter 1993): 95–98.
Knapp, Bettina L., ed. *Critical Essays on Albert Camus*. Boston: G. K. Hall, 1988.
McBride, Joseph. *Albert Camus: Philosopher and Litterateur*. New York: St. Martin's, 1992.
McDermott, John V. "Albert Camus's Flawed Guest." *Notes on Contemporary Lit-erature* 14.3 (May 1984): 5–7.

Meagher, Robert E., ed. *Albert Camus: The Essential Writings.* New York: Harper Colophon, 1979.

Ethan Canin

The Carnival Dog, the Buyer of Diamonds (p. 218)

When this story was published the author was only in his midtwenties. The instructor will be conscious of the paradox that younger writers such as Canin and Gish Jen have turned away from the concept of a narrative as an indeterminate text to reposit the idea of a narrative as a series of agreed assumptions between the reader and the writer. In other words, these younger writers — and they are representative of a widespread movement in their literary generation — have turned their backs on modernist literary theory and rediscovered the older conventions of literary practice. Stories like this one, or Jen's "In the American Society," would have fit comfortably into any quality magazine of the 1920s. These writers have returned to the mainstream literary tradition, and they are reaching a new generation of readers who had never abandoned their enthusiasm for the conventional story. The instructor might find it useful to teach this story and Jen's story together, since they share their literary approach as well as a common theme.

Canin's story is an especially typical part of this redeployment within the tradition because it is an immigrant story, as is Jen's. The immigrant here is Jewish, in Jen's story Chinese. But in both stories the immigrant fits uncomfortably into the new society and attempts to impose his values on his children. Although Canin doesn't tell the reader whether the protagonist's father is the immigrant himself or a first-generation child of immigrants, it is clear from the description of the man that he is still new to the society, and uncomfortable in it, in ways that his son is not.

The story of the Jewish American son struggling to free himself from the immigrant father was a staple of midcentury American fiction when waves of Jews fleeing the pogroms of Russia and Poland were being absorbed into American life. Consciously or unconsciously, Canin may have turned to this conventional style of writing fiction because his story is a conventional one. The fictional elements of the story reflect the realities of the situation he describes. The obvious difference between this story and almost every earlier one is that in Canin's story the son is defeated. Today's generation doesn't have the certainty of success of its predecessors.

Questions for Discussion

1. Although the author doesn't make the father specifically an immigrant, he presents him as an outsider. How is he outside the conventional society?
2. What does the protagonist mean when he calls himself a "sometime Jew"?
3. Has Myron finished his medical studies? How do we know?
4. What was significant about Hank Greenberg hitting a home run? Why hasn't Greenberg been celebrated in the same way as the African American baseball player Jackie Robinson?

5. Why does Myron let his father win the footrace? Why does he attack him later?
6. As the story opens it is clear that Myron has forgiven his father for tricking him five years earlier. Why has he forgiven him?

Topics for Writing

1. Sport has been a traditional entry for immigrants into the social mainstream. Describe other sports and other immigrant sport figures or groups who have made this transition.
2. **CONNECTIONS** Compare the theme and the literary methods of this story and Gish Jen's "In the American Society."

Suggested Reading

Canin, Ethan. *Emperor of the Air.* Boston: Houghton Mifflin, 1988.

ANGELA CARTER

The Company of Wolves (p. 228)

In her collection *The Bloody Chamber,* Carter included two stories based on the Little Red Ridinghood tale. She placed "The Company of Wolves" after "The Werewolf," a shorter narrative in which the grandmother is a witch who can take the form of a wolf. In this version, the girl meets the wolf in the forest on the way to her grandmother's house and fearlessly slashes off its right forepaw. She puts it in her basket and continues her walk to her grandmother's cottage. There the paw falls out of the basket and is transformed into a human hand that the girl recognizes as her grandmother's by the wart on the index finger. Little Red Ridinghood calls in the neighbors, who drive the old woman out into the snowy forest and stone her to death. This version empowers Little Red Ridinghood to vanquish the wolf with the support of her community, united in their effort to replace pagan superstition with Christian belief.

"The Company of Wolves" is a longer story imagining Little Red Ridinghood as a feminist hero. Christianity is absent, paganism rules with its complex superstitions, and the girl is on her own. But she is a hero in her society because reason, not superstition or faith in the supernatural, is her support, and it does not let her down. When "this strong-minded child" enters her grandmother's house, after flirting with the attractive hunter in the forest with whom she has entered into a bet about which of them will come first to the cottage, the girl finds "[n]o trace at all of the old woman [whom the hunter has eaten] except for a tuft of white hair that had caught in the bark of an unburned log." For the first time in her life, the girl shivers with fear, recognizing that the young man/wolf is a murderer. But then Carter tells the reader that "since her fear did her no good, she ceased to be afraid." Many readers will experience this sentence as the climax of the story. Little Red Ridinghood takes off her clothes and goes to bed with the wolf, and the tale ends with her "sweet and sound" in her grandmother's bed, safe "between the paws of the tender wolf."

Carter's version is true to the original in that it remains a fantasy tale with a happy ending, but she has created it as a story for grownups instead of children. The celebration of female sexuality is the theme here, not the fear of death or strangers.

Questions for Discussion

1. What does Carter accomplish in the first five paragraphs of her tale, before introducing the voice of Little Red Ridinghood's mother?
2. How does Carter gradually make the girl older in the story, from "the good child" at the beginning of the narrative to the satisfied young woman sleeping with the wolf at the end? Is she a round or a flat character?
3. How important is the setting of the story? Why does the hunter take out a compass and explain how it works to Little Red Ridinghood?
4. What does Carter's description of the way the grandmother has furnished her cottage suggest about the old woman?
5. Why did Little Red Ridinghood owe the hunter a kiss?

Topics for Writing

1. Analyze "The Company of Wolves" from a feminist critical perspective.
2. **CONNECTIONS** Compare and contrast Carter's tale with Hawthorne's "Young Goodman Brown" or with Irving's "Rip Van Winkle."

Related Commentary

Salman Rushdie, On Angela Carter's *The Bloody Chamber*, p. 1537.

Suggested Readings

Carter, Angela. *Burning Your Boats: The Collected Short Stories*. New York: Holt, 1996.
———. *Come Unto These Yellow Sands*. Newcastle upon Tyne: Bloodaxe, 1985.
———. *Fireworks: Nine Profane Pieces*. New York: Penguin, 1987.
———. *Nothing Sacred: Selected Writings*. London: Virago, 1982.
Fowl, Melinda G. "Angela Carter's 'The Bloody Chamber' Revisited." *Critical Survey* 3.1 (1991): 71–79.
Michael, Magali Cornier. "Feminism and the Postmodernist Impulse: Doris Lessing, Marge Piercy, Margaret Atwood, and Angela Carter." *Dissertation Abstracts International* 51.5 (Nov. 1990): 1609A.
Rushdie, Salman. "Angela Carter, 1940–92: A Very Good Wizard, A Very Dear Friend." *New York Times Book Review* Mar. 8, 1992, p. 5.
Wilson, Robert Rawdon. "SLIP PAGE: Angela Carter, in/out/in the Postmodern Nexus." *Ariel: A Review of International English Literature* 20.4 (Oct. 1989): 96–114.

Raymond Carver

Cathedral (p. 237)

"Cathedral" is a story about alienation, isolation, and the cure for both. The narrator is an insecure, jealous man, more dead than alive — a man who has constructed a virtual prison in which he exists emotionally detached from his wife and cut off from any active participation in what makes life worth living. He anesthetizes his pain with drink and marijuana while making comments that reveal his feelings of inferiority, confusion, and resentment.

When the story opens, the narrator's tone is anecdotal and familiar ("This blind man, an old friend of my wife's, he was on his way to spend the night. . . . I wasn't enthusiastic about his visit"); at the conclusion, however, his tone has become one of awe ("'It's really something,' I said"). We are aware that he has undergone an important transformation, an almost mystical experience that comes to him at an unexpected moment from an unexpected source and literally frees him from the prison his life had become. Despite his jealousy of blind Robert, and his professed resistance to the other's intrusion, the narrator unwittingly makes a friend of the blind man and in the process comes to understand something about himself. As he begins, ironically, to see through Robert's eyes, to experience the world through Robert's perceptions, his own horizons are expanded ("My eyes were still closed. I was in my house. I knew that. But I didn't feel like I was inside anything"). Robert contradicts every stereotypical idea the narrator holds about the blind, and with his commanding presence, his vitality, his sensitivity, and his engagement with life, he forces the narrator to see.

Contrasts abound between Robert and the narrator and between their respective relationships with the narrator's wife. The blind man is infinitely more alive than the narrator ("I don't have any blind friends," the narrator tells his wife; "you don't have *any* friends," she replies. "The blind man was also a ham radio operator. He talked in his loud voice about conversations he'd had with fellow operators in Guam, in the Philippines, in Alaska, and even in Tahiti. He said he'd have a lot of friends there if he ever wanted to go visit those places"). Robert and the narrator's wife (whom the narrator never calls by name but refers to, significantly, as "my wife") have a special and long-lasting friendship that involves a level of intimacy conspicuously absent from the narrator's marital relationship, the cause of much jealousy and resentment. An underlying tension is constantly present in the conversations between the couple, but with Robert the woman is a different person: "I saw my wife laughing as she parked the car. I saw her get out of the car and shut the door. She was still wearing a smile. Just amazing." We infer from this observation that she does not laugh much with her husband. His wife and Robert approach the house, "talking all the way." Earlier the narrator had commented, "right then my wife filled me in with more detail than I cared to know." Talking and the emotional sharing that results have played a vital role in the enduring relationship between the woman and the blind man; they are obviously not an integral part of the marital relationship.

"I want you to feel comfortable in this house," the wife says to her friend. "I am comfortable," Robert replies. Oddly, it is the narrator who is uncomfortable, and this discomfort prompts his pathetic attempts to feel superior to the blind man. Offering him marijuana, the narrator observes: "I could tell he didn't know the first thing." But soon he grudgingly acknowledges, "it was like he'd been doing it since he was nine years old," and the dynamics of the relationship slowly begin to change. After his wife falls asleep, the narrator offers to take Robert up to bed, but Robert declines and the narrator comments, "I'm glad for the company" and adds, "and I guess I was." They watch television together, Robert telling his host, "Whatever you want to watch is okay. I'm always learning something. Learning never ends. It won't hurt me to learn something tonight," but it is the narrator, not the blind man, who will learn something important tonight. The image of the two men's hands tracing the cathedral together is dramatic, striking, and poignant. Robert asks him if he is religious, and the narrator realizes that he truly does not know how to talk to Robert, but the difference now is that he begins to care that he doesn't ("I guess I don't believe in it. In anything. Sometimes it's hard. You know what I'm saying?" "Sure, I do," Robert answers. "Right," the narrator replies).

As the two men's hands trace the cathedral, we are reminded of the time when Robert touched the woman's face. Perhaps the connection that has been forged between the men will influence the marriage as well. The narrator's awkward and inadequate attempts at conversation with Robert are a form of engagement, and his hand speeding across the page drawing windows and arches and buttresses is truly a liberating experience. Inspired by the man who cannot see, he has literally drawn himself out of the prison to which his own limited perceptions had restricted him.

Questions for Discussion

1. Is the narrator a sympathetic protagonist? Does our opinion of him change as the story progresses?
2. What does the narrator learn from his encounter with Robert? Do you believe that there will be a significant change in his outlook from this point on?
3. What is the significance of Carver's choice of a cathedral as catalyst for the narrator's learning experience? What added dimension does this symbol bring to our understanding of the story? Can you tie it to any previous detail?
4. Contrast the author's tone and the narrator's mood at the opening of the story with the tone and mood at the end. How does the change in style reflect the change that has occurred in the narrator?
5. What is the narrator's attitude toward his wife? What kind of marriage do they have, and what evidence do you find to support your conclusion? Is the narrator's jealousy of Robert irrational?
6. What are the primary emotions displayed by the narrator throughout, and how can we understand them in terms of the life he leads? What are some adjectives you would use to characterize him? What role does alcohol play in his life?
7. What is it about Robert that unsettles the narrator? How do his appearance and bearing resist every stereotypical image the narrator has about blind people, and why is this so upsetting?

Topics for Writing

1. For Carver, salvation lies in human contact and connection. Comment critically.
2. Create a conversation between the narrator and his wife after Robert's departure.
3. Discuss "Cathedral" as a story about "the blind leading the blind."

Related Commentaries

Robert Altman, Collaborating with Carver, p. 1644.
Raymond Carver, The Ashtray, p. 1586.
Raymond Carver, Creative Writing 101, p. 1583.
Raymond Carver, On Writing, p. 1579.
Robert Coles, For Compassion, Read Carver. For Male Swagger, See Altman, p. 1646.
Tom Jenks, The Origin of "Cathedral," p. 1594.

Related Story

Tess Gallagher, Rain Flooding Your Campfire, p. 555.

Suggested Readings

See page 48.

RAYMOND CARVER

Errand (p. 248)

Raymond Carver's story may be instructively compared with the excerpt from Henri Troyat's biography of Anton Chekhov describing Chekhov's death (included with other commentary in the Carver Casebook in this anthology). In addition to providing a considerable amount of factual background about Chekhov and the last years of his century, this comparison may shed light on a question that could conceivably be asked by students in the course: What is the difference between a short story and an essay?

In comparing the fiction and nonfiction descriptions of Chekhov's last days, students will notice that Carver has based a good deal of his story on Troyat's biography of Chekhov, which Carver read and enjoyed. A knowledgeable and highly skilled literary biographer, Troyat wrote prose that (even in translation) moves briskly along almost like a short story, since Troyat eliminates editorial digressions and commentary in his desire to dramatize his account of Chekhov's last illness.

Carver has absorbed Troyat's style in addition to information about the people and places involved in Chekhov's death. The pace of the narrative is calm and unhurried, the tone unassuming and authoritative. To make "Errand" complete unto itself as a short narrative, Carver includes information about Chekhov's life — the hemorrhage he suffered while dining with Suvorin, his marriage to the actress Olga Knipper — found in earlier pages in Troyat's biography. These details provide the reader with the information necessary to appreciate the background of the story.

Perhaps most significant, Carver, unlike Troyat, invents details in telling the story of Chekhov's death. "Errand" contains the fictional character of the blond young man who works at the hotel. He brings up the bottle of champagne that Doctor Schwöhrer has ordered for Chekhov in the middle of the night. Later in the morning, the young man reappears at the door of the suite with a vase containing three yellow roses to announce to Olga Knipper that breakfast will be served that day in the garden of the hotel because of the heat wave.

Carver ingeniously introduces this fictional character by having Doctor Schwöhrer summon him from the hotel kitchen by using the telephone in Chekhov's room. This would have been a newfangled gadget in 1904, and the doctor's meticulous way of following the "instructions for using the device" makes his action believable to the reader, thus preparing the way for a fictional rather than a historical character to enter the story. Carver then tells us everything we need to know to accept the "lie": First we visualize the appearance of the young man, who was awakened from sleep and who dressed so hastily that his jacket is carelessly buttoned. Then we see what he sees when he brings his tray into Chekhov's hotel suite, and hear what he hears — the "dreadful, harrowing sound" of the dying writer's "ratchety breathing."

With the young man's reappearance in the concluding paragraphs of the story, Carver's imagination sets to work dramatizing the way that Chekhov's widow entrusts the waiter with the precious errand of notifying the mortician of Chekhov's death. Olga Knipper was an actress, and her way of explaining the errand is an actress's visualization technique. "If it would help keep his movements purposeful he should imagine himself as someone moving down the busy sidewalk carrying in his arms a porcelain vase of roses that he had to deliver to an important man." Chekhov, of course, is the precious "porcelain vase of roses," but to keep the story from veering off into sentimentality, Carver must keep imagining. He succeeds by balancing the widow's beautiful image of the precious vase with the prosaic fact of the champagne cork in the last paragraph of the narrative. The young servant, totally alive and believable as he functions in the story, has been superbly trained in this elegant Swiss hotel to do his duty. "He leaned over. Without looking down, he reached out and closed it into his hand."

Questions for Discussion

1. Why does Carver begin "Errand" with an account of Chekhov's meeting with Alexei Suvorin in 1897, four years before the writer's death?
2. Why does Carver allow Leo Tolstoy to appear in this story?
3. What have you learned about the difference between Tolstoy and Chekhov from this fictionalized encounter? (Refer to Tolstoy's commentary on Chekhov's "The Darling" in this anthology.)

4. What do Chekhov's efforts to minimize the seriousness of his tuberculosis tell you about him?
5. How effective was the medical treatment of tuberculosis at the turn of the century, judging from Doctor Schwöhrer's prescription for Chekhov's diet?
6. Why does Doctor Schwöhrer try to muffle "the festive explosion" when he uncorks the champagne? Why does he push the cork back into the bottle after he pours three glasses of the wine? Why does the champagne cork reappear in the story?

Topics for Writing

1. Write a short story based on an incident you have read in a biography of a famous person.
2. **CONNECTIONS** Write an essay comparing and contrasting Carver's treatment of death and dying with Tolstoy's in "The Death of Ivan Ilych."

Related Commentaries

Robert Altman, Collaborating with Carver, p. 1644.
Raymond Carver, The Ashtray, p. 1586.
Raymond Carver, Creative Writing 101, p. 1583.
Raymond Carver, On "Errand," p. 1588.
Raymond Carver, On Writing, p. 1579.
Robert Cole, For Compassion, Read Carver. For Male Swagger, See Altman, p. 1646.
Olga Knipper, Remembering Chekhov, p. 1589.
Henri Troyat, From "Chekhov's Last Days," p. 1590.

Suggested Readings

See page 48.

RAYMOND CARVER

What We Talk About When We Talk About Love (p. 256)

The scarcely veiled animosity between Dr. Mel McGinnis and his wife, Terri, gives tension to this story of three married couples. Through Mel's thoughts and experiences, Carver is investigating the nature of married love. Like the naive boy in Sherwood Anderson's classic short story "I Want to Know Why," Mel insists on asking an impossible question: What is the nature of love? What is the meaning of sharing?

The three pairs of lovers represent different stages of marriage. At one end of a spectrum are Laura and Nick (the narrator), married only a year and a half, still infatuated, glowing with the power of their attraction for each other.

At the other end of the spectrum are the old married pair in the hospital whom Mel and the other doctors have patched up after a catastrophic highway accident. Glad to learn his wife has survived, the old man — as Mel tells the story — is depressed, not because of their physical suffering but because he can't see his wife through the eye holes in his bandages. As Mel says, "Can you imagine? I'm telling you, the man's heart was breaking because he couldn't turn his goddamn head and *see* his goddamn wife."

Between the two extremes of perfect love, Mel and Terri are veterans (four years married to each other), who are past the bliss of their first attraction and not yet two halves of a whole because they've survived the long haul together. Each has been married before, and each is obsessed with the earlier partner. First Terri talks too much about her sadistic ex-husband Ed; then Mel reveals that he hates his first wife because she kept their kids. Terri says, "she's bankrupting us." The talk appears to ramble, but Carver keeps it under control by sticking to his subject — specific examples of the different varieties of love — and organizing the four friends' conversation by chronicling the stages of their drunkenness as they go through two bottles of gin in the afternoon.

The passing of time is brilliantly described, paralleling the waxing and waning of the stages of love. When the story opens, sunlight fills the New Mexico kitchen where the four friends with their gin and tonics are talking around the table. Midway, when the narrator is beginning to feel the drinks, he describes the sun like the warmth and lift of the gin in his body. "The afternoon sun was like a presence in this room, the spacious light of ease and generosity." As the conversation wears on and Mel tells Terri to shut up after she's interrupted one too many times, the light shifts again, the sunshine getting thinner. The narrator is a shade drunker, and his gaze fixes on the pattern of leaves on the windowpanes and on the Formica kitchen counter, as if he's staying alert by focusing deliberately on the edges of the objects around him. "They weren't the same patterns, of course." Finally, mysteriously, the light drains out of the room, "going back through the window where it had come from." The alcoholic elation has evaporated. At the end of the story, the couples sit in darkness on their kitchen chairs, not moving. The only sound the narrator hears is everyone's heart beating, separately.

The person we know least about is the narrator, Nick. Perhaps Carver deliberately echoes the name of Nick Adams, Hemingway's autobiographical narrator in his stories of initiation; or Nick Carraway, the narrator of Fitzgerald's *The Great Gatsby*. The role of Carver's Nick in the story is also like that of Marlow in Conrad's "Heart of Darkness," as Nick voyages through the conversation of Mel and Terri into uncharted, deep waters of the heart. But this Nick is also a participant, through the gin and the sunlight, in the feelings of his troubled, overworked doctor friend.

Questions for Discussion

1. As the story opens, what is the setting in time, place, and situation?
2. How would you describe Terri? What type of person is Mel?
3. What was Terri's experience with her first husband, Ed? In what way was Mel involved in this experience? How does Terri's view of Ed contrast with Mel's view of him? What does this contrast reveal about the character of Mel and Terri's relationship?

4. In the discussion about Ed, what do we discover about the couple with whom Mel and Terri are socializing? What is their relationship both to each other and to Mel and Terri? Compare and contrast their marriage with Terri and Mel's.
5. What is the point of view in this story? Who is the narrator? How reliable is he?
6. Does Mel view his first wife in the same way he does Terri? What are we told about his first wife?
7. What are some of the questions about love that Carver raises through his characters? Does he offer any answers to these questions?
8. A third couple is introduced in the story. What astonishes Mel about their relationship?
9. What changes in the setting, if any, can you identify over the course of the story? In what way does the setting mirror Carver's message about the stages of love?
10. What does each of the couples represent? What is the significance of the last paragraph?

Topics for Writing

1. Write an essay discussing theme and characterization in "What We Talk About When We Talk About Love."
2. Explore the question posed by the title of this story: What does Carver (and the reader) talk about when he (and we) talks about love?
3. Think about married couples you know and discuss what their views on love might be as well as the quality of their relationships.
4. **CONNECTIONS** Compare and contrast the types of love in Carver's story and Joyce's "The Dead."

Related Commentaries

Robert Altman, Collaborating with Carver, p. 1644.
Raymond Carver, The Ashtray, p. 1586.
Raymond Carver, Creative Writing 101, p. 1583.
Raymond Carver, On Writing, p. 1579.
Robert Coles, For Compassion, Read Carver. For Male Swagger, See Altman, p. 1646.
Arthur M. Saltzman, A Reading of "What We Talk About When We Talk About Love," p. 1595.

Suggested Readings

Adelman, Bob. *Carver Country — The World of Raymond Carver.* New York: Scribner's, 1991. A photographic essay with quotations from Carver's writing.
Carver, Raymond. "The Art of Fiction LXXVI." Interview in the *Paris Review*, No. 88 (Summer 1983).
———. *Fires: Essays, Poems, Stories.* Santa Barbara, CA: Capra, 1983.

———. *Where I'm Calling From: New and Selected Stories*. New York: Atlantic Monthly, 1988.

Gentry, Marshall B., and William A. Stull, eds. *Conversations with Raymond Carver*. Jackson: UP of Mississippi, 1990.

Halpert, Sam, ed. *When We Talk About Raymond Carver*. Layton, UT: Gibbs Smith, 1991.

Simpson, M. "Art of Fiction: Raymond Carver." *Paris Review* 25 (1983): 193–221.

Stull, W. L. "Beyond Hopelessville: Another Side of Raymond Carver." *Philological Quarterly* 64 (1985): 1–15.

Troyat, Henri. *Chekhov*. Trans. Michael Henry Heim. New York: Dutton, 1986.

WILLA CATHER

Paul's Case (p. 267)

Students may feel repelled by this story and reject its ending as heavy-handed. The structure of the plot, which pits a sensitive adolescent against an ugly and confining bourgeois society, invites us to admire Paul's rebellion and to glamorize his suicide, but Cather takes great pains to make Paul as unattractive in his way as the family, school, and neighborhood he hates. Quite apart from his supercilious mannerisms, which his teachers feel some inclination to forgive, Paul's quest for brightness and beauty in the world of art and imagination is subjected to Cather's devastating criticism, so readers who were ready to make a stock tragic response to his demise may find it difficult to care.

Try meeting this objection directly by examining the implications of the story's concluding passage. The vision presented here comes close to formulaic naturalism. Paul is not only caught in a universal machine, he is himself a machine. The imagination that has sustained him against the ugliness of his surroundings is dismissed as a "picture making mechanism," now crushed. The world against which Paul rebels is plain, gray, narrow, and monotonous. Its combination of saints (Calvin, Washington) and customary homilies precludes all that is in itself beautiful, pleasant, and fulfilling in the present moment. Paul's reaction, however, is merely the obverse. His habitual lies reflect his general resort to the artificial. He may be "artistic," but not in the sense of being creative, and his romantic fantasies involve no more satisfactory relations with others than does his ordinary life. Paul's world is so intolerable to his sensitivity that he is driven to escape from it, even at the cost of sitting in the cellar with the rats watching him from the corners. His escape inevitably becomes a form of self-destruction, as manifested in his criminal act — which to him feels like confronting "the thing in the corner" — and finally in his suicide. Paul passes through the "portal of Romance" for good, into a dream from which "there would be no awakening."

If it could be termed a choice, it would clearly be a bad choice, but Cather presents it rather as a symptom of Paul's "case," a disease of life from which he suffers, has suffered perhaps since his mother died when he was an infant, and for which, at first glance, there seems to be no cure. No wonder readers may be inclined to dismiss the story as unduly negative because unduly narrow. But Cather, at the same time that she meticulously documents the inexorable progress of Paul's illness, defines by implication a condition of health whose possible existence gives meaning to Paul's demise. As Philip L. Gerber explains: "Although [Cather] extolled the imaginative, her definition of imagination is all-important; for rather than meaning an ability 'to weave pretty stories out of nothing,' imagination conveyed to her 'a response to what is going on — a sensitiveness to which outside things appeal' and was an amalgam of sympathy and observation."

Paul's refuge is the product of the first, false kind of imagination, but the reality and the power of an imagination of the second sort is evident throughout the story, in the masterful evocations of Cordelia Street, of the school and its all-too-human teachers, and not least of Paul himself. When Paul's case finally becomes extreme enough to break through the insensitivity of bourgeois Pittsburgh, the world of the street that bears the name of King Lear's faithful daughter at last begins to live up to its name, sympathizing with Paul's plight and offering to embrace him with its love. To Paul, however, whose own unregenerate imagination is still confined to making pretty pictures rather than sympathetic observations, the advances of Cordelia Street seem like tepid waters of boredom in which he is called upon to submerge himself. The potential for growth and change that is reflected in his father's abandoning his usual frugality to pay back the money Paul has stolen and in his coming down from the top of the stairs into Paul's world to reach out to him, escape Paul's notice — but not that of the reader.

WILLIAM E. SHEIDLEY

Questions for Discussion

1. Describe Paul's personality as Cather sets it forth in the opening paragraph of the story. Is this someone we like and admire?
2. Why do Paul's teachers have so much difficulty dealing with him? What does the knowledge that Cather was a teacher in Pittsburgh at the time she wrote this story suggest about her perspective on Paul's case?
3. What techniques does Cather use to establish the reader's sympathy for Paul? What limits that sympathy?
4. Contrast the three worlds — school, Carnegie Hall, and Cordelia Street — in which Paul moves. Why does Cather introduce them in that order?
5. What is the effect of Cather's capitalizing the word *Romance*?
6. Discuss the three decorations that hang above Paul's bed. What aspects of American culture do they refer to? What do they leave out?
7. Explore the allusion embodied in the name "Cordelia Street." Why does Paul feel he is drowning there?
8. Discuss Paul's fear of rats. Why does he feel that he has "thrown down the gauntlet to the thing in the corner" when he steals the money and leaves for New York?
9. Explicate the paragraph that begins "Perhaps it was because, in Paul's world, the natural nearly always wore the guise of ugliness." To what extent does this paragraph offer a key to the story's structure and theme?
10. Describe the effect of the leap forward in time that occurs in the white space before we find Paul on the train to New York. Why does Cather withhold for so long her account of what has taken place?
11. What is admirable about Paul's entry into and sojourn in New York? What is missing from his new life?
12. Why does Paul wink at himself in the mirror after reading the newspaper account of his deeds?

13. On the morning of his suicide, Paul recognizes that "money was everything." Why does he think so? Does the story bear him out?
14. What is the effect of Paul's burying his carnation in the snow? of his last thoughts?

Topics for Writing

1. Analyze "Paul's Case" as an attack on American society.
2. In an essay argue that Cather's commentary on Mansfield (printed in Part Two, p. 1440) is a basis for criticism of "Paul's Case."
3. Cather's story is punctuated by several recurrent images and turns of phrase. Locate as many as you can and take note of their contexts. What does this network of internal connections reveal?
4. **CONNECTIONS** Compare Cather's account of Paul's death with accounts of dying in other stories, such as Tolstoy's "The Death of Ivan Ilych" and Bierce's "An Occurrence at Owl Creek Bridge."

Related Commentary

Willa Cather, The Stories of Katherine Mansfield, p. 1440.

Suggested Readings

Arnold, Marilyn. *Willa Cather: A Reference Guide.* Boston: G. K. Hall, 1986.
———. *Willa Cather's Short Fiction.* Athens: Ohio UP, 1984.
Brown, E. K., and Leon Edel. *Willa Cather: A Critical Biography.* Lincoln: U of Nebraska P, 1987.
Callander, Marilyn B. *Willa Cather and the Fairy Tale.* Ann Arbor: UMI Research P, 1989.
Cather, Willa. *Collected Short Fiction 1892–1912.* Introduction by Mildred R. Bennett. Lincoln: U of Nebraska P, 1965.
———. *Early Novels and Stories.* The Library of America. New York: Viking, 1986.
Daiches, David. *Willa Cather: A Critical Introduction.* Ithaca: Cornell UP, 1951. 144–47.
Gerber, Philip L. *Willa Cather.* Twayne's United States Authors Series 258. Boston: Hall, 1975. 72–73, 101, 141, 163.
Murphy, John J. *Critical Essays on Willa Cather.* Boston: G. K. Hall, 1984.
Thomas, Susie. *Willa Cather.* Savage, MD: Barnes and Noble, 1990.
Wasserman, Loretta. *Willa Cather: A Study of Short Fiction.* Boston: Twayne, 1991.

JOHN CHEEVER

The Swimmer (p. 283)

One way to reconstruct a naturalistic time scheme for the story, so Neddy's "misfortunes," the awareness of which he seems to have repressed, can be dated with regard to the other events in the narrative, is to imagine a gap in time covered by the line "He stayed in the Levys' gazebo until the storm had passed." The authoritative point of view in the opening paragraphs seems to preclude placing the misfortunes before Neddy begins his swim, while the gathering clouds and circling de Haviland trainer assert the continuity of the first phase of his journey. After the storm, however, signs of change appear, and it is possible to reconcile Neddy's subsequent encounters with the proposition that he is continuing his swim on another day or days under quite different circumstances. Before the storm, he visits the Grahams and the Bunkers, who greet him as the prosperous and popular Neddy Merrill described at the beginning of the story, but after the storm Neddy visits only the empty houses of the Lindleys and the Welchers; the public pool where any derelict may swim; the peculiar Hallorans, who mention his troubles; the Sachses, who have problems of their own and refuse him a drink; the socially inferior Biswangers, who snub him; and his old mistress Shirley, who implies that this call is not the first he has paid in this condition.

But Cheever is not interested in a realistic time scheme. If he were, he would not have burned the 250-page novelistic version of the story (mentioned in the headnote) that presumably filled in the blanks. Instead, he has constructed the story so Neddy's recognition of his loss strikes the reader with the same impact it has on Neddy. By telescoping time, Cheever thrusts us forward into a state of affairs that exists only as a dim cloud on the horizon on the day the story begins and at first seems to be entirely taking place.

What accounts for the reversal in Neddy's life? Surely it is possible to tax Neddy for irresponsibility and childishness in turning his back on his friends and family and so casually setting off on an odyssey from which he returns far too late. Neddy's own view of his adventure is considerably more attractive. The only member of his society who seems free from a hangover on this midsummer Sunday, Neddy simply wishes to savor the pleasures of his fortunate life: "The day was beautiful and it seemed to him that a long swim might enlarge and celebrate its beauty." Although he has been (or will be) unfaithful to his wife with Shirley Adams, and although he kisses close to a dozen other women on his journey, Neddy does not construe his departure as infidelity to Lucinda. Rather, to swim the string of pools across the suburban county is to travel along "the Lucinda River." As "a pilgrim, an explorer, a man with a destiny," Neddy plunges into this river of life aware of the gathering storm on the horizon but regarding it with pleasurable anticipation. When it finally breaks over the Levys' gazebo, he savors the exciting release of tension that accompanies the arrival of a thunder shower, but with the explosion of thunder and the smell of gunpowder that ensues, Neddy finds his happy illusions, his world of "youth, sport, and clement weather," lashed by a more unpleasant reality, just as the "rain lashed the Japanese lanterns that Mrs. Levy had bought in Kyoto the year before last, or was it the year before that?"

What Neddy now confronts, though he tries gamely to ignore it, are the twin recognitions that his youth is not eternal and that the pleasant society of the "bonny and lush . . . banks of the Lucinda River" is unstable, exclusive, and cruel. Grass grows in the Lindleys' riding ring, the Welchers have moved away, and the sky is now overcast. Crossing Route 424 in his swimming suit, Neddy is subjected to the ridicule of the public, and at the Recreation Center he finds that swimming does not convey the same sense of elegance, pleasure, and freedom that it does in the pools of his affluent friends. The validity of the society Neddy has previously enjoyed is called further into question by the very existence of the self-contradictory Hallorans, whose personal eccentricity is matched by their political hypocrisy. Neddy's visits to the Biswangers and to Shirley Adams complete the destruction of his illusions, but it is Eric Sachs, disfigured by surgery and (with the loss of his navel) symbolically cut off from the human community, who embodies the most troubling reflection of Neddy's condition. "I'm not alone," Shirley proclaims, but Neddy is, and as this man who "might have been compared to a summer's day" recognizes that his summer is over, it is not surprising that for "the first time in his adult life" he begins to cry. While the reader may relish Cheever's indictment of a society whose values have so betrayed Neddy, it is hard not to feel some admiration for a man who, by executing his plan to swim the county through the now icy autumn waters, has indeed become a legendary figure, an epic hero of a sort.

WILLIAM E. SHEIDLEY

Questions for Discussion

1. Who is referred to by the word "everyone" in the opening sentence? Who is not?
2. How does Neddy Merrill relate to the world in which he moves? Why does he decide to swim home?
3. Why does Neddy name his route "the Lucinda River"? The Levys live on "Alewives Lane." Alewives are a kind of fish that swim up rivers to spawn. Is there a sexual component to Neddy's journey?
4. Is the storm that breaks a surprise? How does Neddy feel about the beginning of the rain?
5. What differences can be noticed between what Neddy experiences before and after the storm? How might they be explained?
6. What new elements enter the story when Neddy crosses Route 424? Why do the drivers jeer at him?
7. Before he dives into the unappealing public swimming pool, Neddy tells himself "that this was merely a stagnant bend in the Lucinda River." How characteristic is this effort to assuage his own doubts and discontents?
8. Based on what the Hallorans, the Sachses, the Biswangers, and Shirley Adams say to Neddy, what is the truth about himself and his life of which he is unaware?
9. Cheever has his hero discover the season by observing the stars. What effect does that choice among various possibilities have on our attitude toward Neddy?
10. It is not difficult to say what Neddy has lost. What has he gained?

Topics for Writing

1. Explain why Neddy Merrill talks only with women.
2. Analyze the characters Rusty Towers, Eric Sachs, and Neddy Merrill.
3. Write an essay discussing Neddy Merrill's voyage of exploration and discovery.
4. Evaluate Cheever's attitude toward the swimmer.

Related Commentary

John Cheever, Why I Write Short Stories, p. 1444.

Suggested Readings

Cheever, John. *The Journals of John Cheever*. New York: Knopf, 1991.
Cheever, Susan. *Home before Dark*. Boston: Houghton, 1984.
Coale, Samuel. *John Cheever*. New York: Ungar, 1977. 43–47.
Collins, R. G., ed. *Critical Essays on John Cheever*. Boston: G. K. Hall, 1982.
O'Hara, James E. *John Cheever: A Study of the Short Fiction*. Boston: Twayne, 1989.
Waldeland, Lynne. *John Cheever*. Boston: Twayne, 1979.
Writers at Work, Fifth Series. New York: Penguin, 1981. Interview with John Cheever
    by Annette Grant, Fall 1976.

ANTON CHEKHOV

The Darling (p. 293)

One of the liveliest discussions about a short story in this anthology could be started by a class debate based on the contradictory interpretations of "The Darling" by Leo Tolstoy and Eudora Welty included in Part Two (pp. 1556 and 1568). Tolstoy was convinced that Chekhov was misguided in satirizing women's tendency to depend on men for meaning and direction in their lives. In Tolstoy's view, Chekhov had allowed himself to become a women's rights advocate under the pernicious influence of his "liberated" wife, the actress Olga Knipper. Welty, in contrast, reveals the subtle emotional tyranny of the protagonist, Olenka. In Welty's interpretation, the schoolboy shows us at the end of the story that men want their "space" too. Students could be assigned Tolstoy's or Welty's interpretation and asked to support or refute it. Certainly neither interpretation is unassailable.

Other critical perspectives can also be applied to this provocative story. A feminist reader could argue that Olenka has been handicapped by the environment around her: Uneducated for a profession, she can have no ideas or life of her own. A psychological interpretation could concentrate on the darling's early, possibly traumatic fixation on her father and his long mortal illness just as she reaches manageable age. A formalist approach might look closely at the words the schoolboy uses as he cries out in his sleep: "I'll give it you! Get away! Shut up!" Welty assumes that the boy is dreaming of Olenka. He could just as well be dreaming of his teacher at school, other students fighting with him in the schoolyard, or his own mother, who appears to have abandoned him. He could even be repeating the cruel words his mother might have said to drive him away from her before she left him with Olenka.

The English short story writer H. E. Bates interpreted the story yet another way. Comparing Chekhov's technique with Maupassant's, Bates writes, "Both like to portray a certain type of weak, stupid, thoughtless woman, a sort of yes-woman who can unwittingly impose tragedy or happiness on others. Maupassant had no patience with the type; but in Olenka, in the 'The Darling,' it is precisely a quality of tender patience, the judgment of the heart and not the head, that gives Chekhov's story its effect of uncommon understanding and radiance."

Bates saw Chekhov as subtle: His

> receptivity, his capacity for compassion, are both enormous. Of his characters he seems to say, "I know what they are doing is their own responsibility. But how did they come to this, how did it happen? There may be some trivial thing that will explain." That triviality, discovered, held for a moment in the light, is the key to Chekhov's emotional solution. In Maupassant's case the importance of that key would have been inexorably driven home; but as we turn to ask of Chekhov if we have caught his meaning aright, it is to discover that we must answer that question for ourselves — for Chekhov has gone. . . . Both [Maupassant and Chekhov] knew to perfection when they had said enough; an acute instinct continually reminded them of the fatal tedium of explanation, of going on a second too long. In Chekhov this sense of impatience, almost a fear, caused him frequently to stop speaking, as it were, in mid-air. It was this which gave his stories an air of remaining unfinished, of leaving the reader to his own explanations, of imposing on each story's end a note of suspense so abrupt and yet refined that it produced on the reader an effect of delayed shock.

Questions for Discussion

1. How does Chekhov characterize Olenka at the beginning of the story?
2. Why does he have the "lady visitors" be the first ones to call her a "darling"?
3. Olenka "mothers" each of her husbands. Could she have been both a good wife and a good mother if she had had children of her own? Why or why not?

Topics for Writing

1. Interpret Sasha's words at the end of "The Darling." Identify the person he is talking to, and find details in the story that justify your interpretation.
2. Continue "The Darling," supposing that the "loud knock at the gate" is a message from Sasha's mother, who wants him to join her in Harkov.

Related Commentaries

Anton Chekhov, Technique in Writing the Short Story, p. 1446.
Olga Knipper, Remembering Chekhov, p. 1589.
Leo Tolstoy, Chekhov's Intent in "The Darling," p. 1556.
Henri Troyat, "Chekhov's Last Days," p. 1590.
Eudora Welty, Plot and Character in Chekhov's "The Darling," p. 1568.

(text pp. 302–314)

Suggested Readings

See page 58.

ANTON CHEKHOV

The Lady with the Pet Dog (p. 302)

Anna Sergeyevna comes to Yalta because she wants "to live, to live!" Gurov begins his affair with her because he is bored and enjoys the freedom and ease of a casual liaison. At the outset both are undistinguished, almost clichés — a philandering bank employee escaping from a wife he cannot measure up to, a lady with a dog and a "flunkey" for a husband. By the end of the story, however, after having been captured and tormented by a love that refuses to be filed away in memory, the two gain dignity and stature by recognizing that life is neither exciting nor easy; and, by taking up the burden of the life they have discovered in their mutual compassion, they validate their love.

Chekhov develops the nature of this true love, so ennobling and so tragic, by testing it against a series of stereotypes that it transcends and by showing a series of stock expectations that it violates. Anna Sergeyevna reacts differently from any of the several types of women Gurov has previously made love to, and Gurov finds himself unable to handle his own feelings in the way he is accustomed to. Anna Sergeyevna proves neither a slice of watermelon nor a pleasant focus of nostalgia. Most important, as the conclusion implies, she will not remain the secret core of his life, bought at the price of falsehood and suspicion of others.

In observing the evolution of the lovers, the reader is led through a series of potential misconceptions. We may want to despise Gurov as a careless breaker of hearts, but it is clear that he has one of his own when he sees Anna Sergeyevna as a Magdalene. Later, when Gurov is tormented by his longings for Anna Sergeyevna, we are tempted to laugh the superior realist's laugh at a romantic fool: Surely when Gurov arrives at S——, disillusionment will await him. And in a sense it does. Just as there was dust in the streets at Yalta, the best room in the hotel at S—— is coated with dust; reality is an ugly fence; and even the theater (where *The Geisha* is playing) is full of reminders of how unromantic life really is. But Anna Sergeyevna has not, as Gurov supposes at one point, taken another lover, nor has she been able to forget Gurov.

The antiromantic tone is but another oversimplification, and the story comes to rest, somewhat like Milton's *Paradise Lost*, at a moment of beginning. The lovers' disillusionment about the nature of the struggle they face creates in them a deep compassion for each other, which finds its echo in readers' final attitude toward them as fellow human beings whose lives are like our own and who deserve a full measure of our sympathy. Or perhaps they draw our pity; surely their fate, which Chekhov so skillfully depicts as probable and true, inspires tragic fear. Gurov and Anna Sergeyevna have met the god of love, and Chekhov awes us by making him seem real.

WILLIAM E. SHEIDLEY

Questions for Discussion

1. Why does Gurov call women "the inferior race"?
2. At the end of section I, Gurov thinks that there is "something pathetic" about Anna Sergeyevna. Is there? What is it?
3. Why is Anna Sergeyevna so distracted as she watches the steamer putting in?
4. How does Anna Sergeyevna differ from other women Gurov has known, as they are described in the paragraph that ends "the lace on their lingerie seemed to him to resemble scales"? Compare this passage with the paragraph that begins "His hair was already beginning to turn gray."
5. In view of what follows, is it appropriate that Gurov should see Anna Sergeyevna as a Magdalene?
6. What is the function of the paragraph that begins "At Oreanda they sat on a bench not far from the church"?
7. What "complete change" does Gurov undergo during his affair with Anna Sergeyevna at Yalta? Is it permanent?
8. Explain Gurov's remark at the end of section II: "High time!"
9. Why is Gurov enraged at his companion's remark about the sturgeon?
10. Discuss the possible meanings of the objects Gurov encounters in S——: the broken figurine, the long gray fence, the cheap blanket, and so on.
11. Seeing Anna Sergeyevna enter the theater, Gurov "understood clearly that in the whole world there was no human being so near, so precious, and so important to him." What is Chekhov's tone in this statement?
12. Explain Anna Sergeyevna's reaction to Gurov's arrival. Why does she volunteer to come to Moscow?
13. Discuss the implications of Gurov's "two lives" as Chekhov explains them in section IV. Do you agree with the generalizations about the desire for privacy with which the paragraph ends? Relate these ideas to the story's ending.
14. What will life be like for Gurov and Anna Sergeyevna? Anna has previously said, "I have never been happy; I am unhappy now, and I never, never shall be happy, never!" Is she right?

Topics for Writing

1. Write an essay describing Chekhov's characterization of the wronged spouse in "The Lady with the Pet Dog."
2. Discuss the meaning of the three geographical locales in "The Lady with the Pet Dog."
3. On your first reading of the story, stop at the end of each section and write down your judgment of Gurov and Anna Sergeyevna and your prediction of what will happen next. When you have finished reading, compare what you wrote with what turned out to be the case and with your final estimate of the protagonists. To the extent that your initial impressions were borne out, what points in the text helped to guide you? To the extent that you were surprised, explain what led you astray. What might Chekhov have wanted to accomplish by making such misconceptions possible?
4. **CONNECTIONS** Explore the themes of geography and adultery in Chekhov's "The Lady with the Pet Dog" and Bessie Head's "Life."

Related Commentaries

Anton Chekhov, Technique in Writing the Short Story, p. 1446.
Olga Knipper, Remembering Chekhov, p. 1589.
Henri Troyat, "Chekhov's Last Days," p. 1590.
Vladimir Nabokov, A Reading of Chekhov's "The Lady with the Little Dog," p. 1515.

Suggested Readings

Bates, H. E. *The Modern Short Story.* Boston: The Writer, 1972.
Eekman, Thomas. *Critical Essays on Anton Chekhov.* Boston: G. K. Hall, 1989.
Friedland, Louis S., ed. *Anton Tchekhov's Letters on the Short Story, the Drama, and Other Topics.* Salem, NH: Ayer, 1965.
Kramer, Karl D. *The Chameleon and the Dream: The Image of Reality in Chekhov's Stories.* The Hague: Mouton, 1970. 171.
Matlaw, Ralph E., ed. *Anton Chekhov's Short Stories.* New York: Norton, 1979.
Meister, Charles W. *Chekhov Criticism, 1880 through 1986.* New York: St. Martin's, 1990.
Pritchett, V. S. *Chekhov: A Spirit Set Free.* New York: Random, 1988.
Rayfield, Donald. *Chekhov: The Evolution of His Art.* New York: Barnes, 1975. 197–200.
Smith, Virginia Llewellyn. "The Lady with the Dog." Anton Chekhov's Short Stories: Texts of the Stories, Backgrounds, Criticism. Ed. Ralph E. Matlaw. New York: Norton, 1979. Excerpted from Smith, *Anton Chekhov and the Lady with the Dog* (New York: Oxford UP, 1973). 96–97, 212–18.
Troyat, Henri. *Chekhov.* Trans. Michael Henry Heim. New York: Dutton, 1986.

Charles Chesnutt

The Sheriff's Children (p. 315)

Webster's Dictionary defines "melodrama" as a work characterized by the predominance of plot and physical action over characterization. Plot is plentiful in Chesnutt's story; first he begins with leisurely opening paragraphs to set the time and place of the story in the backwoods of North Carolina a decade after the Civil War, and then in a few rapid paragraphs he presents the reader with a murder, the capture of the murder suspect, and the formation of a mob determined to lynch the suspect before he can be brought to trial. The characters in Chesnutt's story are types: the angry, self-righteous members of the lynch mob; the brave white southern sheriff faithful to his duty who confronts the mob in order to see justice done (rather than to protect the prisoner); his obedient, loving daughter, who courageously saves his life; and the prisoner, the sheriff's unrecognized illegitimate son, who commits suicide rather than face southern justice (or, it might be argued, chooses to become a hero and take his own life rather than compromise his father's respected position in local society by revealing his identity).

Plot may dominate this "old-fashioned" story, but the thoughtful reader may have occasion to reflect upon the manner of Chesnutt's telling of his tale. He delineates wooden, stereotypical characters, but he is passionately involved in dramatizing the tragic legacy of racism flourishing in the United States after the Civil War, and to this end he skillfully suggests subtle undercurrents beneath the surface of the father-son relationship. Writing at the turn of the century, Chesnutt can be categorized as a naturalist like his American contemporaries Theodore Dreiser and Jack London, deeply engaged in the debates of his time over the relative importance of the influences of nature and nurture in the formation of human character.

The sheriff's daughter, unlike his illegitimate son, shares her father's sense of responsibility and bravery. When the sheriff learns he is the prisoner's father, he thinks in terms of the careful nurturing he received, which his own life reflects: "He saw in this mulatto what he himself might have become had not the safeguards of parental restraint and public opinion been thrown around him." Unlike the sheriff's daughter, the mulatto has had none of the opportunities due him by right of birth, namely, the privileges of his father's social class and the protection of his father's position. Instead, race has ruled his life in the United States. Born the son of a black slave mother, his opportunities to succeed in life have been restricted from birth, despite his intelligence. He tells the sheriff that in school "I learned to feel that no degree of learning or wisdom will change the color of my skin and that I shall always wear what in my own country is a badge of degradation."

The mulatto prisoner is thus a "natural" man, his character bereft of the civilizing effects of a nurturing family upbringing. We first see him through the sheriff's eyes as he sits in his cell, a yellow-faced (read cowardly), "cowering wretch," protesting his innocence in a way that evokes the sheriff's contempt. Uppermost in the nameless mulatto's mind is his own survival. When he gets control of the sheriff's gun, his character changes dramatically. The sheriff is overcome with "an involuntary feeling of apprehension.... The keen-eyed, desperate man before him was a different being altogether from the groveling wretch who had begged so piteously for life a few minutes before."

Readers may analyze the spirited exchange between father and son in which the son's innate courage and intellectual superiority are apparent in his rational judgment that death is preferable to life as a mulatto in the United States. Like his father, he is also aware of the nature/nurture controversy: "It is the animal in me, not the man, that flees the gallows." He is prepared to kill his father to save his own life, and has "raised his arm to fire," when his half-sister Polly wounds him in the arm with her own pistol. Chesnutt skillfully diverts our attention from the mulatto's feelings at this point by describing Polly's action. When we next see the prisoner, he has changed once again: "His bravado had given place to a stony apathy. There was no sign in his face of fear or disappointment or feeling of any kind." When his father bandages the wound, the son "utter[s] no word of thanks or apology, but [sits] in sullen silence." Chesnutt tells us no more. He lets us put ourselves in the mulatto's situation to imagine what he might have been thinking and feeling locked overnight in his cell, making his decision to tear the bandage from his wound in order to bleed to death.

Questions for Discussion

1. Why does Chesnutt go into such detail in describing the setting of the story? What is the importance of the "sequestered," "conservative" nature of Branson County, North Carolina?

2. Analyze the process by which the lynch mob persuades itself to take justice into its own hands, ending in Chesnutt's simple statement, "a white man had been killed by a negro."

3. Why does the sheriff invite the negro Sam to have some dinner?

4. Why is the sheriff a hero to the people in the town?

5. Analyze the foreshadowing that Chesnutt has written into the passage beginning, "He had sworn to do his duty faithfully, and he knew what his duty was . . ." and continuing to the end of the paragraph.

6. Why is the sheriff able to talk the mob out of lynching the prisoner?

7. Why do you feel the prisoner took his own life? How does his action relate to the statement he made to his father, "You gave me a white man's spirit, and you made me a slave, and crushed it out"?

Topics for Writing

1. Research the history of the changing social position of African Americans in the southern states after the Civil War.

2. Analyze Chesnutt's explanation of why the sheriff hesitates to promise *not* to go after the mulatto after he escapes from jail: "[T]he baleful influence of human slavery poisoned the very foundations of life, and created new standards of right. The sheriff was conscientious: his conscience had merely been warped by his environment."

3. Analyze the racial stereotypes in the story.

4. **CONNECTIONS** Compare and contrast Chesnutt's dramatization of black-white relations in the South with that in the stories by William Faulkner and Zora Neale Hurston.

Suggested Readings

Chesnutt, Charles Waddell. *The Conjure Woman and Other Conjure Tales.* Ed. R. Broadhead. Durham, NC: Duke UP, 1993.

———. *The Wife of His Youth, and Other Stories of the Color Line.* Ridgewood, NJ: Gregg, 1967.

Render, Sylvia Lyons. *Charles W. Chesnutt.* Boston: Twayne, 1980.

———, ed. *The Short Fiction of Charles W. Chesnutt.* Washington, D.C.: Howard UP, 1974.

KATE CHOPIN

Désirée's Baby (p. 329)

It is difficult to imagine a reader who would not be horrified and disgusted by the tragic results of the racism and sexism that permeate this story. No one could believe that Armand Aubigny's inhuman cruelty to his wife Désirée and his child is warranted. The only real uncertainty the reader confronts regards Armand's foreknowledge of his own parentage: Did he know that his mother had "negro blood" before he married Désirée, or did he discover her revealing letter later on? If he *did* know beforehand (and it is difficult to believe that he did not) his courtship of and marriage to Désirée were highly calculated actions, with Désirée chosen because she was the perfect woman to be used in an "experimental" reproduction. If their child(ren) "passed" as white, everything would be fine. If not, Désirée, the foundling, would be the perfect victim to take the blame.

This may seem to be judging Armand too harshly, because the narrator does describe his great passion for Désirée, so suddenly and furiously ignited. Certainly Armand behaves like a man in love. But Chopin inserts a few subtle remarks that allow us to question this, at least in hindsight: "The wonder was that he had not loved her before; for he had known her since his father brought him home from Paris, a boy of eight, after his mother died there." It does seem unlikely that a man of Armand's temperament would conceive this sudden intense desire for "the girl next door," a sweet, naive young woman whom he has known for most of his life. Right from the beginning, Chopin also reveals details about his character that are unsettling, even to the innocent and loving Désirée. The basic cruelty of Armand's nature is hinted at throughout the story, particularly regarding his severe treatment of "his negroes," which is notably in sharp contrast to his father's example.

Armand's reputation as a harsh slavemaster supports the presumption that he has known about his own part-negro ancestry all along. He did not learn this behavior from his father, who was "easy-going and indulgent" in his dealings with the slaves. The knowledge that some of his own ancestors spring from the same "race of slavery" would surely be unbearable to the proud, "imperious" Armand, and the rage and shame that his knowledge brings would easily be turned against the blacks around him. In much the same way, when Armand realizes that his baby is visibly racially mixed, he vents his fury viciously on his slaves, the "very spirit of Satan [taking] hold of him."

Modern readers will find many disturbing aspects to this story. The seemingly casual racism is horrifying. And feminists will be likely to take exception (as they sometimes do to Chopin's *The Awakening*) to Désirée's passive acceptance of Armand's rejection of her and his child, and her apparently deliberate walk into the bayou. Suicide is not the strong woman's answer to the situation, but Désirée is definitely not a strong woman. What she does have is wealthy parents who love her and are willing to take care of her and the baby. So why would she feel that she has to end her life? Discussion of this issue will have to focus on the historical period and social setting of the story. Gender and class roles and structures were so rigid that it was impossible for a woman to cross those lines very far. If she tried, what would the cost be to her children? And of course, the most rigid barrier of all was racial. No mixing of black and white blood would ever be condoned in that society (thus, Armand's mother remained in France, keeping her family secrets), so Désirée's baby would never have acceptance anywhere. Désirée isn't able to see any viable way out of her terrifying situation, and her view is not entirely unrealistic, considering her time and place. Once again, Kate Chopin realistically depicts the cruelty and horror of a social structure that totally denies power to women, children, the poor, and most of all, to blacks.

Questions for Discussion

1. Describe your feelings toward Armand at the end of the story. What aspect of this last scene do you find the most shocking? Are you completely surprised by his behavior here? See if you can trace Chopin's gradual building of Armand's character, noting the things she chooses to reveal to us throughout the story.
2. What kind of person is Désirée? Does she seem to be a good match for Armand? Does your opinion of her change as the story progresses? How consistent is she as a character?
3. How do you feel about Désirée's final choice? Is suicide an understandable choice, or is she simply a weak character? What other options do you think she may have?
4. Should Madame Valmondé have told Désirée of her realization about the baby? When she sees the baby at four weeks of age, she obviously is startled by something in its appearance, but doesn't mention it. Then, she returns home and seems to wait for disaster to strike, never returning to visit Désirée. How do you explain this behavior, coming from an obviously protective, loving mother?
5. Armand is shown to be a very cruel master to his slaves, a direct contrast to the way in which his father ran the plantation. Does learning his family secret in the last scene suggest any explanation for this?
6. Do you think Armand knew about his own mother's negro ancestry before he courted and married Désirée? Look for evidence from the story to support your opinion.

Topics for Writing

1. Discuss the way the setting affects the action in this story.
2. Should Désirée have returned to her family home with her baby? Consider the pros and cons of her future there.
3. According to the critic Wai-chee Dimock, the racial injustice in "Désirée's Baby" is "only a necessary background against which Chopin stages her deadly dramatic irony. . . . The injustice here is not the injustice of racial oppression but the injustice of a wrongly attributed racial identity." Agree or disagree with this interpretation of the story.
4. **CONNECTIONS** Compare and contrast "Désirée's Baby" and Chesnutt's "The Sheriff's Children," two stories about mulatto offspring.

Related Commentary

Kate Chopin, How I Stumbled upon Maupassant, p. 1448.

Suggested Readings

See page 64.

KATE CHOPIN

The Story of an Hour (p. 333)

Does the O. Henryesque trick ending of this story merely surprise us, or does Chopin arrange to have Louise Mallard expire at the sight of her unexpectedly still living husband in order to make a thematic point? Students inclined to groan when Brently Mallard returns "composedly carrying his gripsack and umbrella" may come to think better of the ending if you ask them to evaluate the doctors' conclusions about the cause of Mrs. Mallard's death. Although Richards and Josephine take "great care . . . to break to her as gently as possible the news of her husband's death," what actually kills Mrs. Mallard is the news that he is still alive. The experience of regeneration and freedom that she undergoes in the armchair looking out upon a springtime vista involves an almost sexual surrender of conventional repressions and restraints. As she *abandons herself* to the realization of her freedom that *approaches to possess her*, Mrs. Mallard enjoys a hitherto forbidden physical and spiritual excitement. The presumption that she would be devastated by the death of her husband, like the presumption that she needs to be protected by watchful, "tender" friends, reduces Mrs. Mallard to a dependency from which she is joyful at last to escape. Chopin best images this oppressive, debilitating concern in what Mrs. Mallard thinks she will weep again to see: "the kind, tender hands folded in death; the face that had never looked save with love upon her, fixed and gray and dead." Although had she lived Mrs. Mallard might have felt guilty for, as it were, taking her selfhood like a lover and pridefully stepping forth "like a goddess of Victory," Chopin effectively suggests that the guilt belongs instead to the caretakers, the "travel-stained" Brently, the discomfited Josephine, and Richards, whose "quick motion" to conceal his error comes "too late."

WILLIAM E. SHEIDLEY

Questions for Discussion

1. In view of Mrs. Mallard's eventual reactions, evaluate the efforts of Josephine and Richards to break the news of her husband's death gently.
2. What purpose might Chopin have in stressing that Mrs. Mallard does not block out the realization that her husband has died?

3. What might be the cause or causes of the "physical exhaustion that haunted her body and seemed to reach into her soul" that Mrs. Mallard feels as she sinks into the armchair?
4. Describe your reaction to the view out the window the first time you read the story. Did it change on a second reading?
5. Mrs. Mallard's face bespeaks repression. What has she been repressing?
6. Discuss the imagery Chopin uses to describe Mrs. Mallard's recognition of her new freedom.
7. What kind of man is Brently Mallard, as Mrs. Mallard remembers him? In what ways does he resemble Josephine and Richards?
8. Describe your feelings about Mrs. Mallard as she emerges from her room. Is the saying "Pride goeth before a fall" relevant here?
9. In what way is the doctors' pronouncement on the cause of Mrs. Mallard's death ironic? In what sense is it nonetheless correct?

Topics for Writing

1. Discuss the imagery of life and the imagery of death in "The Story of an Hour."
2. Write a paper analyzing "The Story of an Hour" as a thwarted awakening.
3. Describe the tragic irony in "The Story of an Hour."
4. On a second reading of "The Story of an Hour," try to recall how you responded to each paragraph or significant passage when you read it the first time. Write short explanations of any significant changes in your reactions. To what extent are those changes the result of knowing the story's ending? What other factors are at work?
5. Can falsehood be the key to truth? Narrate a personal experience in which your own or someone else's reaction to misinformation revealed something meaningful and true.
6. How long is a turning point? Tell a story covering a brief span of time — a few minutes or an hour — in which the central character's life is permanently changed. Study Chopin's techniques for summarizing and condensing information.

Related Commentary

Kate Chopin, How I Stumbled upon Maupassant, p. 1448.

Suggested Readings

Bender, B. "Kate Chopin's Lyrical Short Stories." *Studies in Short Fiction* 11 (1974): 257–66.

Chopin, Kate. *The Complete Works of Kate Chopin.* Baton Rouge: Louisiana State UP, 1970.

Dimock, Wai-chee. "Kate Chopin." *Modern American Women Writers.* Ed. Elaine Showalter et al. New York: Collier, 1993.

Fluck, Winifred. "Tentative Transgressions: Kate Chopin's Fiction as a Mode of Symbolic Action." *Studies in American Fiction* 10 (1982): 151–71.

Miner, Madonne M. "Veiled Hints: An Affected Stylist's Reading of Kate Chopin's 'Story of an Hour.' " *Markham Review* 11 (1982): 29–32.

Seyersted, Per. *Kate Chopin: A Critical Biography.* Baton Rouge: Louisiana State UP, 1969. 57–59.

Skaggs, Peggy. *Kate Chopin.* Boston: Twayne, 1985.

Toth, Emily. *Kate Chopin.* New York: Morrow, 1990.

SANDRA CISNEROS

The House on Mango Street (p. 337)
Hairs (p. 338)
My Name (p. 338)
The Monkey Garden (p. 339)
Mango Says Goodbye Sometimes (p. 341)

THE HOUSE ON MANGO STREET, HAIRS, AND MY NAME

Cisneros opens her collection *The House on Mango Street* with these three stories, and they are so short that, read together as a unit, they can serve the student well as an introduction to the author's narrative approach. Cisneros credits Jorge Luis Borges's *Dreamtigers* as an important influence on her choice of form in *The House on Mango Street.* Like Borges in "Everything and Nothing," a short piece from *Dreamtigers,* Cisneros works within short narrative forms, writing sketches rather than stories. Where Borges develops an idea about Shakespeare as his theme, Cisneros dramatizes emotions in her sketches. These emotions belong to the young narrator as she tells about her experiences of economic hardship and social marginalization within a Mexican American family. The economic and social realities of her life are difficult, but the emotional security she finds within her tightly knit family appears to have given her the strength to survive the difficulties she faces and enables her to speak in the positive tone of her stories.

"The House on Mango Street" starts in a voice that suggests muted protest, foreshadowing our awareness of the narrator's developing strength of character. In the opening paragraph, the narrator names the various streets her family has lived on as they moved from apartment to apartment during her early childhood. Her memories center on the difficult living conditions in the different rental apartments — for example, broken water pipes and a hostile landlord "banging on the ceiling with a broom" if the six members of her family made too much noise. Her parents have told their four children that they would eventually own their own home, and this promise gives them hope. Cisneros's book begins when the family has achieved its dream of home ownership. Then the author takes the difference between the American dream and its economic and social reality as the subject of her book.

Students should be aware that Cisneros and her young narrator are not identical. Cisneros has chosen the persona of a young girl to tell her stories, and this choice of first-person point of view adds considerable poignancy to her narratives. Reading "The House on Mango Street," we are aware that the (imaginary) narrator's naiveté is part of the emotional effect of what she tells us. We become emotionally involved in the story through her shy pride at moving into her "own" house on Mango Street, and through her confusion after she realizes that the dream house her parents have promised her isn't at all what she dreamed it would be.

We understand how important the house is to the narrator when she tells us about the apartment on Loomis where the family lived before moving to Mango Street. There a nun from her school made her "feel like nothing" by tactlessly wondering how her young pupil could live in a building that had been so brazenly burglarized. Yet among the descriptive details of the way the Loomis building looked, the narrator discloses that her father had nailed wooden bars on the windows of the family's third-floor apartment so that she and her brother Carlos and sister Nenny and the baby Kiki wouldn't fall out. The significance of this detail doesn't weigh as heavily on the narrator as her memory of her shame before the nun, but we register the father's concern for his young children's safety. There is little character description in Cisneros's stories, but the essential details giving coherence to the narrative are there.

"Hairs" describes the narrator's perception of the different types of hair within her immediate family. Reading her description as metaphor, we can understand each character's personality traits. Once again the reader is shown the importance of the family's emotional support to the narrator's sense of well-being. Her father's "hair is like a broom" (that is, he is an industrious man, working hard to support his family). Her hair "is lazy" (that is, she is still an irresponsible child, with a mind of her own). The baby Kiki "has hair like fur" (the child narrator perceives the demanding little sister as more animal than human). The longest description is of the mother's hair, as the narrator's relationship with her mother is central to the girl's sense of emotional security. Her hair "is the warm smell of bread before you bake it," complete sustenance and acceptance, the staff of life itself.

"My Name" follows "Hairs" as the narrator places herself in the center of this third sketch. The reader learns that her name is Esperanza, but only midway through the sketch. She is named after her great-grandmother, giving us a sense of the girl's pride in the continuity and longevity of her family. The name means "hope" in Spanish, and it has a faintly old-fashioned ring, reminiscent of the Puritans' tradition of naming their daughters Hope, Faith, and Charity. Now the Mexican, not the English, are the immigrants to the New Land, and Cisneros's stories are the literature of this new cultural wave, as Hawthorne's were to readers in the United States in the preceding century.

The Monkey Garden and Mango Says Goodbye Sometimes

In the three earlier stories, Cisneros introduces the setting, plot, and characters of her narrative. Esperanza's family background is central to these introductory sketches, but as she begins to grow up on Mango Street, she spends more time with her friends. Then she discovers that the strongest sense of conflict in her life can come from her own feelings.

"The Monkey Garden" begins abruptly with a statement of the absence of the monkey. This is odd, as the monkey is featured in the story's title. There are more highly developed characters and action in the plot of this story, but ironically the sense of absence is at the narrative's emotional center. Esperanza experiences happiness playing as a tomboy with her young friends in the monkey garden. She thinks she has found the Garden of Eden, where she and her neighborhood gang can escape the complexities of the adult world. It contains treasure ("Nenny found a dollar and a dead mouse") and perfect peace ("Eddie Vargas laid his head beneath a hibiscus tree and fell asleep there like a Rip Van Winkle").

Conflict is introduced into the plot when Esperanza discovers that her friend Sally would rather flirt with the boys than continue to play in the garden. The narrator experiences peer pressure to exchange the innocence of childhood for the sexual knowledge of adolescence. The girl is so reluctant to leave her earthly paradise that she tries to imagine suicide as a way to quell her anger about what is happening to her. She learns that willing death is not as easy as it appears in the books she has read. At the end of the story she is left with a headache and an undefined sense of loss: "The garden that had been such a good place to play didn't seem mine either."

Cisneros's first-person narrator has attempted, all unknowingly, to turn Washington Irving's "Rip Van Winkle" into its opposite statement. Her immature heroine is unaware that responsible, productive adult life is elsewhere than in the garden. When little Eddie Vargas falls asleep, she presents it as a positive act — he and the others playing in the garden are free in paradise, "Far away from where our mothers could find us." But life intervenes, and our brief time on earth is no paradise, as both Irving and Cisneros show us in their different ways.

In the sketch "Mango Says Goodbye Sometimes," Cisneros creates a humorous meditation on storytelling through her young narrator's explanation of why she makes up stories. Esperanza is a survivor. She tells stories for at least ten reasons:

1. for companionship ("The mailman says, Here's your mail.")
2. for self-dramatization ("She trudged up the wooden stairs.")
3. for pleasure ("I like to tell stories.")
4. to express rebellion ("I am going to tell you a story about a girl who didn't want to belong.")
5. to keep memory alive ("We didn't always live on Mango Street.")
6. to comfort herself in the face of perceived adversity ("I put it down on paper and then the ghost does not ache so much.")
7. to free herself from the pain of the past ("Mango says goodbye sometimes.")
8. to create something tangible that gives her the sense of belonging to a larger community ("One day I will pack my bags of books and paper.")
9. to impress others ("Friends and neighbors will say, What happened to that Esperanza?")
10. to help others trapped by a similarly harsh experience of life ("I have gone away to come back. For the ones I left behind. For the ones who cannot out.").

Questions for Discussion

1. How does your awareness of the author's background help you to understand her stories in *The House on Mango Street*?
2. What clues does Cisneros give you to help you understand that she has created a fictional narrator in these five stories?
3. How does Cisneros's choice of a first-person narrator shape the way she tells her stories?

4. Why is the image of bread appropriate for the smell of Esperanza's mother's hair? What feelings does it suggest to the reader?
5. What clues does the narrator give us to help us sense a continuing passage of time between the stories "My Name" and "The Monkey Garden"?
6. Why does the reference to "Rip Van Winkle" seem appropriate in "The Monkey Garden"?
7. What is the role of the monkey in "The Monkey Garden"?
8. What is the effect of Cisneros's repetition of lines from her opening story "The House on Mango Street" in her concluding story "Mango Says Goodbye Sometimes"?

Topics for Writing

1. Summarize one of the commentaries in the Cisneros casebook.
2. Write a sketch of your earliest memories of the home(s) you lived in as a young child.
3. **CONNECTIONS** Compare and contrast the themes in Irving's "Rip Van Winkle" and Cisneros's "The Monkey Garden."

Related Commentaries

Sandra Cisneros, Straw into Gold, p. 1597.
Ellen McCracken, On Cisneros's *The House on Mango Street*, p. 1600.
Julian Olivares, *The House on Mango Street* and the Poetics of Space, p. 1604.
Alvina E. Quintana, The House as Symbol, p. 1608.
Marc Zimmerman, U.S. Latino Literature: History and Development, p. 1610.

Suggested Reading

Cisneros, Sandra. *Woman Hollering Creek.* New York: Random, 1991.

JOSEPH CONRAD

Heart of Darkness (p. 344)

At the center of the concentric layers out of which Conrad constructs this story lies a case of atavism and the collapse of civilized morality. Kurtz casts aside all restraint and becomes as wild as his surroundings; or rather, the darkness around him calls out the darkness within his innermost being. Kurtz is a man of heroic abilities and exemplary ideals, yet at the end of the story, he explodes, unable to control his own strength.

Conrad does not provide an intimate inside view of Kurtz. To do so would destroy the aura of mystery and special significance that marks the story's theme as a profound revelation, the "culminating point of [Marlow's] experience," gained at "the farthest point of navigation." Instead, Conrad positions Kurtz in the midst of an impenetrable jungle, at "the very heart of darkness," as far from home and as remote from familiar frames of reference as possible. Then he causes the reader to approach Kurtz through a series of identifications that make the revelation of his debasement a statement not just about Kurtz, but about us all.

Conrad creates this effect mainly through his use of Marlow as narrator, and no discussion of the story can avoid exploring his function. He is on one hand a kind of prophet — his pose resembles that of an idol or Buddha — whose wisdom arises from his having looked beyond the veil that screens the truth from common view ("the inner truth is hidden — luckily, luckily"), and on the other hand an adventurer like the heroes of epic poems, descending into Hades and emerging shaken with his dark illumination. But Marlow's vision is neither of heaven nor of hell. His journey up the Congo River is in fact a descent into the inner reaches of the human soul. Forced by a combination of circumstances and preconceptions into a special association with Kurtz, Marlow recognizes in that "shadow" the intrinsic darkness of human nature, in which he shares. When he plunges into the jungle to redeem Kurtz, who has crawled away on all fours to rejoin the "unspeakable rites" of his worshipers, Marlow embraces what Kurtz has become no less than what he once was or might have been, acknowledging his own kinship with the deepest depravity. Kurtz dies crying, "The horror! The horror!" — apparently having regained from his rescuer enough of his moral bearings to recoil from his own behavior. Marlow, who judges the truth "too dark — too dark altogether," preserves the innocence of Kurtz's "Intended," leaving her "great and saving illusion" intact.

Conrad may be suggesting that only by a conscious lie or by willful blindness can we avoid sinking into the savagery that surrounds us, that dwells under externally maintained restraint within us, and that animates our civilization in various guises, such as the "flabby, pretending, weak-eyed devil of a rapacious and pitiless folly." The conquest of the earth, which is what the civilized society portrayed in the story is engaged in, "is not a pretty thing when you look into it too much," Marlow says. "What redeems it is the idea only . . . an unselfish belief in the idea — something you can set up, and bow down before, and offer sacrifice to." But such idolatry of our own idea is not far from its horrible perversion into the worship of himself that the would-be civilizer Kurtz sets up. It leads to a civilization aptly portrayed in Kurtz's symbolic painting of a blindfolded woman carrying a torch through darkness. If Conrad offers a glimmer of light in the dark world he envisions, it is in the sympathetic understanding that enables Marlow to befriend Kurtz and to lie for Kurtz and his Intended, even at the cost of having to taste the "flavor of mortality" he finds in lies, which he detests like the death it suggests to him.

WILLIAM E. SHEIDLEY

Questions for Discussion

1. What does Conrad gain by having his story told by Marlow to a group of important Londoners on a yacht in the Thames estuary? What is implied by the association of the Thames with the Congo? by Marlow's assertion, "And this also . . . has been one of the dark places on the earth"?

2. Marlow enters on his adventure through a city he associates with "a whited sepulcher"; he passes old women knitting who remind him of the Fates; the Company office is "as still as a house in a city of the dead." Locate other

indications that Marlow's journey is like a trip into the underworld. What do they suggest about the story's meaning?

3. In what ways is the French warship "shelling the bush" an apt image of the European conquest of Africa? What does this historical theme contribute to our understanding of Marlow and Kurtz?

4. Discuss the Company's chief accountant. Why is it appropriate that Marlow first hears of Kurtz from him?

5. Marlow calls the men waiting for a post in the interior "pilgrims." Explain the irony in his use of the term.

6. Marlow is associated with Kurtz as a member of "the gang of virtue." Explain the resonance of that phrase.

7. Describe the journey up the Congo as Marlow reports it in the pages that follow his remark, "Going up that river was like traveling back to the earliest beginnings of the world." In what ways does Conrad make it a symbolic journey as well as an actual one?

8. Discuss Marlow's attitudes toward the natives. What do they mean to him?

9. As the boat draws near Kurtz's station, people cry out "with unrestrained grief" from the jungle. Why?

10. After the attack of the natives is repulsed and the narrative seems at the point of reaching the climax toward which so much suspense has been built — the meeting with Kurtz — Conrad throws it away by having Marlow stop to light his pipe and speak offhandedly and abstractly about what he learned. Why? Does this passage actually destroy the suspense? Is the story rendered anticlimactic? Or is the climax changed? What is the true climax of the story?

11. Why do you think the heads on stakes are facing Kurtz's house?

12. Discuss the Russian and his attitude toward Kurtz. Why does Conrad trouble to add this European to Kurtz's train of cultists?

13. Marlow is astonished that the Manager calls Kurtz's methods "unsound." Why? What does this passage reveal about each of them?

14. Explain what happens to Marlow when he goes into the bush after Kurtz. Explain what happens to Kurtz. Why does Marlow call Kurtz "that shadow"?

15. Marlow claims to have "struggled with a soul"; he tells Kurtz that if he does not come back he will be "utterly lost." Is Marlow a savior for Kurtz? Is Kurtz saved?

16. Why does Marlow lie to Kurtz's "Intended"?

17. Contrast the last paragraph of the story with the opening.

18. Comment on the title of Kurtz's pamphlet, about the "Suppression of Savage Customs," and on the significance of its scrawled postscript, "Exterminate all the brutes."

Topics for Writing

1. In an essay, explore Conrad's use of foreshadowing.

2. Discuss traditional symbolism and literary allusion as a way of universalizing the theme of "Heart of Darkness."

3. Analyze the function of the frame in this novella.

4. Marlow frequently concludes a segment of his narrative with a generalization that sums it up and takes on a quality of special significance, such as, "I felt as though, instead of going to the center of a continent, I were about to set off for the center of the earth"; or, "It was like a weary pilgrimage among

hints for nightmares." Locate as many such passages as you can. What do they reveal about the mind of the narrator?
5. Conrad frequently uses an impressionist technique that Ian Watt has called "delayed decoding." When the steamboat is attacked, for example, Marlow first sees "little sticks" flying about, and only later recognizes them as arrows. Find other instances of delayed decoding in the story, and then write a narrative of your own using a similar method.
6. **CONNECTIONS** Analyze the journey into madness in Conrad's "Heart of Darkness" and Gilman's "The Yellow Wallpaper."

Related Commentaries

Chinua Achebe, An Image of Africa: Conrad's "Heart of Darkness," p. 1411.
Edward Said, The Past and the Present: Joseph Conrad and the Fiction of Autobiography, p. 1541.
John Simon, Coppola's *Apocalypse Now* and Conrad's "Heart of Darkness," p. 1649.
Lionel Trilling, The Greatness of Conrad's "Heart of Darkness," p. 1559.

Suggested Readings

Bender, Todd K. *Concordances to Conrad's "The Shadow Line" and "Youth": A Narrative.* New York: Garland, 1980.
Bennett, Carl D. *Joseph Conrad.* New York: Continuum, 1991.
Berthoud, Jacques. *Joseph Conrad: The Major Phase.* New York: Cambridge UP, 1978. 41–63.
Billy, Ted. *Critical Essays on Joseph Conrad.* Boston: G. K. Hall, 1987.
Cohen, Michael. "Sailing through *The Secret Sharer:* The End of Conrad's Story." *Studies in English* 10.2 (Fall 1988): 102–09.
Conrad, Joseph. *Heart of Darkness: An Authoritative Text, Backgrounds and Sources, Criticism.* Ed. Robert Kimbrough. Rev. ed. New York: Norton, 1971.
———. *Portable Conrad.* New York: Penguin, 1991.
Gekoski, R. A. *Conrad: The Moral World of the Novelist.* New York: Barnes, 1978. 72–90.
Gillon, Adam. *Joseph Conrad.* Boston: Twayne, 1982.
Graver, Lawrence. *Conrad's Short Fiction.* Berkeley: U of California P, 1969.
Hynes, Samuel, ed. *The Complete Short Fiction of Joseph Conrad. The Stories, Volume I.* New York: Ecco, 1991.
Page, Norman. *A Conrad Companion.* New York: St. Martin's, 1986.

JULIO CORTÁZAR

A Continuity of Parks (p. 407)

Students may be familiar with the kind of geometric drawings that present a pattern of lines that seem to create a perfectly logical form, except that the lines overlap and appropriate each other's space, resulting in a seemingly normal drawing of a physical impossibility. Cortázar's story has the same quality of a logical and reasonable appearance that turns itself inside out in the final lines of the story. A character from a book that a man has been reading suddenly turns up behind him in the room, poised to stab him to death. Since it seems to be a human instinct to try to "understand" any story we read, we make an effort to understand Cortázar's conundrum.

In the beginning of the story it is clear that the man is reading a novel. We are given the details about his reading, and we are told that "word by word" he has been "caught up in the sordid dilemma of the hero and heroine." Then the characters begin to take on a life of their own, and we are presented with a love scene with imprecise implications. As the love scene ends, the man who has been presented to us as a character in a novel leaves on a mission that has been described for him by the woman. Then, in a twist of reality, we are told in the final sentence of the story that his mission is to kill the man who sits reading. The opening of the story cannot be reasonable if that is its ending. Cortázar has presented us with the verbal equivalent of the geometric drawing that seems reasonable, but leaves us with an object that has no rational equivalent.

The student may ask why Cortázar has chosen to present us with this puzzle. On a direct and immediate level he could be showing us how powerfully we react to stories — so powerfully the characters can seem to come alive for us. Since the beginning of his career, however, Cortázar has again and again confronted his readers with the ambiguity of writing itself, teasing us for our insistence on trying to "understand" a story, even when there is nothing on the page but words and scenes that the writer can manipulate at will. In his first novel, the modernist classic *Hopscotch*, the chapters are deliberately left in no rational order, only listed in possible combinations at the end of the book, so the reader is forced to hop from one chapter to another. "A Continuity of Parks" could be read as a literary exercise that the author has deliberately created to emphasize his point. The story also could serve as a demonstration of "modernist" literary theory. If the student is interested in contemporary modernist stories, there are further examples in the text by Allen, Barth, Borges, and Calvino.

Questions for Discussion

1. Is there any way this story might be explained on a logical basis?
2. Is it true that readers can lose themselves so deeply in a book that they begin to believe that the characters have a life of their own?
3. What is the last reference the author makes to the fact that the man is reading a book?
4. What kind of story does the author suggest that the novel describes?
5. Why does he say "and underneath liberty pounded"?
6. Why does the killer expect the dogs to be silent and the estate manager to be away? How does he know how to find his way through the house?
7. Have both fictional characters now begun to direct the story themselves?

Topics for Writing

1. Compare this story with another of the modernist stories in the anthology and discuss their similarities and their differences.

2. Examine the aesthetic and historical basis of modernist writing through a study of source material from your college library.

Suggested Readings

Alazraki, Jaime, and Ivar Ivask, eds. *The Final Island: The Fiction of Julio Cortázar.* Norman: U of Oklahoma P, 1978.

Cortázar, Julio. *Around the Day in Eighty Worlds.* Trans. Thomas Christensen. San Francisco: North Point, 1986. Esp. 17–23, 158–67.

———. *Blow Up and Other Stories.* London: Panther, 1967.

———. *Unreasonable Hours.* Trans. Alberto Manguel. Toronto: Coach House, 1995.

STEPHEN CRANE

The Open Boat (p. 410)

Crane's story fictionalizes an actual experience. A correspondent himself, Crane happened to be aboard the *Commodore* when it went down, and he included in his newspaper report of the event this passage (as quoted by E. R. Hagemann):

> The history of life in an open boat for thirty hours would no doubt be instructive for the young, but none is to be told here now. For my part I would prefer to tell the story at once, because from it would shine the splendid manhood of Captain Edward Murphy and of William Higgins, the oiler, but let it suffice at this time to say that when we were swamped in the surf and making the best of our way toward the shore the captain gave orders amid the wildness of the breakers as clearly as if he had been on the quarter deck of a battleship.

It is good that Crane did not write "at once" but let his experience take shape as a work of art which, instead of celebrating the "splendid manhood" of two or four individuals, recognizes a profound truth about human life in general — about the puniness of humankind in the face of an indifferent nature and about the consequent value of the solidarity and compassion that arise from an awareness of our common fate. Crane's meditation on his experience "after the fact" enables him to become not simply a reporter but, as he puts it in the last line of the story, an *interpreter* of the message spoken to us by the world we confront.

Crane portrays the exertions of the four men in the boat without glamorizing them. His extended and intimate account of their hard work and weariness wrings out any false emotion from the reader's view of the situation. By varying the narrative point of view from a coolly detached objective observer to a plural account of all four men's shared feelings and perceptions to the correspondent's rueful, self-mocking cogitations, Crane defeats our impulse to choose a hero for adulation, at the same time driving home the point that the condition of the men in the dinghy — their longing, their fear, and their powerlessness before nature and destiny — reflects our own. By the end, what has been revealed is so horrible that there can be no triumph in survival. The good fortune of a rescue brings only a reprieve, not an escape from what awaits us. Billie the oiler drowns, but there is no reason it should have been he, or only he. His death could be anybody's death.

Crane's narration builds suspense through rhythmic repetition, foreshadowing, and irony. We hear the surf periodically: Our hopes for rescue are repeatedly raised and dashed; night follows day, wave follows wave, and the endless struggle goes on. The correspondent's complaint against the cruelty of fate recurs in diminuendo, with less whimsy and self-consciousness each time.

These recurrences mark the men's changes in attitude — from the egocentric viewpoint they start with, imagining that the whole world is watching them and working for their survival, to the perception of the utter indifference of nature with which the story ends. Some stages in this progression include their false sense of security when they light up the cigars; their isolation from the people on shore, epitomized by their inability to interpret the signal of the man waving his coat (whose apparent advice to try another stretch of beach they nonetheless inadvertently follow); their experience of aloneness at night; their confrontation with the hostility of nature in the shark; and, finally, their recognition that death might be a welcome release from toil and suffering. They respond by drawing together in a communion that sustains them, sharing their labor and their body heat, huddled together in their tiny, helpless dinghy. Even their strong bond of comradeship, however, cannot withstand the onslaught of the waves. When the boat is swamped, it is every man for himself: Each individual must face death alone. Because of the fellowship that has grown up among them, however, when Billie dies, each of the others feels the oiler's death as his own. The reader, whom Crane's narrative has caused to share thirty hours at sea in an open boat, may recognize the implication in what is spoken by "the sound of the great sea's voice to the men on shore."

WILLIAM E. SHEIDLEY

Questions for Discussion

1. Contrast the imagery and the tone of the first paragraph with those of the second. Why does Crane continually seek to magnify nature and to belittle the men who are struggling with it? Find other instances of Crane's reductive irony, and discuss their effects.
2. How does Crane convey the men's concentration on keeping the boat afloat?
3. Explain Crane's use of the word "probably" in the first paragraph of section II.
4. Why does the seagull seem "somehow gruesome and ominous" to the men in the boat? Compare and contrast the seagull with the shark that appears later.
5. Comment on the imagery Crane uses to describe changing seats in the dinghy (stealing eggs, Sèvres).
6. What is it that the correspondent "knew even at the time was the best experience of his life"? Why is it the best?
7. What is the purpose of Crane's understatement in the line "neither the oiler nor the correspondent was fond of rowing at this time"?
8. What is the effect on the reader of the men's lighting up cigars?
9. Discuss the meaning of the correspondent's question "Was I brought here merely to have my nose dragged away as I was about to nibble the sacred cheese of life?"

10. What do you think the man waving a coat means? Why is it impossible for him to communicate with the men in the boat?

11. "A night on the sea in an open boat is a long night," says Crane. How does he make the reader feel the truth of that assertion?

12. At one point the correspondent thinks that he is "the one man afloat on all the oceans." Explain that sensation. Why does the wind he hears sound "sadder than the end"? Why does he later wish he had known the captain was awake when the shark came by?

13. Why does the correspondent have a different attitude toward the poem about the dying soldier in Algiers from the one he had as a boy?

14. Examine the third paragraph of section VII. How important are the thoughts of the correspondent to our understanding of the story? What would the story lose if they were omitted? What would the effect of this passage have been if Crane had narrated the story in the first person? If he had made these comments in the voice of an omniscient third-person narrator?

15. Define the correspondent's physical, mental, and emotional condition during his final moments on the boat and during his swim to the beach.

16. Characterize and explain the tone of Crane's description of the man who pulls the castaways from the sea.

17. Why does Crane make fun of the women who bring coffee to the survivors?

Topics for Writing

1. Consider Crane's handling of point of view in "The Open Boat."
2. Discuss the importance of repetition in Crane's narrative.
3. Analyze imagery as a key to tone in "The Open Boat."
4. After reading the story once rapidly, read it again with a pencil in hand, marking every simile and metaphor. Then sort them into categories. What realms of experience does Crane bring into view through these devices that are not actually part of the simple boat-sea-sky-beach world in which the story is set? Why?
5. Write an eyewitness account of some experience you have undergone that would be suitable for newspaper publication. Then note the changes you would make to turn it into a fictional narrative with broader or more profound implications — or write that story.

Related Commentary

Stephen Crane, The Sinking of the *Commodore*, p. 1453.

Suggested Readings

Adams, Richard P. "Naturalistic Fiction: 'The Open Boat.' " *Stephen Crane's Career: Perspectives and Evaluations.* Ed. Thomas A. Gullason. New York: New York UP, 1972. 421–29. Originally published in *Tulane Studies in English* 4 (1954): 137–46.

Cady, Edwin H. *Stephen Crane.* Twayne's United States Authors Series 23. Rev. ed. Boston: G. K. Hall, 1980. 150–54.

Colvert, James B. *Stephen Crane*. New York: Ungar, 1987.

Follett, Wilson, ed. *The Work of Stephen Crane*. New York: Knopf, 1925.

Fryckstedt, O. W., ed. *Stephen Crane: Uncollected Writings*. Uppsala: Studia Anglistica Upsaliensia, 1963.

Hagemann, E. R. "'Sadder Than the End': Another Look at 'The Open Boat.'" *Stephen Crane in Transition: Centenary Essays*. Ed. Joseph Katz. DeKalb: Northern Illinois UP, 1972. 66–85.

Johnson, Glen M. "Stephen Crane." *American Short-Story Writers, 1880–1910. Dictionary of Literary Biography*, vol. 78. Detroit: Gale, 1989.

Katz, Joseph, ed. *The Portable Stephen Crane*. New York: Viking, 1985.

Kissane, Leedice. "Interpretation through Language: A Study of the Metaphors in Stephen Crane's 'The Open Boat.'" Gullason, cited above. 410–16. Originally published in *Rendezvous* (Idaho State U) 1 (1966): 18–22.

Knapp, Bettina L. *Stephen Crane*. New York: Ungar, 1987.

Stallman, R. W. *Stephen Crane: A Critical Bibliography*. Ames: Iowa State UP, 1972.

———. *Stories and Tales/Stephen Crane*. New York: Vintage, 1955.

Wolford, Chester L. *Stephen Crane: A Study of the Short Fiction*. Boston: Twayne, 1989.

DON DELILLO

Videotape (p. 429)

To tell his story, DeLillo has used second-person narration, a form that is not commonly used because it forces the reader into a position of assumed intimacy with the narrator. Perhaps this explains why DeLillo brings the narrator's wife into the second half of the story — to show him bullying someone else into watching the videotape that has fascinated him of a random murder on a Texas highway.

The central character in this story is the narrator, rather than the unnamed twelve-year-old girl making the video in the back seat of her parents' car or the unwary forty-year-old victim of the crime. The narrator's mind is central here. He speculates on the "crude power" of the footage he is watching and equates it with his own subconscious mind and its unlimited capacity to imagine acts of violence: "It is the jostled part of your mind, the film that runs through your hotel brain under all the thoughts you know you're thinking."

DeLillo has told interviewers that in preparation for writing *Libra*, his novel about Lee Harvey Oswald, he spent hours watching amateur videotapes of the assassination of President John F. Kennedy in Dallas. In "Videotape," DeLillo has imagined that a Texas Highway Killer is the murderer, but the effect of the videotape suggests a similar fascination for the author. At the end of the story, the narrator speculates about contemporary culture and asks whether "this is a crime that has found its medium, or vice versa — cheap mass production, the sequence of repeated images and victims." He strains to find meaning in the videotape, trying to convince himself that he is not a voyeur, that "it is instructional." Perhaps it is, but DeLillo needed to write a story about it in order to convince us.

Questions for Discussion

1. What is your response to second-person narration? Do you find the narrator of this story more or less sympathetic as the story progresses?
2. Are the girl making the video and the murder victim round or flat characters?
3. How does the tone of the story contribute to DeLillo's dramatization of his theme?
4. Analyze the plot of "Videotape." Does it proceed in the stages you have studied in other stories in this anthology?

Topics for Writing

1. Discuss DeLillo's use of videotape as a metaphor for human consciousness, or the video camera as a metaphor for the world.
2. **CONNECTIONS** Compare and contrast DeLillo's story with Lorrie Moore's use of second-person narration in "How to Become a Writer."

Suggested Reading

DeLillo, Don. *Underworld.* New York: Scribner, 1997.

JUNOT DÍAZ

Fiesta, 1980 (p. 434)

Junot Díaz's story is one that is common in the American experience — the story of a child of immigrant parents who is destined to become a writer and who will bear witness to the difficulties that parents and family face in making a new life in the United States. The instructor will probably be familiar with Henry Roth's novel *Call It Sleep*, published in the 1930s, which describes similar tensions and trauma experienced by Jewish immigrants in New York City's Lower East Side. The first novel of Beat writer Jack Kerouac, *The Town and the City*, published in 1950, reflects the struggle of the young protagonist — Kerouac himself — to liberate himself from the constricted social outlook of his French Canadian immigrant family. This theme is so ubiquitous to American literature that the instructor will be able to supply many other examples.

Díaz's story is distinctive for several reasons, among them the use of colorful vernacular speech mirroring the narrator's youthful experiences. Another distinctive element of the story is the level of brutality and violence that he describes. There have been many difficult fathers in this literary genre, but few as threatening as the father Díaz presents to his readers. A continuing motif in the story is the nausea the narrator experiences when he rides in his father's van. The vomiting could be explained in psychological terms as the boy's helpless reaction to what he witnesses in the family, and to the physical abuse he is forced to endure. He can say nothing, so his body spews out what he is too frightened to say. The boy was also riding in the van the first time he was taken by his father to meet the woman his father is seeing outside the marriage, and the van will always be associated in his mind with the meeting.

Students who do not speak Spanish may have difficulty with some of the language, and it would be helpful if the instructor would familiarize the class with words such as *tío* and *tía* before assigning the story. The use of vernacular terms is one of the stylistic characteristics of stories describing immigrant life. If students have read any of the work of other immigrant writers, they will already have encountered words in Yiddish, Hebrew, Italian, Irish, and a dozen other languages. Perhaps in another generation it will be the young writers of the group of Russians living in Brighton Beach who will describe their experience in the New World, and the vernacular expressions in their stories will be in Russian.

The instructor will find other examples of this genre in the volume. Ethan Canin's "The Carnival Dog, the Buyer of Diamonds" describes a first-generation Jewish father and son. Gish Jen's "In the American Society" describes a Chinese immigrant father through the sympathetic eyes of his daughter. Helena María Viramontes's "The Moths" depicts an entire family who treats a young girl with anger and rejection.

Questions for Discussion

1. Do the Spanish words present a difficulty for the students? Would students prefer that these terms were translated into English in the text? Why did the author use them?
2. The story is set in 1980. Would a family in these circumstances today be able to get protection from the father's brutality?
3. In the story, one brother (Rafa) is following in the father's footsteps. Why would he do this? Does the story suggest any reasons why Rafa would emulate his father?
4. Could a family survive long with this level of anger and insensitivity?
5. What is the role of the mother's sister, called Tía, in the story? Is it a traditional role in this society?
6. Before the family leaves to drive to the party the boy's mother throws three pieces of candy out of the car window as "an offering to Eshu." What does this tell us about her?
7. Is Rafa older or younger than the narrator? How do we know? How old are they?

Topic for Writing

1. Read Díaz's book *Drown*, the collection of linked stories from which this one is taken, and analyze the placement of "Fiesta, 1980" in the book.

Suggested Reading

Díaz, Junot. *Drown*. New York: Riverhead, 1996.

Isak Dinesen

The Blue Jar (p. 446)

"The Blue Jar" is an enigmatic story that illustrates Dinesen's use of fiction as an "anecdote of destiny." The narrative doesn't define the life of Lady Helena, yet after reading it we have an intuitive sense of who she is.

Lady Helena's "mind has suffered from her trials," so we cannot look too closely for rational patterns and explanations of her quest for "the right blue" jar or bowl. Perhaps she is seeking the impossible union of body and spirit, or perhaps the integration of her own soul. "Surely there must be some of it [the perfect color blue] left from the time when all the world was blue."

The image that Lady Helena describes of a parallel ship on the other hemisphere, a perfect reflection of herself, in harmony with the moon and the tides, may suggest to some students the idea of a lover (the young sailor who shared the lifeboat with her after the shipwreck?) or the more abstract projection of her "destiny" in life. This short story is rich in ambiguity and leaves a bittersweet impression of Dinesen's craft as a writer.

Questions for Discussion

1. We know that fairy tales enchant children, and we know, from works such as Bruno Bettelheim's *The Uses of Enchantment*, what strong psychological demands lie behind that enthrallment. Would you expect a fairy tale for adults to differ from those you read as a child? What expectations does the fairy-tale form of "The Blue Jar" set up for you?
2. What is the function of Lady Helena's father in this story? What plot elements of her life does he control? Why does she mimic his search for "ancient blue china"?
3. Her life now devoted to searching for the right color, Lady Helena cries, "Surely there must be some of it left from the time when all the world was blue." Can we know exactly what blue symbolizes for Lady Helena? Does this story give us enough information to be able to say that it suggests a nostalgia for paradise? What might paradise be made of? When she discovers the right blue, she says, "Oh, how light it makes one. Oh, it is as fresh as a breeze, as deep as a deep secret, as full as I say not what." What is common to these four categories? What does the common element suggest about paradise?
4. After the shipwreck, Lady Helena is compelled to do two things: search and sail. What do you make of her saying "We two are like the reflection of one another, in the deep sea, and the ship of which I speak is always exactly beneath my own ship, upon the opposite side of the globe"? Yet Lady Helena seems to see herself as the prime mover in this duality: "I draw it to and fro wherever I go, as the moon draws the tides, all through the bulk of the earth." Analyze the sexual references in this sentence.
5. Lady Helena can die after the successful completion of her task: She has found the right blue. When, after her death, her heart is cut out and laid in the jar, "everything will be as it was then." Again, Lady Helena refers to

something in the past. But immediately the following sentence directs our attention to a particular time: "My heart will be innocent and free, and will beat gently, like a wake that sings, like the drops that fall from an oar blade." Why does Lady Helena compare her heartbeat to a wake, to a drop from an oar blade?

6. "The Blue Jar" is an example of what Dinesen called an "anecdote of destiny." Is destiny the implicit subject of the penultimate sentence: "Is it not a sweet thing to think that, if only you have patience, all that has ever been, will come back to you?" In what moments in this story do you see the suggestion of Lady Helena's destiny?

Topics for Writing

1. Compare physiological vision with psychological vision in "The Blue Jar."
2. Discuss "innocence" as defined and explored in "The Blue Jar."

Suggested Readings

Dinesen, Isak. *Winter's Tales.* New York: Random, 1942, 1970.
Hannah, Donald. "In Memoriam Karen Blixen: Some Aspects of Her Attitude to Life." *Sewanee Review* 71 (1963): 585–604.
Landry, M. "Anecdote as Destiny: Isak Dinesen and the Story-Teller." *Massachusetts Review* 19 (1978): 389–406.

RALPH ELLISON

Battle Royal (p. 449)

In the headnote to his comments on "Battle Royal" reprinted in Part Two (p. 1457), Ellison is quoted expounding on the importance of "converting experience into symbolic action" in fiction. One of the major triumphs of "Battle Royal" (and of *Invisible Man* as a whole) is Ellison's success in the realistic rendering of experiences that are in themselves so obviously significant of larger social, psychological, and moral truths that explication is unnecessary. From the small American flag tattooed on the nude dancer's belly to the "rope of bloody saliva forming a shape like an undiscovered continent" that the narrator drools on his new briefcase, Ellison's account of the festivities at the men's smoker effectively symbolizes the condition of blacks in America while remaining thoroughly persuasive in its verisimilitude. Both the broader structure of the evening and the finer details of narration and description carry the force of Ellison's theme. The young blacks are tortured first by having the most forbidden of America's riches dangled before them, then by being put through their paces in a melee in which their only victims are their fellows and the whites look on with glee, and finally by being debased into groveling for money (some of it counterfeit) on a rug whose electrification underlines their own powerlessness. In one brief passage, the nightmare of such an existence appears in a strange subaqueous vision of primitive life: "The boys groped about like blind, cautious crabs crouching to protect their midsections, their heads pulled in short against their shoulders, their arms stretched nervously before them, with their fists testing the smoke-filled air like the knobbed feelers of hypersensitive snails."

Because his actual experience forms itself into such revealing images, the narrator's dream of his grandfather seems all the more credible as a statement of his position. "Keep This Nigger-Boy Running," he dreams the message of his brief-case says — not far from "You've got to know your place at all times." The narrator's grandfather knew his place and played his role, but he never believed a word of it. It is this assurance of an inner being quite different from the face he turned toward the world that makes him so troubling to his descendants. In his effort to please the white folks and in so doing to get ahead, the narrator seeks alliance rather than secret enmity with his antagonists. As a result he subjects himself to the trickery and delusions the white community chooses to impose on him. Dependent for his sense of himself on his ability to guess what they want him to do, the narrator finds himself groping in a fog deeper than the swirls of cigar smoke that hang over the scene of the battle royal. When the smoke clears and the blindfold comes off, he will recognize, as he puts it at the start, that he is invisible to the whites and may therefore discover his own identity within himself.

The first episode of a long novel does not accomplish the narrator's enlightenment, but it constitutes his initiation into the realities of the world he must eventually come to understand. Ellison says (in the Commentary in Part Two, p. 1457) that the battle royal "is a ritual in preservation of caste lines, a keeping of taboo to appease the gods and ward off bad luck," and that "it is also the initiation ritual to which all greenhorns are subjected." This rite of initiation bears a revealing relation to the primitive initiation ceremonies known to anthropologists. The battle royal, for example, separates the boys from their families, challenges them to prove their valor, and subjects them to instruction by the tribal elders in a sort of men's house. The boys are stripped and introduced to sexual mysteries. But the hazing of women that is a frequent feature of such initiations is not carried on here by the boys but by the gross elders, whose savagery is barely under control; the ritual ends not with the entry of the initiates into the larger community but with their pointed exclusion; and the sacred lore embodied in the narrator's recital of his graduation speech makes explicit the contradictions inherent in the society it describes. To cast down his bucket where he is forces him to swallow his own blood. The narrator is delighted with the scholarship to "the state college for Negroes" that he wins by toeing the line and knowing his place, and he does not object that the "gold" coins he groveled for are fraudulent. His education in the meaning of his grandfather's troubling injunctions will continue, but the reader has already seen enough to recognize their validity.

WILLIAM E. SHEIDLEY

Questions for Discussion

1. In the opening paragraph the narrator says, "I was naive." In what ways is his naiveté revealed in the story that follows?
2. Why does the narrator feel guilty when praised?
3. What is the message to the narrator behind the suggestion "that since I was to be there anyway I might as well take part in the battle royal"? Explain his hesitation. What is the most important part of the evening for the whites?

4.   Who is present at the smoker? Discuss the role of the school superinten-
     dent.
5.   What techniques does Ellison use to convey to the reader the impact that
     seeing the stripper has on the boys?
6.   What does the stripper have in common with the boys? Why are both a
     stripper and a battle royal part of the evening's entertainment?
7.   During the chaos of the battle, the narrator worries about how his speech
     will be received. Is that absurd or understandable?
8.   Does the deathbed advice of the narrator's grandfather offer a way to handle
     the battle royal?
9.   Why does Tatlock refuse to take a dive?
10. Explain the narrator's first reaction to seeing the "small square rug." In
     what sense is his instinct correct?
11. What is the meaning of the electric rug to the whites? What do they wish it
     to demonstrate to the blacks?
12. Explain Mr. Colcord's reaction when the narrator tries to topple him onto
     the rug.
13. Analyze the narrator's speech. What is the implication of his having to de-
     liver it while swallowing his own blood?
14. Why is the school superintendent confident that the narrator will "lead his
     people in the proper paths"?
15. Why does the narrator stand in front of his grandfather's picture holding
     his briefcase? Who gets the better of this confrontation?

Topics for Writing

1.   Make a study of seeing and understanding in "Battle Royal."
2.   Analyze the role of sex, violence, and power in Ellison's "Battle Royal."
3.   Write an essay exploring the battle royal and black experience in America.
4.   Describe the "permanent interest" of "Battle Royal." (See Ellison's Com-
     mentary in Part Two, p. 1457).
5.   Examine the blonde, the gold coins, and the calfskin briefcase in "Battle
     Royal."
6.   Select a passage of twenty lines or less from this story for detailed explica-
     tion. Relate as many of its images as possible to others in the story and to
     the general ideas that the story develops. To what extent does the passage
     you chose reflect the meaning of the story as a whole?
7.   Recall an experience in which you were humiliated or embarrassed. What
     motives of your own and of those before whom you were embarrassed put
     you in such a position? Narrate the incident so these underlying purposes
     become evident to the reader.
8.   Write a description of a game or ceremony with which you are familiar.
     What set of principles or relationships (not necessarily malign) does it ex-
     press?

Related Commentary

Ralph Ellison, The Influence of Folklore on "Battle Royal," p. 1457.

Suggested Readings

Blake, Susan L. "Ritual and Rationalization: Black Folklore in the Works of Ralph Ellison." *PMLA* 94 (1979): 121–26, esp. 122–23.

Horowitz, Ellin. "The Rebirth of the Artist." *Twentieth-Century Interpretations of Invisible Man.* Ed. John M. Reilly. Englewood Cliffs, NJ: Prentice, 1970. 80–88, esp. 81. (Originally published in 1964.)

O'Meally, Robert G. *The Craft of Ralph Ellison.* Cambridge, MA: Harvard UP, 1980. 12–14.

Vogler, Thomas A. *"Invisible Man:* Somebody's Protest Novel." *Ralph Ellison: A Collection of Critical Essays.* Ed. John Hersey. Englewood Cliffs, NJ: Prentice, 1974. 127–50, esp. 143–44.

LOUISE ERDRICH

The Red Convertible (p. 460)

The story takes place in 1974, when Henry Junior comes back to the Chippewa Indian reservation after more than three years as a soldier in Vietnam. He is mentally disturbed by his experiences in the war, and, as his brother Lyman (who narrates the story) says laconically, "the change was no good."

Erdrich has structured her story in a traditional manner. It is narrated in the first person by Lyman, who uses the past tense to describe the finality of what happened to his brother and the red Oldsmobile convertible they once shared. The plot moves conventionally, after a lengthy introduction giving the background of the two brothers and their pleasure in the car. They are Indians who work hard for what they earn, but they also enjoy their money. As Lyman says, "We went places in that car, me and Henry." An atmosphere of innocence pervades this part of the story. They enjoy sightseeing along the western highways, going when and where they please, spending an entire summer in Alaska after they drive a female hitchhiker with long, beautiful hair home.

The story moves forward chronologically (although it is told as a flashback after the opening frame of four paragraphs), organized in sections usually several paragraphs long. Its structure is as loose and comfortable as the brothers' relationship. Then, midway, the story darkens when Henry goes off to Vietnam. For three sections, Lyman describes Henry's disorientation after the war. Then Henry fixes the convertible, the boys get back behind the wheel, and it seems briefly as if the good times are again starting to roll. But Henry feels internal turmoil similar to that of the flooded river they park alongside. The story reaches its climax when Henry suddenly goes wild after drinking several beers, deteriorating into what he calls a "crazy Indian." Lyman stares after him as he jumps into the river, shouting, "Got to cool me off!" His last words are quieter, "My boots are filling," and then he is gone.

The last paragraph of the story is its final section, Lyman describing how he drove the car into the river after he couldn't rescue Henry. It has gotten dark, and he is left alone with the sound of the rush of the water "going and running and running." This brings the story full circle, back to the beginning, where Lyman told us that now he "walks everywhere he goes." His grief for his brother is as understated as the rest of his personality. Erdrich has invented a natural story-teller in Lyman. We feel his emotional loss as if it were our own.

Questions for Discussion

1. In the opening paragraph, Lyman says that he and Henry owned the red convertible "together until his boots filled with water on a windy night and he bought out my share." When does the meaning of this sentence become clear to you? What is the effect of putting this sentence in the first paragraph?

2. Also in the opening paragraph, Erdrich writes: "his youngest brother Lyman (that's myself), Lyman walks everywhere he goes." If Lyman is narrating this story, why does he name himself? Does speaking of himself in the third person create any particular effect?

3. What is the function of the third section of the story? Why does the narrator tell us about their wandering, about meeting Susy? What associations does the red convertible carry?

4. Watching Henry watching television, Lyman says, "He sat in his chair gripping the armrests with all his might, as if the chair itself was moving at a high speed and if he let go at all he would rocket forward and maybe crash right through the set." How would you describe the diction in this sentence? What effect does the sentence's length — and its syntax — create? What is the tone? What does this line, and the paragraphs around it, tell you about Lyman's reaction to Henry's change?

5. Where do Lyman and Henry speak directly to each other in this story? Where do they speak indirectly? How do they communicate without speech? Describe how Erdrich presents the moments of emotion in this story.

6. Why is Lyman upset by the picture of himself and his brother? When does the picture begin to bother him? Do we know if it's before or after Henry's death? Does it make a difference to our interpretation of the story? What burden of memory does this picture carry?

7. Consider the tone of the final paragraph, in which Lyman is describing how he felt when he gave his car to his dead brother. Look at the diction surrounding the red convertible here: It plows into the water; the headlights "reach in . . . go down, searching"; they are "still lighted. . . ." What attribute does the diction give the car? How is the car different now from the way it's been in the rest of the story? Does this transformation of the car invoke a sense of closure in the story?

8. The closing sentence says "And then there is only the water, the sound of it going and running and going and running and running." How does this statement comment on the relationship between the two brothers?

Topics for Writing

1. Write an essay considering brotherhood in "The Red Convertible."
2. Discuss Erdrich's use of setting to determine tone.
3. Rewrite the story from the third-person point of view.

4. **CONNECTIONS** Compare and discuss Lyman's initiation into maturity with that of Julian in Flannery O'Connor's "Everything That Rises Must Converge."

Suggested Readings

Erdrich, Louise. "Excellence Has Always Made Me Fill with Fright When It Is Demanded by Other People, but Fills Me with Pleasure When I Am Left to Practice It Alone." *Ms.* 13 (1985): 84.

———. "Where I Ought to Be: A Writer's Sense of Place." *New York Times Book Review* 28 (July 1985): 1+.

Howard, J. "Louise Erdrich." *Life* 8 (1985): 27+.

WILLIAM FAULKNER

A Rose for Emily (p. 469)

Few stories, surely, differ more on a second reading than does "A Rose for Emily," which yields to the initiate some detail or circumstance anticipating the ending in nearly every paragraph. But Faulkner sets the pieces of his puzzle in place so coolly that the first-time reader hardly suspects them to fit together into a picture at all, until the curtain is finally swept aside and the shocking secret of Miss Emily's upstairs room is revealed. Faulkner makes it easy to write off the episodes of the smell, Miss Emily's denial of her father's death, the arsenic, and the aborted wedding (note the shuffled chronology) as the simple eccentricities of a pathetic old maid, to be pitied and indulged. The impact of the final scene drives home the realization that the passions of a former generation and its experience of life are no less real or profound for all their being in the past — whether we view them through the haze of sentimental nostalgia, as the Confederate veterans near the end of the story do, or place them at an aesthetic distance, as the towns-people do in the romantic tableau imagined in section II.

In his interviews with students at the University of Virginia (excerpted in Part Two, p. 1461), Faulkner stressed Miss Emily's being "kept down" by her father as an important factor in driving her to violate the code of her society by taking a lover, and he expressed a deep human sympathy for her long expiation for that sin. In the narrative consciousness of the story, however — the impersonal "we" that speaks for the communal mind of Jefferson — Miss Emily Grierson is a town relic, a monument to the local past to be shown to strangers, like the graves of the men slain at the battle of Jefferson or the big houses on what long ago, before they put the sidewalks in, was the "most select street." Because all relics are to a degree symbolic, one should not hesitate to take up the challenge found in Faulkner's ambiguous claim quoted in the headnote, that "the writer is too busy . . . to have time to be conscious of all the symbolism that he may put into what he does or what people may read into it." Miss Emily, for example, may be understood to express the part of southern culture that is paralyzed in the present by its inability to let go of the past, even though that past is as dead as Homer Barron, and even though its reality differed from the treasured memory as greatly as the Yankee paving contractor — "not a marrying man" — differs from the husband of Miss Emily's desperate longings. Other details in Faulkner's economical narration fit this reading: the prominence of Miss Emily's iconic portrait of her father; her refusal to acknowledge changing laws and customs; her insistence that the privilege of paying no taxes, bestowed on her by the chivalrous Colonel Sartoris, is an inalienable right; her dependence on the labors of her Negro servant, whose patient silence renders him an accomplice in her strange crime; and, not least, her relationship of mutual exploitation with Homer, the representative of the North — a relationship that ends in a morbid and grotesque parody of marriage. In this context, the smell of death that reeks from Miss Emily's house tells how the story judges what she stands for, and the dust that falls on everything brings the welcome promise of relief.

But Faulkner will not let it lie. Seen for what she is, neither romanticized nor trivialized, Miss Emily has a forthright dignity and a singleness of purpose that contrast sharply with those representatives of propriety and progress who sneak around her foundation in the dark spreading lime or knock on her door in the ineffectual effort to collect her taxes. And as the speechless townsfolk tiptoe aghast about her bridal chamber, it is Miss Emily's iron will, speaking through the strand of iron-gray hair that lies where she has lain, that has the final word.

WILLIAM E. SHEIDLEY

Questions for Discussion

1. The story begins and ends with Miss Emily's funeral. Trace the chronology of the intervening sections.
2. Emily is called "a fallen monument" and "a tradition." Explain.
3. Why does the narrator label Miss Emily's house "an eyesore among eyesores"?
4. Define the opposing forces in the confrontation that occupies most of section I. How does Miss Emily "vanquish them"?
5. Discuss the transition between sections I and II. In what ways are the two episodes parallel?
6. Apart from her black servant, Miss Emily has three men in her life. What similarities are there in her attitudes toward them?
7. Why is Homer Barron considered an inappropriate companion for Miss Emily?
8. Consider Faulkner's introduction of the rat poison into the story in section III. What is the narrator's avowed reason for bringing it up?
9. At the beginning of section IV, the townspeople think Emily will commit suicide, and they think "it would be the best thing." Why? What is the basis of their error regarding her intentions?
10. Why do you think Miss Emily gets fat and develops gray hair when she does?
11. Why does Miss Emily's servant disappear after her death?
12. Describe Miss Emily's funeral before the upstairs room is opened. In what way does that scene serve as a foil to what follows?
13. Discuss the role of dust in the last few paragraphs of the story.
14. Why does Faulkner end the story with "a long strand of iron-gray hair"?

Topics for Writing

1. Contrast the various attitudes toward the past in "A Rose for Emily."
2. Discuss the meaning of time and Faulkner's handling of chronology in "A Rose for Emily."
3. Construct a profile of Emily Grierson: Is she a criminal, a lunatic, or a heroine?
4. Explain the title of "A Rose for Emily."
5. Consider the relationship between "A Rose for Emily" and the history of the South.
6. What can you discern about the narrator of "A Rose for Emily"?
7. Were you surprised by the story's ending? On a second reading, mark all the passages that foreshadow it.
8. Imitate Faulkner by telling the events that lead up to a climax out of chronological order. What new effects do you find it possible to achieve? What problems in continuity do you encounter?

Related Commentary

William Faulkner, The Meaning of "A Rose for Emily," p. 1461.

Suggested Readings

See page 88.

William Faulkner

That Evening Sun (p. 476)

"That Evening Sun" is one of a handful of American short stories that have been so frequently anthologized and discussed that they almost define the style and the method of American short fiction. For the instructor the question may not be so much presenting the story for its literary qualities, but in seeing how well the story still relates to the political and social attitudes of students today, more than sixty years since it was first published. It isn't as acceptable now for a white writer to deal with themes of African American life, and for many feminists there can be questions about a white male author's presentation of a black woman's experience. Does the story still have the powerful effect on its readers that it had in the harsh years of the Great Depression and the cruelest decades of legalized segregation?

The answer is that the narrative device that gave the story so much of its first impact still is as effective today. By weaving through the story the uncomprehending chorus of children's voices, Faulkner succeeds in making the brutal violence of the story frighteningly real. There is no more desperate moment in American literature than when Nancy's attempt to keep the children amused in her lonely cabin ends with the broken popcorn popper. The reader's realization that the children don't understand what is happening only sharpens the effect. For women readers the story perhaps will reflect some of their own emotions and responses as the society is ready now to listen to the stories of battered wives and of women threatened by lovers or friends. The terror that is stalking Nancy is no different from the fear that a woman feels when she knows that a restraining order issued by a distant judge won't protect her from the rage of a disturbed ex-husband.

From the perspective of sixty years, it is also possible to see the racial dimensions of the story in a different way. Perhaps part of what gave Faulkner his great international reputation — and his Nobel Prize — was an understanding that what he was describing was the bitter reality of life for any underclass. The black underclass outside the white neighborhoods of this southern town has been forced into the way of life of the peasants of the older European societies. Faulkner's Nancy could have been a servant in a renter's cottage outside the manor walls in nineteenth-century England, or a woman forced outside the social framework — as she would be by her unwed pregnancy — in any European small town before World War I. Faulkner's story still forces us to face this very real inhumanity in a world we realize has not left this legacy of violence behind.

Questions for Discussion

1. Compare the ages of the children with the responses to Nancy's fear. How much more awareness do the older children have?
2. How does Faulkner describe the small town's ability to help someone like Nancy?
3. Why is Jesus still able to go free, despite the awareness of the children's father of what is happening?

Topics for Writing

1. Faulkner describes the uneasy boundary where the white and the black societies of this small town meet. What are the real effects of this boundary?
2. Compare the situation Nancy faces with a similar situation today.
3. The children's father acts in a way that he would consider sympathetic and protective but would be considered paternalistic today. Discuss his character and role in the story.

Suggested Readings

Basset, John E. *Vision and Revisions: Essays on Faulkner.* West Cornwall, CT: Locust Hill, 1989.

Bloom, Harold. *William Faulkner.* New York: Chelsea House, 1986.

Blotner, Joseph. *Faulkner: A Biography.* New York: Random, 1991.

Brooks, Cleanth. *A Shaping Joy.* New York: Harcourt, 1971.

Gwynn, Frederick, and Joseph Blotner, eds. *Faulkner in the University.* Charlottesville: U of Virginia P, 1959.

Hall, Donald. *To Read Literature: Fiction, Poetry, Drama.* New York: Holt, 1981. 10–16.

Heller, Terry. "The Telltale Hair: A Critical Study of William Faulkner's 'A Rose for Emily.' " *Arizona Quarterly* 28 (1972): 301–18.

Hoffman, Frederick J. *William Faulkner, Revised.* Boston: Twayne, 1990.

Howe, Irving. *William Faulkner: A Critical Study.* 2nd ed. New York: Vintage, 1962. 265.

Leary, Lewis. *William Faulkner of Yoknapatawpha County.* Twentieth-Century American Writers. New York: Crowell, 1973. 136.

Millgate, Michael. *The Achievement of William Faulkner.* New York: Random, 1966.

F. Scott Fitzgerald

Babylon Revisited (p. 490)

"Babylon Revisited" develops a paradox about the past: It is irretrievably lost, but it controls the present inescapably. Charlie Wales revisits the scenes of "the big party" carried on by stock-market rich Americans in Paris during the 1920s — a party at which he was one of the chief celebrants — and shakes his head over how much things have changed. His memories of those times come into focus only gradually, and as they do his nostalgia modulates to disgust. His guilt-ridden desire to repudiate his past behavior reaches a peak *not* when his negotiations to get his daughter back remind him that he brought on his wife's pneumonia by locking her out in the snow, but only when Lorraine's *pneumatique* reminds him that for several years his life was given over to trivial foolishness. For a man trying to reestablish himself as a loving and responsible father, the memory of harming his wife in wild anger at her flirtation with "young Webb" is less embarrassing than the memory of riding a stolen tricycle all over the Étoile with another man's wife.

The problem for Charlie Wales is that his past — for the moment embodied in the pathetic relics Duncan and Lorraine — clings to him despite his efforts to repudiate it. The reader (like Marion) is inclined to fear that Charlie might return to his past ways, but Charlie is not tempted by Lorraine or by the lure of alcohol. His lesson has been learned, but that does not prevent the past from destroying his plans for the future. Or perhaps, as David Toor argues, it is Charlie who clings to the past; perhaps he ambivalently punishes himself out of a guilt he refuses to acknowledge, as when he sabotages his campaign to get Honoria from the Peterses by leaving their address for Duncan with the bartender at the Ritz. As the story ends, history is repeating itself. Just as Charlie caused Helen's sickness, the inopportune arrival of his old friends has sickened Marion. As a result he loses Honoria, at least for six months of her fast-waning and irretrievable childhood — just as he has lost Helen for good.

WILLIAM E. SHEIDLEY

Questions for Discussion

1. Why does Fitzgerald begin the story with what seems to be the end of a conversation that then begins when Charlie walks into the bar in the next paragraph?

2. As Charlie rides through Paris on his way to see his daughter, he thinks, "I spoiled this city for myself." What reason might Fitzgerald have for treating this subject so mildly and in such vague terms here?

3. Characterize the Peters family. To what extent are we to approve of their attitudes?

4. What is the effect of Charlie's repeatedly taking "only one drink every afternoon"? Does the reader expect him to regress into alcohol abuse?

5. What does Charlie's brief encounter with the woman in the *brasserie* contribute to the story?

6. Why does Charlie identify the fine fall day as "football weather"?

7. Discuss the impact of the appearance of Duncan and Lorraine after Charlie's lunch with Honoria.

8. Why is Marion reluctant to release Honoria to her father? Why is Charlie able to win her consent, temporarily?

9. When Marion suggests that Charlie may have caused Helen's death, "an electric current of agony surged through him," but Lincoln says, "I never thought you were responsible for that." Was he? What does Charlie himself think? Explain his reaction.

10. Explain Charlie's reaction to Lorraine's *pneumatique*. Why does he ignore it? Why does that tactic fail?

11. Why does Fitzgerald introduce the arrival of Duncan and Lorraine precisely where he does, and in the way he does?

12. What does Paul mean when he supposes that Charlie "lost everything [he] wanted in the boom" by "selling short"? What does Charlie mean when he replies, "Something like that"?

13. Explain the irony of Charlie's present financial success, apparently unique among his old friends.

14. What does the title mean?

Topics for Writing

1. Analyze Fitzgerald's use of recurring motifs and foreshadowing in "Babylon Revisited."

2. Consider Charlie Wales as a study of remorse.

3. Write an essay describing the techniques of characterization in "Babylon Revisited" of the secondary characters.

4. Consider Charlie's daughter's name as the key to his underlying motives.

5. After reading each of the five sections of the story, write a paragraph giving your assessment of Charlie Wales and your prediction of what will happen to him. Is there consistency, or a progression, in your judgments?

Suggested Readings

Gallo, Rose Adrienne. *F. Scott Fitzgerald*. Modern Literature Monographs. New York: Ungar, 1978. 101–05.

Gross, Seymour. "Fitzgerald's 'Babylon Revisited.' " *College English* 25 (1963): 128–35.

Male, Roy R. " 'Babylon Revisited': The Story of the Exile's Return." *Studies in Short Fiction* 2 (1965): 270–77.

Toor, David. "Guilt and Retribution in 'Babylon Revisited.'" *Fitzgerald/Hemingway Annual 1973*. Ed. Matthew J. Bruccoli and C. E. Frazer Clark, Jr. Washington, D.C.: Microcard Eds., 1974. 155–64.

GUSTAVE FLAUBERT

A Simple Heart (p. 507)

Students may find Flaubert's long narrative boring and pointless, its central character too narrow and insignificant for such extended treatment, and its plot lacking the qualities of conflict, suspense, and climax customary in well-structured fiction. Rather than assuring them of the work's recognized perfection or quoting Ezra Pound's judgment that "A Simple Heart" embodies "all that anyone knows about writing," you might try placing the work in contexts that will make it more interesting and accessible.

That the tale is an autobiographically intimate recollection of the people and places of Flaubert's childhood, some of them revisited while it was being written, underlines the degree to which his objective narration controls strong personal feelings. Add that Félicité is run down by the mail coach at precisely the same spot on the road where Flaubert suffered the first onset of the epilepsy that led him to choose a life of retirement and dedicated labor at his art — a life in many ways comparable to Félicité's own obscure and laborious existence — and students may find themselves ready to give the story a second look.

Flaubert wrote "A Simple Heart" during the last years of his life as one of three interrelated tales, the *Trois Contes*, on religious themes. By this time Flaubert had suffered the humiliation of seeing Normandy and his own home occupied by the invading Prussians; he had lost most of his money through misguided generosity to the husband of an ungrateful niece; and he had watched his friends die off. One of them was the novelist George Sand, for whom he was writing "A Simple Heart" in response to her chiding him for insensitivity in his detached style of fiction. The *Trois Contes*, each in a different way, embody Flaubert's reaction to these losses. Each subjects pride and worldliness to a devastating confrontation with humility and self-abnegation.

The genre of "A Simple Heart" is the saint's life; its deceptively simple chronological structure traces the stages by which the protagonist throws off selfishness and worldly desires and, in the process, attains the spiritual purity requisite for miracles, martyrdom, and assumption into bliss. With the loss of Théodore, Félicité leaves ordinary erotic love behind her and enters upon a lifelong devotion to selfless labor. She does this not as a self-conscious and would-be heroic rejection of the world but only because she knows of nothing else to do. The love she feels subsequently, however, is as selfless as her labor. It goes virtually unrewarded by Paul, Virginie, and Victor, but it is in a sense its own reward, for it enables Félicité to experience a vicarious life of the imagination seemingly more real than her own, as in Virginie's first communion or Victor's trip to Havana. As the world relentlessly strips her of each beloved person and finally even of the very senses by which to apprehend them, Félicité can resort to the power of her imagination, unrestrained by any conventional critical intellect. Imagination blooming into faith allows her not only to find the answer to her loneliness in a parrot but also to endow the dead, stuffed bird with spiritual life and to experience her final beatific vision of the parrotlike Holy Ghost spreading over her from heaven.

Flaubert worried that his tale would seem ironic and Félicité's confusion of the parrot Loulou with the deity absurd. On the contrary, he insisted, "it is in no way ironic, as you may suppose, but . . . very serious and very sad" (quoted by Stratton Buck, p. 105). The question of tone should lead a class discussion straight to the fundamental issues raised by the story. Félicité's utter lack of pretension, as Jonathan Culler argues, defeats the impulse toward irony because it allows nothing for irony to deflate, while Flaubert, by avoiding commentary and committing himself to the pure and precise rendering of the facts of the case, presents the reader with the necessity, in order to give meaning to Félicité's life, of imagining a sacred order in which her vision of the parrot is not a mockery but a divine blessing and a fit reward.

WILLIAM E. SHEIDLEY

Questions for Discussion

1. One critic (Peter Cortland) remarks that in a way Félicité's life is "entirely covered" by Flaubert's opening sentence. How is that so? In what sense does that sentence miss everything?
2. Why does Flaubert introduce his second section by defeating any excitement or special interest the reader might feel about Félicité's affair with Théodore?
3. What is the effect of Flaubert's detailed descriptions of the Norman countryside as well as the other settings and circumstances of the story?
4. Explain the purpose of Félicité's musings about the Holy Ghost in the third section.
5. Why is Virginie's first communion more meaningful to Félicité than her own reception of the sacrament?
6. Compare the reactions of Félicité and Mme Aubain to the death of Virginie. What do the differences reveal about their characters?
7. What is the effect on the reader's attitude toward Félicité of the passage that begins when she is whipped by the coachman?
8. Why does Flaubert have Mère Simon tell herself, as she sponges the sweat from the dying Félicité's temples, "that one day she would have to go the same way"?
9. *Félicité* means happiness, good fortune, or bliss. Is the name of Flaubert's heroine ironic?

Topics for Writing

1. Examine the episode of Loulou's disappearance and return, and the consequences of Félicité's search for him as an epitome of the story.
2. Discuss the circumstances of Félicité's death as a key to Flaubert's theme.
3. Analyze the function of the brief, one-sentence paragraphs that punctuate the text at certain points.

4. Review the story and make a list of everything Félicité loses. Is it possible to make a corresponding list of things she gains?
5. Study Flaubert's description of Mme Aubain's house in the first section and write a similar description of a house you know.
6. Write an obituary for Félicité such as might have been published in the Pont-l'Évêque newspaper. Are you satisfied with the result?

Suggested Readings

Buck, Stratton. *Gustave Flaubert*. Twayne's World Authors Series 3. New York: Twayne, 1966. Esp. 103–08.
Cortland, Peter. *A Reader's Guide to Flaubert*. New York: Helios, 1968. 127–46.
Cross, Richard K. *Flaubert and Joyce: The Rite of Fiction*. Princeton: Princeton UP, 1971. 17–25.
Culler, Jonathan. *Flaubert: The Uses of Uncertainty*. Ithaca: Cornell UP, 1974. Esp. 11–19, 208–11.

MARY E. WILKINS FREEMAN

The Revolt of "Mother" (p. 533)

In "The Revolt of 'Mother,'" Freeman draws a sharp but subtle portrait of a woman character whom most students will find appealing, although she acts in a devious, underhanded way to assert her will over her husband. Freeman is careful to enlist our sympathies for the wife in the beginning of the story, yet she is presented in humorous terms at the end to minimize the implications of her domestic rebellion. A close reading of the opening paragraphs will reveal the skillful ways Freeman makes Mrs. Penn a sympathetic character in the conflict with her husband.

The story opens with an exchange of dialogue between the husband and wife. Really, though, *dialogue* is not quite the term, since Mr. Penn tries to avoid his wife's direct question: "What are them men diggin' over there in the field for?" He is silent until his wife repeats the question. Then he tells her to go back in the house and mind her own business. Implacable, she stands her ground.

The dialect used in the conversational exchange is colloquial, and Freeman takes pains to make us *hear* the characters. The husband "ran his words together, and his speech was almost as inarticulate as a growl." Freeman's language as narrator is more sophisticated than her fictional characters' speech. Reading the story, we accept her view of the situation as an informed bystander, even if we suspect that she is not an impartial one.

The characters in these opening paragraphs are defined by what they do as well as what they say and how they say it. The husband's face drops at his wife's question, and he jerks the collar roughly over his bay mare and slaps on the saddle. Mrs. Penn is less physically aggressive than her husband, but her will is at least as strong as his. Freeman takes pleasure in describing her inner strength as she waits for her husband to answer her. "Her eyes, fixed upon the old man, looked as if the

93

meekness had been the result of her own will, never of the will of another." She is like John's sister in Gilman's "The Yellow Wallpaper," a conventional woman who is (as Gilman wrote) a "perfect and enthusiastic housekeeper, and hopes for no better profession."

"The Revolt of 'Mother'" is a realistic local-color story, but the New England landscape and lives depicted in it have symbolic overtones too. It is spring, a time of growth and renewal. Mrs. Penn's will is like the dandelions in the vivid green grass, determined to survive even if unencouraged by her husband. Mr. Penn sees his wife in symbolic terms: "She looked as immovable to him as one of the rocks in his pasture-land, bound to the earth with generations of blackberry vines." In due time, Mrs. Penn, a "perfect and enthusiastic housekeeper," will be preserving these blackberries and baking her family delicious berry pies. She is no infertile rocklike earth goddess or unconventional rebel girl. She is the living spirit of the domestic hearth, and she deserves a home larger than the "infinitesimal" one her husband has provided for her, "scarcely as commodious for people as the little boxes under the barn eaves were for doves."

Mrs. Penn's actions at the end of the story continue on the larger-than-life level introduced so carefully with the symbolism in these early paragraphs, only now Freeman shifts her tone to suggest burlesque. Mother's feat moving into the new barn "was equal in its way to Wolfe's storming of the Heights of Abraham," an allusion to the war between the English and the French in Quebec, when the British general James Wolfe led his troops to victory on the Plains of Abraham. Mrs. Penn's action has "a certain uncanny and superhuman quality" when she takes over her husband's new barn. Its threshold "might have been Plymouth Rock from her bearing." Freeman meant her readers to find this symbolism and hyperbole funny, but today's readers (even if they aren't feminists) may see the revolt of "mother" in a different light. Was Freeman too sympathetic toward her heroine in the early pages of the story or too heavy-handed in the later ones? Don't let students miss the ambivalence in the treatment of Mrs. Penn.

Questions for Discussion

1. What does the opening scene of this short story establish about the character of Sarah Penn? How does her husband, Adoniram, view her? Is this view similar to or different from the narrator's presentation of her?

2. How would you describe Adoniram Penn? Based on the opening scene of the story, what would you say is the nature of the relationship between the Penns?

3. Are the characters defined only by their conversations, or by their actions as well? Give examples.

4. Note the colloquial dialect used by Sarah and Adoniram Penn. How does this differ from that used by the narrator of the story? What devices does Freeman employ to make us "hear" the conversation of the characters?

5. What is the point of view of this story? In your opinion, can we trust the judgment of the narrator? Why or why not? How impartial do you feel the narrator is?

6. What is the setting of the story? How is it one of the main sources of conflict?

7. Note the fact that only the narrator refers to Sarah and Adoniram by name. Within the story itself, these characters are referred to, and refer to each

other, only as "mother" and "father." To what extent do the characters fulfill these symbolic roles? Has Freeman given them any individuality outside these roles?

8. What is the function of Sammy and Nanny? Are they necessary to the story?
9. Toward the end of the story, Sarah Penn becomes larger than life and almost superhuman. Where does this shift of treatment take place? How does Freeman accomplish it? What problems does this ambivalent treatment of Sarah Penn create in the story?
10. Freeman's treatment of Adoniram Penn also changes. How would you describe this shift, and what does it contribute to your understanding of Adoniram as an individual?
11. What significance would you attach to Freeman's putting the word "mother" in quotation marks in the title of the story?

Topics for Writing

1. Examine the dilemma of individuality versus societal expectations and roles as shown in the characters of the story.
2. What is the importance of the relationship of children to parents and the tendency of children to emulate their parents as elements in "The Revolt of 'Mother'"?
3. Discuss the importance of setting to the conflict of the story.
4. State the themes of Freeman's story as they relate to philosophy and social criticism.
5. Try to rewrite the story from the point of view of Adoniram Penn; from the point of view of Nanny or Sammy.

Suggested Readings

Pryse, M. "An Uncloistered New England Nun." *Studies in Short Fiction* 20 (1983): 289–95.
Toth, S. A. "Defiant Light: A Positive View of Mary Wilkins Freeman." *New England Quarterly* 46 (1973): 82–93.

MARY GAITSKILL

Tiny, Smiling Daddy (p. 545)

Gaitskill explains the meaning of her title at the end of the story, when the "daddy" who is her protagonist thinks about his relationship with his dead father and contrasts his devastating memories with the psychological phrase "the good parent in yourself," which he considers a cliché: "What did the well-meaning idiots who thought of these phrases mean by them? When a father dies, he is gone, there is no tiny, smiling daddy who appears, waving happily, in a secret pocket in your chest." Gaitskill uses third-person narration to tell her story, which explores the feelings of Stew, a father who feels himself wronged because his daughter Kitty has left home to live an independent life as a lesbian. As a boy,

Stew's own father was insensitive to him, and Stew retaliates by being brutal to his daughter after she tells her parents that she is a lesbian. He says to her, "And if you ever try to come back here I'm going to spit in your face. I don't care if I'm on my deathbed, I'll still have the energy to spit in your face."

Stew is presented in a harsh light as a father, deliberately offending his daughter by acts of coarseness. In his own eyes he has been a "good daddy," but Gaitskill lets us understand the way his daughter has experienced his love. He never physically abused her, but Kitty has felt that he emotionally dominated the household. She resents the way that he devalued her feelings and left her without self-respect by treating her and her mother Marsha as if the two women formed a small harem for his pleasure alone. Stew can only see a situation in terms of good and bad, with no shadings in between. Since his daughter is a lesbian, she is not normal in his eyes. A normal woman would grow up, get married, and give him a son-in-law and grandchildren. She would stay "his beautiful, happy little girl" all her life, instead of turning into a "glum, weird teenager" who leaves home in rebellion. When Kitty publishes an article in a national magazine, he asks himself, "How could she have done this to him? She knew how he dreaded exposure of any kind."

The reader asks, "Exposure of what?" What were his hidden feelings toward his daughter? Was incest at the back of his mind while she was growing up in his house? Is he genuinely sorry for brutally rejecting her when she told him she was a lesbian, and for being incapable of accepting her as his daughter after that? Or is he fiercely protective of his privacy because he believes that she is still emotionally immature, and that her feelings toward him will change as she grows older? Or is Stew's fear of exposure based on his experience as an astute student of the media, understanding the vulgar commercial exploitation fueling "feel-good" talk shows on television and "true-story" articles based on pop psychology in national magazines? Stew isn't critical of the society he lives in, except to mourn the passing of the good old days of his boyhood. There is no bridging the gulf between him and his daughter, as everyone in his "tiny" family is sadly aware.

Questions for Discussion

1. What is Gaitskill suggesting about Stew in her opening sentence, when she tells us that "the phone rang five times before he got up to answer it"?
2. Define the basic conflict in the story between Stew and Kitty. Is either one of them a sympathetic character?
3. What role does Marsha play in her marriage with Stew? What details in the story tell you how well he understands her? Does Marsha share Stew's hostility toward their daughter?
4. In what way would you call the family in this story dysfunctional? In what way is it functional?
5. How would the story have been different if Gaitskill had chosen a first-person instead of a third-person narrator?

Topics for Writing

1. Write an essay analyzing Gaitskill's characterization of Kitty in the story.

2. Continue Gaitskill's narrative by imagining a devastating telephone conversation between Stew and Kitty about her magazine article, after which Marsha persuades him to go to a family therapist to explore the reasons he is so angry with his daughter.

Suggested Reading

Gaitskill, Mary. *Because They Wanted To.* New York: Simon & Schuster, 1997.

TESS GALLAGHER

Rain Flooding Your Campfire (p. 555)

Gallagher's story is her version of what happened on the evening when her recently widowed blind friend spent an evening with her and her companion Raymond Carver, ate dinner, watched television, and stayed overnight. Carver's story based on the same real-life incident is "Cathedral." Gallagher tells us that she was "bummed" out after reading his story, so she decided to tell it again. In the middle of her narrative she confides that she and her blind friend (called Norman in her story, Robert in Carver's) often comforted each other in the old days by sharing a private joke when things were difficult. They "had a saying" when something made them feel bad: "rain flooding your campfire." Reading Carver's story was like "rain flooding your campfire" for Gallagher, because she thought he didn't do justice to the memory of her blind friend. What Carver (called Mr. G. in Gallagher's story) omitted in "Cathedral" was everything she considered important about the visit — "the tender, painful things about my friend Mr. G. hadn't known to tell."

After reading the two different versions of the same visit, the reader may understandably feel some confusion. What details are invented in the two stories, and what really happened? Gallagher invents a persona for her first-person narrator, who is clearly not herself — in her story she works at the gas company and lives with a man named Ernest. She also invents a different persona for Carver, turning him into a colleague at the gas company who spends his time on the job writing fiction so bad that it never gets published. These characterizations are both tongue-in-cheek, of course. Ernest and two other gas company employees, the couple Sal and Margaret, who are dinner guests, are so thinly described that they never emerge in the story, except when Sal's dog, Ripper, noses Norman's crotch and tries to bite him in the hallway after the blind man has emerged from his tearful breakdown in the bathroom. Perhaps they are in Gallagher's story because they were there in "real life" so she felt bound to include them in her fictional narrative. Or perhaps she imagined them in order to differentiate her plot from Carver's — Gallagher leaves the reader free to speculate.

The strength of Gallagher's story is her description of the narrator's attachment to her blind friend. Her observations of the effect of his physical presence on her are the strongest part of her story. Describing Norman as she sits next to him, for example, she notices that "He's bald, except for close-shaven sideburns and a band of hair at the back of his neck. Because his eyes are clouded he's always seemed balder to me than he is." The narrator in Carver's "Cathedral" is subconsciously aware of his wife's depth of feeling for her old blind friend and reacts with flippant hostility toward his innocent guest before what Gallagher recognizes as his profound epiphany at the end of the story, when he "experiences blindness through his blind visitor." Gallagher, on the other hand, is flippantly hostile not so much toward the insensitive Mr. G. as toward the apparently too-real existence of what she calls Carver's "patched-up" story. She refers to it repeatedly throughout her narrative, even rewriting it for him (as a joke) to improve it, "bringing in Norman's intrusive mother-in-law."

Questions for Discussion

1. How does Gallagher contribute to the characterization of her narrator and the blind man, as well as develop the implications of her title, by describing the camping trip they took in happier days with his wife Caroline?
2. Why does Gallagher change the object drawn by the blind man after watching television to a missile, instead of a cathedral? Does this effectively foreshadow the last scene of her story?
3. How does the narrator establish intimacy between herself and Ernest in the story? How does the language she uses to describe their time together in the bedroom at the end of the story suggest the depth of their relationship?
4. What does the narrator suggest about the emotional bond between herself and the blind man by her vision of him standing outside alone in the dark front yard?
5. Explain what Gallagher means by having her narrator stand naked beside Norman outdoors at night before guiding him back into the house. In what way is she attempting to parallel the ending to Carver's story?

Topics for Writing

1. Create your own version of this story from the blind man's point of view.
2. **CONNECTIONS** Compare and contrast the voices of the narrators in "Rain Flooding Your Campfire" and "Cathedral." What different types of humor do they illustrate? Consider, for example, the narrator's use of slang in the title of Gallagher's story and in expressions such as "he gouges himself with the truth."
3. Imagine you are the blind man and have just listened to someone reading aloud Carver's and Gallagher's stories about you. Which one would you prefer, and why?

Related Commentary

Tom Jenks, The Origin of "Cathedral," p. 1594.

Related Story

Raymond Carver, Cathedral, p. 237.

Suggested Reading

Gallagher, Tess. *At the Owl Woman Saloon.* New York: Scribner, 1997.

Mavis Gallant

1933 (p. 565)

Mavis Gallant, in her essay "What Is Style?" (p. 1462 of this anthology), makes an arresting analogy between fiction and life:

> Style is inseparable from structure, part of the conformation of whatever the author has to say. What he says — this is what fiction is about — is that something is taking place and that nothing lasts. Against the sustained tick of a watch, fiction takes the measure of a life, a season, a look exchanged, the turning point, desire as brief as a dream, the grief and terror that after childhood we cease to express. The lie, the look, the grief are without permanence. The watch continues to tick where the story stops.

Gallant's story "1933" is an evocation of a distant time and place, the first of several linked stories about the French-Canadian widow Mme. Carette and her daughters Berthe and Marie published in *Across the Bridge.* The opening pages of the story have a stillness so quiet that the ticking of Gallant's watch is hardly noticed as she skillfully and swiftly sketches in the background of her narrative. The widow's financial situation, her decision to move to a smaller and less expensive apartment, the careful disposition of the furniture, the fatherless family's cautious adjustment to the new neighborhood — all the details proceed at a funereal pace in the story, as stylized as in an early Ingmar Bergman film. We know that nothing lasts, because death is behind all the decisions being made: The widow and her children are survivors, but in their Catholic Quebeçois world, death is just a matter of time.

What makes Gallant's story so poignant is that the act of imagination creating it, rather than the austere religion shaping its every detail, is what resurrects the life being described. Like the fiction of Isaac Bashevis Singer, Gallant's presentation of a distant and lost past preserves its memory for posterity. The author's narrative is alive. It breathes in the accuracy of its details and the passion of its telling. The spirit of the mother's stern renunciation of life in her widowhood moves on the page in sentences such as "Mme. Carette told Berthe that her days of entertaining and cooking for guests were over. She was just twenty-seven." Later her exhaustion and sense of humiliation at being forced to earn money for her children by sewing in other people's houses leads her to express spiteful thoughts about the marriage of the couple downstairs who have taken care of Berthe and Marie overnight, and she is appalled at herself: "No sooner had she said this than she covered her mouth and spoke through her fingers: 'God forgive my unkind thoughts.' She propped her arms on each side of her plate, as the girls were forbidden to do, and let her face slide into her hands."

As Gallant says, "The watch continues to tick where the story stops," reminding us that nothing in life is permanent. Memories can keep the past alive, and stories are as close to permanent as we get.

(text pp. 571–575)

Questions for Discussion

1. Where does the story take place? How does Gallant suggest the French-Canadian background of her characters?
2. How does the death of M. Carette affect his family?
3. What is the symbolic significance of the location of the family's new apartment near the Institute for the Deaf and Dumb?
4. How religious is Mme. Carette? What does the narrator imply about the role of religion in the children's daily life?
5. Why are so few English words needed between Rue Saint-Denis and Parc Lafontaine?
6. Why can't Mme. Carette become friends with M. Grosjean's Irish wife?

Topic for Writing

1. Write a story about a death in your family, and describe how it affected your life.

Related Commentary

Mavis Gallant, What Is Style?, p. 1462.

Suggested Readings

Gallant, Mavis. *Across the Bridge.* New York: Random, 1933.
———. *Paris Notebooks.* Toronto: Macmillan, 1985.

GABRIEL GARCÍA MÁRQUEZ

A Very Old Man with Enormous Wings (p. 571)

The word "allegories" in the headnote presents a challenge to readers of this story, and the inevitable failure of any simple scheme of interpretation to grasp fully the mystery at its heart, reflects García Márquez's central theme exactly. Like the crabs, which come into the human world from an alien realm, the "flesh-and-blood angel" constitutes an intrusion of something strange and unfathomable into the comfortable world of reality as we choose to define it. Everybody, from the "wise" woman next door to the pope, takes a turn at trying to find a slot in which to file the winged visitor, but no definition seems satisfactory, and even Pelayo and Elisenda, whom the angel's presence has made wealthy, spend their money on a house "with iron bars on the windows so that angels wouldn't get in." When at last the old man flies away, Elisenda feels relief, "because then he was no longer an annoyance in her life but an imaginary dot on the horizon of the sea."

In discussing how he receives artistic inspiration, García Márquez says, "There's nothing deliberate or predictable in all this, nor do I know when it's

100

going to happen to me. I'm at the mercy of my imagination." Without intending to limit the story's implications, one might associate the angel with this sort of unpredictable intrusion of the visionary and wonderful into everyday life. As an old man with wings, the angel recalls the mythical symbol of the artist, Daedalus, except that his wings are "so natural on that completely human organism that [the doctor] couldn't understand why other men didn't have them too." Bogged down in the mud, the angel seems less an allusion to Daedalus's son, the over-reacher Icarus, than a representation of the difficulty of the artistic imagination in sustaining its flight through the unpleasant circumstances of this "sad" world. True artists are often misunderstood, ill treated, and rejected in favor of more practical concerns or of the creators of ersatz works that flatter established preju-dices. Just so, nobody can understand the angel's "hermetic" language, and when he performs his aggressively unpractical miracles, no one is delighted. Exploited by his keepers, to whom he brings vast wealth, the angel receives as royalties only his quarters in the chicken coop and the flat side of the broom when under-foot. Popular for a time as a sideshow attraction, the angel is soon passed over in favor of the horrible "woman who had been changed into a spider for having disobeyed her parents," a grotesque and slapdash creation of the lowest order of imaginative synthesis, whose "human truth" gratifies both sentimentality and narrow-mindedness. But the artistic imagination lives happily on eggplant mush, possesses a supernatural patience, and though functionally blind to the bumping posts of ordinary reality, ever again takes wing. The angel has, perhaps rightly, appeared to his human observers "a cataclysm in repose," but near the end, as he sings his sea chanteys under the stars, he definitely comes to resemble "a hero taking his ease," preparing to navigate the high seas beyond the horizon.

WILLIAM E. SHEIDLEY

Questions for Discussion

1. Why are there crabs in the house? Is it for the same reason the old man with enormous wings has fallen in the courtyard? What other associations does the story make between the old man and the crabs?
2. Pelayo first thinks the old man is a nightmare. What other attempts are made to put this prodigy into a familiar category?
3. How does the old man differ from our usual conceptions of angels? What is the essential difference?
4. Explain Father Gonzaga's approach to the angel. What implications — about the angel and about the church — may be derived from his failure to com-municate with him effectively?
5. Comment on the angel's career as a sideshow freak. Who receives the ben-efit of his success? Why does he fall? Compare what he has to offer with what the spider-woman has. What reasons might people have to prefer the latter?
6. Why do you think the angel tolerates the child patiently?
7. What are the implications of the angel's examination by the doctor?
8. How do we feel as the angel finally flaps away at the end? Does Elisenda's response adequately express the reader's?

Topics for Writing

1. Consider the ordinary and the enormous in "A Very Old Man with Enormous Wings." (Consider the etymological meaning of "enormous.")
2. Is García Márquez's fallen angel a fairy tale, a myth, or an allegory?
3. Recharging the sense of wonder: How does García Márquez make the reader believe in his angel?
4. Read the story aloud to a selected spectrum of people (at least three) of various ages and educational levels. Tabulate their responses and opinions, perhaps in an interview. Combining this evidence with your own response to the story, try to define the basis of its appeal.
5. Select a supernatural being from a fairy tale or other familiar source (the cartoons involving talking animals that wear clothes and drive cars might be worth considering), and imagine the being as a physical reality in your own ordinary surroundings. Write a sketch about what happens.
6. **CONNECTIONS** Compare "A Very Old Man with Enormous Wings" with other presentations of the supernatural (Hawthorne's, for example).

Suggested Readings

Bell-Villada, Gene H. *García Márquez: The Man and His Work.* Chapel Hill: U of North Carolina P, 1990.

Byk, John. "From Fact to Fiction: Gabriel García Márquez and the Short Story." *Mid-American Review* 6.2 (1986): 111–16.

Fau, Margaret Eustella. *Bibliographic Guide to Gabriel García Márquez 1979–1985.* Westport, CT: Greenwood, 1986.

García Márquez, Gabriel. *Collected Stories.* New York: Harper, 1984.

———. *Strange Pilgrims: Twelve Stories.* New York: Knopf, 1993.

McMurray, George R. *Gabriel García Márquez.* New York: Ungar, 1977. 116–19.

McNerney, Kathleen. *Understanding Gabriel García Márquez.* Columbia: U of South Carolina P, 1989.

Morello Frosch, Marta. "The Common Wonders of García Márquez's Recent Fiction." *Books Abroad* 47 (1973): 496–501.

Oberhelman, Harley D., ed. *Gabriel García Márquez: A Study of the Short Fiction.* Boston: Twayne, 1991.

Ortega, Julio. *Gabriel García Márquez and the Powers of Fiction.* Austin: U of Texas P, 1988.

Williams, Raymond L. *Gabriel García Márquez.* Boston: Twayne, 1984.

Zhu, Jingdong. "García Márquez and His Writing of Short Stories." *Foreign Literatures* 1 (1987): 77–80.

CHARLOTTE PERKINS GILMAN

The Yellow Wallpaper (p. 577)

Gilman wrote "The Yellow Wallpaper" between 1890 and 1894, during what she later recalled were the hardest years of her life. She had left her first husband and child to live alone in California after a nervous breakdown, and she was beginning to give lectures on socialism and freedom for women while she kept a boardinghouse, taught school, and edited newspapers. During this time, her husband married her best friend, to whom Gilman relinquished her child. The emotional pressures and economic uncertainties under which Gilman lived contributed to the desperate tone of this story.

Early readers of "The Yellow Wallpaper" compared it with the horror stories of Edgar Allan Poe (William Dean Howells said it was a story to "freeze our . . . blood" when he reprinted it in 1920 in *Great Modern American Stories*). Like Poe's homicidal narrators, Gilman's heroine tells her story in a state of neurotic compulsion. But she is no homicidal maniac. Unlike Poe, Gilman suggests that a specific social malady has driven her heroine to the brink of madness: the bondage of conventional marriage.

Her husband is her physician and keeper, the father of her beloved but absent child, the money earner who pays the rent on the mansion where she is held captive for her "own good." When she begs to get away, he replies practically, "Our lease will be up in three weeks, and I can't see how to leave before." Insisting that he knows what is best for her, he believes that the cure for her mysterious "weakness" is total rest. The husband is supported in his view by the opinion of the foremost medical authority on the treatment of mental illness, Dr. S. Weir Mitchell, a name explicitly mentioned in the story. Gilman had spent a month in Dr. Mitchell's sanitorium five years before. In her autobiography she later reported that she almost lost her mind there and would often "crawl into remote closets and under beds — to hide from the grinding pressure of that profound distress."

Gilman transferred the memory of her physical debilitation and "absolute incapacity" for normal (read "conventional") married life into her heroine's state in "The Yellow Wallpaper." The story dramatizes Gilman's fear while living with her first husband that marriage and motherhood might incapacitate her (as it apparently had Gilman's mother) for what she called "work in the world." She felt imprisoned within her marriage, a victim of her desire to please, trapped by her wedding ring. Gilman left her husband, but in "The Yellow Wallpaper" her heroine is sacrificed to the emotional turmoil she experiences.

As a symbolic projection of psychological stress, "The Yellow Wallpaper" has resemblances to Kafka's "The Metamorphosis," although it is more specific in its focus on social injustice to women. Like Gregor Samsa, Gilman's heroine is victimized by the people she loves. The yellow wallpaper surrounding her is "like a bad dream." It furnishes the central images in the story. The reader can use it like a Rorschach test to understand the heroine's experience of entrapment, confinement, and sacrifice for other family members. Like Gregor Samsa, she regresses to subhuman behavior as a self-inflicted punishment following her psychological rebellion — the wallpaper's bad smell, its bars and grid, its fungus and toadstools, and its images of the creeping (dependent, inferior) woman. But unlike Gregor Samsa, Gilman's heroine thinks she is freed from the "bad dream" by telling her story, not to a "living soul," but to what she calls (nonjudgmentally) "dead paper."

Telling her story enables her to achieve her greatest desire — the symbolic death of her husband. The story ends, "Now why should that man have fainted? But he did, and right across my path by the wall, so that I had to creep over him every time!" The central irony of the story, however, is that by the time she realizes the twisted ambition fostered by obediently following "like a good girl" her passive role as a conventional member of the "weaker sex," she has been driven insane.

Questions for Discussion

1. Why have the narrator and her husband, John, rented the "colonial mansion"? What is its history, and what is the reaction of the heroine to this estate? Does she feel comfortable living in the house?
2. Give a description of John. Why does the heroine say that his profession is *"perhaps . . .* one reason I do not get well faster"? How does the narrator view her husband? Does she agree with John's diagnosis and treatment? Who else supports John's diagnosis? What effect does this have on the heroine?
3. What clue does the narrator's repeated lament, "what can one do?" give us about her personality? Describe other aspects of the woman's personality that are revealed in the opening of the story. What conflicting emotions is she having toward her husband, her condition, and the mansion?
4. How would you characterize the narrator's initial reaction to, and description of, the wallpaper?
5. Describe the narrator's state after the first two weeks of residence. Has John's relationship with his wife changed at all?
6. Who is Jennie? What is her relationship to the narrator, and what is her function in the story?
7. How has the narrator changed in her description of the wallpaper? Is it fair to say that the wallpaper has become more dominant in her day-to-day routine? Explain.
8. By the Fourth of July, what does the narrator admit about the wallpaper? What clues does Gilman give us about the education of the narrator and her increasingly agitated state? Is she finding it more and more difficult to communicate? Explain.
9. As the summer continues, describe the narrator's thoughts. What is her physical condition? Is there a link between her symptoms and psychological illness?
10. How does the narrator try to reach out to her husband? What is his reaction? Is this her last contact with sanity? Do you think John really has no comprehension of the seriousness of her illness?
11. Why do you think Gilman briefly changes the point of view from first person singular to the second person as the narrator describes the pattern of the wallpaper? What effect does the narrator say light has on the wallpaper?
12. Who does the narrator see in the wallpaper? How have her perceptions of John and Jennie changed from the beginning of the story?
13. Abruptly the narrator switches mood from boredom and frustration to excitement. To what does she attribute this change? How does John react to this? What new aspects of the wallpaper does she discuss?
14. By the final section of the story, what is the narrator's relationship to her husband? to Jennie? to the wallpaper? How has the narrator's perspective changed from the start of the story? What change do we see in her actions?
15. Identify what has driven the narrator to the brink of madness. How does she try to free herself from this element? What is her greatest desire? What is the central irony of the story?

Topics for Writing

1. Compare and contrast the husband-wife relationship and its outcome in Gilman's "The Yellow Wallpaper" and Henrik Ibsen's play "A Doll's House."
2. **CONNECTIONS** Compare and contrast the monologue in Gilman's "The Yellow Wallpaper" with that in Poe's "The Cask of Amontillado" or "The Tell-Tale Heart."
3. **CONNECTIONS** Compare and discuss the concept of marriage in Gilman's "The Yellow Wallpaper," Carver's "What We Talk About When We Talk About Love," and Walker's "Roselily."

Related Commentaries

Sandra M. Gilbert and Susan Gubar, A Feminist Reading of Gilman's "The Yellow Wallpaper," p. 1465.

Charlotte Perkins Gilman, Undergoing the Cure for Nervous Prostration, p. 1467.

Suggested Readings

Bader, J. "The Dissolving Vision: Realism in Jewett, Freeman and Gilman." *American Realism: New Essays*. Ed. Eric J. Sundquist. Baltimore: Johns Hopkins UP, 1982. 176–98.

Delaney, Sheila. *Writing Women: Women Writers and Women in Literature, Medieval to Modern*. New York: Schocken, 1983.

Feminist Papers: From Adams to de Beauvoir. Ed. Alice S. Rossi. New York: Columbia UP, 1973.

Hanley-Peritz, J. "Monumental Feminism and Literature's Ancestral House: Another Look at 'The Yellow Wallpaper.'" *Women's Studies* 12.2 (1986): 113–28.

Hill, Mary A. "Charlotte Perkins Gilman: A Feminist's Struggle with Womanhood." *Massachusetts Review* 21 (1980): 503–26.

———. *Charlotte Perkins Gilman: The Making of a Radical Feminist, 1860–1896*. Philadelphia: Temple UP, 1980.

Lane, Ann J. "Charlotte Perkins Gilman: The Personal Is Political." *Feminist Theorists*. Ed. Dale Spender. New York: Pantheon, 1983.

Nies, Judith. *Seven Women*. New York: Viking, 1977. 127–45.

Shumaker, C. "'Too Terribly Good to Be Printed': Charlotte Gilman's 'The Yellow Wallpaper.'" *American Literature* 57 (1985): 588–99.

Nikolai Gogol

The Overcoat (p. 590)

"The Overcoat," like Gogol's work in general, has been the subject of widely differing critical responses, some of which will surely be replicated in class discussion. A humanitarian view that sees the story as the vindication of a downtrodden little man coordinates fairly well with an interpretation that stresses the story's satiric attack on the rigid Czarist bureaucracy. Readers who note the grim joke with which the story ends, however, find its report on the destruction of a being too paltry even for contempt to be harrowingly cynical and heartless, while those who closely attend to the shifting narrative tone praise Gogol for producing a masterpiece of that combination of comedy and horror that we designate as the grotesque.

In some ways an obverse of romantic or Laforguian irony, which expresses a self-conscious revulsion from one's own emotional enthusiasms, the grotesque vision dissolves in grim laughter the appalled revulsion from a world devoid of any positive value. Neither Akaky Akakievich Bashmachkin (whose name in Russian alludes to dung on a shoe) nor the social and physical world with which he is at odds offers anything admirable, and the narrator's continuously shifting understatements, overstatements, verbal ironies, and bathetic juxtapositions repeatedly prevent the reader from any mistaken investment of esteem. Nonetheless, the possibility that Akaky Akakievich is our brother in ways not considered by his sentimental young colleague remains the source of the story's grip on our imagination.

Before time, which ages his coat, and the chill of the St. Petersburg winter combine to impose a need on him, Akaky Akakievich lives in a static and self-contained world of meaningless alphabetic letters, which he finds fulfillment and delight in replicating. He is a "writer" of sorts, but a writer who — like Gogol himself, according to Charles C. Bernheimer — hesitates to express himself in what he writes. With his fall from this undifferentiated condition into his struggle to acquire an overcoat, he is born into temporal human existence. His isolation breaks down, and so does his innocence: He makes a friend; he participates in a creative act; he experiences stirrings of sensuality; and he eventually manages to assert himself in words. He also becomes guilty of vanity, pride, lust, and deception. Having gained an identity as a man with a new coat, he becomes vulnerable to the destruction of that identity and consequently of the self it defines, which happens in three rapid stages.

Because we have seen him emerge from a state approximating nonexistence, Akaky Akakievich's brief history as a suffering human being does not appear to be much different from the radically reduced quintessence of the fate we imagine to be our own. That the retribution carried out by the shade of Akaky Akakievich — which suggests his vindication and the exaltation of his overcoat-identity to the stature of a myth — can finally be nothing more than a fantasy or a joke only serves to underline the inescapable dilemma that the story propounds between the meaninglessness of remaining locked within the circle of the self and the danger of aspiring beyond it.

WILLIAM E. SHEIDLEY

Questions for Discussion

1. Characterize the narrative mode of the opening paragraphs. Can you define a consistent tone?
2. In what sense was it "out of the question" to give Akaky Akakievich any other name?
3. Does Gogol share the feelings of "the young man" who thinks Akaky Akakievich's complaints mean "I am your brother"?

4. Describe Akaky Akakievich's life before his coat wore out.
5. Why does Gogol bother to make Petrovich such an unsavory character?
6. Describe Akaky Akakievich's feelings about his new overcoat once he decides to acquire it.
7. What possible attitudes might one take toward Akaky Akakievich's experience at the party? about his visit to the "Person of Consequence"?
8. Near the end, the narrator speaks of how "our little story unexpectedly finishes with a fantastic ending." What is the effect of this and the narrator's other implicit acknowledgments of the fictionality of his story — made as implausible assertions of its veracity — on the reader?
9. Consider Nabokov's commentary on "The Overcoat." What "gaps and black holes in the texture of Gogol's style" seem to you to "imply flaws in the texture of life itself"?

Topics for Writing

1. Discuss satire as a diversionary tactic in "The Overcoat."
2. Consider the "Person of Consequence" and a person of little consequence: two sides of the same coin?
3. Write an essay arguing that disappointed expectation is the goal of Gogol's style.
4. Study the long sentence on page 593 that begins "Even at those hours . . ." and continues nearly to the end of the paragraph it opens. Write a similar sentence about a community with which you are familiar (e.g., college students on a campus; the residents of your neighborhood). Try to follow Gogol as closely as possible: clause for clause, phrase for phrase. How would you define the tone of what you have written? Is it the same as Gogol's tone?
5. Nabokov concludes his commentary on this story (p. 1512) by suggesting that "after reading Gogol one's eyes may become gogolized and one is apt to see bits of [Gogol's irrational] world in the most unexpected places." Write a sketch in which, by manipulating style and diction, you cause your reader to glimpse a darker world beyond the surface appearances of things.
6. **CONNECTIONS** Compare and discuss Gogol's Akaky Akakievich and Melville's Bartleby as versions of the artist.

Related Commentary

Vladimir Nabokov, Gogol's Genius in "The Overcoat," p. 1512.

Suggested Readings

Bernheimer, Charles C. "Cloaking the Self: The Literary Space of Gogol's 'Overcoat.' " *PMLA* 90 (1975): 53–61.
Erlich, Victor. *Gogol.* Yale Russian and East European Studies 8. New Haven: Yale UP, 1969. Esp. 143–56.
Karlinsky, Simon. *The Sexual Labyrinth of Nikolai Gogol.* Cambridge, MA: Harvard UP, 1976. 135–44.
Lindstrom, Thaïs S. *Nikolay Gogol.* Twayne's World Authors Series 299. New York: Twayne, 1974. Esp. 88–96.

NADINE GORDIMER

Country Lovers (p. 613)

This tale is about race relations in South Africa. A mixed-race couple from the country become lovers and are brutally separated by social conventions. The story suggests the power of the attraction between all lovers — intangible, mysterious, beyond description in words. It overcomes differences of background, education, job status, and race. Yet, as Gordimer shows in this story, it cannot survive the virulence of unjust social conventions.

The country lovers are children together and grow up to become lovers. He is Paulus Eysendyck, the white son of the farm owner employing the black girl's father. She is named Thebedi; she is pretty, and clever with her hands. Her affection for Paulus is returned, and their lovemaking — which he instigates — is lyrically described: "They were not afraid of one another, they had known one another always; he did with her what he had done that time in the storeroom at the wedding, and this time it was so lovely, so lovely, he was surprised . . . and she was surprised by it, too."

The outcome of this love affair is a mixed-blood colored baby with straight fine hair and Paulus's hazel eyes. When he sees his child, Paulus cries out of anger and self-pity. His life will be ruined, his family shamed (later his father says, "I will try and carry on as best I can to hold up my head in the district"). Paulus murders the infant, Thebedi buries it, but the police come and dig it up. Someone has reported that it died mysteriously. Evidence in court is insufficient, so the verdict is "not guilty." The affair is over; as the black girl says to the newspaper reporter, "It was a thing of our childhood, we don't see each other anymore."

Questions for Discussion

1. The story ends with the protagonists in court. Why does Gordimer close the story with the court scene? Why does she give the quotations carried by the Sunday papers? How would you compare the story given to the public — both legal and journalistic — and the more private story you have had access to through reading "Country Lovers"?
2. After Paulus sees his baby for the first time, he says, "I feel like killing myself." Why does this make both Thebedi and Paulus sense a return of the "feeling between them that used to come when they were alone down at the river-bed"?
3. While Paulus is murdering the baby, Thebedi thinks she hears "small grunts . . . the kind of infant grunt that indicates a full stomach, a deep sleep." She tells her husband the baby is sleeping. When she first testifies, she is hysterical, and says things that we know are not true. More than a year later she retestifies, and tells the truth. At no point does Gordimer give the reader any explicit commentary on Thebedi's feelings and actions. How do you interpret the flat description of events in these most highly charged moments in the story?

Topics for Writing

1. In Gordimer's essay "The Flash of Fireflies," she says that "the short story is a fragmented and restless form, a matter of hit or miss, and it is perhaps for this reason that it suits modern consciousness — which seems best expressed as flashes of fearful insight alternating with near-hypnotic states of indifference." Analyze the language and structure of "Country Lovers" with reference to this definition.
2. Discuss the effects of apartheid on human relationships.
3. Discuss the effects of repressive policies on human rights in "Country Lovers."
4. Consider other legislation that you feel violates human rights and write a short story illustrating its effects.

Suggested Readings

Clayton, Cherry, ed. *Women and Writing in South Africa: A Critical Anthology.* Marshalltown: Heinemann Southern Africa, 1989, 183ff.

Cooke, J. "African Landscapes: The World of Nadine Gordimer." *World Literature Today* 52 (1978): 533–38.

Eckstein, B. "Pleasure and Joy: Political Activism in Nadine Gordimer's Short Stories." *World Literature Today* 59 (1985): 343–46.

Gordimer, Nadine. *Jump and Other Stories.* New York: Farrar, 1991.

Gray, S. "Interview with Nadine Gordimer." *Contemporary Literature* 22 (1981): 263–71.

Heywood, Christopher. *Nadine Gordimer.* Windsor, ONT: Profile, 1983.

Hurwitt, J. "Art of Fiction: Nadine Gordimer." *Paris Review* 25 (1983): 83–127.

Jacobs, J. U. "Living Space and Narrative Space in Nadine Gordimer's 'Something Out There.'" *English in Africa* 14.2 (Oct. 1987): 31–43.

Lazar, Karen. "Feminism as 'Piffling'? Ambiguities in Some of Nadine Gordimer's Short Stories." *Current Writing* 2.1 (Oct. 1990): 101–16.

Mazurek, Raymond A. "Nadine Gordimer's 'Something Out There' and Ndebele's 'Fools' and Other Stories: The Politics of Literary Form." *Studies in Short Fiction* 26.1 (Winter 1989): 71–79.

Newman, Judie. *Nadine Gordimer.* New York: Routledge, 1988.

Ross, Robert L., ed. *International Literature on Major Writers.* New York: Garland, 1991. 762ff.

Smith, Rowland. *Critical Essays on Nadine Gordimer.* Boston: G. K. Hall, 1990.

Smyer, R. I. "Africa in the Fiction of Nadine Gordimer." *Ariel* 16 (1985): 15–29.

Trump, Martin. "The Short Fiction of Nadine Gordimer." *Research in African Literature* 17.3 (Fall 1968): 341–69.

NATHANIEL HAWTHORNE

My Kinsman, Major Molineux (p. 620)

The critic Lewis Leary has said that "in the hand of a master, [the short story] becomes consummately an art, suggesting more than it seems at first to reveal." This statement is certainly true about "My Kinsman, Major Molineux," which has attracted a massive number of critical interpretations. In Part Two, Simon O. Lesser brings a psychological approach to his reading of this classic tale (p. 1496).

One way to approach the story in the classroom is to compare and contrast it with "Young Goodman Brown." Both describe the experience of immature, arrogant young men who seek something outside the familiar circle of their experience; both underestimate the impediments in their paths as they search for enlightenment. Hawthorne's distance from both Robin and Brown allows him to present them ambivalently, displaying simultaneous contradictory attitudes toward their quests so that both stories suggest a good deal more than they seem "at first to reveal."

Robin sets a high value on himself, yet he is woefully ignorant of the political climate of his times; self-interest is his only concern. In the beginning paragraph of "My Kinsman, Major Molineux," Hawthorne tells us more about the hardships faced by colonial governors than Robin appears to know. Thus Robin lacks political savvy in the eyes not only of the townspeople but also of the reader. Hawthorne adopted this strategy, carried on in popular fiction writing in our own time, to give historical weight to his magazine tale. But few writers inject historical material this way, to tell the reader something the protagonist does not know. Thus Hawthorne ensures that the reader will also be emotionally distanced from Robin.

Why did the author make Robin such a bumpkin? The customary answer is that Hawthorne wrote tales of initiation, dramatizing male rites of passage in the New England community. A more politicized reading would suggest that in both "My Kinsman, Major Molineux" and "Young Goodman Brown" Hawthorne is investigating the darker side of the American dream of self-fulfillment, putting personal ambition before community involvement. Material advancement drives Robin, spiritual ambition rules Brown; both are the products of a society whose traditions are so recent that its citizens hope to attain power just by asking for it. Hawthorne shows us that the road to hell is paved with good intentions: which way the road to heaven?

Questions for Discussion

1. What is the importance of the historical background in the opening paragraph of "My Kinsman, Major Molineux"?
2. What are Robin's good qualities? his limitations?
3. Trace Robin's search for his kinsman. What kind of picture does Hawthorne paint of pre-Revolutionary New England life?
4. What is your interpretation of the grotesque character with his face painted in two colors whom Robin meets in the inn and later sees on the street?
5. How does the description of the moonlight help to set the scene and prepare for the end of the story?
6. What is the importance of Robin's dreams of home just before he meets the "gentleman in his prime" who befriends him?
7. How do you react to the description of Major Molineux "in tar-and-feathery dignity" on the uncovered cart? Would you have reacted the way Robin did to the sight of his uncle? What does his reaction tell you about Robin?

8. Interpret the last words of the "gentleman in his prime" at the end of the story. Does he have good or bad intentions toward Robin?

9. Do you think Hawthorne intended "My Kinsman, Major Molineux" to be read as a realistic tale or as an allegory? Explain.

Topics for Writing

1. Rewrite the story making Robin a contemporary young man who goes to a state capital seeking political favor from a distant relative.

2. **CONNECTIONS** Contrast and compare "My Kinsman, Major Molineux" and "Young Goodman Brown."

Related Commentaries

Edgar Allan Poe, The Importance of the Single Effect in a Prose Tale, p. 1531.
Simon O. Lesser, A Psychological Reading of Hawthorne's "My Kinsman, Major Molineux," p. 1496.

Suggested Readings

See page 113.

Nathaniel Hawthorne

Young Goodman Brown (p. 633)

Teaching "Young Goodman Brown," you should encourage students to read "The Elements of Fiction" (p. 1683) carefully, since different aspects of Hawthorne's story are analyzed throughout the discussion of the elements of short fiction. "Writing about Short Stories" (p. 1696) also has student essays developing different ideas about "Young Goodman Brown."

Students often need help recognizing stories that are not intended to be read as realistic narrative. Some readers tend to take every word in the story literally; Hawthorne, however, meant "Young Goodman Brown" to be a moral allegory, not a realistic story. While most students will be able to recognize the use of symbolism, you might have to introduce them to the idea of allegory, in which the entire story is an extended metaphor representing one thing in the guise of another.

An allegory is a story that has a dual meaning — one in the events, characters, and setting; and the other in the ideas they are intended to convey. At first, "Young Goodman Brown" holds our interest on the level of the surface narrative. But the story also has a second meaning, which must be read beneath, and concurrent with, the surface narrative. This second meaning is not to be confused with the theme of the story — all stories have themes, but not all stories are allegories. In an allegory, the characters are usually personifications of abstract qualities (faith) and the setting is representative of the relations among the abstractions (Goodman Brown takes leave of his "Faith" at the beginning of the story).

A story is an allegory only if the characters, events, and setting are presented in a logical pattern so that they represent meanings independent of the action described in the surface story. Most writers of allegorical fiction are moralists. In this moral allegory, Hawthorne is suggesting the ethical principle that should govern human life. The *unpardonable sin* for Hawthorne is a "want of love and reverence for the Human Soul" and is typified by the person who searches the depths of the heart with "a cold philosophical curiosity." The result is a separation of the intellect from the heart, which is fatal in relationships among human beings, as shown in what happens to Goodman Brown when he returns to Salem village at the end of the story.

Questions for Discussion

1. When is a careful reader first aware that Hawthorne intends this story to be read as a moral allegory?
2. One of the characters in a Hawthorne story says, "You know that I can never separate the idea from the symbol in which it manifests itself." Hawthorne's flat characters — such as Deacon Gookin, Goody Cloyse, and the minister — represent social institutions. Why does Hawthorne include them in the story?
3. On page 634, Hawthorne writes, "But the only thing about him that could be fixed upon as remarkable was his staff, which bore the likeness of a great black snake, so curiously wrought that it might almost be seen to twist and wriggle itself like a living serpent. This, of course, must have been an ocular deception, assisted by the uncertain light." What is the assertion contained in the first sentence? What effect do the words "might almost" have on that assertion? Why does Hawthorne immediately qualify the first sentence in the second? On page 640, Hawthorne writes: "Either the sudden gleams of light flashing over the obscure field bedazzled Goodman Brown, or he recognized a score of the church members of Salem village famous for their especial sanctity." Discuss the function of this sentence and find others like it throughout the story. What is their cumulative effect?
4. Why is it important that most of the action in this story takes place in the forest? Looking through Hawthorne's story, isolate the particular words that are associated with the woods. Consider the paragraph on page 639 that begins "And, maddened with despair." List the characteristics of forests that are responsible for this long literary tradition. Consider, too, whether the idea of wilderness remains static throughout history. In the late nineteenth century, with industrialization such a potent force, would people have conceived of the forest in the same way the early settlers did? Why or why not?
5. Where does this story take place (besides in the forest)? On page 634 a man addresses the protagonist, saying, "You are late, Goodman Brown. . . . The clock of the Old South was striking as I came through Boston, and that is full fifteen minutes agone." What does this detail — that the traveler was in Boston fifteen minutes ago — mean to our interpretation of the story?
6. One page 640, "the dark figure" welcomes his listeners to "the communion of your race." What is usually meant by the word "communion"? How is it

meant here? What does the speaker mean by the phrase in which he uses it? What kinds of powers does the "sable form" promise the crowd? Discuss the kinds of knowledge that will henceforth be accessible to his listeners' senses. Who is speaking in this passage on page 641: "Herein did the shape of evil dip his hand and prepare to lay the mark of baptism upon their foreheads, that they might be partakers of the mystery of sin, more conscious of the secret guilt of others, both in deed and thought, than they could now be of their own"? How does this sentence guide your judgment of Young Goodman Brown in the closing paragraph of the story? How does the sable figure's sermon comment on the closing paragraph?

7. How much time does this story cover? Where do the first seven paragraphs take place? How many paragraphs are set in the forest? What do the final three paragraphs address? What might be some reasons for the story to be built this way?

Topic for Writing

1. Show how a knowledge of seventeenth-century New England history and Puritan theology can enhance a reading of the story.

Related Commentaries

Herman Melville, Blackness in Hawthorne's "Young Goodman Brown," p. 1505.
Edgar Allan Poe, The Importance of the Single Effect in a Prose Tale, p. 1531.

Suggested Readings

Arvin, Newton. *Hawthorne.* New York: Russell and Russell, 1961.
Bloom, Harold. *Nathaniel Hawthorne.* New York: Chelsea House, 1990.
Cowley, Malcolm, ed. *Portable Hawthorne.* New York: Penguin, 1977.
Crowley, J. Donald, ed. *Centenary Edition of the Works of Nathaniel Hawthorne.* Columbus: Ohio State UP, 1974. Vol IX, *Twice-Told Tales;* Vol. X, *Mosses from an Old Manse;* Vol. XI, *The Snow Image and Uncollected Tales.*
Ferguson, J. M., Jr. "Hawthorne's 'Young Goodman Brown.' " *Explicator* 28 (1969): Item 32.
Fetterley, Judith. *The Resisting Reader.* Bloomington: Indiana UP, 1978.
Gallagher, Edward J. "The Concluding Paragraph of 'Young Goodman Brown.' " *Studies in Short Fiction* 12 (1975): 29–30.
McIntosh, James, ed. *Nathaniel Hawthorne's Tales.* New York: Norton, 1987.
Newman, Lea Bertani. *A Reader's Guide to the Short Stories of Nathaniel Hawthorne.* Boston: G. K. Hall, 1979.
Robinson, E. Arthur. "The Vision of Goodman Brown: A Source and Interpretation." *American Literature* 35 (1963): 218–25.
Von Frank, Albert J., ed. *Critical Essays on Hawthorne's Short Stories.* Boston: G. K. Hall, 1991.
Whelan, Robert E. "Hawthorne Interprets 'Young Goodman Brown.' " *Emerson Society Quarterly* 62 (1971): 3–6.

Bessie Head

Life (p. 643)

This story opens with a paragraph of explanation about its background, reminiscent of the beginning of "My Kinsman, Major Molineux." As Hawthorne tells us that the colonial governors appointed by the king of England often ran into trouble with their subjects in the New World, Head explains that the village people in Botswana rejected city habits that were harmful to them and that "the murder of Life had this complicated undertone of rejection." In their introductory paragraphs, both Head and Hawthorne eliminate a large measure of suspense in their stories by giving broad hints of both the plot and theme to come. What, then, makes the reader want to continue?

This question is a useful one to begin a discussion about "Life." For one thing, Head's protagonist has an unusual name, and most readers will entertain the possibility that Head is writing an allegory investigating the human situation, and that the specific twenty-seven-year-old woman named Life is a literary symbol in addition to being a realistic character.

This sense of a larger dimension to the character in Head's story — as in Hawthorne's depiction of Robin's adventures searching for his uncle — is strengthened by the author's description of the setting. In a very few pages, "Life" tells us a great deal about how people live in the villages of Botswana. We read about the traditional custom of continuing to offer a home in the village to members of families who left for Johannesburg, even as long as seventeen years after a family has departed. We learn of the village women's willingness to help Life by working to make her yard and house habitable. Traditional food, references to the feasting at weddings, the villagers' matter-of-fact attitude toward sex ("that it ought to be available whenever possible like food and water"), the division of labor between men and women, the careers available to educated women, the social differences between the respectable housewives and the beer-brewing women — all these details paint a rich picture and develop our awareness of the moral structure of village customs.

The narrator's point of view is close and balanced, not distant and ironic like Hawthorne's attitude toward Robin. Head is an omniscient storyteller; she tells us that "one evening death walked quietly into the bar" when she introduces Lesego, the cattleman who becomes Life's husband. Head succinctly defines their attraction for us: "[T]hey looked at each other from their own worlds and came to fatal conclusions." The tragedy of their marriage is the second half of the story, and what happens to them focuses the moral dimension of "Life."

Questions for Discussion

1. Is suspense lacking in the story because Head tells you the ending in her first paragraph? Explain.
2. What is attractive about Life? Is her "undertone of hysteria" attractive or unattractive?
3. Why is Lesego so confident that Life will change her promiscuous ways if he marries her?

4. Explicate the paragraph of commentary beginning "She hadn't the mental equipment to analyse what hit her" after Lesego tells Life that he will kill her if she is unfaithful to him.
5. Head's description of the activity of Life's yard — the blaring transistor radio, the people reeling around "dead drunk," the prostitution — is not presented in a judgmental way. How do you know what Head thinks of such behavior?
6. Is Head more sympathetic to the village women or to Life? Explain.

Topics for Writing

1. Analyze the function of food and drink in "Life."
2. Use a feminist critical strategy to analyze the ending of "Life," Lesego's action and his punishment.
3. In the final paragraph, Head suggests that the beer-brewing women have the last word "on the whole affair." Agree or disagree with this statement and explain your response.

Suggested Readings

Head, Bessie. *The Collector of Treasures and Other Botswana Village Tales.* London: Heinemann, 1977.

———. *Tales of Tenderness and Power.* Portsmouth, NH: Heinemann International, 1990.

ERNEST HEMINGWAY

Hills Like White Elephants (p. 653)

Hemingway wrote this story in May 1927, while on his honeymoon in the Rhône delta with his second wife, Pauline. According to his biographer Kenneth Lynn, the story was a dramatization of a fantasy he had about his first wife, Hadley: "[I]f only the two of them had not allowed a child to enter their lives they would never have parted." Throughout his biography, Lynn interprets the fiction in terms of Hemingway's relationships. How much this approach sheds light on the fiction each reader must judge.

This story is an early example of a minimalist technique. Characterization and plot are mere suggestions, and it is possible for some young readers to finish the story for the first time with no idea that the couple are discussing an abortion. The setting Hemingway chooses for the couple's conversation is more richly developed. The symbolism of the "two lines of rails" at the station (the choice either to end the pregnancy or have the child); the fields of grain and trees along the Ebro River, which the girl sees on the other side of the station (fertility, a settled life) compared with the barren hills, long and white like white elephants (something considered unlucky, unwanted, and rejected); the bar and the station building (the temporary escape offered by alcohol, the sense of people in transit) —

one can interpret these details in perfect harmony with the couple's emotional and physical dilemma.

The man's bullying of the girl drives the story. His ignorance about abortion and his insensitivity to what she is feeling or will have to endure physically ("It's not really anything. It's just to let the air in") are not presented as weakness. They are simply part of his insistence on persuading Jig to do what he wants her to do. The girl is also worthy of discussion. Her vulnerability is idealized, yet she is not stupid. Without the suggestion of her intelligence, there would be no story.

Hemingway regarded "Hills Like White Elephants" as one of his best stories, reserving a prominent place for it in his second collection, *Men Without Women*, published in the fall of 1927. Lynn states that in choosing this title for the book, Hemingway meant to suggest "that the alienation of women from men (as well as vice versa) was one of his themes."

Questions for Discussion

1. In what ways could you categorize this story as a minimalist work?
2. What do we know about the man? About the girl? Why isn't Jig called "a woman" in the story?
3. What is a "white elephant"? How does this expression suit the story?
4. What do you think will happen to this couple after the story ends?
5. Read the story aloud in class, assigning two students the roles of the man and the girl. Is the story as effective read as dialogue as it is on the page as a literary text?

Topic for Writing

1. Rewrite the story in a different setting to discover the importance of the railroad station and the Spanish landscape in "Hills Like White Elephants."

Suggested Readings

Baker, Carlos, ed. *Ernest Hemingway: A Life Story.* New York: Macmillan, 1976.
———. *Ernest Hemingway: Selected Letters 1917–1961.* Scribner's, 1981.
Beegel, Susan F., ed. *Hemingway's Neglected Short Fiction: New Perspectives.* Ann Arbor: UMI Research Press, 1989.
Benson, Jackson. *The Short Stories of Ernest Hemingway: Critical Essays.* Durham, NC: Duke UP, 1975.
———, ed. *New Critical Approaches to the Short Stories of Ernest Hemingway.* Durham, NC: Duke UP, 1990.
Brenner, Gerry, and Earl Rovit. *Ernest Hemingway, Revised Edition.* Boston: Twayne, 1990.
Flora, Joseph M. *Ernest Hemingway: A Study of the Short Fiction.* Boston: Twayne, 1989.
Hays, Peter L. *Ernest Hemingway.* New York: Continuum, 1990.
Lynn, Kenneth S. *Hemingway.* New York: Simon, 1987.
Martin, Terence. *Ernest Hemingway: Revised Edition.* Boston: Twayne, 1990.

Reynolds, Michael S., ed. *Critical Essays on Ernest Hemingway's* In Our Time. Boston: G. K. Hall, 1983.

AMY HEMPEL

In the Cemetery Where Al Jolson Is Buried (p. 658)

The dialogue between the two friends in Hempel's story is often funny, but the humor never lightens the underlying somber mood of the piece. One of the two unnamed characters is in an intensive care room in a private hospital north of Malibu, suffering through the terminal stage of cancer, aware that her medical treatment has been unsuccessful and that she will soon die. Her friend (the narrator) has come to the hospital only after overcoming a deep reluctance to visit the sickroom. Both women are afraid of dying, but the first-person narrator is doubly frightened, both of her own mortality and that of her friend. The only respite for the two women is in their avoiding discussion about why they are together in the hospital room. The jittery visitor is so afraid of losing her self-control that she rattles off trivial facts and jokes about media stars and chimpanzees, while the patient, in contrast, attempts to control her feelings by making jokes about herself to avoid self-pity. They are inspired in their attempts at conversation because each one is feeling her situation very intensely. It is beyond anything they have experienced in their lives thus far.

The individuality of the two characters is so fully delineated that the reality of their life-and-death drama is activated for the reader by their first exchange. The patient knows she won't leave the hospital alive, so she begins the dialogue by asking her visitor to "tell me things I won't mind forgetting." The round of trivia begins, until the narrator grows self-conscious in front of the camera on the ceiling that monitors the sickroom. They joke about "feminist bitching," keeping up the facade that they are in control of the situation. Yet the patient is so emaciated from her radiation therapy that her summer-weight blanket is painful on her legs. Looking at her friend makes the narrator "understand the law that requires two people to be with the body at all times," that is, the television surveillance that allows the nurses to keep constant watch on their patient so they can immediately intervene in any suicide attempt.

Requested to leave the sickroom during a doctor's examination, the visitor sits on the beach, thinking obsessively about earthquakes. A metaphor for the emotional shock she is enduring, the tremors of the earth suggest the profundity of her grief at losing someone she considers a sister. She is fearful, yet she can still joke when she returns with a newspaper to her friend's bedside. The fragments of the story get shorter and shorter. The visitor leaves the hospital. The sick woman dies and is buried in Forest Lawn Cemetery in Los Angeles, where Al Jolson lies in state (he starred in *The Jazz Singer,* the first feature-length sound film made in Hollywood). The narrator has experienced the death of her friend, and she is still afraid — not of dying, but of loss, as she makes clear at the end of the story with her anecdote about the chimp mother with the talking hands. Ironically enough, the animal, unlike the narrator, does not understand that she too is mortal, yet she is instinctively fluent "in the language of grief."

Questions for Discussion

1. Is "In the Cemetery Where Al Jolson Is Buried" a sketch or a short story? Explain your choice of terminology.
2. Discuss how Elizabeth Kübler-Ross would analyze what the patient and her visitor are going through in the story.
3. What is the significance of the references to pop songs and television shows in the story? How do they relate to the situation of the patient and her visitor?
4. What role does the California setting play in the story? How would it differ if Hempel set it in a public hospital located in a less glamorous place?
5. How can the incident when the patient breaks out of her isolation chamber and crouches on the floor of the broom closet be understood as a suicide attempt? (Remember that her advanced cancer treatment has made it necessary for her to be placed in a sterile room.)

Topics for Writing

1. Analyze the function of the metaphors of either *words* (the talking chimp, the pop stars, or the title) or *earthquakes* in the story.
2. Analyze the way Hempel has organized the episodes of her narrative. How do they suggest a plot? What, if anything, has she omitted in her sequential order?
3. Discuss the use of irony in Hempel's story.
4. **CONNECTIONS** Compare and contrast Hempel's story about a person suffering a terminal illness with Tolstoy's "The Death of Ivan Ilych."
5. **CONNECTIONS** Define minimalism in contemporary short fiction, using the stories in this anthology by Hemingway and Hempel as your examples. How does Hemingway's analogy of the iceberg to describe his literary technique also apply to Hempel's dramatization of her characters' situation?

Suggested Reading

Hempel, Amy. *Tumble Home: A Novella and Short Stories*. New York: Scribner,1997.

Langston Hughes

Thank You, M'am (p. 666)

Langston Hughes believed that writing, in its small way, could help change the world. "Thank You, M'am" is not a realistic story. It is a lesson in possibilities, not a presentation of reality. Most readers will be conscious that any teenage thief they might encounter in daily life would probably be too strung out on drugs to respond to any sympathetic treatment, and usually there would be a gang or at least an accomplice lurking somewhere in the background. At the same time, readers want to believe that Mrs. Jones could bring Roger home to her small, shabby apartment and with a dinner of ham and lima beans turn him into a repentant former delinquent. Hughes presents his story so directly and so matter-of-factly, as if the matter were already decided when the boy chose that particular woman to rob, that we are forced to accept and understand what he is telling us. Hughes believes harsh punishment and emotional indifference have less effect in saving a young criminal than kindness and understanding. We accept his opinion for at least as long as we are reading the story, and if we should let the story influence our reaction in the unhappy event that we meet someone like Roger, then Hughes would feel that his story was successful.

As any reader who is familiar with Hughes's poetry or stories is aware, one of his insistent themes is that people can understand each other, despite their racial and social differences. At the same time, he never lost his intense anger at the racism that he felt permeated American life. Much of his writing is a direct protest against the American racial situation, but he was just as insistent that the African American community had to accept responsibility for its own failures. When the boy tells Mrs. Jones that he hasn't eaten because there's nobody at home to fix dinner for him, Hughes is scolding the parents of boys like Roger for their neglect of their children. He understood that one of the strongest foundations of life in Harlem, where he lived for most of his life, was the indomitable spirit of women like Mrs. Jones. He wrote often about women like her, always with sympathy, and always with respect for their religious feelings and their refusal to give in to life's difficulties. As Mrs. Jones tells Roger, "I have done things, too, which I would not tell you, son — neither tell God, if He didn't already know. Everybody's got something in common." Hughes's heart was with the ordinary people of black America, and in stories like this one he tells his readers of his love and his hope that the future can be saved from a bleak and seemingly hopeless past.

Questions for Discussion

1. In the story the boy tries to steal the purse of an African American woman. How might the situation have been different if he had been caught robbing a white woman?
2. Why doesn't the boy run out of the apartment when he has the chance?
3. What do the details of the room tell us about the woman's economic status?
4. What does Hughes tell us about the woman when he gives us her full name, Luella Bates Washington Jones?
5. Is the woman's statement "Shoes got by devilish ways will burn your feet" a folk saying, or could it be a biblical reference?
6. What is Mrs. Jones telling the boy when she leads him outside and closes the door?

Topic for Writing

1. Using any collection of Hughes's poetry, find a poem about a woman like Mrs. Jones and compare the two women Hughes has created. An example is his poem from 1926, "Mother to Son."

Suggested Reading

Hughes, Langston, ed. *The Best Short Stories by Black Writers 1899–1967.* Boston: Little, Brown, 1967.

ZORA NEALE HURSTON

The Gilded Six-Bits (p. 670)

An instructor presenting this story may find that it is difficult to reconcile some of the contemporary commentary on the work of Zora Neale Hurston with the realities of her short fiction. The tendency has been to idealize her and her work, overlooking the bitter realities that she describes. It may be that she grew up in an isolated community, and that a current writer could comment, as did scholar Mary Helen Washington, that the community was "neither ghetto, nor slum, nor black bottom, but a rich source of black cultural traditions . . . ," but the violence and the near collapse of the strong familial tradition that Hurston describes in a story like "The Gilded Six-Bits" reflects a society that has been degraded by years of systematic racism and economic repression.

It is sometimes emphasized that Hurston learned much about her little community through her research into the oral folk tradition, but the story doesn't relate to any of the characteristics of the oral folktale. Despite the muted sentimentality of the ending, the story is a realistic description of a clumsy infidelity on the part of a young wife. Hurston described how she loved to listen to the men of the community vying with each other as they told the old folktales on the grocery steps, but the story certainly doesn't have anything to do with Brer Rabbit.

At a point in American social consciousness when there is much concern about the effect of negative images in the portrayal of minority groups, it is interesting that the story has recently enjoyed a widespread popularity. Perhaps this is because Hurston's opening descriptions of the young couple, Joe and Missie May, present them as childlike and innocent. What she describes in the short story is almost a child marriage. Joe is so delighted with Missie May's girlishness that, when she is seduced by a newcomer to town, he punishes her the way a child would be punished, with silence and withdrawal.

Joe is almost as childlike as Missie May in his eventual acceptance of her infidelity. The newcomer had impressed him the way an adult impresses a child, with his swagger, his pretense of sophistication and wealth. For Joe this is summarized by the gold piece the man wears on his watch chain. When Joe surprises the man in bed with Missie May there is a short fight, and Joe pulls loose the man's chain with the gold piece. When he looks at it later he finds that it's only a fifty cent piece that has been gilded to look like gold, and it's obvious all the man's claims were lies. After some weeks Joe and Missie May mend their marriage, and she bears him a son. A week after the child is born Joe tells the storekeeper that he was never fooled by the other man at all, and he uses the fifty cent piece to buy candy for his wife and son. When he returns home they play again the youthful game of their marriage that opened the story.

In the real world of the dirt road, tar-paper shack communities that Hurston is describing, adultery was much more harshly punished. Perhaps the story has earned some of its popularity with student readers by describing the world as we wish it were, instead of how it is.

Questions for Discussion

1. How would you describe the economic conditions of Joe and Missie May's life?
2. Would this description only be real for the community of Eatonville, Florida, where Hurston grew up, or would it apply to black rural communities everywhere in the South?
3. How does the author make us aware of Joe's lack of sophistication? Is this presented in a negative way?
4. Why does the author make a point of Joe's being excited that the newcomer has lived in a city?
5. How is the newcomer different from the other men in the small town?
6. Hurston never tells the reader what finally happens to Slemmons. Why isn't this important to her?
7. What is likely to happen to Missie May in the future?

Topics for Writing

1. Discuss the images of coins and money that occur in the story, beginning with the title.
2. Consider the possibilities that Joe and Missie May have to change their life for the better.
3. Analyze the economic factors that make a man like Slemmons fascinating to people in the small town.
4. Describe the elements of racism that have conditioned Joe and Missie May to accept their life as it is.

Related Commentaries

Rosalie Murphy Baum, The Shape of Hurston's Fiction, p. 1430.
Zora Neale Hurston, What White Publishers Won't Print, p. 1476.
Alice Walker, Zora Neale Hurston: A Cautionary Tale and a Partisan View, p. 1564.

Suggested Readings

See page 123.

Zora Neale Hurston

Sweat *(p. 678)*

"Sweat" is interesting for the modern reader on many levels. For the student familiar with the regional authors of the previous generation — writers such as Sarah Orne Jewett and Kate Chopin — the style of the story will be familiar. The story is set in a small, isolated community; the central figure is an older woman; and the story is concerned with her personal tragedy. As in most regional stories, the line of the horizon is the boundary of the action. In "Sweat" there is no suggestion that there is a world beyond the limits of the small town and the woman's cabin on a dirt road just on the outskirts. The carefully rendered dialogue is written in the colloquial speech favored by the regionalists, and, as in their work, the descriptions of the house and the dirt roads set the scene with precise detail.

For the student who has read such contemporary black women writers as Alice Walker and Toni Morrison, the theme of the story will also be familiar. Hurston presents the same bitter anger and despair between black men and women in the rural South that Walker and Morrison present later. Hurston is perhaps even more important as a precursor of current openness than she is as a writer who is simply continuing an older, regional literary style.

In reading a story like "Sweat" it is useful to forget Hurston's studies in black folklore, which in fact were done *after* the story was published. At this point in her career she was part of a very sophisticated and socially conscious movement that was attempting to give the black minority in the United States a literary voice. Unlike many of the writers of a generation before who modeled their work on Maupassant, Hurston is much closer to the French realist Émile Zola, whose grim novels of small-town life in the French provinces were widely read in the United States at this time. There is in his work, as in Hurston's, an uncompromising hardness, and he would have approved of Hurston's heroine as she creeps back in the shadows to let her husband die of the rattlesnake bite he had intended for her. It is a description that Alice Walker would appreciate.

Questions for Discussion

1. Why doesn't Delia go to the sheriff when her husband terrorizes her with the snake?
2. Why is it this "other" woman of Sykes's who finally drives Delia to try to do something to save what is left of her life?
3. What will happen to Delia now that her husband is dead?
4. Why didn't people in the community try to help Delia when they learned of her husband's open infidelities?
5. Why does Delia decide to go to a different church?
6. Why is her husband still permitted to take part in church services, even though he is not trying to hide his "sinful ways"?
7. Will there be any investigation into the circumstances of Delia's husband's death?

Topics for Writing

1. Discuss the role of the white families in the small town in making it possible for Delia to eke out her hard living. What could the community have done to make her life better?
2. Discuss the social attitudes that accept Delia's husband's right to brutalize her physically and emotionally.
3. CONNECTIONS   Compare the description of Delia's situation in "Sweat" with Nancy's situation in Faulkner's "That Evening Sun." How do the different authors resolve their plots?

Related Commentaries

Rosalie Murphy Baum, The Shape of Hurston's Fiction, p. 1430.
Zora Neale Hurston, What White Publishers Won't Print, p. 1476.
Alice Walker, Zora Neale Hurston: A Cautionary Tale and a Partisan View, p. 1564.

Suggested Readings

Edwards, Lee R. *Psyche as Hero: Female Heroism and Fictional Form.* Middletown, CT: Wesleyan, 1984.
Gates, Henry Louis, ed. *Black Literature and Literary Theory.* New York: Methuen, 1984.
Hemenway, Robert. *Zora Neale Hurston: A Literary Biography.* Urbana: U of Illinois P, 1977.
Howard, Lillie P. *Zora Neale Hurston.* Boston: Twayne, 1980.
Hull, Gloria T. *Color, Sex, and Poetry: Three Women Writers of the Harlem Renaissance.* Bloomington: Indiana UP, 1987.
Hurston, Zora Neale. *The Gilded Six-Bits.* Minneapolis: Redpath, 1986.
———. *I Love Myself When I Am Laughing . . . and Then Again When I Am Looking Mean and Impressive.* Ed. Alice Walker. Old Westbury, NY: Feminist, 1979.
———. *Mules and Men.* Westport, CT: Greenwood, 1969.
Lupton, Mary Jane. "Zora Neale Hurston and the Survival of the Female." *Southern Literary Journal* 15.1 (Fall 1982): 45–54.
Washington, Mary Helen, ed. *Invented Lives: Narratives of Black Women, 1860–1960.* Garden City, NY: Anchor, 1987.
Yates, Janelle. *Zora Neale Hurston: A Storyteller's Life.* Staten Island, NY: Ward Hill, 1991.

WASHINGTON IRVING

Rip Van Winkle (p. 689)

Class discussion of this story could center on the statement that Nachtigal's folktale "Peter Klaus the Goatherd" tends to *summarize* the action, while Irving's short story *develops* it. One of the ways that Irving developed the tale was to add more details about the protagonist's wife. In "Rip Van Winkle," Dame Winkle henpecks her husband so mercilessly that he runs off to hunt squirrel in the Catskill Mountains in order to avoid her. Feminist readers have criticized Irving for his unflattering portrait of Rip's wife. On further reflection, you can see that Irving paid a substantial price for his humorous tone in the story — including the verbal irony in his portrait of Dame Winkle. It forced him to sacrifice the tragic undertones suggested in Nachtigal's transcription of the folktale.

Questions for Discussion

1. In what ways did Irving rewrite Nachtigal's folktale to make it an American story?
2. Why did Irving begin his tale with the poem by Cartwright (an unidentified poet) and the cumbersome explanation of the origin of the tale in Diedrich Knickerbocker's papers?
3. What different kinds of humor are present in "Rip Van Winkle"?
4. Do you think any less (or any more) of Irving's story after reading "Peter Klaus the Goatherd"? How important is evidence of an author's originality in judging the success or failure of a literary work?
5. Do you think the portrait of Dame Winkle is fair or unfair? How essential is her role in Rip's story?

Topics for Writing

1. Investigate and report on other mythical stories about a human being's encounter with the spirit world.
2. **CONNECTIONS** Compare and contrast the plots in "Peter Klaus the Goatherd" and "Rip Van Winkle."

Related Commentary

J. C. C. Nachtigal, Peter Klaus the Goatherd, p. 1520.

SHIRLEY JACKSON

The Lottery (p. 702)

The interpretive suggestions in the headnote should guide students toward a recognition of the main themes of "The Lottery." The near universality of the ritual sacrifice of year gods and scapegoats in primitive cultures to ensure fertility, the continuation of life, and the purgation of society has been a common assumption since the publication of James G. Frazer's *The Golden Bough*. Jackson does not explore the transmutations of these old ceremonies in the accepted religious practices and psychological mechanisms of modern humanity; rather, she attempts to shock her readers into an awareness of the presence of raw, brutal, and superstitious impulses within us all. A fruitful approach for class discussion might involve exploring how the story achieves its impact. Jackson's comments (included in Part Two, p. 1480) provide incontrovertible documentation of the power of "The Lottery" to stir the dark instincts dwelling below the surface of the civilized psyche, perhaps the same regions from which the story emerged fully formed — as Jackson claims — in the mind of the writer. No wonder readers, from the author's agent on, have found "The Lottery" disturbing.

But they have also found it compelling, fascinating, and irresistible, and the reason may have partly to do with Jackson's technical skill. For the inattentive first reader, the natural suspense of any drawing, contest, or lottery provides strong motivation to hurry through to the ending, and when the realization of what is at stake comes, it strikes with redoubled force because of the reader's increased velocity. For the more careful reader, or for the reader already aware of the ending, the subtle foreshadowing — the boys are gathering stones, the box is black, Tessie Hutchinson "clean forgot what day it was" — triggers an uncomfortable double awareness that also urges haste, a haste like that which spurs Mr. Summers's final, horrible remark, "All right, folks. . . . Let's finish quickly," and the cries of "Come on" and "Hurry up" by other villagers.

For Jackson has succeeded in gaining the reader's vicarious participation in the lottery. Even the backwoods New England quaintness of the setting draws not the kind of condescending laughter that would distance the reader but the warm sentimental indulgence we reserve for the cutest Norman Rockwell illustrations. Little boys are being little boys as they pick up the stones, the villagers are walking clichés, and even Tessie Hutchinson, singled out from the rest by her tardiness, is tardy for the most housewifely of reasons. (How different the story would be if she appeared nervous and flustered, a few moments ahead of, say, a disheveled Steve Adams!) The reader is drawn to sink into this warm bath of comfortable stereotypes, illusions intact. Totally off guard against the possibility that the good hearts of these neighborly folks might beat in time with an ancient and brutal rhythm, that superstitious fears of hunger and death might easily outweigh feelings of friendliness and compassion, the reader may well recoil from any previous fascination and, in an effort to deny involvement, recoil from the story, too. Except that we do not reject it; "The Lottery" continues to exert such power over the imagination of its readers that it clearly must be providing a catharsis for instincts similar to those that move the villagers to pick up stones.

WILLIAM E. SHEIDLEY

Questions for Discussion

1. What associations does the word *lottery* have for you? Are they relevant to the story?
2. Comment on the ending of the first paragraph.
3. On what other occasions might the people of the village gather in the way they do for the lottery? Mr. Summers is in charge of "civic activities." Is the lottery one of these? Explain.
4. Discuss the degree to which the tradition of the lottery has been kept. Why does no one want to make a new box? Why is the whole institution not abandoned?
5. Examine the character of Tessie Hutchinson. She claims that her fate is not *fair*. Is there any reason why she should be singled out? Is she a tragic heroine? Consider her cry, "There's Don and Eva. . . . Make *them* take their chance!"

6. On your first reading, when did you begin to suspect what happens at the end of the story? How soon might it become evident? What are the most important hints?

7. One reason the ending can surprise a reader is that the villagers never speak directly of what they are about. Why not? Are they ashamed? afraid?

8. Comment on the conversation between the Adamses and Old Man Warner. What is the implication of Steve Adams's last appearance in the story?

9. Does the rhyme "Lottery in June, corn be heavy soon" adequately explain the institution of the lottery? What other reasons might people have for such behavior? What is the social function of a scapegoat?

10. After her family has received the black spot, Tessie complains, but Mrs. Delacroix tells her, "Be a good sport, Tessie." Comment on this choice of words.

11. Discuss the reaction of the Hutchinson family. Why does the lottery single out a family first, then a victim?

12. Old Man Warner says, "People ain't the way they used to be." Are they? What does he mean?

13. Why are the people in such a hurry to "finish"?

14. What is the implication of "someone gave little Davy Hutchinson a few pebbles"?

Topics for Writing

1. Discuss Jackson's techniques for building suspense in "The Lottery."

2. Write an essay exploring the usefulness of stereotypes in "The Lottery."

3. Examine the behavior of groups of people with which you are familiar. Can you find actual instances of formal or informal practices similar to the one described in "The Lottery" — even though they may not lead to such a brutal finale? Have you or has anyone you know been made a scapegoat? Write an essay showing how one such case reflects and confirms the implications of Jackson's story.

4. **CONNECTIONS** Compare and contrast Jackson's "The Lottery" and Le Guin's "The Ones Who Walk Away from Omelas."

Related Commentary

Shirley Jackson, The Morning of June 28, 1948, and "The Lottery," p. 1480.

Suggested Reading

Freidman, Lenemaja. *Shirley Jackson.* Twayne's United States Authors Series 253. Boston: G. K. Hall, 1975. 63–67.

HENRY JAMES

Paste (p. 710)

A Maupassant biographer, Francis Steegmuller, has said that James was unaware of Maupassant's "The Jewels of M. Lantin" when he wrote "Paste," but the similarities between the two stories are so pronounced that Steegmuller's statement is difficult to believe. Certainly James knew of Maupassant's "The Necklace," which was widely popular at the time.

In Maupassant's "The Jewels of M. Lantin" the implication that the jewels are proof of the wife's infidelity are finally shrugged aside by her husband, who simply sells the jewels and uses the money to quit his job. In his commentary on Maupassant, James spoke of his cynicism and his hardness. As an American living in England, and writing for the most refined magazines of his time, James couldn't allow himself the luxury of the French writer's casual acceptance of an immoral situation. He gives the revelation of the story to a poor governess, who is presented the jewels — which include a genuine pearl necklace — by her cousin, who is certain they are false, but who wants her to have some souvenir of her aunt, who had been his stepmother.

James, however, has a cynicism of his own, and after the girl agonizes over the moral implications of the pearls when she inadvertently finds that they are real, she is cheated by her cousin and her employer of any of the money that could have come to her from the cousin's offhand gift. The cousin takes them back from her with an angry denial that they could have any implications about his stepmother's conduct when she was a young actress, and then he lies to her when he tells her that he has "smashed" them. Her employer lies to her as well when she tells her that she found them again quite by chance in a shop window.

The most significant difference in James's approach to his material is to separate the moral question from the central character. Charlotte never wavers in her sense of what is right and wrong in the situation. She doesn't feel that she is entitled to any sum of money that the sale of the pearls might bring. Whatever qualms she might have about the cousin's actions, she would never question him about what he has done. By casting her as a governess, the classic situation of young women of "heightened sensibilities and straightened circumstances," James is expressing one of the accepted attitudes of his day — that the upper classes had fewer moral scruples than the people below them in the social scale. Implicit in this, as James makes clear, is the exploitation the lower classes faced in every aspect of their lives and work.

In reading the story it should be natural for the student to identify with the young woman, and certainly her moral agonizing will seem familiar to anyone who has listened to all-night student discussions of social issues. As in the story that James probably has used as a model for his more elaborate treatment, jewelry has become the device for measuring a character's moral fiber. Of all the characters in the three stories only Charlotte, James's heroine, survives with any decency, and for many readers there may be perhaps some impatience at her obtuseness and her passive willingness to let everybody cheat her out of something that could have been hers.

Questions for Discussion

1. How does James describe the jewels in such a way as to make us think they must be false?
2. The story suggests that women appearing on the stage are morally suspect. Was this a common attitude at the time?
3. Do you think James feel sympathetic to Charlotte, or is he also impatient with her inability to make something of the opportunity to sell the pearls?
4. What are some reasons why women at the time of the story would find owning valuable jewelry important?

Topics for Writing

1. Contrast the moral attitudes of Charlotte and her employer toward the implications of the pearls as a gift to an actress.
2. Discuss the limitations of women's right to own property at the time of the story.
3. **CONNECTIONS** Contrast the story by James and the treatment of the same theme by Maupassant.

Related Commentary

Henry James, From *The Art of Fiction*, p. 1483.

Related Story

Guy de Maupassant, The Necklace, p. 976.

Suggested Readings

Hocks, Richard A. *Henry James: A Study of the Short Fiction*. Boston: Twayne, 1990.
Kraft, James. *The Early Tales of Henry James*. Carbondale: Southern UP, 1969.
Stowell, H. Peter. *Literary Impressionism, James and Chekhov*. U of Georgia P, 1980.

GISH JEN

In the American Society (p. 723)

Jen's story of a father's difficulties with the American system can be compared to Ethan Canin's story, "The Carnival Dog, the Buyer of Diamonds," which also has as its subject a father who stubbornly resists accepting the mores of American society. Both stories are told from the point of view of the man's child, and both have a relaxed air of autobiography. They are not stories constructed as narratives in the accepted sense. They are written as reminiscences of scenes remembered with forgiveness and acceptance, and the instructor could present the two stories together. Although Canin's story has clear models in the traditional American short story, Jen's is constructed with an open, free-wheeling fluidity. The artistic model for her story is the television sitcom, in which the dogged but loveable father gets himself into difficulties but is forgiven by his family, who exhibit an amused tolerance for his foibles. Students will have no difficulty following Jen's narrative, but they will probably miss the laugh track and the musical cues that are usually a feature of this kind of entertainment.

The instructor could also compare this story with Sherman Alexie's "The Lone Ranger and Tonto Fistfight in Heaven," which presents the theme of the outsider unable to find a role in American society, but with a brooding unhappiness that is not present in Jen's narrative. Although Jen as a first-generation Chinese American might be expected to feel a sense of alienation from the society, she does not feel the strains that drive the Native American Alexie. In her story, it is the father who has difficulties. Though the characters in any story are never quite the same as the writer of the story itself, the daughter narrating the events in Jen's story is clearly comfortable with her place in today's America. Jen herself has had the support of a middle class family who provided her with a university education. Although they didn't encourage her when she decided to become a writer, she was supported by a series of grants and awards to help her through her apprentice years. Her nickname in itself is a reflection of her ease with American life. Her given name is Lillian, which is also the first name of the actress Lillian Gish, whom Jen admired. Classmates at college began calling her Gish, and she kept the name for her writing. Her mother still calls her Lillian.

The story, like all plots for television sitcoms, moves quickly. The characters who appear, such as the cooks and part-time workers at the narrator's father's pancake house, are stock figures — from the humorous inability of her father's illegal-immigrant employees to speak or write proper English to the hip sarcasm of a younger sister who is more at home in America than anyone else in the family. The half-hearted attempt on the part of the mother to join the local country club functions as a subplot to keep the story moving and to introduce the secondary character, Mrs. Lardner, the mother of a friend of the narrator's younger sister, who in turn invites the family to the party that is the setting for the finale in which the father is humiliated. The humiliation, however, goes no deeper than the water that soaks the father's clothes, and the story ends on a note of bemused cheerfulness.

Questions for Discussion

1. In a story like this, intended for quick amusement, there is never serious tragedy or genuine unhappiness. Does Jen suggest at any point in her narrative that there is the possibility of deeper emotion?
2. Some commentators, discussing Jen's work, have described her sense of conflict between her values and the mainstream American culture. Is there anything in the story to suggest that it is not the narrator's father, but the narrator herself, who feels alienated from people around her?
3. Is the narrator's mother coming to terms with American life? How is this presented in the story?
4. Does the narrator feel a sense of shared identity with her father's employees, the Chinese workers, who are illegal immigrants?

5. The story is written from the point of view of someone who has been economically comfortable all of her life. What does the narrator tell us about her father's family in China? How is this reflected in her attitudes toward her new life in the United States?

Topics for Writing

1. In several of her poems, including "How I Got that Name," another young Chinese American writer, the poet Marilyn Chin, has written about her difficulty finding a place in today's America. Compare Chin's response to her situation and Jen's response to some of the same experiences.

2. **CONNECTIONS** Compare "In the American Society" to stories by Ethan Canin or Sherman Alexie and discuss the differences between each author's representation of life in the United States.

Suggested Readings

Chin, Marilyn. *Dwarf Bamboo*. Greenfield Center, NY: Greenfield Review Press, 1987.

———. *The Phoenix Gone, the Terrace Empty*. Minneapolis: Milkweed Editions, 1994.

Hagedorn, Jessica, ed. *Charlie Chan Is Dead: An Anthology of Contemporary Asian American Fiction*. New York: Penguin, 1993.

Sarah Orne Jewett

A White Heron (p. 736)

Jewett portrays Sylvia, whose very name associates her with the woodland, as torn between the natural world in which she is so fully at home and the first stirrings of the "great power" of love in her "woman's heart." Her project of pleasing the young hunter and winning the treasure of his gratitude, in the form of ten dollars, leads her out of her shyness and into the heroic adventure of climbing the great pine tree. As a result of her efforts, Sylvia grows within herself. The reader worries that she may be tempted into betraying the white heron and thus into surrendering something essential to her own integrity, but Sylvia, in her vision from the top of the tree and her face-to-face meeting with the heron, has gained the perspective necessary to hold firm.

Jewett's rich evocation of the landscape and the emotional intensity with which she narrates the climactic action contribute to the story's deeper resonances. If Sylvia recalls the woodland goddess Diana — and similarly guards her chastity — she also resembles those heroes and heroines of myth and folklore who must go to some symbolic world-navel or towering height in quest of wisdom, or who must suffer an initiation that involves mastering their fear of the (sometimes phallic) *other* and reintegrating their identities in order to cope with it. Sylvia rejects the destructive gun and mounts the pine tree, "a great main-mast to the voyaging earth," electing the fecund life of a natural world she is still discovering over the destructive promises of the "ornithologist," whose grounds are populated with dead, stuffed birds. While the narrator ends fretting over Sylvia's having consigned herself to loneliness and love-longing, nothing in the story suggests that she would be better off having sold herself for ten dollars and a whistle.

Students may find it easier to approach the story through its autobiographical dimensions. According to Eugene Hillhouse Pool, who builds on F. O. Matthiessen's early study, Jewett remained childlike and single all her life, treasuring the love of her father, who used to take her on long rambles through the countryside when she was a girl. "As Sylvia elects to keep her private and meaningful secret, so is she choosing for Miss Jewett too. . . . She chooses, psychologically, to remain a child, with Sylvia." But if Jewett chose to remain a child, it is a child in terms she met in reading Wordsworth, whom she admired: as one privy to the indwelling spirit of the natural world.

The imagery that surrounds Sylvia is uniformly associated with *mother* nature until she ventures up the tree and meets the heron. Her adventure enables her to reject assertively the young man and the advancing modern world of science and machinery with which he is associated. This is a step forward from her original strategies of withdrawal and concealment. The antinomy, however, is not resolved. The only perfect marriage in the story is between the nesting herons; and Jewett offers no key to a satisfactory union between the world of nature and the civilization that threatens to despoil it.

WILLIAM E. SHEIDLEY

Questions for Discussion

1. Jewett is known as a local colorist. To what extent is the locale of this story its subject? To what extent does the story transcend its specific Maine setting?
2. Discuss the presentation of the cow Sylvia is driving as the story opens. What does her "loud moo by way of explanation" actually explain?
3. Comment on the men, apart from the hunter, mentioned in the story. Is the absence of men from Sylvia's world a significant factor in the story?
4. As a child in town, Sylvia has the reputation of being "afraid of folks." Is she? Does she have reason?
5. Explain Sylvia's reaction when she hears the hunter's whistle. Why does Jewett briefly switch to the present tense here? Does she do so elsewhere?
6. Comment on the omniscient-narrative point of view in this story. How is it controlled? What does the narrative voice contribute?
7. Describe the character and appurtenances of the young hunter, and contrast them with those of Sylvia. How important are his evident gentleness and good intentions?
8. How does Jewett charge the pine tree and Sylvia's climb to the top of it with special meaning? What does Sylvia see up there that she has never seen before?
9. What do Sylvia and the heron have in common?
10. Analyze the last paragraph. What has Sylvia lost? What has she preserved? What has she gained?

Topics for Writing

1. Research elements of folk and fairy tale in "A White Heron."
2. Analyze Sylvia's nighttime excursion as a journey into the self.
3. Examine maternal and sexual imagery in "A White Heron."
4. Consider "A White Heron" as a rejection of modern industrial society.

Related Commentary

Sarah Orne Jewett, Looking Back on Girlhood, p. 1488.

Suggested Readings

Brenzo, Richard. "Free Heron or Dead Sparrow: Sylvia's Choice in Sarah Orne Jewett's 'A White Heron.' " *Colby Library Quarterly* 14 (1978): 36–41.

Cary, Richard. *Sarah Orne Jewett.* Albany, NY: New Collections UP, 1962.

Donovan, Josephine L. *Sarah Orne Jewett.* New York: Ungar, 1980.

Hovet, Theodore R. "America's 'Lonely Country Child': The Theme of Separation in Sarah Orne Jewett's 'A White Heron.'" *Colby Library Quarterly* 14 (1978): 166–71.

———. "'Once Upon a Time': Sarah Orne Jewett's 'A White Heron' as a Fairy Tale." *Studies in Short Fiction* 15 (1978): 63–68.

Keyworth, Cynthia, et al. *Master Smart Women: A Portrait of Sarah Orne Jewett.* Belfast, ME: North Country, 1988.

Nagel, Gwen. *Critical Essays on Sarah Orne Jewett.* Boston: G. K. Hall, 1984.

Pool, Eugene Hillhouse. "The Child in Sarah Orne Jewett." *Appreciation of Sarah Orne Jewett.* Ed. Richard Cary. Waterville, ME: Colby College P, 1973. 223–28, esp. 225. Originally published in *Colby Library Quarterly* 7 (1967): 503–09.

Westbrook, Perry D. *Acres of Flint: Sarah Orne Jewett and Her Contemporaries*, Rev. Ed. Metuchen, NJ: Scarecrow, 1981.

CHARLES JOHNSON

Menagerie, A Child's Fable (p. 745)

Despite the subtitle of "Menagerie" ("A Child's Fable"), Johnson's interest in psychology, philosophy, religion, history, and folk and popular culture contributes such a wealth of references to people, ideas, images, and events in this story that it jumps out of the category of Children's Literature to become a story for adults (or precocious children). Yet Johnson's writing is so clear, steady, and lucid that his references, far from seeming obscure, explain themselves with little fuss or fanfare. Of course a flighty aerobic dance teacher would own a flirtatious little female poodle. Of course a cruel pet shop owner with a heart condition would live alone and fail to show up one fine Monday morning. By the time readers finish "Menagerie," there's a good chance they will have empathized so closely with the narrator Berkeley, the German shepherd, that they will feel that they are also on his intellectual wavelength: "Not the smartest, but steady."

Children's stories with fabulous talking animals that dramatize a moral are not unusual (Aesop's fables come immediately to mind), but adult stories "peopled" with talking animals instead of human beings are rare indeed. Johnson's irrepressible sense of humor — and his unwavering moral sense — underpin the narrative, but it is his ability to create realistic "human" characters in the bodies of dog, monkey, turtle, fish, rabbit, and Siamese that holds our interest.

Take Monkey, for example. We're told right from the start that Berkeley didn't care "a whole lot" for him, and then we're shown his uninhibited wickedness: He is "a comedian always grabbing his groin to get a laugh, throwing feces, or fooling with the other animals." He's the Freudian amoral id in action, doing just as he pleases, totally devoid of any higher instincts of conscience, justice, or gratitude, entirely capable of biting the hand that feeds him. Tortoise, on the other hand, is at the other extreme, so repressed by his dizzying week of freedom after escaping from his cage that "he hadn't spoken in a year."

"Menagerie, A Child's Fable" is included in Johnson's collection of what he calls "tales and conjurations," *The Sorcerer's Apprentice*. (*Webster's Dictionary* defines "conjuration" as the act of conjuring, or practicing magic; the word also has a second meaning, "a solemn appeal.") Johnson uses as an epigraph a quotation from chapter XXIII of Herman Melville's *The Confidence Man:* "It is with fiction as with religion; it should present another world, and yet one to which we feel the tie." "Menagerie" presents a fictional world that has such clear ties to our own muddled state of humanity that students should understand the allegory without much explanation. If they need help interpreting the chaos of the last scene, a suggestion that they watch the evening news on television or read the front page of their local newspaper might help to illuminate Johnson's meaning for them.

Questions for Discussion

1. When do you become aware that the story will be narrated solely from the point of view of the animals in the pet shop?
2. What is the larger point Johnson is making when he tells us that Berkeley mistakes the gunfire on television for the real thing?
3. What is the basic conflict in the story?
4. How does Johnson make you sympathetic to some of the animals and hostile to others?
5. Is Monkey right in saying that Berkeley is being a fascist by keeping the animals locked up? In what ways is Monkey smarter than Berkeley? In what ways is Monkey less intelligent?
6. Why is Berkeley unsympathetic to Rabbit's organization of the females into a radical group hostile to the males? What does Berkeley suggest to smooth relations between the sexes? Why does his rational suggestion fall upon deaf ears?
7. Why does Berkeley fret over the idea that "truth was decided in the end by those who could be bloodiest in fang and claw"? How does this idea reflect Darwin's theory of evolution? Does Monkey's use of the store owner's gun challenge nineteenth-century evolutionary theory?
8. Why does Johnson give Tortoise the last grim word in the story?

Topics for Writing

1. Create a story in which animals who think and speak and interact are the only characters.
2. Write an essay in which you discuss the implications of Johnson's fable as a moral allegory.
3. Rewrite "Menagerie" as a comic strip.

Suggested Reading

Johnson, Charles. *The Sorcerer's Apprentice.* New York: Penguin, 1987.

JAMES JOYCE

Araby (p. 753)

The rich texture of imagery and allusion that Joyce weaves into "Araby" may delight the sophisticated reader, but for the classroom instructor it represents a temptation comparable to the temptation that may be brought to mind by the apple tree in the "wild garden" mentioned in the second paragraph. Students should not be asked to contemplate the story's symbolism until they grasp its plot. To begin class discussion of "Araby" with the question What happens? may well be to discover that, for a novice reader, no meaningful action seems to have been completed. When the confusion arising from this sense of anticlimax is compounded by the difficulties presented by the unfamiliarity of florins, bazaars, hallstands, and other things old and Irish, "Araby" may strike students as pointless and unnecessarily obscure.

Once it is seen, however, that the narrator's disappointment at the bazaar resolves the tension built up by his attraction to Mangan's sister and his quest to fetch her a symbol of his love, the many specific contrasts between the sensuous and romantic world of the narrator's imagination and the banal and tawdry world of actual experience become meaningful keys to understanding what has happened. The opposition between fantasy and reality continues throughout: "Her image accompanied me even in places the most hostile to romance." The story's pivotal paragraph ends with the narrator cooling his forehead against the window in one of the empty upper rooms, staring out not really at Mangan's sister but at "the brown-clad figure cast by my imagination." Before this moment, his excited fancy has transformed the "decent" and somewhat dilapidated neighborhood of North Richmond Street into a fitting backdrop for such a tale as one might find in a yellow-leaved romance. Mangan's sister, kissed by lamplight, becomes in his view a work of art like a painting by Rossetti. The narrator's soul luxuriates in a dream of exotic beauty soon to be possessed by means of a journey to Araby: "I imagined that I bore my chalice safely through a throng of foes." But after the protracted visit from the tedious Mrs. Mercer and the even longer delayed return of the narrator's uncle with the necessary coin, the limitations of the romantic imagination begin to emerge. The "chalice" is replaced by a florin, held "tightly in my hand"; the quest is made by "third-class carriage"; and the bazaar itself, its potential visionary qualities defeated by failing illumination, turns out to be an ordinary market populated by ordinary shop girls from no farther east than England. At Araby, what matters is not purity of heart but hard cash.

The pitiful inadequacy of the narrator's two pennies and sixpence to master "the great jars that stood like eastern guards" at the door of the bazaar stall completes his painful disillusionment, but Joyce allows his hero one last Byronic vision of himself "as a creature driven and derided by vanity." When the lights go out in Araby, its delusive magic collapses, and the bazaar becomes as "blind" as North Richmond Street. Well might the narrator's eyes burn, for they have been working hard to create out of intractable materials a much more beautiful illusion than Araby. This imaginative power cannot be entirely vain, however, since in the mind that tells the story it is capable of evoking experiences like those described in the story's third paragraph, against which even the hoped-for transports of Araby would have paled.

William E. Sheidley

Questions for Discussion

1. Why does the narrator want to go to the bazaar?
2. Why does he arrive so late?
3. Why doesn't he buy anything for Mangan's sister?
4. Enumerate the activities taking place at Araby. To what extent do they sustain its "magical name"?
5. What had the narrator expected to find at Araby? What was the basis of his expectation?
6. Define the narrator's feelings for Mangan's sister. To what extent is she the cause of those feelings? What, as they say, does he *see* in her?
7. What purpose might Joyce have had in choosing not to mention the object of the narrator's affections until the middle of the third paragraph? Describe the context into which she is introduced. In what ways is she part of the world of North Richmond Street?
8. What is the role of the narrator's uncle in the story? What values and attitudes does he represent? Are they preferable to those of the narrator?

Topics for Writing

1. Make a study of light, vision, and beauty in "Araby."
2. Compare "Araby" and the quest for the Holy Grail.
3. Analyze the function of nonvisual sense imagery in "Araby."
4. Explore Joyce's control of tone in "Araby."
5. On a second reading of the story, keep two lists. In the first record ideas, images, and allusions that suggest contexts remote from the immediate situation, jotting down associations that they bring to mind. In the second list note anything mentioned in the story with which you are unfamiliar. Look some of these items up. Then write an informal paragraph or two showing to what extent tracking Joyce's mind in this fashion helped you to understand and enjoy the story.
6. Using the first three paragraphs of "Araby" as a model, write a recollection of the way you spent your evenings at some memorable period of your

childhood. Use specific sensory images to evoke the locale, the activities, and the way you felt at the time.

7. Narrate an experience in which you were disappointed. First show how your erroneous expectations were generated; then describe what you actually encountered in such a way that its contrast with your expectations is clear.

Suggested Readings

See page 138.

JAMES JOYCE

The Dead (p. 757)

"The Dead" is an apprehension of mortality. Joyce's carefully detailed scrutiny of the party, with all its apparent vivacity, serves only to reveal the triviality, transience, and emptiness of what passes for life in Dublin. The story involves a series of supersessions. Miss Ivors's friendliness is superseded by rigid politics, and she departs. Her kind of fervor is superseded by the "hospitality" of the dinner table that Gabriel feels so good about and that he celebrates in his speech. That conviviality, however, is exposed as mostly hypocritical, as each person reveals a selfish preoccupation — including Gabriel, who uses his oration to reassure himself after his self-esteem has been wounded by Miss Ivors. The long evening, however, generates in the heart of Gabriel a strong surge of love for Gretta that supersedes his selfishness. It is edged with jealousy and self-contempt, Gabriel's habitual weaknesses; nonetheless, the reader feels for a while that out of the waste of the soiree at least this rejuvenation has been salvaged. But Gabriel is longing for something just as dead as Michael Furey, and Gretta's devastating disclosure of a dead lover's power over her mind brings the "thought-tormented" Gabriel to his final recognition of the predominance of death. Like the monks of Mount Melleray, all people in Ireland, dead or alive — from the aged Aunt Julia on down — seem to be sleeping in their coffins.

While Gabriel's vision is triggered by the revelation of a dead man's sway over the emotions of his wife and of his consequent power to thwart Gabriel's desire, it is supported by the pervasive imagery of snow, chill, and death that comes to fulfillment in the last paragraph. The snow has been falling intermittently throughout the story. Gabriel is blanketed with it when he arrives on the scene, and images of cold and dampness pervade the narration. Last year "Gretta caught a dreadful cold"; Bartell D'Arcy has one this year. The girl in the song he sings holds her death-cold infant in a soaking rain. Not only are the physical descriptions of some characters so vivid that one almost sees the skulls beneath the flesh; even the warm, lively, cheerful elements of the story contribute to the final impression of morbidity. The Misses Morkan are giving what may be their final dance. The alcoholic antics of Mr. Browne and Freddy Malins consist only of ersatz good humor. And Gabriel himself, on whom everyone depends, can barely sustain his nerve and perform his function as master of the revels, keeper of order, and sustainer of life.

In the moribund and sterile world presided over by his three spinster aunts, Gabriel is called upon to play a role not unlike that of a year god at this Christmas season. (The party probably takes place on Epiphany, January 6.) From the outset he is willing, but in three sequential encounters he fails. Each failure strikes a blow at his naiveté, his self-confidence, and his sense of superiority. His first two defeats are followed by accomplishments (handling Freddy, his performance at dinner), but their effect on him is cumulative. Gabriel's cheerful banter with the pale, pale Lily does not suit her, as one who has been hurt in love, and his Christmas gift of a coin can do little to ease her "great bitterness." Afterward, his pretensions to take care of people are subjected to merciless ridicule in the "goloshes" passage. With Miss Ivors, Gabriel is more circumspect than with Lily, but that does not prevent him from being whipsawed between her political hostility and her personal affection. This confusing interaction not only causes Miss Ivors to abandon the company and Gabriel in his speech to reject the entire younger generation of Ireland, it also sets the stage for his ultimate failure with Gretta. Gretta's favorable response to Miss Ivors's plan for a trip to Galway now seems to Gabriel a betrayal, and the association of this trip with Gretta's love for the long-dead Michael compounds the feelings of alienation and self-contempt that Miss Ivors's disapproval fosters in him.

Gabriel's failures and self-doubts should not diminish him unduly in the reader's eyes: Joyce portrays him as aesthetically sensitive, charitable, and loving. The "generous tears" he sheds out of sympathy for Gretta's sorrow may not redeem anyone in a world devoted to death, but they are the distillation of a compassion quite opposite to the self-serving hypocrisy that has passed for friendly conversation at the Misses Morkan's ball. By the end of the story Gabriel no longer feels superior to his compatriots. He recognizes that when Aunt Julia dies his speechifying will be useless. He turns his mind away from the past and toward a future in which, as he feels his old identity fade and dissolve, at least the theoretical possibility of growth and change exists. The ambiguity of Gabriel's much-debated "journey westward" reflects the uncertainty of any future, but Gabriel's readiness to embrace it represents a major step forward from his rejection of Miss Ivors's proposition in favor of cycling the European continent again.

WILLIAM E. SHEIDLEY

Questions for Discussion

1. Contrast the mood of the first paragraph with that of the second. Why does Joyce move from anticipation to rigidity?
2. Why are the Misses Morkan so eager for Gabriel to arrive?
3. What is the basis of Gabriel's error with Lily?
4. Explain Gabriel's hesitation to quote Browning.
5. What does Gabriel's interest in galoshes reveal about him?
6. Comment on the men present at the dance besides Gabriel. Why does Joyce limit his cast so narrowly?
7. Discuss the reception of Mary Jane's "Academy piece."
8. What does Miss Ivors want from Gabriel? Why is he so upset by his conversation with her? Why does she leave early? Figuratively, what does she take with her when she goes?
9. Explain Gabriel's longing to be out in the snow. Is Gabriel "thought-tormented"?

10. Explain the irony of Julia's singing "Arrayed for the Bridal" to Mary Jane's accompaniment. What, in this regard, is the effect of the subsequent conversation?
11. Comment on the relevance of the dinner-table conversation to the themes of the story.
12. Why is Gabriel so cheerful when carving and when proposing his toast? Is he justified? Why does he imagine people standing in the snow before he begins to speak?
13. What is the effect of Joyce's ending the tribute to the Misses Morkan with a glimpse of Freddy conducting the singers with his fork?
14. Comment on Gabriel's anecdote about "the never-to-be-forgotten Johnny." Can it be read as a summation in a minor key of the party now ending? of the life of the Morkan family? of their society?
15. Discuss the scene in which Gabriel watches Gretta listening to D'Arcy. What is Gabriel responding to? What is Gretta responding to? What do they have in common? Trace their moods as they proceed to the hotel.
16. Why is Gabriel so humiliated when he learns that Michael Furey is dead? What other effects does this revelation have on him? Explain what he realizes in the last section of the story.
17. Discuss the final paragraph. What does its poetic beauty contribute to the story? What is our final attitude toward Gabriel?

Topics for Writing

1. Discuss the relationship between Gabriel Conroy and women in general.
2. Would you say "The Dead" is a Christmas story? Why or why not?
3. Comment upon Gabriel Conroy's death wish.
4. Consider Gabriel Conroy as a failed redeemer.
5. Explore habit and hypocrisy in "The Dead."
6. After your first reading of the story, scan it again, marking the following: all references to cold, dampness, and snow; all references to death, illness, or people dead at the time of the story; all references to warmth, light, fire, and the like; all references to youth, young people, children, and the like. Catalog your findings and write a paragraph on the importance of these elements in the story.
7. For a specific occasion, plan and compose an after-dinner speech with several headings like Gabriel's. Then analyze your speech, explaining what you were trying to accomplish for your audience — and for yourself. Compare your intentions with Gabriel's.

Related Commentaries

Lesley Brill, Filming James Joyce's "The Dead": The Camera as Character, p. 1652.
Richard Ellmann, A Biographical Perspective on Joyce's "The Dead," p. 1458.
Frank O'Connor, Style and Form in Joyce's "The Dead," p. 1524.

Suggested Readings

Anderson, Chester G. *James Joyce.* New York: Thames Hudson, 1986.

Attridge, Derek, ed. *The Cambridge Companion to James Joyce.* New York: Cambridge UP, 1990.

Beck, Warren. *Joyce's "Dubliners": Substance, Vision, and Art.* Durham, NC: Duke UP, 1969. 303–60.

Beckett, Samuel, et al. *An Examination of James Joyce.* Brooklyn: Haskell, 1974.

Benstock, Bernard, ed. *Critical Essays on James Joyce.* Boston: G. K. Hall, 1985.

Brugaletta, J. J., and M. H. Hayden. "Motivation for Anguish in Joyce's 'Araby.'" *Studies in Short Fiction* 15 (1978): 11–17.

Cronin, E. J. "James Joyce's Trilogy and Epilogue: 'The Sisters,' 'An Encounter,' 'Araby,' and 'The Dead.'" *Renascence* 31 (1979): 229–48.

Ellmann, Richard. *James Joyce. New and Revised Edition.* New York: Oxford UP, 1982.

Levin, Harry. *James Joyce: A Critical Introduction.* New York: New Directions, 1960.

Loomis, C. C., Jr. "Structure and Sympathy in 'The Dead.'" *Twentieth Century Interpretations of "Dubliners."* Ed. Peter K. Garrett. Englewood Cliffs, NJ: Prentice, 1968. 110–14. Originally published in *PMLA* 75 (1960): 149–51.

Mason, Ellsworth, and Richard Ellmann, eds. *The Critical Writings of James Joyce.* Ithaca, NY: Cornell UP, 1989.

Morrissey, L. J. "Joyce's Narrative Struggles in 'Araby.'" *Modern Fiction Studies* 28 (1982): 45–52.

Riqueline, John P. *Teller and Tale in Joyce's Fiction: Oscillating Perspectives.* Baltimore: Johns Hopkins UP, 1983.

Roberts, R. P. "'Araby' and the Palimpsest of Criticism, or Through a Glass Eye Darkly." *Antioch Review* 26 (1966–67): 469–89.

San Juan, Epifanio, Jr. *James Joyce and the Craft of Fiction: An Interpretation of "Dubliners."* Rutherford, NJ: Fairleigh Dickinson UP, 1972, 209–23.

Scott, Bonnie. *James Joyce.* Atlantic Highlands, NJ: Humanities P International, 1987.

Stone, H. "'Araby' and the Writings of James Joyce." *Antioch Review* 25 (1965): 375–410.

FRANZ KAFKA

A Hunger Artist (p. 788)

This "brief but striking parable of alienation" (to quote Kafka biographer Ernst Pawel) was probably written in February 1922, shortly before Kafka began *The Castle.* He had just returned to Prague after a four-week winter vacation prescribed by his doctor as a sort of "shock treatment" to arrest his advancing tuberculosis and deepening depression. Back at his desk, in his room in his parents' apartment, Kafka described his activities in a letter to a friend: "In order to save myself from what is commonly referred to as 'nerves,' I have lately begun to write a little. From about seven at night I sit at my desk, but it doesn't amount to much. It is like trying to dig a foxhole with one's fingernails in the midst of battle."

"A Hunger Artist" was among the few works Kafka allowed to be published in his lifetime. Ironically, he read the galley proofs only a few days before his death. Pawel describes the scene:

> On May 11, [his friend Max] Brod came for what he knew would be his last visit, pretending merely to have stopped off on his way to a lecture

in Vienna so as not to alarm his friend. Kafka, by then quite unable to eat, was wasting away, dying of starvation [because of throat lesions] and immersed in the galley proofs of "A Hunger Artist." Fate lacked the subtle touch of Kafka's art.

The effort drained him. "Kafka's physical condition at this point," Klopstock [a medical student] later wrote, "and the whole situation of his literally starving to death, were truly ghastly. Reading the proofs must have been not only a tremendous emotional strain but also a shattering kind of spiritual encounter with his former self, and when he had finished, the tears kept flowing for a long time. It was the first time I ever saw him overtly expressing his emotions this way. Kafka had always shown an almost superhuman self-control."

As a parable, "A Hunger Artist" may be interpreted in as many ways as there are readers finding words to describe their response to the text. Kafka created in his fiction a metaphorical language akin to music, touching emotions at a level beyond the denotations of the words he used to dramatize his imaginary characters' situations. The title is significant: "*A* Hunger Artist," not "*The* Hunger Artist." There are many kinds of hungers, and many kinds of artists expressing different needs for substance. Students may define the "hunger" as a desire for religious certainty and the "fasting" as the stubborn abstention from a faith without God. Or the key to the parable may lie in the Hunger Artist's statement at the end of the story: "I have to fast. I can't help it. . . . Because I couldn't find the food I liked. If I had found it, believe me, I should have made no fuss and stuffed myself like you or anyone else." Kafka was tormented by a failure of nourishment — from his faith, his family, his talent, his art.

Questions for Discussion

1. What is a parable? Is "A Hunger Artist" a parable?
2. Is it possible to read Kafka's story literally, as a realistic tale? What gives you the sense that there is more to "A Hunger Artist" than its plot and characters?
3. Is Kafka describing an unimaginable situation? Explain.
4. Gaping spectators, butchers, theatrical managers, circus people — the world of the Hunger Artist is mercenary and materialistic. He is described as a "martyr." A martyr to what?
5. As the Hunger Artist loses his popularity, he joins the circus, and his cage is put on display near the animal cages. What does this symbolize? What does this action foreshadow?
6. Explicate the last paragraph of the story. Analyze the function of the panther and his "noble body."

Topics for Writing

1. Write a parable of your own.
2. Agree or disagree with this statement by Primo Levi, the Italian author who translated Kafka's *The Trial*:

    Now I love and admire Kafka because he writes in a way that is totally unavailable to me. In my writing, for good or evil, knowingly or not, I've always strived to pass from the darkness into the light. . . . Kafka forges his path in the opposite direction: he endlessly unravels the hallucinations that he draws from incredibly profound layers, and he never filters them. The reader . . . never receives any help in tearing through the veil or circumventing it to go and see what it conceals. Kafka never touches ground, he never condescends to giving you the end of Ariadne's thread.

But this love of mine is ambivalent, close to fear and rejection: it is similar to the emotion we feel for someone dear who suffers and asks us for help we cannot give. . . . His suffering is genuine and continuous, it assails you and does not let you go.

3. **CONNECTIONS** "It was not the hunger artist who was cheating, he was working honestly, but the world was cheating him of his reward." Compare and contrast "A Hunger Artist" and "The Metamorphosis," taking this statement as the theme of both stories.

Related Commentary

Milan Kundera, Kafka and Modern History, p. 1491.

Suggested Readings

See page 143.

Franz Kafka

The Metamorphosis (p. 794)

This story admits the broadest range of explications — biographical, psychoanalytical, religious, philosophical. Here is one way it might be read: As the sole supporter of his family after the collapse of his father's business, Gregor Samsa has selflessly devoted himself to serving others. Bringing home "good round coin which he could lay on the table for his amazed and happy family" has given him great satisfaction, and his only ambition has been to send his sister, "who loved music, unlike himself," to study at the Conservatorium. After his metamorphosis, Gregor can no longer justify his existence by serving others. Instead, he must come to terms with himself *as* himself, an alien being whose own nature and needs are perhaps only by a degree more strange to Gregor than those of the human Gregor Samsa would have been, if somehow he had confronted them rather than deferring to the version of himself projected by the supposed needs of his family.

Kafka simultaneously traces Gregor's painful growth to self-willed individuality and the family's liberation from dependence upon him, for the relationship of dependence and exploitation has been crippling to both parties. Gregor learns what food he likes, stakes his sticky claim to the sexually suggestive picture of the woman with the fur muff (which may represent an objectification of his libido), and, no longer "considerate," at last *comes* out, intruding his obscene existence upon the world out of a purely self-assertive desire to enjoy his sister's music and to be united with its beauty. With this act Gregor has become fully himself; his death soon after simply releases him from the misery of his existence.

It is also a final release of the family from dependence and from the shame and incompetence that it entails. As an insect, Gregor becomes quite obviously the embarrassment to the family that they allowed him to be when he was human. Step by step they discover their ability to support themselves — taking jobs, coping with what is now merely the troublesome burden of Gregor, and learning finally the necessity of escaping from the prison that his solicitousness has placed them in. Gregor's battle with his father strangely transmutes the Oedipal conflict. It is triggered by Gregor's becoming a being for whom there is no longer room in the family, just as if he were a youth growing to sexual maturity, but the result is that the father, who has previously been reduced to a state of supine inertia by Gregor's diligent exertions, returns to claim his full manhood as husband and paterfamilias.

Emerging from their apartment, "which Gregor had selected," the family members grow into an independent purposiveness that Gregor himself is never able to attain. The story may be said to end with a second metamorphosis, focused in the image of Grete stretching her young body — almost like a butterfly newly emerged from her cocoon. Gregor, left behind like the caterpillar whose demise releases her, is denied all but a premonitory glimpse of the sexual and reproductive fulfillment for which his sister seems destined.

WILLIAM E. SHEIDLEY

Questions for Discussion

1. Describe the effect of Kafka's matter-of-fact assertion of the bizarre incident with which the story begins. Are you very interested in how it came to pass? How does Kafka keep that from becoming an issue in the story?
2. What are Gregor's concerns in section I? To what degree do they differ from what would matter to him if he had *not* been transformed into an insect?
3. When Gregor is trying to get out of bed, he considers calling for help but then dismisses the idea. Why?
4. What seems most important to the members of Gregor's family as he lies in bed? his health?
5. Describe the reaction of Gregor's parents to their first view of the metamorphosed Gregor. What circumstances in ordinary life might elicit a similar response?
6. Discuss the view from Gregor's window.
7. Trace Gregor's adaptation to his new body. In what ways do the satisfactions of his life as an insect differ from the satisfactions of his life as a traveling salesman?
8. When Gregor's father pushes him back into his room at the end of section I, Kafka calls it "literally a deliverance." Comment on the possible implications of that description.
9. Describe Grete's treatment of Gregor in section II. Is Gregor ill?
10. What are Gregor's hopes for the future? Is there anything wrong with those hopes?
11. For a time, Gregor is ashamed of his condition and tries to hide from everyone. In what way might this be called a step forward for him?

12. Discuss the conflicting feelings Gregor has about the furniture's being taken out of his room. Why does he try to save the picture? What might Kafka's intention be in stressing that it is on this occasion that Grete calls Gregor by his name for the first time since his metamorphosis?

13. "Gregor's broken loose." What does Gregor's father do? Why? Explain the situation that has developed by the end of section II.

14. How does the charwoman relate to Gregor? Why is she the one who presides over his "funeral"?

15. Compare the role of the lodgers in the family with that of Gregor. Have they supplanted him? Why does Gregor's father send them away in the morning?

16. Why does Gregor, who previously did not like music, feel so attracted to his sister's playing? What change has taken place in his attitude toward himself? What might Kafka mean by "the unknown nourishment he craved"?

17. Comment on Grete's use of the neuter pronoun "it" to refer to Gregor.

18. What is the mood of the final passages of the story?

Topics for Writing

1. Write an essay describing how Kafka gains the reader's "willing suspension of disbelief."

2. Consider Gregor Samsa's metamorphosis as a triumph of the self.

3. Analyze Kafka's "The Metamorphosis" as a study of sublimated incest.

4. Consider Kafka's use of apparently symbolic images whose complete meaning seems impossible to state in abstract terms — the apples, the fur muff, or the hospital beyond the window, for example. Write a vignette in which symbolic objects play a role without becoming counters in a paraphrasable allegory. Some examples of symbols: a candle, a cup, the sea, broken glass, ants.

5. **CONNECTIONS** Compare and discuss Tolstoy's "The Death of Ivan Ilych" and Kafka's "The Metamorphosis" as two studies of dying.

Related Commentaries

Gustav Janouch, Kafka's View of "The Metamorphosis," p. 1486.
Milan Kundera, Kafka and Modern History, p. 1491.
Jane Smiley, Gregor: My Life as a Bug, p. 1550.
John Updike, Kafka and "The Metamorphosis," p. 1561.

Related Story

Philip Roth, "I Always Wanted You to Admire My Fasting"; or, Looking at Kafka, p. 1169.

Suggested Readings

Anderson, Mark. *Reading Kafka*. New York: Schocken, 1990.
Canetti, Elias. *Kafka's Other Trial: Letters to Felice*. New York: Schocken, 1988.
Greenberg, Martin. "Kafka's 'Metamorphosis' and Modern Spirituality." *Tri-Quarterly* 6 (1966): 5–20.

Gross, Ruth V. *Critical Essays on Franz Kafka*. Boston: G. K. Hall, 1990.

Kafka, Franz. *The Diaries of Franz Kafka*. New York: Schocken, 1988.

———. *The Metamorphosis*. Trans. and ed. Stanley Corngold. New York: Bantam, 1972. (Contains notes, documents, and ten critical essays.)

Levi, Primo. "Translating Kafka." *The Mirror Maker*. New York: Schocken, 1989.

Moss, Leonard. "A Key to the Door Image in 'The Metamorphosis.'" *Modern Fiction Studies* 17 (1971): 37–42.

Nabokov, Vladimir. *Lectures on Literature*. New York: Harcourt, 1980. 250–83.

Pascal, Roy. *Kafka's Narrators: A Study of His Stories and Sketches*. New York: Cambridge UP, 1984.

Pawel, Ernst. *The Nightmare of Reason: A Life of Franz Kafka*. New York: Farrar, 1984.

Spann, Meno. *Franz Kafka*. Boston: G. K. Hall, 1976.

Tauber, Herbert. *Franz Kafka: An Interpretation of His Works*. Brooklyn: Haskell, 1969.

Taylor, Alexander. "The Waking: The Theme of Kafka's 'Metamorphosis.'" *Studies in Short Fiction* 2 (1965): 337–42.

Wolkenfeld, Suzanne. "Christian Symbolism in Kafka's 'The Metamorphosis.'" *Studies in Short Fiction* 10 (1973): 205–07.

JAMAICA KINCAID

Girl (p. 829)

Kincaid's one-paragraph story is a dialogue between a mother and a daughter, consisting mostly of the mother's litany of advice about how to act in a ladylike manner. Students might enjoy reading it aloud. The West Indian prose rhythms are subtly beautiful, and the humor of the mother's advice is revealed in the audible reading process for anyone who has missed it by scanning too quickly. The conflict between the girl and her mother is evident in the mother's fears that her daughter will grow up to be a "slut." Everything the mother says is twisted in light of that fear. The daughter wonders, *"But what if the baker won't let me feel the bread?"* And the mother replies, "You mean to say that after all you are really going to be the kind of woman who the baker won't let near the bread?" The speech rhythm is reminiscent of James Joyce's interior monologues. In fact, we are not amiss to ask whether the mother is actually speaking to her daughter in the story, or whether the daughter has internalized her mother's voice and written it down for us to read to the accompaniment of our own laughter.

Questions for Discussion

1. What are the major subjects in this litany of advice? What kind of life do they describe?

2. The title of the story is "Girl," yet the girl seems to have only two lines of her own, one a protest and the other a question. Why might the author have decided to call the story "Girl" rather than "Mother" or "Woman" or "Advice" or "Memory"?

3. Identify and discuss Kincaid's use of humor in "Girl." What contribution does it make to the story?

4. What is the effect of fairly precise household rules alternating with comments such as "on Sundays try to walk like a lady and not like the slut you are so bent on becoming." String together the lines that admonish the potential slut. What do we think of the mother? What connection is there between the subjects the mother is speaking of and the idea of a slut? Why does it keep popping up from the most innocuous of items? What does this refrain make us think of the daughter? Is the slut refrain a joke or is the author making a suggestion about the construction of self?

5. Some of the advice seems like it could never have been spoken, but only inferred: "this is how you smile to someone you don't like too much; this is how you smile to someone you don't like at all; this is how you smile to someone you like completely." Throughout the whole piece, do you think the mother is speaking to her daughter? What other possibilities could underlie the story's composition?

6. On page 829 the kind of advice changes: "this is how to make a good medicine to throw away a child before it even becomes a child," says the mother. Surely she's not speaking to a young girl here. In the final line, the mother calls her a "woman," the only direct address in the story; earlier the listener has been addressed as a potential slut and been told she's "not a boy." What's the difference between the advice that precedes and follows the reference to aborting a child? Which is more concrete? More abstract? Why does the advice change because of the listener's age? What kinds of knowledge is her mother able to offer?

Topics for Writing

1. Analyze Kincaid's use of humor to indicate conflict in "Girl."
2. Expand the story through the use of descriptive prose. Is the result more or less effective than Kincaid's original?
3. Write a short story in which you use only dialogue.

Suggested Readings

Kincaid, Jamaica. *At the Bottom of the River.* New York: Vintage, 1985.
———. Interview. *New York Times Book Review* 7 Apr. 1985: 6+.

W. P. Kinsella

Shoeless Joe Jackson Comes to Iowa (p. 832)

Many students will have seen the movie *Field of Dreams,* which was based on Kinsella's short story, and the instructor might choose to add the film to the list of outside materials that students can use to supplement the text. Some students also might have seen the nine-part television documentary on baseball by Ken Burns, which was presented on PBS and is also available on video. In each of these films, baseball is presented as one of the central realities of the American experience. Kinsella's story is a loving homage to the American national sport, and the only irony is that Kinsella himself is Canadian. It would seem more likely that a Canadian writer would feel this kind of emotion for ice hockey, but Kinsella has spent many years in the United States. Also, for some years now Canada has been home to two passionately loved baseball teams playing in the American leagues, even though the players are the same assortment of Caribbean and American athletes as the players on other teams.

For a student who is not a fan of baseball, the story will probably seem implausible, since no one but a fan would make the emotional and physical sacrifices of the story's protagonist for the memory of a long-dead player. If, however, the students can think of some figure who would inspire the same kind of enthusiasm in themselves, they will have no difficulty responding to the story. A classroom exercise might be to compile a list of the names of figures for whom the students *would* make this kind of sacrifice. Would they build a stage in their back yard if they felt certain that John Lennon or Jimi Hendrix would come and play? Would they build a basketball court on the front lawn if they thought Michael Jordan might show up some day to shoot a few hoops? Kinsella is that kind of fan, and for someone who shares his emotions the only stretch required to follow the story is the writer's calm assurance that the narrator's wife doesn't think he's nutty as a fruitcake, which is an expression that the narrator's father would have been familiar with.

Kinsella has actually presented his reader with two love stories: One is the narrator's love for Shoeless Joe Jackson, and the other is his love for Iowa. In the third paragraph, the sky is described as "robin's-egg blue," and the wind is "as soft as a day-old chick." When the narrator digs away at the playing field he is putting next to his house, he says that he "stirred the earth with my fingers and knew I loved Iowa as much as a man could love a piece of earth." With the memory of a baseball player his father had seen, the love he feels for the soil, and his even more embracing love for his wife and daughter, he is one of the happiest and most fulfilled figures in contemporary short fiction.

Although the story takes on a supernatural character as the figure of Jackson appears on the homemade, partially completed field, we never feel that we have entered the world of modernist writing. The story is, simply, too down to earth. For once the title of the film better describes the story than the writer's title. The narrator *has* created a field of dreams, and he invites us to dream with him. If students ask about Jackson, the facts in Kinsella's story are true, and for generations he was a folk hero, the simple, trusting figure who had been tricked by dishonest friends. Every boy in America could repeat the plea of the boy who met Jackson outside the courthouse after he'd been convicted of conspiring with the rest of the team to lose the World Series for a gambling syndicate: "Say it ain't so, Joe." Kinsella still feels the boy's pain almost eighty years later.

Questions for Discussion

1. Is baseball still as important to American life as Kinsella feels it is, or have other sports taken its place?
2. What part does the narrator's love for his father play in his love for baseball? Have the students followed a sport with the same enthusiasm because their father or their mother played the sport as a youth?
3. Could the narrator's passion for his playing field be interpreted as a compensation for the difficulties of the rest of his life?

4. When the narrator's wife first sees the player out on the field her husband has constructed, are we expected to believe that it is the figure of Jackson who has appeared? Why does she see him first?
5. Are there other kinds of experiences in which the strength of one person's belief influences someone else's beliefs?
6. What does Jackson mean when he says the field "is true"?
7. Who is the minor league catcher to whom the narrator asks Jackson to give a trial when the entire team is assembled?

Topics for Writing

1. Write a paper discussing the role of baseball in American life today, and compare this to Kinsella's story.
2. There are many descriptions of Iowa in the story. In a paper, list them and compare this fictional Iowa with what you can find out about the real Iowa.
3. Because of its supernatural figure, the story has been described as an example of modernist literary technique. Discuss why this is or is not valid.
4. Compare this story and the film *Field of Dreams*, and analyze which is more effective in presenting Kinsella's imaginative concept.

Suggested Reading

Kinsella, W. P. *Go the Distance: Baseball Stories*. Dallas: Southern Methodist UP, 1995.

Margaret Laurence

The Mask of the Bear (p. 842)

Although the title of Margaret Laurence's story has prepared the reader for a portrait of a man who has some of the characteristics of a bear, it still is difficult for a modern reader to accept the rough and insensitive character she presents. The man, the narrator's grandfather, is described in the opening sentences as wearing his heavy bearskin coat (rare even in rural Canada), and it is clear that Laurence intends for us to see the coat as a metaphor for the old man's conduct. He dominates his house with the ferocity of a caged grizzly bear, bullying his wife, his daughters, and his granddaughter into frightened silence. Describing her own struggle to present a passive face to her grandfather, the narrator states, "I felt, as so often in the Brick House, that my lungs were in danger of exploding, that the pressure of silence would become too great to be borne." A modern woman would simply have left him, especially after he had been unfaithful, saving herself and her children from a life of emotional deprivation and psychological scarring.

Another element of the story is the narrator's description of her first efforts to write stories by using phrases from the Bible. Her struggle to find a way to break out of her silence through the written word is one that is common to many other writers, especially women writers who have grown up in households like the one she describes.

The story develops unexpected depth in the final scene, when three of the man's children are gathered in the house after their mother's funeral, discussing their parents' relationship. The old man is obviously distraught, and his son, who has used alcohol as a defense against his father's surliness and disapproval, attempts to justify his father's treatment of his wife by suggesting that their mother was too good, too patient and forgiving for her husband — "an angel," as he expresses it. "Can you feature going to bed with an angel . . . ?" he asks.

His sisters have spent much of their lives attempting to deal with their father's irascible nature, and the unmarried sister has lost her last possible chance at marriage because of her father, so the two women refuse to accept their brother's explanation. The effort of the three to understand the lives of their father and mother lapses into another unresolved silence.

It is only the narrator who achieves some kind of emotional resolution in her feelings toward her grandfather. At the opening of the story, she remembers his bearskin coat, a metaphor for her grandfather's conduct. At the story's end, when she is much older and has more understanding, she feels his presence again in a bear mask carved by one of Canada's Northwest Indian tribes. This time she sees beyond the surface. The mask becomes a new metaphor as she senses a bewildered presence behind the opening of the mask's eyes. She recognizes it as the person who was truly her grandfather. What she finally understands is that just as in her grandfather's hard face, "the mask had concealed a man."

Questions for Discussion

1. Why does the author distinguish among three kinds of bears — kodiak bears, grizzly bears, and brown bears — in the opening paragraph?
2. What does the little girl mean when, seeing her grandfather in the bearskin coat, she simpers to herself, "It's you"?
3. In her memories of her grandfather, is there anything that he accepts or is pleased with?
4. What is she telling us about her little village when she says that it was her family's lack of money that made it impossible for her to find the books she wanted? Do many writers come from these kinds of isolated communities?
5. What does the canary represent to the narrator's grandmother?
6. Would it have been common for someone in a northern village in Canada in the 1930s to have a canary?
7. Is there any way Aunt Edna could have met the man who came to see her without her father knowing what was happening?
8. What was the basis for the father's belief in his right to control the lives of his wife and children?
9. Is this an acceptable basis for a man's conduct today?
10. Is it expected that people in this rural area during the 1930s would doubt the reality of heaven, as the narrator implies in her memory of the adults talking after her grandmother's funeral?
11. Is it significant that the narrator, when she is older, sees her grandfather mirrored in an Indian artifact, instead of an object from her own culture?

Topics for Writing

1. Using examples from the story, discuss the role of women in rural society in the years that the author describes, then compare this role with women's lives today.
2. Explicate the author's meaning when she says of her grandfather that the "new week's beginning would release him into the only freedom he knew, the acts of work."

Suggested Readings

Gunnars, Kristjana, ed. *Crossing the River: Essays in Honor of Margaret Laurence.* Winnipeg: Turnstone, 1988.
Laurence, Margaret. *Birds in the House.* New York: Knopf, 1970.

D. H. Lawrence

Odour of Chrysanthemums (p. 859)

Because of its unusual vocabulary and emotional complexity, this can be a difficult story for many students to understand. Before they read it, their attention should be directed to the first paragraph of the headnote, which suggests an approach. Elizabeth Bates, the protagonist, is bitter because she feels trapped in her marriage. She is caught between her attempt to relate to her husband and her struggle to break free from her marital bondage. Her husband drinks away most of the meager wages he earns at the coal mine, leaving her to tend the children in a dark, squalid cottage she calls a "dirty hole, rats and all." She is fiercely protective of their two children — daughter, Annie, and young son, John. There is another baby on the way. Consumed with anger toward her husband, Elizabeth channels her love and tenderness toward her children. She feels herself "absolutely necessary for them. They were her business."

Recognizing the pattern of Lawrence's use of symbolism in the story may be one of the best ways to approach it. In the opening paragraph, Elizabeth's emotional situation is prefigured in the image of the nameless woman forced back into the hedge by the oncoming train. The female-male opposition in the story is symbolized here: marriage and home (the hedge) versus the mine and the pub (the train). A little later on, Lawrence has Elizabeth comment explicitly on the symbolism implied in the title of the story. When her young daughter is charmed to see her mother wearing the chrysanthemums — "You've got a flower in your apron" (pregnancy = flowering), Elizabeth tells her that she's speaking nonsense. To the mother, the flowers are not beautiful anymore. Most emphatically she does not treasure them as a hardy symbol of fertility in her otherwise bleak existence. To her, they are a symbol of death: "It was chrysanthemums when I married him, and chrysanthemums when you were born, and the first time they ever brought him home drunk, he'd got brown chrysanthemums in his button-hole."

Ironically, near the end of the story, when Elizabeth lays out her dead husband on the parlor floor, she smells "a cold, deathly smell of chrysanthemums in the room." One of the miners coming in with the stretcher knocks the vase of flowers to the floor, and she mops up the spilled water. In this action she is a servant of death, "her ultimate master" at the end of the story.

For most of the story, however, her master is her husband. The word "master" is the common name for husband among the village wives, but Elizabeth has refused to submit to her destiny. The line between female and male is clearly drawn in her world, where the sight of twelve children living at home on a miner's salary is not uncommon. But Elizabeth feels herself apart from the other housewives and miners. She judges everyone she comes in contact with, except herself. Then, as she begins to wash the naked body of her dead husband, she feels herself "countermanded. She saw him, how utterly inviolable he lay in himself. She had nothing to do with him. She could not accept it."

The final scene of "Odour of Chrysanthemums," the description of the mother and the wife laying out the body of the dead man, is one of the most unforgettable moments in Lawrence's fiction. The physicality of the dead man is unmistakable, and it affects the two women differently. Now Elizabeth fully accepts the reality of her individuality, her separate existence in the world. Before, she felt herself apart as an emotional defense against her disappointment with her marriage. Now she knows "the utter isolation of the human soul." The husband she hated existed only in her mind. With his death, she is free to ask, "Who am I? What have I been doing? . . . What wrong have I done? . . . There lies the reality, this man." The story ends with her horrified by the distance between them. Yet she is at peace.

Questions for Discussion

1. "Odour of Chrysanthemums" is set in the kind of mining village Lawrence grew up in. The first four paragraphs "pan in" on the social world of the story, establishing a relationship among the industrial landscape, wild nature, and human beings. Read the opening carefully, noting the diction of the passage, and try to state Lawrence's vision of the relationship among these elements.
2. Note how Elizabeth Bates appears on the scene merely as "a woman." How does the author go on to establish a closer relationship to her? What is she like when we first meet her? Describe the world she inhabits.
3. When Elizabeth sets out to find Walter, she notes "with faint disapproval the general untidiness" of the Rigleys. Consider the use of dialect in this passage. Who uses it? Can you determine Elizabeth's relationship to her neighbors and her class position? Might it be connected to her general satisfaction with her marriage?
4. In section I the family awaits Walter Bates's return from the mines — and yet his presence seems to haunt the family. What influence does even his absence exert on his wife and children?
5. Elizabeth's mother-in-law arrives, and the two women discuss Walter. How does Lawrence subtly and comically establish their relationship to each other and to Walter?
6. Miners stripped down to work underground; half-naked, white Walter is strangely beautiful as he is brought home. Her husband's body is a revelation to Elizabeth: "And she knew what a stranger he was to her." Try to

explain the epiphany Elizabeth undergoes; what does she now understand about her marriage?

7. Lawrence said of literary symbols, "You can't give a symbol a meaning anymore than you can give a cat a 'meaning.' Symbols are organic units of consciousness with a life of their own, and you can never explain them away because their value is dynamic, emotional, belonging to the sense-consciousness of the body and soul, and not simply mental. An allegorical image has a *meaning*" (from an essay that appears in *Dragon of Apocalypse: Selected Literary Criticism*, ed. Anthony Beal [New York: Viking, 1966]). Trace the meaning that chrysanthemums take on in each stage of this story. Is it possible to give them a "full" meaning? According to Lawrence, are the flowers symbolic or allegorical?

8. Given the portrait of the social world in the story and the portrayal of this unhappy marriage, how might the two be related? Is Lawrence explicit about the relationship or might you like to argue with him about the causes of feeling in it?

9. One of the difficulties in understanding "Odour of Chrysanthemums" is its vocabulary. Consult a good dictionary to discover the meanings of words such as "gorse," "coppice," "hips," "spinney," "cleaved," "whimsey," "reedy," "pit-pond," "alders," "tarred," "pit-bank," "headstocks," and "colliery." How does this increase your understanding of Lawrence's story?

Topics for Writing

1. Analyze light and dark imagery in "Odour of Chrysanthemums."
2. Discuss the use of sound and silence in "Odour of Chrysanthemums."
3. **CONNECTIONS** Compare the isolation and alienation of marriage in Lawrence's "Odour of Chrysanthemums" and Bobbie Ann Mason's "Shiloh."

Related Commentaries

D. H. Lawrence, Draft Passage from "Odour of Chrysanthemums," p. 1492.
D. H. Lawrence, The Lust of Hate in Poe's "The Cask of Amontillado," p. 1494.
Jay Parini, Lawrence's and Steinbeck's "Chrysanthemums," p. 1530.

Related Story

John Steinbeck, The Chrysanthemums, p. 1255.

Suggested Readings

See page 154.

D. H. LAWRENCE

The Rocking-Horse Winner (p. 873)

Lawrence's masterful technical control wins the reader's assent to the fantastic premise on which the story is built; without that assent, the thematic statement the story propounds would lack cogency. Rather than confronting us boldly with his improbable donnée, as Kafka does in "The Metamorphosis," Lawrence edges up to it. The whispering voices in the house that drive Paul to his furious rocking begin as a thought in the mother's mind and then become a figure of speech that crystallizes imperceptibly into a literal fact — or rather, into an auditory hallucination heard by the children that expresses their perception of their mother's unquenchable need for funds. Paul's ability to pick a winner by riding his rocking horse to where he is lucky requires even more circumspect handling. Like the family members, we learn about it after the fact, putting together bits of information to explain a set of peculiar but at first not at all implausible circumstances — Paul's claim, "Well, I got there!", his familiarity with race horses, Bassett's reluctance "to give him away" to Oscar, Paul's giving Oscar a tip on a long shot that comes in a winner, and only then, with Oscar's skepticism always preempting that of the reader, the revelation of how much he has won. It is not until the very end that we, with his astonished mother, actually witness Paul in the act of receiving revelation — just as he slips beyond the world of everyday probability for good and into the uncharted supernatural realm from whence his "luck" seems to emanate.

Although no explanation, supernatural or otherwise, is necessary to account for good fortune at the race track, Lawrence persuades the reader that Paul's success is caused by his exertions and therefore has a moral meaning. In Paul's household the lack of love is perceived as a lack of money and the lack of money is attributed to a lack of luck. Since luck is by definition something that happens *to* one, to blame one's troubles on luck is to deny responsibility for them and to abandon any effort to overcome them. As the event makes clear, Paul's mother will never be satisfied, no matter how much money falls her way, because no amount of money can fill the emptiness left by the absence of love. The "hard little place" in her heart at the beginning of the story has expanded until, at the end, she feels that her whole heart has "turned actually into a stone." Paul sets out by the force of will to redefine luck as something one can acquire. He places belief before evidence and asserts, "I'm a lucky person. . . . God told me," and then makes good on his promise by riding his rocking horse to where luck comes from. " 'It's as if he had it from heaven,'" Bassett says, "in a secret, religious voice."

In his single-minded devotion to winning money for his mother at the racetrack by riding his rocking horse (which W. D. Snodgrass has likened to masturbation as Lawrence understood it), Paul diverts his spiritual and emotional forces to material aims, and Lawrence symbolically represents the effect of this *materialization* in the process of petrification by which the mother's heart and Paul's blue eyes, which have throughout the story served as an emblem of his obsession, turn to stone. At the end Oscar states the case with epigrammatic precision: Hester's son has been transformed into eighty-odd thousand pounds — a tidy sum, but of course it will not be enough.

WILLIAM E. SHEIDLEY

Questions for Discussion

1. How is Paul's mother portrayed at the outset? Does Lawrence suggest that she is blameworthy? Why or why not?
2. Explain the family's "grinding sense of the shortage of money." Why do the voices get even louder when some money becomes available? What would it take to still the voices?
3. Discuss the implications of Paul's confusing *luck* with *lucre*. How accurate is his mother's definition of luck? What would constitute true good luck for him?
4. Explain Paul's claim to be lucky. In what sense is he justified? In what sense is he very unlucky?
5. What function do Oscar and Bassett play in the story, beyond providing Paul with practical access to the racetrack and the lawyer?
6. "Bassett was serious as a church." Is this a humorous line? Does it suggest anything beyond the comic?
7. What is the effect on the reader of the episode in which Oscar takes Paul to the track and Paul's horse Daffodil wins the race?
8. Explain the mother's response to her birthday gift. What is its effect on Paul? Why?
9. Before the Derby, Paul does not "know" for several races. Can this dry spell be explained? What brings it to an end?
10. Analyze Paul's last words in the story. What does he mean by *"get there"*? Where, in fact, does he go? Is *absolute* certainty possible? How? Why is Paul so proud to proclaim that he is lucky to his mother? Finally, comment on her reaction.
11. Evaluate Oscar's remarks, which end the story. Was Paul a "poor devil"? In what senses?

Topics for Writing

1. Describe the handling of the supernatural in Lawrence's "The Rocking-Horse Winner."
2. Explore the religious theme of "The Rocking-Horse Winner."
3. Consider luck, will, and faith in "The Rocking-Horse Winner."
4. Analyze the realistic elements and the social theme of Lawrence's supernatural tale.
5. Consider luck, lucre, and love in "The Rocking-Horse Winner."
6. Look up a newspaper story about some unexplained phenomenon, ghost, or poltergeist, and work it into a narrative whose meaning is finally not dependent on an interest in the supernatural.

Related Commentaries

Janice H. Harris, Levels of Meaning in Lawrence's "The Rocking-Horse Winner," p. 1469.

D. H. Lawrence, The Lust of Hate in Poe's "The Cask of Amontillado," p. 1494.

Suggested Readings

Boulton, J. T., ed. *The Letters of D. H. Lawrence*. New York: Cambridge UP, 1989.

Clayton, J. J. "D. H. Lawrence: Psychic Wholeness through Rebirth." *Massachusetts Review* 25 (1984): 200–21.

Harris, Janice. *The Short Fiction of D. H. Lawrence*. New Brunswick, NJ: Rutgers UP, 1984.

Hyde, G. M. *D. H. Lawrence*. New York: St. Martin's, 1990.

Jackson, Dennis, and Felda Jackson. *Critical Essays on D. H. Lawrence*. Boston: G. K. Hall, 1988.

Kalnins, M. "D. H. Lawrence's 'Odour of Chrysanthemums': The Three Endings." *Studies in Short Fiction* 13 (1976): 471–79.

Lawrence, D. H. *Portable D. H. Lawrence*. New York: Penguin, 1977.

Meyers, Jeffry. *D. H. Lawrence: A Biography*. New York: Knopf, 1990.

Olson, Charles. *D. H. Lawrence and the High Temptation of the Mind*. Santa Barbara, CA: Black Sparrow, 1980.

Rice, Thomas Jackson. *D. H. Lawrence: A Guide to Research*. New York: Garland, 1983.

Rose, S. "Physical Trauma in D. H. Lawrence's Short Fiction." *Contemporary Literature* 16 (1975): 73–83.

Sager, Keith. *D. H. Lawrence: Life into Art*. Athens: U of Georgia P, 1985.

San Juan, E., Jr. "Theme versus Imitation: D. H. Lawrence's 'The Rocking-Horse Winner,'" *D. H. Lawrence Review* 3 (1970): 136–40.

Schneider, Daniel J. *The Consciousness of D. H. Lawrence: An Intellectual Biography*. Lawrence: UP of Kansas, 1986.

———. *D. H. Lawrence: The Artist as Psychologist*. Lawrence: UP of Kansas, 1984.

Shaw, M. "Lawrence and Feminism." *Critical Quarterly* 25 (1983): 23–27.

Snodgrass, W. D. "A Rocking Horse: The Symbol, the Pattern, the Way to Live." *D. H. Lawrence: A Collection of Critical Essays*. Ed. Mark Spilka. *Twentieth Century Views*. Englewood Cliffs, NJ: Prentice, 1963. Originally published in *Hudson Review* 11 (1958).

Squires, Michael, and Keith Cushman. *The Challenge of D. H. Lawrence*. Madison: U of Wisconsin P, 1990.

Widmer, Kingsley. *The Art of Perversity: D. H. Lawrence's Shorter Fictions*. Seattle: U of Washington P, 1962. 92–95, 213.

DAVID LEAVITT

We Meet at Last (p. 885)

Leavitt's unhappy story is a description of one of the crises of contemporary gay life — a crisis that is only partially exposed and still ridden with secrets and insecurity. It is a simple story that students will have no difficulty following. A man waits in a park for his first meeting with a man he has known only as a voice over the phone. Their phone conversations have been so exciting that they have had a mutual sexual experience simply talking to each other. The man waiting in the park has pressed for a meeting, but the other man has hesitated, certain that he couldn't live up to the expectations of the man waiting for him. When the other man finally appears, he understands immediately that the man waiting is stricken with disappointment, and with a desperate apology he quickly leaves.

Within its small dimensions, the story expresses a tangled web of emotions. Each of the men has made a significant emotional investment in the meeting, and they are each deeply affected by its unhappy outcome. What they experience is not unique to gay life — there is as much disappointment in a failed meeting between a heterosexual couple who have known each other only through phone calls or letters — but because of the hesitations that still surround overt expressions of homosexual affection, Leavitt's story has a particular poignancy. A description of such a meeting in terms of a homosexual relationship is relatively new to our literature, and would have been virtually impossible to publish only a generation ago.

Leavitt is still a young writer, but he achieved an early success because he was writing frankly about what were still new subjects. In recent years, one of his books had to be withdrawn from publication because it was based too closely on an earlier book by the English writer Stephen Spender, and a new novel received generally unenthusiastic reviews. As this small sketch makes clear, however, he is a writer of considerable sensitivity and skill and an important contributor to the gay literary tradition.

Questions for Discussion

1. Why is Jack taking such care with his appearance when we first encounter him in the park? Why does he pretend to be reading the metro section of the newspaper instead of the business section?
2. Stewart, when he appears, is physically just as he described himself on the telephone. Why is Jack disappointed?
3. Is there any chance that a fantasy relationship that has been shattered by a momentary glimpse of reality could be rekindled?
4. What is Leavitt trying to understand with his question, "What does it mean, to 'meet'?"

Topic for Writing

1. Analyze whether it is social pressure that makes it impossible for the two men in Leavitt's story to have more than a fantasy relationship, or whether it is something in their own personalities.

Suggested Readings

Leavitt, David. *Family Dancing: Stories*. New York: Knopf, 1984.

Leavitt, David, and Mark Mitchell, eds. *Pages Passed from Hand to Hand: The Hidden Tradition of Homosexual Literature in English from 1748 to 1914*. Boston: Houghton, 1997.

——. *The Penguin Book of Gay Short Stories*. New York: Viking, 1984.

"The New Lost Generation." *Esquire* 103 (1985): 85–88.

"New Voices and Old Values." *New York Times Book Review* 12 May 1985: 1+.

Ursula K. Le Guin

The Ones Who Walk Away from Omelas (p. 889)

The tone of Le Guin's story deserves special mention, because it supports the humane wisdom of her theme. Rational, unhurried, calm, and composed, her words flow in long paragraphs like the deep bed of a river. She subtitles her story "Variations on a theme by William James." Read her explanation of the source of her story in Part Two (p. 1495), where she quotes two paragraphs by James, the American philosopher and experimental psychologist (1842–1910) and older brother of the writer Henry James. Students will recognize that Le Guin's tone is similar to James's in his philosophical discourse, which she so admires.

The tone of Le Guin's story is animated by her choice of narrator. Simultaneously certain and uncertain, she is both assured and tentative in her description of the happy, peace-loving community. (Remember *Omelas* means "O-peace," as well as Salem, Oregon, spelled backward.) Le Guin is too modest in her assertion of writing about "fortune cookie ideas." She possesses great authority in her definitions: "Happiness is based on a just discrimination of what is necessary, what is neither necessary nor destructive, and what is destructive." Perhaps students need to discuss this philosophical point to make sure they understand it. Major themes of the story — that ideals are the probable causes of future experience, and that what you touch, touches you — are based on this definition of happiness. The ones who walk away from Omelas have used it in formulating their decision to leave the utopian community.

Le Guin is also wise in matters of human psychology. She purposely leaves the details of the good life in Omelas vague, so that readers can imagine their own utopias, complete with as many or as few drugs and as much or as little sex as they are comfortable with. She also knows that her readers will find her vision of the good life more believable after her description of the tormented child on whom everything depends. For human beings, the ideal becomes real only with the introduction of pain and loss, "the terrible justice of reality." The destination of those who leave Omelas is less imaginable than the city of near-perfection. The ones who leave are unwilling to be bound by the terrible laws of this "utopia"; they must create their own futures. Le Guin's fantasy isn't escapist literature. It's as real and inescapable as life itself.

Questions for Discussion

1. What is the tone of this story?
2. What is the point of view in the story? Who is the narrator? Briefly discuss the dual attitudes of the narrator.
3. How accurate is Le Guin's contention that "happiness is based on a just discrimination of what is necessary, what is neither necessary nor destructive, and what is destructive"? How central is this idea to the themes of the story?
4. What type of society is Omelas? Did you find the narrator's description substantive or vague? Discuss possible reasons the author constructed the story in this manner.

5. What role does the tormented child play in the story? How does it affect the citizens of Omelas?
6. Why do some citizens desert Omelas? What is the place that is "even less imaginable to most of us than the city of happiness"?
7. What is the source of conflict in the story? Who is the protagonist? the antagonist?
8. Discuss the major themes of the story.
9. How would you characterize Le Guin's narrative style? Do you feel her use of the short question is effective? Why?
10. What is your reaction to the story?

Topics for Writing

1. Analyze the idea of the utopian society in "The Ones Who Walk Away from Omelas."
2. **CONNECTIONS** Compare and contrast the societies and philosophies in Omelas and in the small town in Jackson's "The Lottery."

Related Commentary

Ursula K. Le Guin, The Scapegoat in Omelas, p. 1495.

Suggested Readings

Cogell, E. C. "Setting as Analogue to Characterization in Ursula Le Guin." *Extrapolation* 18 (1977): 131–41.
Manlove, C. N. "Conservatism in the Fantasy of Le Guin." *Extrapolation* 21 (1980): 287–97.
Moylan, T. "Beyond Negation: The Critical Utopias of Ursula K. Le Guin and Samuel R. Delany." *Extrapolation* 21 (1980): 236–53.
Wood, S. "Discovering Worlds: The Fiction of Ursula K. Le Guin." *Voices for the Future: Essays on Major Science Fiction Writers.* Ed. J. D. Clareson. Bowling Green: Bowling Green U Popular P, 1976–79. 2:154–79.

DORIS LESSING

The Old Chief Mshlanga (p. 895)

It used to be thought that the aesthetic experience of art was universal, that all people confronted with something like Bach's "St. Matthew Passion" would experience the same exaltation, or that everyone reading *Moby Dick* would be swept up into the same rush of excitement when the crew's chase goes into the third day. What the new concerns of women readers and readers from other cultures have made us conscious of, however, is that this response to words on a page is as strongly culturally conditioned as the creative impulse that wrote the words initially. Reading the African stories of white writers like Doris Lessing or

Nadine Gordimer, in this light, presents us with complex problems, which the instructor might want to bring the students.

Taking as her defense the surface of her story, "The Old Chief Mshlanga," Lessing probably would say that she has parried any charges that could be made against her of moral complicity by writing a sketch — it is almost a memoir — that describes a white girl growing up in an African society and becoming conscious for the first time of the crime that has been committed by the white settlers who have seized the land and destroyed the native culture. Certainly Lessing's consciousness of this crime was one of the factors that led to her long involvement in the Communist Party in Britain, but the presentation of this coming to knowledge is presented almost obliquely, as one of many things that the girl learns as she begins to go beyond the boundaries of the family farm. She is more upset by her feeling that she has lost her way when she is unsure of the direction to the African village than she is by the vague awareness forced upon her that perhaps the Africans have a right to the land. The question for the instructor is to decide how much Lessing is trying to say about the enormity of the crime, and how well she succeeds by presenting it so indirectly.

It would seem obvious that someone from the displaced African cultures would have a different response to the story. In the early pages, when the girl describes letting her dogs force any Africans she meets to climb a tree to escape the dogs' savagery, her description is so offhand — despite our inference that she knows better as an adult — that the passages could be infuriating to someone who feels what is happening as an African. When she grows older and becomes dimly aware of what this might mean, and simply greets some of the Africans she meets, we are never told that she could feel or understand the moral responsibility for what she has done. As the last, cruel irony, when her impulsive visit to the African village leads to her understanding the extent of the later destruction of the village and its people, she tells us that the white person who will be given the land may find that his corn grows tall in the place where the village had been.

Lessing's great talent as a writer lies in her ability to empathize with her characters. She is a natural writer of fiction, who has apparently only to consider a character and have a story suggest itself. In a few sentences she is inside the character and she sees and feels the experience as her character feels it. Because she works this way it isn't possible for her to draw back, as Nadine Gordimer can, and consider for a moment the whole social issue that is involved. She can suggest — as her young girl does when she begins to understand the significance of the old chief — but she can't step far enough out of her character to draw larger social inferences.

In her later work, when Lessing's subject was making a new life for herself in England, or her own difficulties as a single parent, or the ideological confusion of young political radicals, the issues seem to have presented less complex problems so she could dramatize them fully. Here, in the African stories, the reader is drawn into the rich weave of description and emotion, and presented with an appealing portrait of a young white girl. At the same time, unlike Gordimer's African story "Country Lovers," we are left wondering uncomfortably what an African reader would feel about Lessing's simple anecdotes.

Questions for Discussion

1. What is the historical background for the white farms Lessing describes in her story?
2. What is the girl's first response when she hears that the land had once belonged to the old chief's people?
3. Why doesn't she say anything when her father is about to seize the village's goats?
4. Why does the girl go out with a rifle and dogs?
5. Why does she never do any work?
6. Do you feel the girl ever really understands what is destroying the African culture?
7. There is an irony in the dependence of the people on mealie — which is the South African word for corn. What is this irony?
8. Do you think the story is a portrait of Lessing herself?

Topics for Writing

1. Discuss the way of life that the girl describes and contrast it with the situation in South Africa today.
2. Discuss the implications of the following: A story that has clear political overtones, like this one, presents us again with the dilemma of how explicit a work of art should be in its treatment of moral issues.
3. Discuss the symbolism in the young girl's feeling of having lost her way when she walks to the village.
4. Contrast the life on the farm, and the role the white girl plays on it, with the glimpse Lessing gives us of the way of life of the African tribe.
5. **CONNECTIONS** Compare the growing awareness of social injustice in Lessing's young girl with a similar situation in the story by Gordimer or in Mansfield's "The Garden-Party."

Suggested Readings

Pickering, Jean. *Understanding Doris Lessing*. Columbia: U of South Carolina P, 1990.
Sprague, Claire, and Virginia Tiger, eds. *Critical Essays on Doris Lessing*. Boston: G. K. Hall, 1986.
Whittaker, Ruth. *Doris Lessing*. New York: St. Martin's, 1988.

Clarice Lispector

The Smallest Woman in the World (p. 904)

Julia Alvarez's commentary on this story in the text can provide students with an approach to Lispector's narrative. Another idea that sheds light on Lispector's theme has been provided by the critic Giovanni Pontiero, who recognized that Lispector's characters — like the smallest woman in the world — are "free from psychological conflicts, [so] they show a greater participation in what is real, the greater space that includes all spaces." This is perhaps Little Flower's possession of "the most perfect feeling," her knowledge that "not to be devoured is the secret goal of a whole life."

Questions for Discussion

1. Lispector has framed the beginning and ending of her story by setting it "in the depths of Equatorial Africa," where the French explorer Marcel Pretre has discovered the smallest woman in the world. In the middle of the story, Lispector dramatizes the responses of the "civilized world" to the newspaper reports of Little Flower. How does Lispector keep our interest in the story despite her unconventional organization of her plot?
2. In the fifth paragraph, Lispector refers to "the heart of Africa," which the white explorer has penetrated to find Little Flower. What is Lispector's view of "the heart of Africa" in this story? How does it compare to conventional views of Africa, as in Joseph Conrad's story "Heart of Darkness"?
3. What kinds of humor do you find in "The Smallest Woman in the World"?
4. Why do the people reading about Little Flower in the newspaper react so differently to her? What is Lispector trying to show about our so-called civilized life?
5. How does Lispector shape the conclusion of her story by giving the last word to "one old lady, folding up the newspaper decisively"?

Topics for Writing

1. Summarize Julia Alvarez's commentary on Lispector's story (p. 1417). How did it help you to understand the story?
2. **CONNECTIONS** Compare and contrast "The Smallest Woman in the World" with Gabriel García Márquez's "A Very Old Man with Enormous Wings" as examples of magical realism.

Related Commentary

Julia Alvarez, On Lispector's "The Smallest Woman in the World," p. 1417.

Suggested Readings

Cixous, Helene. *Reading with Clarice Lispector.* Ed. and trans. by Verena Andermatt Conley. Minneapolis: U of Minnesota P, 1990.
Peixoto, Marta. *Passionate Fictions: Gender, Narrative, and Violence in Clarice Lispector.* Minneapolis: U of Minnesota P, 1994.

JACK LONDON

To Build a Fire (p. 910)

While the protagonist of "To Build a Fire" lacks sufficient imagination to concern himself with "significances" or to "meditate upon . . . man's place in the universe," London's story leads us directly to these issues. Its setting and structure strip man's confrontation with death in an alien and indifferent or even hostile universe down to a starkly simple example, while its slow and detailed pace brings home the reality of that confrontation with all the force of actual experience.

The nameless traveler across the blank Arctic landscape is as well equipped as any man for coping with his situation. He is resourceful, cautious, tenacious, and able to tolerate a great deal of discomfort. More experience in the Yukon would not have improved his ability to cope: It would simply have supplied him with such wisdom as is propounded by the old-timer: Don't try it, or don't try it alone. But avoidance can only be temporary. Man must face death, and face it alone. London places his character on "the unprotected tip of the planet," exposed to the frigid emptiness of the universe, and the story details how it overcomes him.

London defines the man's condition by contrasting it with that of the dog, which is at home in the hostile environment. Fitted by nature with adequate defenses against the cold and guided by unfailing instinct in deciding what to do, the dog provides an unsentimental perspective on the man's struggles. Although the man's judgment is a poor substitute for canine instinct and although his improvised technology, despite its provision of fire, proves disastrously less reliable than husky fur, the man's consciousness of his situation, his errors, and his eventual dignity in accepting his death earn him a heroic stature impossible for the dog, which London portrays *as* a dog, not as a person deserving credit for his decisions and hence his survival. At the end, the husky has more in common with "the stars that leaped and danced and shone brightly in the cold sky" than with the human spirit that has passed from the frozen corpse, leaving behind its mark in the dignity of the posture that the corpse retains.

Readers may disagree over whether the story — which, as Earle Labor has shown, corresponds remarkably with Greek tragedy as defined by Aristotle — conveys a tragic sense of order or the black pessimism characteristic of the mature London. Surely all readers will, however, acknowledge the powerful effect that the story creates, thanks to London's artful use of foreshadowing, repetition, and close observation of authentic detail. As numbness and frost invade and gradually seize the body of the man, the metaphysical chill accompanying the recognition of mortality creeps irresistibly into the reader's mind. Each detail of the story contributes to this single impression — the atmosphere; the cold ironic voice of the narrator; and most poignantly, perhaps, the contrasting moments of warmth by the fire at lunch, the remembered comfort of which is strangely echoed in the repose of the dying man's last thoughts.

Questions for Discussion

1. Describe the atmosphere established in the first two paragraphs.

2. What techniques does London use to impress the reader with the man's solitude? Why does he refrain for so long from mentioning the dog?
3. How cold is it? How does London make clear what such cold is like? Why is it important for him to do so?
4. London tells us that the man lacks imagination. What good would imagination have done him?
5. Why is the dog reluctant to follow the man? Why does it follow him anyway? Trace the dog's attitudes throughout the story.
6. The man keeps close track of time and distances. Why are they important to him? What significance might they have for the reader?
7. What is the reason for London's careful introduction of the hazards of the hidden spots of water in such detail before the man actually slips into one? What would be the difference if he withheld these explanations until afterwards?
8. What does the man do at half past twelve when he arrives at the forks? What does his behavior reveal about his character? In what way are those traits important to the subsequent action?
9. The words of an old-timer from Sulphur Creek enter the man's memory at intervals in the story. Trace the changes in his response to them. What does the old-timer have in common with the dog?
10. Several times London associates the cold with outer space. Consider the possible implications of this connection.
11. Why does London wait until after lunch to have the man fall into the water?
12. What mistake does the man make in building his second fire? Why does he commit that error?
13. While his second fire is getting started, the man indulges in some distinctly prideful thoughts. Is pride his downfall? Explain.
14. How do we feel about the man as he struggles to build his third fire?
15. What is wrong with the man's plan to kill the dog, warm his hands in the dog's body, and then start another fire?
16. At one point the man crawls after the dog on all fours, like an animal; at another he feels that he is flying like the god Mercury. What do you think London means to imply by these comparisons?
17. Although the man readily accepts the likelihood that he will lose parts of his body to the frost, he refuses to acknowledge that he is going to die until nearly the end. Contrast his behavior before and after he makes that recognition.
18. By the end, does the man still lack imagination?
19. Explain the effect of the last paragraph's being narrated from the dog's point of view.

Topics for Writing

1. Write an essay contrasting the use of instinct and judgment in "To Build a Fire."
2. Discuss London's use of foreshadowing and repetition.
3. Discuss London's treatment of the partial source of the story, Jeremiah Lynch's *Three Years in the Klondike* (London, 1904). (Quoted in Franklin Walker, *Jack London and the Klondike*, pp. 256–57; see Suggested Readings, next page.)

4. After reading the story, make a list of the elements that compose it, such as *man, dog, cold, old-timer, fire, water,* and so on. Read it again, classifying each passage into the appropriate category or categories. Invent new categories as needed, but keep your list as short as possible. Draw a diagram showing how the elements are related. Does your diagram reveal or confirm anything about the meaning of the story?

5. Write a story or vignette involving a human being and an animal. Imitate London by telling part of it from the animal's point of view but without anthropomorphizing the animal in any way.

Suggested Readings

Labor, Earle. *Jack London.* Twayne's United States Authors Series 230. New York: Twayne, 1974. 63–70.

McClintock, James I. *White Logic: Jack London's Short Stories.* Grand Rapids, MI: Wolf House, 1975. 116–19.

Walker, Franklin. *Jack London and the Klondike: The Genesis of an American Writer.* San Marino, CA: Huntington Library, 1966. 254–60.

Lu Xun

Diary of a Madman (p. 923)

Translated by William A. Lyell

This story can serve the instructor as an excellent example of cross-cultural literature. American college students reading the story can get a feeling for what is considered important by their contemporaries in Chinese literature classes. Required reading in China for every college student, the story is regarded as a classic by Communist leaders today because its author has dramatized the need for his fellow citizens' continuing progress toward social enlightenment. Lu Xun acknowledges that progress is difficult because people instinctively resist change, but he urges the Chinese people to abandon the "old ways" of their prerevolutionary society and adopt more modern views. "Diary of a Madman" is also a fine example of cross-cultural literature because its Chinese author is so clearly influenced by the earlier "Diary of a Madman" written by the great Russian writer Nikolai Gogol, whom Lu Xun read while a student in Japan.

One must always be cautious when talking about the literary style of short fiction read in translation, but here the second footnote informs the reader that Lu Xun wrote the introductory section of his story "in classical Chinese, while the diary entries that follow are all in the colloquial language." This is an important point, since it suggests that in China short story literature written in the colloquial is a fairly recent phenomenon. Lu Xun is considered a pioneer in this form by Chinese literary historians. He made his use of colloquial language acceptable to his readers (who expected the entire story to be written in the more formal classical Chinese) by attributing his words to a man suffering from temporary insanity. An irony, of course, is that the "temporary" insanity of the story's unnamed protagonist has lasted for what should have been the most productive three decades of the man's life.

Another aspect of the cross-cultural element in "Diary of a Madman" is that Lu Xun is describing a society of cannibals. It is difficult for most people to imagine how cannibalism would be justified in any society, but Lu Xun has done it for us. Everyone around the madman in his story is reluctant to discuss the practice, yet apparently it happens all the time. A woman on the street who is angry at her son tells him, "Damn it all, you've got me so riled up I could take a good bite right out of your hide." Does she mean it literally? Or is she speaking metaphorically, her feelings of aggression beyond her control? "Diary of a Madman" is a fantasy story that can be read along with Shirley Jackson's "The Lottery" as a dramatization of how unexamined ritual behavior from the past can continue to influence contemporary social action.

Questions for Discussion

1. What is the setting of the story? In what year are the events taking place? Could you imagine it happening in contemporary China?
2. Who are the characters in the story? What do we know about the narrator? How do we know that the other characters think that he is ill?
3. How does the diary form of the story contribute to your sense that the narrator is suffering from mental illness? How reliable is he as a witness to what is going on among the people who live close to him?
4. How does section 10 of the story clarify the author's intent in writing it?

Topic for Writing

1. **CONNECTIONS** Compare and contrast "Diary of a Madman" with "The Lottery," analyzing the different ways the two authors use the elements of fiction to make the reader "suspend disbelief" in their fantasies.

Topic for an Oral Report

1. Read the work of a contemporary Chinese author of short stories and report on it to the class.

Suggested Readings

Lyell, William A. *Lu Hsun's Vision of Reality.* Berkeley: U of California P, 1976.
———. *Lu Xun's* Diary of a Madman *and Other Stories.* Honolulu: U of Hawaii P, 1990.

BERNARD MALAMUD

The Jewbird (p. 933)

A remarkable story of the effects of anti-Semitism, "The Jewbird" is an example of the literary genre of magical realism, like García Márquez's "A Very Old Man with Enormous Wings." Schwartz is a talking bird with a human personality, more humane in his relations with the family than Cohen, the father who bullies his wife, Edie, and son, Maurie, into doing what he wants. Malamud's perspective on the characters is compassionate (Cohen's mother is dying, after all, so no wonder he's on edge), but he reserves his full sympathy for Schwartz, the black crow who is the epitome of the Wandering Jew: homeless, hungry, and harried. As the Jewbird says, "I'm running. I'm flying but I'm also running."

The human characters in this story are drawn boldly. Cohen is the typical working-class father, belligerent and aggressive, insisting on his authority over his wife and son. Edie is the kind, dutiful wife, a clever shopper who fits herring for the bird into the family budget and gets her evening out at the movies every once in a while. Maurie is the Milquetoast son, shy of violence, slow in school, screechy on the violin. The setting is minimally sketched in, a Lower East Side Manhattan apartment, where the family eats in the kitchen. The plot moves swiftly through the exchange of dialogue between Schwartz and the three human characters. Malamud draws his characters, background, and action like a cartoonist, without subtlety but with clarity, vigor, and strength.

The poignancy of the situation lies in the character of the Jewbird. Anti-Semitism is primitive and crude, and it releases stronger feelings than those normally evoked in a domestic sitcom. Malamud takes pains to establish Schwartz's Jewish background — his name, his habits of prayer, food preferences, and language. There is no mistaking his authenticity. Schwartz speaks the Pidgin English (no bird pun intended) of old European Jews, who express themselves more comfortably in Yiddish. He speech is fully of homey metaphors: When the cat stops trying to get him, he tells Edie, "we will both be in Paradise." Malamud's point seems to be that there is a pecking order even among Jews. Edie knows that — and she has the final word in the story.

Questions for Discussion

1. Malamud compresses an enormous amount of information about the Cohen family into the opening paragraph. What do we know about the family by the end of this paragraph? What does a sentence like "The frozen foods salesman was sitting at supper with his wife and young son . . ." tell us about the kind of family this is? And what do you make of the first five sentences of this story? Who's speaking here? Notice how these sentences are all about the same length; what effect does that fact create? How are these ideas — "It's open, you're in. Closed, you're out and that's your fate" — attached to the Cohen family?
2. When Edie asks her husband what he has against the bird, Cohen replies "Poor bird, my ass. He's a foxy bastard. He thinks he's a Jew. . . . A Jewbird, what a chutzpah. One false move and he's out on his drumsticks." Look at

the other passages in this story where Cohen reviles the bird. What does he hate about Schwartz?

3. In the paragraph beginning "But the quarrel," the point of view suddenly shifts. Explain the reason for, and the effect of, this change.

4. Consider the following quotation: "So he ate the herring garnished with cat food, tried hard not to hear the paper bags bursting like fire crackers outside the birdhouse at night, and lived terror-stricken closer to the ceiling than the floor, as the cat, his tail flicking, endlessly watched him." Why do we laugh at this series of tortures, even as we grimace for Schwartz's pain?

5. Consider this exchange between Cohen and Schwartz:

   "For Christ sake, why don't you wash yourself sometimes? Why must you always stink like a dead fish?"

   "Mr. Cohen, if you'll pardon me, if somebody eats garlic he will smell from garlic. I eat herring three times a day. Feed me flowers and I will smell like flowers."

   Compare the form of address and the diction used by each speaker. How would you describe the tone of each speech? What effect does this exchange have on your assessment of each speaker?

6. What does Edie mean when she says "When the cat gets to know you better he won't try to catch you any more"? Schwartz doesn't believe this for a second: "When he stops trying we will both be in Paradise." Why would Edie say what she does, and why does Schwartz reject the idea? Are there some parallels between the cat and Cohen? What are the differences between them?

7. When Cohen finally kills Schwartz, we don't have any access to Schwartz's thoughts. Why might Malamud want to distance us from Schwartz in his final moments? What do we learn from having access to Cohen's mind?

8. Edie and Maurie don't get to say much in this story. Why would Malamud give Edie the last word? Is she correct in her assessment? Why does she speak using Schwartz's dialect?

Topics for Writing

1. Discuss Malamud's use of irony in the theme of anti-Semitism in "The Jewbird."

2. Discuss diction as a conveyor of theme and setting in "The Jewbird."

3. Study the story and list all the ways Malamud delineates Schwartz's Jewish character. Write a paragraph in which you discuss the importance of this characterization to the story.

4. **CONNECTIONS** Compare the uses of magical realism in Malamud's "The Jewbird" and García Márquez's "A Very Old Man with Enormous Wings."

Suggested Readings

Malamud, Bernard. "Long Work, Short Life." *Writers and Their Craft*. Ed. Nicholas Delbanco and Laurence Goldstein. Detroit: Wayne State UP, 1991.
———. *The Stories of Bernard Malamud*. New York: Farrar, 1983.
Stern, D. "Art of Fiction: Bernard Malamud." *Paris Review* 16 (1975): 41–64.

KATHERINE MANSFIELD

Bliss (p. 941)

The life that blooms in Bertha Young presses against the restraints of "idiotic civilization" like a blossom bursting out of its bud case. Through all the incidents leading up to the devastating revelation of the liaison between Harry and Pearl, Mansfield develops Bertha's flowerlike vulnerability. We are attracted by her tolerant and amused appreciation of her husband and guests, the delight she takes in her "absolutely satisfactory house and garden," and her love for Little B. But at the same time we must feel a growing anxiety for this young woman, who herself knows that she is "too happy — too happy!" She is so little in command of her life that she must beg Nanny for a chance to feed her own daughter; her catalog of the wonderful things in her life dwindles off into trivia ("their new cook made the most superb omelettes"); and her husband and "modern, thrilling friends" look to the skeptical eye of the reader more like *poseurs* and hypocrites than the charming and sincere eccentrics Bertha takes them for.

Mansfield defines Bertha's condition and the danger to which it exposes her in the explicit symbol of the pear tree in bloom, to which Bertha likens herself, and in the unsettling glimpse of the cats, a gray one and its black shadow, that creep across the lawn beneath it. On the telephone to Harry, Bertha tries and fails to communicate her state of bliss, but she hopes that her fascinating new "find," Pearl Fulton, with whom she feels a mysterious kinship, will somehow be able to understand. In the moonlight the pear tree resembles the silvery Pearl, just as in the daylight it matched Bertha's green and white apparel, and as the two women gaze at it together, Bertha feels that the ecstatic communion she has desired is taking place. And in a sense it is, for the moment seems to release in Bertha for the first time a passionate sexual desire for her husband that, as she too soon learns, is shared by Pearl.

The reader winces as the long-anticipated blow falls at last, and Eddie Warren intones the line that might end a more cynical version of the story: "'Why Must it Always be Tomato Soup?' It's so *deeply* true, don't you feel? Tomato soup is so *dreadfully* eternal." But Mansfield will not leave it there. As the gray cat Pearl and the black cat Eddie slink off into the night, Bertha returns to the window to find the pear tree, an embodiment of the same energy and beauty that wells up within herself, standing "as lovely as ever and as full of flower and as still."

WILLIAM E. SHEIDLEY

Questions for Discussion

1. Define the impression of Bertha given by the opening section. What is the source of her bliss?
2. What is the function of the scene in which Bertha feeds Little B? Comment on the way the section ends.
3. What does Bertha try and fail to say to Harry on the telephone?
4. What explains Pearl Fulton's limited frankness?
5. Do you agree that Harry's use of phrases like "liver frozen, my dear girl" or "pure flatulence" is an endearing, almost admirable quality? Why or why not?

6. Comment on the juxtaposition of the cats and the pear tree.
7. Can one be "too happy"? Explain.
8. Evaluate Bertha's summary of her situation. Does she indeed have "everything"?
9. Explain the line "Her petals rushed softly into the hall."
10. What techniques does Mansfield use to characterize the Knights and Eddie Warren? What do you think of these people?
11. Comment on the possible implications of Harry's delayed arrival, followed shortly by that of Pearl Fulton.
12. Why is Bertha eager for Pearl to "give a sign"?
13. What transpires as Bertha and Pearl look at the pear tree?
14. Explain Harry's way of offering a cigarette to Pearl and Bertha's interpretation of it.
15. Why does Bertha feel "that this self of hers was taking leave of them forever" as she bids farewell to her guests?
16. What is the effect of Eddie Warren's quoting a poem about tomato soup while the climax of the story takes place?
17. What *is* going to happen now?

Topics for Writing

1. Comment on the names in "Bliss."
2. Discuss the rebirth of Bertha Young.
3. Write an essay analyzing Mansfield's use of light and color in "Bliss."
4. The story is divided by white spaces into a number of sections. On your first reading, stop at each one of these spaces and write a few sentences addressed to Bertha Young. What would you say to her at each of those moments? When you have finished the story, review your previous advice and write one more letter to Bertha in response to her concluding question.
5. Study the way Mansfield characterizes Harry, the Knights, Eddie, and Pearl. Then write a character sketch of your own using some of the same techniques and devices.

Related Commentaries

Willa Cather, The Stories of Katherine Mansfield, p. 1440.
Katherine Mansfield, Review of Woolf's "Kew Gardens," p. 1500.

Suggested Readings

See page 170.

Katherine Mansfield

The Garden-Party (p. 951)

"The Garden-Party," like its protagonist, Laura Sheridan, is brimming with life. Mansfield's lush, sensual descriptions of the sights, sounds, smells, and tastes that are observed by Laura throughout the party preparations help to create a vibrant character filled with a childlike wonder and anticipation. Posed on the brink of adulthood, Laura sees and feels everything so intensely that we feel uneasy for her, sensing that some calamity, or at the very least some major disappointment, is waiting to shake her innocent dream of life's perfection.

For all her sensitivity and good nature, Laura appears, in the opening scenes, to be a typical upper-class young woman, delighted by the prospect of a party, and rather egocentric in her vision of such things as the cooperation of the weather and the blooming of the roses, and of the "absurdity" of the class distinction between herself and the workmen. She naively imagines that taking a bite of her bread and butter in front of these men makes her "just like a work-girl," but, as she will be reminded before the end of the story, there is a much greater difference between her life and that of a workgirl than a simple relaxation of stuffy manners and conventions. Laura is clearly glamorizing the lives of the working class in these imaginings, although it seems that she should know better. Later on, we discover that she and her brother have walked many times through the lane of cottages just below their home, where the poor live, because "one must go everywhere; one must see everything." While this is a perfect description of Laura's enthusiastic willingness to embrace life, we have to wonder what these excursions have really shown her, if she is so easily able to envision herself as a "workgirl."

It is the fate of the cottages that brings Laura's awakening to some of life's realities. The news of the accidental death of a young man from the lane intrudes on Laura's beautiful day. She reacts with characteristically intense emotion to the news, insisting that the party "must be called off." But she quickly discovers that she is the only one of her family and friends who is at all disturbed by the knowledge of the young man's death. In her exchanges with her sister and mother, she begins to discover just how deep are the class distinctions that she had scoffed at earlier. Her mother calmly states "people like that don't expect sacrifices from us," and that she "can't understand how they keep alive in those poky little holes" (as if they had any choice). Laura's sensitivity, which allows her to imagine the pain of the widow, and to recoil at the impropriety of the band playing and people laughing just yards from where a tragedy is occurring, is obviously not shared by her family. She is shaken and confused by the vast difference between her own instinctive sympathy and the cold lack of concern displayed by her mother and sister, but concludes that her mother "must be right," that it would be selfish and silly for her to "spoil the party" for everyone else, and decides to "think about it all later."

After the party, when Laura's mother, Mrs. Sheridan, is reminded of the unpleasant subject of the dead man by her husband, she has the "brilliant idea" of sending some of the leftover party food to the widow. Laura is repelled by this idea, which she finds too patronizing. But, after her own "extravagant" display of sympathy, she can't refuse when she is chosen to take the basket to the dead man's house. There, she has her first unromanticized view of the lives of the lower class, and an acutely painful realization of her own difference from them, as well as her first close-up view of death. However, it is in Laura's "encounter" with the dead man that the truly remarkable strength and beauty of her character emerges. For she is even able to empathize with the dead, to feel death from the man's point of view, a "marvelous" state of peace, rest, and beauty. Laura sees death, in a very realistic but highly unusual way for one so young, as just another aspect of the wondrous, overwhelming beauty and mystery of life.

Questions for Discussion

1. How would you characterize Laura after reading the scene where she "supervises" the workmen?
2. Does your vision of Laura change as the story progresses? Trace the development of her character through the major incidents of the story.
3. How do you think Laura's mother and sisters see her? What do you think creates the close bond between her and her brother Laurie?
4. What is the effect of the detailed, highly sensual description of the setting? How does it contribute to your understanding of Laura as a character?
5. Do you think the party should have been canceled? Why or why not?
6. How do you react to Laura's mother and sister Jose as characters? Compare them to Laura.
7. How do you think the mourners feel about Laura's visit to deliver the food basket? Is the sense that she was "expected" all in Laura's mind? Do the people show any resentment?
8. Were you surprised by Laura's reaction to the dead man? Discuss her attitude toward death. Is it consistent with other things that you have learned about her character?

Topics for Writing

1. Analyze "The Garden-Party" as a story of maturation and development.
2. Discuss Laura's desire to be just like "a work-girl."
3. **CONNECTIONS** Compare and discuss the imagery in "The Garden-Party" and "Bliss."

Related Commentaries

Willa Cather, The Stories of Katherine Mansfield, p. 1440.
Katherine Mansfield, Review of Woolf's "Kew Gardens," p. 1500.

Suggested Readings

Boddy, Gill. *Katherine Mansfield: The Woman and the Writer.* New York: Penguin, 1988.
Fullbrook, Kate. *Katherine Mansfield.* Muskogee: Indiana UP, 1986.
Hanson, Clare, ed. *The Critical Writings of Katherine Mansfield.* New York: St. Martin's, 1987.

Kobler, Jasper F. *Katherine Mansfield: A Study of the Short Fiction.* Boston: G. K. Hall, 1990.

Mansfield, Katherine. *Journal of Katherine Mansfield.* New York: Ecco, 1983.

O'Sullivan, Vincent, and Margaret Scott. *The Collected Letters of Katherine Mansfield.* New York: Oxford UP, 1987.

Rohrberger, Mary H. *The Art of Katherine Mansfield.* Ann Arbor, MI: UMI, 1977.

BOBBIE ANN MASON

Shiloh (p. 964)

The trip to Shiloh is supposed to be a second honeymoon for Leroy and Norma Jean Moffitt, a chance for them to start their marriage all over again, as Leroy says, "right back at the beginning." The trouble is, as Norma Jean is quick to point out to her husband, they had already started all over again after his tractor-trailer accident brought him home for good, and "this is how it turned out."

It's a topsy-turvy world in Mason's story. Husbands are hurt so they take up needlepoint; housewives are self-reliant so they study composition at community college when they aren't working at the drugstore. Thirty-four-year-old "girls" like Norma Jean irrationally turn on their mothers after years of obedience just because their mothers catch them smoking cigarettes. And yet it's a familiar world to readers of fiction by women authors about women's domestic rebellion these past fifteen years: Erica Jong's *Fear of Flying*, Sue Kauffman's *Diary of a Mad Housewife,* and Lisa Alther's *Kinflicks,* for example. Norma Jean might scoff at her husband's suggestion that she has been influenced by the feminist movement — he asks her, "Is this one of those women's lib things?" — but he's no fool. She probably wouldn't have told him she was going to leave him if Betty Friedan hadn't published *The Feminine Mystique* and helped bring a feminist consciousness back to America about the time Norma Jean married her high school sweetheart, Leroy Moffitt.

The old patriarchal consciousness still permeates the story, of course, since this consciousness has a tight hold on the mate and the older fictional characters. Norma Jean is introduced in the first sentence as "Leroy Moffitt's wife, Norma Jean." The story is told in the present tense, making the reader aware of the slow passage of time for the characters caught in a static way of life, as mother Mabel says, "just waiting for time to pass." But Norma Jean feels the need for change. The opening of "Shiloh" is one of the most exhilarating first sentences in contemporary American short fiction. "Leroy Moffitt's wife, Norma Jean, is working on her pectorals." Used to be only boys lifted weights to build up their muscles. Now opportunity beckons even for a thirty-four-year-old married woman who bakes cream-of-mushroom casseroles. She doesn't want to be known as somebody's wife, a hackneyed first name between two commas evoking the more famous "real" name of a departed sex goddess from an era before Betty Friedan.

We don't know much about what she's thinking, this fictional Norma Jean, because Mason has structured the story so that her husband's consciousness and feelings are in the forefront. Through his confusion about what's happening with his wife, the reader senses that probably at this point Norma Jean doesn't know exactly what she wants herself, beyond wanting to break free. On their trip to Shiloh she walks rapidly away from Leroy to stand alone on a bluff by the river. He sees her waving her arms, and he can't tell if she's beckoning him or doing another exercise for her pectorals. One thing they both know is that she won't be needing the dust ruffle his mother-in-law made for their marital bed. If this Wonder Woman has her way, she won't be pushing her jogging shoes under her husband's couch or hiding the dust under his bed one day longer than she has to.

Questions for Discussion

1. After reading the story, look back at the first five paragraphs. What do they say about Norma Jean and Leroy's relationship? Does the rest of the story bear out the opening moment?

2. On the first page we discover that, through building an array of kits, "Leroy has grown to appreciate how things are put together." How does his fascination with building comment on Leroy's marriage? What is the impulse behind building the log cabin? How would you compare Leroy's hobby with Norma Jean's interests?

3. In this passage Mason introduces the background of the Moffitts' marriage: "Perhaps he reminds her too much of the early days of their marriage, before he went on the road. They had a child who died as an infant, years ago. They never speak about their memories of Randy, which have almost faded, but now that Leroy is home all the time, they sometimes feel awkward around each other, and Leroy wonders if one of them should mention the child. He has the feeling that they are waking up out of a dream together — that they must create a new marriage, start afresh. They are lucky they are still married. Leroy has read that for most people losing a child destroys the marriage." The figure of a dead child might be expected to haunt the couple in this story. Does the child control their present actions? We discover later that Randy would be sixteen now, so Leroy has been away from home, basically, for sixteen years. What difference does his sudden presence make to the marriage?

4. "When the first movie ended, the baby was dead. . . . A dead baby feels like a sack of flour." Usually, a subject like the death of infants evokes a particular kind of rhetoric, laden with sentimentality and tragedy. How would you describe these two sentences? Why doesn't the narrator use some euphemisms for death? What effect do these perceptions create? How do these sentences influence your assessment of Leroy's character?

5. Although the title emphasizes the importance of "Shiloh," we don't hear anything about it until page 967, when Mabel Beasley says, "I still think before you get tied down y'all ought to take a little run to Shiloh." What does Shiloh represent for Mabel? What does history itself mean to Leroy and Norma Jean? Can they articulate their shared history? Consider the passage about the baby on page 970.

6. When Norma Jean tells Leroy she's leaving him, he asks her, "Is this one of those women's lib things?" Is this a story about feminism? Consider the point of view; discuss the ideology apparent in the opening line of the story. What do we know about Norma Jean's feelings? Consider how a descriptive sentence such as "She is doing goose steps" gives us some access into her emotional life. How would you describe Mabel Beasley within a feminist framework?

7. How does Leroy's opinion that "nobody knows anything. . . . The answers are always changing" comment on the themes of this story?
8. Leroy concludes that "the real inner workings of a marriage, like most of history, have escaped him." This seems like a poignant realization in the face of Norma Jean's departure. Does Leroy assign blame for the dissolution of his marriage? Does this knowledge imply that he will be able to forge a new, vital marriage with Norma Jean? Is the final paragraph hopeful? What do you make of Leroy's inability to distinguish between Norma Jean's exercise and her signals?

Topics for Writing

1. In an interview Bobbie Ann Mason gave to Lila Havens, she said she's more interested in the male characters in her stories than in the females. How has she selected the details of "Shiloh" to portray Norma Jean's husband, Leroy Moffitt, with compassion?
2. Discuss Mason's use of details to enrich the story's reality.
3. **CONNECTIONS** Compare and contrast the theme of alienation in Mason's "Shiloh" and Lawrence's "Odour of Chrysanthemums."

Related Commentary

Bobbie Ann Mason, On Tim O'Brien's "The Things They Carried," p. 1502.

Suggested Readings

Reed, J. D. "Postfeminism: Playing for Keeps." *Time* 10 Jan. 1983: 61.
Ryan, Maureen. "Stopping Places: Bobbie Ann Mason's Short Stories." *Women Writers of the Contemporary South.* Ed. Peggy Whitman Prenshaw. Jackson: UP of Mississippi, 1984. 283–94.
Smith, W. "Publisher's Weekly Interviews." *Publisher's Weekly* 30 Aug. 1985: 424–25.

GUY DE MAUPASSANT

The Necklace (p. 976)

"The Necklace" has long been one of the most popular of Maupassant's stories, and one of the most interesting aspects of the story is this popularity, since artistically it is far from his best. The story is little more than an anecdote. Mme. Loisel, a woman from the lower middle class, is deeply dissatisfied with her station in life. As she sits down to dinner with her husband — a "little clerk at the Ministry of Public Instructions" — she thinks of "dainty dinners, of shining silverware, of tapestry which peopled the walls with ancient personages and with strange birds in the middle of a fairy forest."

Her husband, sensing her unhappiness, gets a ticket for a grand ball, and, when she is miserable at not having a fine dress, he gives her money he has been saving for a gun and a shooting holiday with his friends. When she is still unhappy at not having jewels, he suggests she borrow some from a wealthy friend, Mme. Forestier. Mme. Loisel borrows what she thinks is a diamond necklace, is a great success at the ball, but loses the necklace on the way home.

Too ashamed to tell the friend what has happened, the couple borrow money to buy a diamond necklace like the one that was lost. They return the necklace and slowly repay the loan. After ten years, during which the wife has become "the woman of impoverished households — strong and hard and rough," she accidentally meets Mme. Forestier and learns that she had lent her only a paste copy of a diamond necklace. Mme. Loisel and her husband have destroyed their lives for nothing.

Unlike in his finest stories, Maupassant here stays on the surface of the characters. Mme. Forestier and Mme. Loisel's husband are only faintly sketched; they seem to exist merely to act out roles. The anecdote itself is so implausible that a single question — why didn't Mme. Forestier notice that a different necklace had been returned to her? why did M. Loisel allow his life to be destroyed without a protest? — would bring it to earth. But most readers are willing to suspend their disbelief.

When we place the story in the time it was written, its themes stand out even more sharply. On its most obvious level this is one of the tales of moral instruction that were so widespread in nineteenth-century popular literature. Mme. Loisel's dreams of clothes and jewels represent the sin of vanity, and someone who has such dreams must be punished. The punishment inflicted on the woman and her husband is memorably out of proportion to their sin, the better to serve as a warning to those reading the story for moral instruction.

A second theme, which may be less obvious to the contemporary reader, is that Mme. Loisel has dreamed of moving to a higher social level. French society was rigidly structured, and Mme. Loisel's ambitions represented a threat, however vague, to the story's privileged audience. They would, of course, want to see her punished for this ambition.

These facts help to explain why the story was so widely read when it was written — but for today's readers other factors seem to be at work. For example, to one young student the necklace became the symbol for everything the world of adults represents. Perhaps it is the story's weaknesses — its implausible simplicities, the lack of definition of its minor characters, the trite obviousness of Mme. Loisel's yearning, and the pious cruelty of her punishment — that make it possible for other generations to give "The Necklace" their own interpretation.

Questions for Discussion

1. Do we use anecdotes like "The Necklace" to point out moral lessons today? What other examples of this kind of moral instruction can you think of in popular literature?
2. How did an evening at a ball offer Mme. Loisel a chance to present herself in a new guise?
3. What do we learn from the story about the structure of French society at the time "The Necklace" was written?

4. What symbols for wealth and station could be used in a story like this written for today?

Topics for Writing

1. Analyze the symbolic implications of the necklace.
2. Consider the contrast between the lives of Mme. Loisel and her friend Mme. Forestier.

Related Commentaries

Kate Chopin, How I Stumbled upon Maupassant, p. 1448.
Guy de Maupassant, The Writer's Goal, p. 1504.

Related Story

Henry James, Paste, p. 976.

Suggested Readings

Fusco, Richard A. "Maupassant and the Turn of the Century American Short Story." *Dissertation Abstracts International* 51.5 (Nov. 1990): 1612A.
James, Henry. *Tales of Art and Life.* Schenectady, NY: Union College P, 1984.
Lohafer, Susan, ed. *Short Story Theory at a Crossroads.* Baton Rouge: Louisiana State UP, 1989. 276–98.
Los Angeles Public Library Staff. *Index to the Stories of Guy de Maupassant.* Boston: G. K. Hall, 1970.
McCrory, Donald. "Maupassant: Problems of Interpretation." *Modern Languages: Journal of the Modern Language Association* 70.1 (Mar. 1989): 39–43.
Poteau-Tralie, Mary L. "Voices of Authority: The Criminal Obsession in Guy de Maupassant's Short Works." *Dissertation Abstracts International* 52.4 (Oct. 1991): 1353A.
Traill, Nancy Helen. "The Fantastic for the Realist: The Paranormal Fictions of Dickens, Turgenev, and Maupassant." *Dissertation Abstracts International* 50.9 (Mar. 1990): 2891A.
Troyat, Henri. *Maupassant.* Paris: Flammarion, 1989.

HERMAN MELVILLE

Bartleby, the Scrivener (p. 984)

Many students have trouble reading this story because they cannot accept what they consider the weirdness of Bartleby's character. On first reading, the story seems to yield this interpretation. Shortly after it appeared in the November and December issues of *Putnam's Monthly Magazine* in 1853, for example, Richard

Henry Dana Sr. wrote to Melville's friend Evert Duyckinck saying that he admired the skill involved in creating the character of Bartleby because "the secret power of such an inefficient and harmless creature over his employer, who all the while has a misgiving of it, shows no common insight." Dana's interpretation will probably also be the way 99 percent of present-day college students will respond to the story, sharing his lack of sympathy for Bartleby.

The question is: Did Melville intend the readers of his story to feel this way? Why did he conclude his tale with the lines "Ah, Bartleby! Ah, humanity!"?

Most sympathetic literary critics see this story as Melville's attempt to dramatize the complex question of an individual's obligation to society. Like the dead letters that Bartleby burned in his previous job after they were no longer needed, his life ends when he is no longer useful to his employer. What standards should we use to judge someone's worth? How should we view those who no longer accept the world they are offered?

Questions for Discussion

1. How does the narrator's viewpoint affect your feelings toward Bartleby? What details particularly influence you one way or the other?
2. Do your feelings toward Bartleby change when the narrator reveals Bartleby's previous job in the Dead Letter Office?
3. How does Melville's humorous description of the two other clerks in the law office relieve his heavy presentation of the Wall Street setting? How do these minor characters set off each other, the lawyer, and Bartleby?
4. Do you ever feel like saying "I would prefer not to" in reply to figures of authority? What do you do when you feel a bit of Bartleby in you?

Topics for Writing

1. Explicate the paragraph beginning "For the first time in my life a feeling of overpowering stinging melancholy seized me." A close reading of this passage may bring you closer to realizing the complexity of Melville's portrayal of the lawyer's relationship to Bartleby.
2. Analyze the conclusion of the story. How can Bartleby's life be compared to a dead letter?
3. This story has an unusually prolonged and discursive exposition before the title character is introduced. Also, Melville doesn't motivate his behavior until the end of the story, after he is dead and the lawyer finds out about his previous job. Breaking the customary rules of starting a short story with a brief exposition and motivating the characters as they are introduced, Melville might be accused of writing a poorly structured tale. Argue for or against this accusation, remembering that the short-story genre was in its infancy when Melville wrote "Bartleby, the Scrivener."
4. Read the excerpt from Melville's review of Hawthorne's *Mosses from an Old Manse* (p. 1505), discussing what Melville calls "the power of blackness" in Hawthorne's tales. Can you find the same "power of blackness" in Melville's description of Bartleby's situation?

Related Commentaries

Herman Melville, Blackness in Hawthorne's "Young Goodman Brown," p. 1505.
J. Hillis Miller, A Deconstructive Reading of Melville's "Bartleby, the Scrivener,"
p. 1507.

Suggested Readings

Boswell, Jeanetta. *Herman Melville and the Critics: A Checklist of Criticism.* Metuchen,
NJ: Scarecrow, 1981.
Budd, Louis J., and Edwin H. Cady, eds. *On Melville.* Durham, NC: Duke UP,
1988.
Dillingham, W. B. *Melville's Short Fiction, 1853–1856.* Athens: U of Georgia P, 1977.
Fogle, R. H. *Melville's Shorter Tales.* Norman: U of Oklahoma P, 1960.
Freeman, John. *Herman Melville.* Brooklyn, NY: Haskell, 1974.
Higgins, Brian. *Herman Melville: A Reference Guide, 1931–1960.* Boston: G. K. Hall,
1987.
Inge, M. Thomas, ed. *Bartleby the Inscrutable: A Collection of Commentary on Herman
Melville's Tale "Bartleby the Scrivener."* Hamden, CT: Shoe String, 1979.
McCall, Dan. *The Silence of Bartleby.* Ithaca, NY: Cornell UP, 1989.
Melville, Herman. *Correspondence.* Evanston, IL: Northwestern UP, 1991.
———. *Pierre, The Piazza Tales and Uncollected Prose.* New York: Library of America,
1984.
Vincent, H. P., ed. *"Bartleby the Scrivener": Melville Annual for 1965.* Kent, OH: Kent
State UP, 1967. Includes Henry Murray's "Bartleby and I," 3–24.
Whitehead, Fred A. "Melville's 'Bartleby the Scrivener': A Case Study." *New York
State Journal of Medicine* 90 (Jan. 1990): 17–22.

Yukio Mishima

Swaddling Clothes (p. 1011)

Mishima's story is a classic third-person narrative in which the author re-
moves himself entirely from the action. We are conscious of his presence only as
an omniscient observer. By the end of the first paragraph, however, Mishima has
already set the story in motion by telling us that the female protagonist is afraid
to return to her house, not only because it is Western in style and uncomfortable,
but also because there are bloodstains on the floor. A sentence later we are told
that the woman is oversensitive. This combination of circumstances is enough to
give us the emotional setting for the story. The events of the night have been so
shocking, however, that even someone who is not oversensitive would be disturbed — disturbed enough to act irrationally in the same way that the woman,
Toshiko, acts.

As the students have learned from the headnote to the story, Mishima was
a complex man with a fascination for violence. For Japanese readers his most
famous story is "Patriotism," a minutely described ritual double suicide, and his
own life ended in a successful attempt to disembowel himself while a young

follower struggled to behead him. There is nothing in the ending of the story to tell us that the young wife will be harmed by the beggar she has surprised sleeping on the park bench, but Mishima has already planted the idea of a knife and a stabbing for us. The shock of the story is Toshiko's numbed belief that twenty years have gone by and that the man on the bench is the child she had seen born on her floor only a few hours earlier to her maidservant.

Although the central theme of the story is the wife's horror at what she has seen and its effect on her consciousness, there is a subtheme in the author's emphasis on her husband's adoption of Western ideas, which to the husband simply means abandoning his wife every evening and forcing her to live in a style of house she finds foreign and uncomfortable. Mishima believed passionately in the purity of Japanese traditions, and he went to his death attacking the softening of the Japanese character under the influence of Western ideas. A traditional husband would have been a shelter and a support for his wife, and a traditional family would never have gotten themselves into their situation. Mishima leaves it to the reader to decide if the wife will also pay for her husband's abandonment of Japanese ideals, but he has so skillfully presented his story that we cannot help believing that the man on the bench does have a knife and that Toshiko will meet the fate she envisioned.

Questions for Discussion

1. Discuss some of the examples of "Westernism" that the author describes.
2. Would a couple such as the actor and his wife really believe in "gastric dilation"?
3. What does it tell us about the husband that he says to his friends that he had "rescued" the good rug?
4. Is the wife being overly emotional in her inability to forget the sight of the newborn baby wrapped in bloody newspapers?
5. The author writes, "[n]o doubt Toshiko derived a certain satisfaction from her somber thoughts." Is Mishima suggesting that what will happen to Toshiko is in some way something that she deserves?
6. When the man seizes her wrist, is her reaction a rational acceptance of what is happening to her, or could it be a shock of terror?

Topics for Writing

1. Discuss the cultural clash that is part of the woman's dilemma, using examples from the story.
2. Write an additional scene about what happens to Toshiko in the park in order to create a closed ending to Mishima's story.

Suggested Readings

Boardman, Gwenn R. "Greek Hope and Japanese Samurai: Mishima's New Aesthetic." *Critique* 12 (1970): 103–15.

Enright, D. J. "Mishima's Way." *Encounter* 36 (1971): 57–61.

Falk, Ray. "Yukio Mishima." *Saturday Review* 16 May 1959: 29.

Mishima, Yukio. *Acts of Worship.* Trans. and with an introduction by John Bester. Tokyo: Kodansha International, 1989.

———. *Death in Midsummer and Other Stories.* New York: New Directions, 1966.

Seidensticker, Edward. "Mishima Yukio." *Hudson Review* 24 (1971): 272–82.

Spurling, J. "Death in Hero's Costume: The Meaning of Mishima." *Encounter* 44 (1975): 56+.

Ueda, Makoto. "Mishima Yukio." *Modern Japanese Writers and the Nature of Literature.* Stanford: Stanford UP, 1976. 219–59.

LORRIE MOORE

How to Become a Writer (p. 1016)

Students reading this humorous story may regard it as a mirror reflecting a "sitcom" version of themselves. It is as familiar as an empty Diet Coke can. The setting of the story is both nonexistent and omnipresent: parents on the verge of divorce, a son in the armed services, a kid sister who's good with little kids. Life swirls around, full of plot action, and what's a crazy girl who wants to become a writer to do? The answer for this affluent family: Advance one painless step — go on to college.

The girl attends college as a child psychology major. Nothing much happens there except a fateful accident: A computer erroneously assigns the girl to a creative writing class instead of "The Ornithological Field Trip" on Tuesdays and Thursdays at 2 P.M. So begins her apprenticeship to her craft, for which she shows more enthusiasm than talent. She apparently never reads short fiction, yet she tries very hard to write it. After graduation, she flirts briefly with the idea of law school before settling for slow starvation at home. Her kind, divorced mother is resigned: "Sure you like to write. Of course. Sure you like to write."

Moore's decision to tell the story in the second person gives her narrative its sense of immediacy. Her sense of humor does the rest, as she carves and serves up her tender victim, a sacrifice to the creative spirit that lives within us all.

Questions for Discussion

1. What is the irony involved in the girl's inability to find good plots for her stories, in the light of her parents' troubled marriage and her brother's military service in Vietnam?
2. Judging from the girl's behavior in her writing classes, does she show any talent? Are creative writing classes in college a good place to find out if one can write?
3. What does Moore gain by organizing her story chronologically?
4. Do you think that the fragments the girl keeps in a folder can be developed into good stories?
5. How does the detail the girl notices about her date at the end of the story suggest that she might have the talent to become a writer after all?

Topic for Writing

1. Moore's story is a goldmine of possibilities for writing other stories. For example, experiment with the point of view of her narrative — rewrite it in the first or the third person. Or, develop her fragments into short stories of your own, humorous if possible, tragic if not.

Suggested Reading

Moore, Lorrie. *Self-Help.* New York: Knopf, 1985.

Bharati Mukherjee

The Management of Grief (p. 1022)

Bharati Mukherjee cites Moghul miniature painting, with "its insistence that everything happens simultaneously, bound only by shape and color," as a model for her fiction. This "sense of the interpenetration of all things" informs "The Management of Grief," which initially situates the reader among a rather bewildering array of characters and actions. Gradually we become aware that Shaila Bhave, who narrates the story, has recently lost her husband and two sons in a plane crash. The disoriented quality of her narrative ("A woman I don't know is boiling tea the Indian way in my kitchen") mirrors the state of her mind as she struggles to make sense of her loss, focusing on memories and odd details. The abruptness of our entry into the story suggests the abruptness of tragedy itself. Kusum, the similarly bereaved neighbor, voices the question that might occur to anyone afflicted with such loss: "Why does God give so much if all along He intends to take it away?"

Mukherjee asks us to consider the manner in which various characters cope with grief. The community looks toward Mrs. Bhave as "a pillar" because she has "taken it more calmly," but she is troubled by her inability to grieve outwardly, referring to herself as "a freak." Her equanimity, we learn, is due as much to Valium as to inner strength. With the help of the drug she is able to "manage" her grief in a way that may be ultimately less healthy than that of the relatives who express their grief more openly. While in Ireland waiting to identify bodies, she admits, "I haven't eaten in four days, haven't brushed my teeth." By the end of the story Shaila experiences a visitation on the streets of Toronto by her departed husband and sons, who urge her, "Go, be brave." While the experience may be interpreted in a positive light, a transition in her grieving process, it also may be seen as an aural hallucination, the result of her mixing tranquilizers in her distraught emotional state. Her dropping her package and directionless walking suggest purposelessness and lack of direction.

While personal tragedy commands center stage in this story, cultural vectors play out across the background. The crash may have been caused by a Sikh bomb. Judith Templeton, the culturally naive social worker, persuades Shaila to try to convince a grieving Sikh couple to take advantage of available aid.

Templeton, while meaning well, has little sensitivity to the cultural and political complications of the situation, and she overlooks the difficulty of the position for which she recruits Shaila — that of helping a potential enemy. The plane crash pulls the relatives, now well assimilated into Canada, back to India and the old ways, which cling with more tenacity than they may have realized.

Questions for Discussion

1. At one point, Shaila observes, "Like my husband's spirit, I flutter between worlds." What does she mean?
2. Review the India section of the story. In what ways have the characters changed in moving from India to Canada?
3. Do you detect a pattern of inhibited emotional response in Shaila? If so, to what extent may this pattern be culturally induced?

Topic for Writing

1. Discuss the grieving processes and coping mechanisms of the various characters. Is Shaila as healthy and calm as she outwardly appears to be? What does Dr. Ranganathan mean when he says, "We've been melted down and recast as a new tribe"? Do the relatives experience successive stages of grief?

Suggested Readings

Boxill, Anthony. "Women and Migration in Some Short Stories of Bharati Mukherjee and Neil Bissoondath." *Literary Half Yearly* 32.2 (July 1991): 43–50.

Mukherjee, Bharati. *The Middleman and Other Stories.* New York: Grove, 1988.

Nelson, Emmanuel S. *Bharati Mukherjee: Critical Perspectives.* New York: Garland, 1993.

———. "Kamala Markandaya, Bharati Mukherjee and the Indian Immigrant Experience." *Toronto South Asian Review* 9.2 (Winter 1991): 1–9.

ALICE MUNRO

Meneseteung (p. 1035)

Alice Munro's richly detailed story shifts subtly between two levels of presentation. On one level it is a story deeply rooted in the earlier genre of "local color" fiction, and the action of the story fits the expected restrictions and explications of the genre. On another level, however, it is a modern story, with a modern consciousness, and Munro shifts with casual skill from one level to the other. The older story is entirely plausible, and her contemporary response to the inner narrative is just as convincing. Look, Munro seems to be saying to her readers, this is what happened to a woman living alone in a small town long ago, and although we see her tragedy now from a modern perspective, we still must respect the attitudes and the social mores that she herself felt guided her life.

Munro's story is so convincing in its setting that we are surprised by her final paragraph, when she tells us, "I may have got it wrong. I don't know if she took laudanum. Many ladies did. I don't know if she ever made grape jelly." The author maintains that she has gotten most of her story from a collection of poetry and notices in an old newspaper, but these, like everything else, are fictional, including the skillful examples of Almeda's poetry and the quotation from "her" autobiographical sketch. An indication to the modern reader that this is not a story from an earlier period is Munro's awareness that we really don't know what life was like in a small western Canadian town in the 1880s. She spends several paragraphs describing the town's appearance and the way of life of its people and giving a short summary of its history up to that point, without interrupting the narrative. Also, although the emotional life of her heroine is lived within the rigid confines of nineteenth-century women's lives that we recognize from the American local color writers of the same period, such as Sarah Orne Jewett, Munro includes details such as Almeda's difficulty with menstrual pain and the prevalence of opiates in medicines prescribed for women that the older writers kept hidden from their readers.

Although "Meneseteung" is a story, its stylistic approach could properly be termed novelistic. We are given much detail about the characters' lives and attitudes. If Munro had chosen to develop the threads she has spun for us, the story would have become a novel, especially since she follows the lives of her two protagonists beyond the moment of revelation, when Jarvis understands that he could marry again and Almeda realizes that marriage, for her, is emotionally impossible. Because of this larger emotional field, Munro's characters and their barren history linger in our memory.

Students might also notice the suggestion that Almeda has turned to writing because of her isolation and her complex relationship with her father. They could compare this description of a young woman beginning to write with the woman who tells her own story in Margaret Laurence's "The Mask of the Bear." She also has begun to write out of a sense of isolation and alienation from the life around her. The most revealing detail in Munro's description of her heroine is the hat Almeda wears in the portrait in the collection of her poems. The hat is "untrimmed, shapeless . . . , something of a soft beret, that makes me see artistic intentions, or at least a shy and stubborn eccentricity." It is the only gesture of freedom that Munro's heroine allows herself.

Questions for Discussion

1. Discuss the point of view of the story, with special attention to the dual level of narrative that Munro maintains throughout.
2. Are the poetic quotations, written by Munro, typical of genteel verse of the period? What does the poetry reveal about the restraints and boundaries of the life of the writer?
3. When Almeda writes of the Canadian West of the 1850s, what part of Canada is she writing about?
4. What is the author telling us when she says of Jarvis Coulter, "A man may keep his house decent, but he will never — if he is a proper man — do much to decorate it"?

5. What is the author telling us when she says of Almeda, "naturally she is in better shape than most married women of her age"?
6. What is the nerve medicine the doctor has prescribed? What are its ingredients?
7. When Almeda tells Jarvis that she cannot meet him to walk to church, is it because of the agitation of the day's events or is it the natural culmination of the life she has led?
8. Is the newspaper's circumspect description of her final years a criticism of her actions, or an acceptance of the difficulties of her loneliness and emotional isolation?
9. Discuss the implications of the story's final paragraph.

Topics for Writing

1. Discuss the institution of marriage as it is described in the story, and compare it to the modern view of marriage.
2. Analyze the life of the town that Munro describes, emphasizing the social differences in the rich and the poor parts of town and the separate lives of men and women.
3. **CONNECTIONS** Compare this story to another story of women's lives during this period, either Sarah Orne Jewett's "A White Heron" or Mary E. Wilkins Freeman's "The Revolt Of 'Mother.'"

Suggested Readings

Bardolph, Jacqueline, ed. *Short Fiction in the New Literature in English: Proceedings. of the Nice Conference of the European Association for the Common Wealth Literature and Language Studies.* Nice: Faculté des Lettres et Sciences Humaines de Nice, 1989. 141–51.

Blodgett, E. D. *Alice Munro.* Boston: Twayne, 1988.

Carrington, Ildiko de Papp. *Controlling the Uncontrollable: The Fiction of Alice Munro.* DeKalb: Northern Illinois UP, 1989.

Hanson, Clare, ed. *Rereading the Short Story.* New York: St. Martin's, 1989. 65–85.

Jansen, Reamy. "Being Lonely: Dimensions of the Short Story." *Crosscurrents* 39.4 (Winter 1989–90): 391–401, 419.

MacKendrick, Louis K., ed. *Probable Fictions: Alice Munro's Narrative Acts.* Downsview, ONT: ECW, 1983.

Martin, W. R. *Alice Munro: Paradox and Parallel.* Edmonton: U of Alberta P, 1987.

Miller, Judith. *The Art of Alice Munro: Saying the Unsayable: Papers from the Waterloo Conference.* Madison: U of Wisconsin P, 1984.

Munro, Alice. *Selected Stories.* New York: Knopf, 1996.

Nischik, Reingard M., ed. *Modes of Narrative: Approaches to American, Canadian, and British Fiction.* Wurzburg: Konigshausen, 1990. 110–18, 141–52.

Rasporich, Beverly J. *Dance of the Sexes: Art and Gender in the Fiction of Alice Munro.* Edmonton: U of Alberta P, 1990.

Stich, K. P., ed. *Reflections: Autobiography and Canadian Literature.* Ottawa: U of Ottawa P, 1988. 176.

JOYCE CAROL OATES

Where Are You Going, Where Have You Been? (p. 1052)

Pointing to Oates's remark that she usually writes "about real people in a real society" should help to keep discussion away from premature allegorization or mythologizing, which — for all its eventual value and interest — smothers the story's impact by diverting attention from its realism. Her further observation that she understands Connie to be "struggling heroically to define personal identity in the face of incredible opposition, even in the face of death itself," may suggest how to go about answering the main question the story poses when considered in naturalistic terms: Why does Connie go out to Arnold Friend?

Connie's life as Oates depicts it takes place in two realms. Within her home and family Connie feels condemned and rejected, and she returns the disapproval. Outside these familiar precincts lies a world defined by movies, the drive-in restaurant, and the ever-present popular music. It is *not* the music of Bob Dylan, as Tom Quirk assures us, but the comparatively mindless, sentimental, and romantic music against which in the early 1960s Dylan stood out in such bold contrast. Connie's idea of the world into which, at the age of fifteen, she is beginning to make her first tentative forays is shaped by these songs and occupied by *boys*: boys who can be snubbed with impunity, boys who merge into one undifferentiated and safe blur in her mind, boys who offer hamburgers and "the caresses of love." And that love is "not the way someone like June would suppose but sweet, gentle, the way it was in movies and promised in songs." To these boys Connie presents herself as undifferentiated *girl,* and she is concerned that she look attractive to them.

The world, however, is occupied not only by frank and tentative boys but also by determined and deceitful men, by evil as well as by innocence, by hypocrisy, perversion, and violence — an exponent of all of which Connie attracts in Arnold Friend. Although in the course of their interview Connie sees through his disguise, the impoverishment of her world provides her no way to resist his advances. Her home offers no refuge, her father does not come when she needs him (he has always been essentially absent anyway), and she is unable to manipulate the telephone because of her panic. Meanwhile, Arnold, who presents himself in the guise of a movie hero, a teenage "boy," and her lover, offers to take charge of her. He places his mark upon her and gives her a role to play in a world of his devising. Because she is cut off from her past and has no idea of a future, she is at his mercy in determining what to do in the present. Like her cultural cousin, Vladimir Nabokov's Lolita, sobbing in Humbert's arms, she simply has nowhere else to go. Not only does Arnold show Connie that she is desired, he also provides her a way to be "good": By going with him she will save her undeserving family from getting hurt. Connie does not so much decide to go out to Arnold as she watches an alien being that Arnold has called into existence in her body respond to his desires. The final ironic horror, of course, is that she will be raped and murdered and buried in the desert not as brown-eyed Connie but as the imaginary "sweet little blue-eyed girl" of Arnold's sick imagination.

Oates acknowledges that her inspiration for the story came in part from reading about an actual case, and Tom Quirk has demonstrated at length the degree to which the circumstances of "Where Are You Going, Where Have You Been?"

seem to be derived from an article in *Life* (4 Mar. 1955) by Don Moser titled (in a reference to some lyrics from a popular song) "The Pied Piper of Tucson." Even some of the most apparently allegorical details, such as Arnold's trouble with his boots, which has been attributed to his having cloven hooves or wolf paws, reflect the facts about Charles Schmid, a wiry gymnast of twenty-three who stuffed things in his boots, wore makeup, and drove around Tucson in a gold car playing the hero to a group of high-school kids until he was arrested for raping and murdering three young girls. Quirk's argument that Oates followed the magazine article's theme in relating this horror in the "golden west" to the emptiness of "the American dream" points out an important dimension of the story, and his emphasis keeps the real horror of the incident in focus.

Gretchen Schulz and R. J. R. Rockwood are aware of the *Life* article, but they focus instead on another acknowledged source of Oates's inspiration, the folktale. Their discussion of the story's allusions to and affinities with "The Pied Piper of Hamelin," "Cinderella," "Little Red Riding Hood," and other tales suggests why "Where Are You Going, Where Have You Been?" is such a disturbing work. Their article offers detailed interpretations of the psychological crises Connie passes through, based on psychoanalytic interpretations of the meaning and developmental function of the analogous tales. (They use Bruno Bettelheim as their chief authority.) But whereas folktales most often smooth the passage of their readers through Oedipal conflicts and reintegration of the childhood identity into the adult by working through to a happy ending, "Where Are You Going, Where Have You Been?" taps these powerful psychic forces in the reader only to pour them out on the sand.

WILLIAM E. SHEIDLEY

Questions for Discussion

1. Define Connie's relationships with her mother, sister, and father. What is missing from this family? Why does Connie wish "her mother was dead and she herself was dead and it was all over"?

2. What are Connie's "two sides"? In your opinion, is Connie's case unusual for a girl her age in our society? In what ways is she atypical? What about June?

3. The girls enter the drive-in with "faces pleased and expectant as if they were entering a sacred building," and the popular music in the background seems "like music at a church service." Explore the drive-in religion further. What are its creeds, its mysteries? Is it a true religion? a guide to the good life? Does Connie believe in anything else?

4. Discuss the similarities between Eddie, who rotates on a counter stool and offers "something to eat," and the emblem of the drive-in on its bottle-top roof. What else does Eddie offer? Compare Eddie with Arnold Friend as we first see him at the drive-in.

5. What does Oates accomplish by returning briefly to Connie's relationship with her family before narrating what happens "one Sunday"?

6. Discuss Connie's daydreams, in which "all the boys fell back and dissolved into a single face that was not even a face, but an idea, a feeling, mixed up with the urgent insistent pounding of the music," and in which she associates sunbathing with the "sweet, gentle" lovemaking "in movies and

promised in song." What is the source of the sexual desire reflected in these dreams? What is its object?

7. Asbestos was formerly used as a noninflammable insulating material. Trace the images of heat and fire associated with it in the story.

8. Compare Connie's gentle breathing as she listens to the "XYZ Sunday Jamboree" with her breath "jerking back and forth in her lungs" when she tries to use the telephone at the climax of the story.

9. Why does Connie whisper "Christ. Christ" when she hears a car coming up the driveway? Does the effort to see Arnold Friend as a Christ figure find further substantiation in the text? Does it yield any meaningful insights?

10. Where does Connie stand during the first part of her conversation with Arnold? Is Oates's blocking of the scene realistic? symbolic?

11. Describe Arnold's car and clothing. What purpose is served by his transparent disguise? Why does it take Connie so long to penetrate the disguise?

12. Does Arnold have supernatural knowledge about Connie, her family, and her friends? Can his apparent clairvoyance about the barbecue be explained in naturalistic terms?

13. Account for Connie's idea that Arnold "had driven up the driveway all right but had come from nowhere before that and belonged nowhere and that everything about him and even the music that was so familiar to her was only half real." Explain the importance of that idea for understanding what happens to Connie.

14. Why does Connie's kitchen seem "like a place she had never seen before"? How has Arnold succeeded in making Connie feel cut off from her past and unprotected in her home? What is the implication of "the echo of a song from last year" in this context?

15. What is the role of Ellie in Arnold's assault on Connie?

16. Arnold implies that Connie can protect her family from harm by coming with him. How important a factor is this in his winning her over to his will?

17. Examine the passage in which Connie tries to telephone her mother and then collapses in panic and hysteria. Notice its associations with sex and birth. What is taking place in Connie at this moment?

18. Arnold asks rhetorically, "What else is there for a girl like you but to be sweet and pretty and give in?" In what sense is this true?

19. Explain Connie's feeling that she is watching herself go out the door. What has caused this split in her consciousness?

Topics for Writing

1. Discuss Arnold Friend's obvious masquerade, and why it succeeds.

2. Comment on popular music and religion in "Where Are You Going, Where Have You Been?"

3. Read the story once while bearing in mind that it is "based on fact" — something very much like this is known to have actually happened. After finishing the story, write a personal essay giving your reaction. What does this account imply about human nature? About the society reflected in the story?

4. Reread the story with an eye to its allusions to folktales and fairy tales with which you are familiar. Arnold's "coach" has a pumpkin on it; Connie is nearly asleep when he awakens her; he has big teeth; and so forth. What are the tales alluded to about? Is this story a fairy tale, too?

5. Select an item from the news that grips your imagination, and ask yourself why it does. Does it have affinities with folktales or myths? Does it suggest disturbing ideas about human nature and society? Write a narrative of the event, perhaps from the point of view of one of the participants, that incorporates these larger implications.
6. **CONNECTIONS** Compare technique and theme in Oates's "Where Are You Going, Where Have You Been?" and Jackson's "The Lottery."
7. **CONNECTIONS** Compare and contrast Arnold Friend and Flannery O'Connor's Misfit.
8. **CONNECTIONS** Study the allusions to religion in the story. How would Flannery O'Connor have handled this material?

Related Commentary

Joyce Carol Oates, *Smooth Talk:* Short Story into Film, p. 1657.

Suggested Readings

Bloom, Harold. *Joyce Carol Oates.* New York: Chelsea House, 1981.

Friedman, Ellen G. "Joyce Carol Oates." *Modern American Women Writers.* Ed. Elaine Showalter. New York: Macmillan, 1991.

Gardner, John. *On Writers and Writing.* Reading, MA: Addison-Wesley, 1994. 75.

Gillis, Christina Marsden. " 'Where Are You Going, Where Have You Been?': Seduction, Space, and a Fictional Mode." *Studies in Short Fiction* 18 (1981): 65–70.

Johnson, Greg. *Understanding Joyce Carol Oates.* Columbia: U of South Carolina P, 1987.

Oates, Joyce Carol. *New Heaven, New Earth.* New York: Vanguard, 1974.

———. *(Woman) Writer: Occasions and Opportunities.* New York: NAL-Dutton, 1989.

Milazzo, Lee. *Conversations with Joyce Carol Oates.* Jackson: UP of Mississippi, 1989.

Pearlman, Mickey, ed. *American Women Writing Fiction: Memory, Identity, Family, Space.* Lexington: U of Kentucky P, 1989. 9–44.

Plimpton, George. *Women Writers at Work: The* Paris Review *Interviews.* New York: Penguin, 1989.

Quirk, Tom. "A Source for 'Where Are You Going, Where Have You Been?' " *Studies in Short Fiction* 18 (1981): 413–19.

Rozga, Margaret. "Threatening Places, Hiding Places: The Midwest in Selected Stories by Joyce Carol Oates." *Midwestern Miscellany* 18 (1990): 34–44.

Schulz, Gretchen, and R. J. R. Rockwood. "In Fairyland, without a Map: Connie's Exploration Inward in Joyce Carol Oates's 'Where Are You Going, Where Have You Been?' " *Literature and Psychology* 30 (1980): 155–67.

Urbanski, Marie Mitchell Olesen. "Existential Allegory: Joyce Carol Oates's 'Where Are You Going, Where Have You Been?' " *Studies in Short Fiction* 15 (1978): 200–03.

Wegs, Joyce M. " 'Don't You Know Who I Am?': The Grotesque in Oates's 'Where Are You Going, Where Have You Been?' " *Journal of Narrative Technique* 5 (1975): 66–72.

Wesley, Marilyn Clarke. "Transgression and Refusal: The Dynamic of Power in the Domestic Fiction of Joyce Carol Oates." *Dissertation Abstracts International* 49.11 (May 1989): 3365A.

Winslow, Joan D. "The Stranger Within: Two Stories by Oates and Hawthorne." *Studies in Short Fiction* 17 (1980): 263–68.

TIM O'BRIEN

The Things They Carried (p. 1065)

In "The Things They Carried," O'Brien has found a brilliant solution to one of the most common problems a writer faces: how to find a new way to approach a subject that has been written about many times before. His subject is men at war, a topic that has occupied writers since remotest antiquity. The earliest epic in the European tradition is Homer's account of the siege of Troy, and the earliest griot narratives from the empires of Africa recount battles fought along the banks of the Niger River.

The Vietnam War has been treated in a stream of stories, books, articles, studies, and debates. O'Brien's innovation is to tell us directly not about the soldiers, or about the meaningless war they find themselves in, but about the things they are carrying on their shoulders and in their pockets. This simple device is startling and effective. The things his "grunts" are carrying are one way to identify them, to bring them to life, and the author also tells us about the things they carry under different circumstances.

This use of the small detail to illuminate the whole picture would not be as effective if it were limited to a simple description of what each of the men is carrying. But as he discusses the items — their use, their importance to the assignment the men are carrying out, and the significance of each thing to each man — O'Brien tells us about the war itself, and the soldiers' attitudes toward what they are doing. By presenting each of these objects as a microcosm of the reality of the war, the author makes the experience more comprehensible. He has found a dimension that shows us the soldiers as human beings, and that is the most important task for a writer who wants to make us face this cruel reality again.

Questions for Discussion

1. What is the effect of O'Brien's use of abbreviations and acronyms: R & R, SOP, M & Ms, USO, Psy Ops, KIA?
2. When the author writes, "Afterward they burned Than Khe," what is he telling us about the attitude of the men toward the people in the villages around them?
3. Why is it important to specify the weight of the equipment each man is carrying?
4. Does the language of the soldiers sound "real"? Do the descriptions of the weapons have the feeling of reality?
5. Why does the lieutenant burn the letters he has been carrying?

Topics for Writing

1. Soldiers from both sides are fighting the war, but the author only tells us about the men from one side. Why doesn't he describe the North Vietnamese soldiers?
2. Discuss the attitudes toward the war in the United States as they are reflected in the attitudes of the soldiers in "The Things They Carried."
3. Stories about men at war usually emphasize heroism and heroic acts; these are completely absent in this story. What has caused this change in attitude?

Related Commentary

Bobbie Ann Mason, On Tim O'Brien's "The Things They Carried," p. 1502.

Suggested Readings

Bonn, Maria S. "A Different World: The Vietnam Veteran Novel Comes Home." *Fourteen Landing Zones: Approaches to Vietnam War Literature.* Ed. Philip K. Jason. Iowa City: U of Iowa P, 1992.
Calloway, Catherine. "Pluralities of Vision: *Going after Cacciato* and Tim O'Brien's Short Fiction." *America Rediscovered: Critical Essays on Literature and Film of the Vietnam War.* Ed. Owen W. Gilman, Jr. New York: Garland, 1990.
———. "Tim O'Brien (1946–): A Primary and Secondary Bibliography." *Bulletin of Bibliography* 50.3 (Sept. 1993): 223–29.

FLANNERY O'CONNOR

Everything That Rises Must Converge (p. 1080)

"Everything That Rises Must Converge" is one of O'Connor's most powerful stories. Although they are emotionally linked as closely as Siamese twins, Julian and his mother are in such fundamental disagreement that only death can bring their souls together, since "everything that rises must converge." O'Connor goes to great lengths to spell out the differences between mother and son. They are so extreme that humor is the one thing that makes them bearable to the sensitive reader. Julian asserts that "true culture is in the mind." His mother says, "It's in the heart." He insists that "nobody in the damn bus cares who you are." She replies, "I care who I am." She always looks on the bright side of things. He glories in scenting out impending disasters. He tells himself he isn't dominated by his mother. She knows he's both financially and emotionally dependent on her, and she gets him to do whatever she asks.

Contrasts and opposites rule this unlikely pair, but the world they inhabit is also in a state of opposition to their sense of themselves. Blacks no longer know their place in the back of the bus; mother and son are exiled from the destroyed family mansion; Julian wants to be a writer after his college education, but he's selling typewriters instead. The only constant is his mother's ridiculous hat. It reappears on the head of the black lady sitting with her little son next to Julian and his mother on the bus. This sight amuses his mother, who hasn't lost her sense of humor, her spirit refusing to be worn down by the remarks and behavior of her critical, hostile son. As a character she is partially redeemed (despite her racial bigotry) by her humor and her fundamental generosity. In contrast, Julian is damned by his sense of pride.

O'Connor makes certain of this damnation by subtly shifting the point of view to Julian's mental outlook during his journey on the bus, when he withdraws "into the inner compartment of his mind where he spent most of his time." He will be alone there, feeling smugly superior to his mother, until he realizes that he has lost her, at which time he will be forced to include her in his emotional state by entering "the world of guilt and sorrow."

Students may enjoy discussing the humor in this story as well as O'Connor's sublime ear for the ridiculous in her characters' speech. "Everything That Rises Must Converge" also lends itself well to different critical perspectives. Since O'Connor wrote from a Christian orientation, the religious implications of the narrative can be traced: the references to Saint Sebastian, or the Negro mother's threat to her little boy, "Quit yo' foolishness . . . before I knock the living Jesus out of you!" Or O'Connor's quiet comment about "guilt and sorrow" at the end. Students who are budding social historians, psychologists, or feminists can also find abundant material in this story to explore from their orientations.

Questions for Discussion

1. O'Connor writes that Julian's mother's eyes, "sky-blue, were as innocent and untouched by experience as they must have been when she was ten." Again, when she turns her eyes, now a "bruised purple," on Julian, he gets an "uncomfortable sense of her innocence." What are we to make of her innocence? How do we reconcile this attribute with her racism?

2. Julian seems to hate almost everything about his mother. Does she hate anything about her son? Why does he despise her? Why does she love him?

3. The idea of family mansion implies family ties. How do family ties appear in this story? Does the "decayed mansion" mean more to Julian or to his mother? What does it mean to him? to her?

4. What point of view controls "Everything That Rises Must Converge"? At which points in the story do we have the most intimate access to Julian's thoughts?

5. Describe Julian's relationships with people other than his mother. Consider the paragraphs beginning "He began to imagine" and "He imagined his mother." Who would he like to be friends with and why? Does his acknowledgment of his mother's racism imply positive things about Julian's own character?

6. On page 1085 we discover that Julian's mother doesn't think Julian knows "a thing about 'life,' that he hadn't even entered the real world" yet. Does the narrator agree with her? Discuss this sentence and the closing sentence of the story together. What does this imply about the characteristics that belong to "real life"?

7. After his mother's stroke, Julian looks "into a face he had never seen before." What is different about her face now? What metaphor is O'Connor

sustaining behind the description of the literal differences brought on by neurological devastation?

8. O'Connor, a devout Catholic, said her stories were meant to be more like parables than true to life. What elements of this story are Christian? Is the preoccupation central to this story available only to Christians?

Topics for Writing

1. Compare and contrast the two mothers and the two sons in the story.
2. Analyze the symbolism of the hat at the convergence of two apparent opposites — the two mothers.
3. Discuss the role of pride and the response to charity in Julian and the black mother.
4. Write an examination of the changing social order between the generations of Julian's mother and Julian.
5. Explore the role of irony in "Everything That Rises Must Converge."

Related Commentaries

Wayne C. Booth, A Rhetorical Reading of O'Connor's "Everything That Rises Must Converge," p. 1634.
Robert H. Brinkmeyer Jr., Flannery O'Connor and Her Readers, p. 1625.
Anthony Di Renzo, A Dialogical Reading of "Everything That Rises Must Converge," p. 1637.
Flannery O'Connor, From Letters, 1954–55, p. 1613.
Flannery O'Connor, Writing Short Stories, p. 1616.
V. S. Pritchett, Flannery O'Connor: Satan Comes to Georgia, p. 1623.

Suggested Readings

See page 196.

FLANNERY O'CONNOR

Good Country People (p. 1091)

In the world of Flannery O'Connor's fiction, characters are seldom who we think they are or even who they think they are. "Good Country People" provides an intriguing twist on the archetypal theme: Events and people are seldom as simple as they seem.

O'Connor revels in the idiosyncrasies of personality, peopling this story with three strong characters in Joy (Hulga), Mrs. Hopewell, and Manley Pointer, as well as an interesting subsidiary character, Mrs. Freeman, with her "special fondness for the details of secret infections, hidden deformities," and "assaults upon children." O'Connor's choice of names figures prominently. Joy changes her name to Hulga to symbolize her sense of her own ugliness. Mrs. Hopewell continually hopes well of things, blathering a stream of banal platitudes that reveal her own lack of depth. The name Manley Pointer strikes the reader as almost humorously phallic and predatory-sounding, given the surprising turn of events in the storage barn.

We don't see how "right" the details of this story are until we reach its sardonic conclusion, Pointer going Hulga's intellectual atheism one better, disappearing with her leg in his "Bible" valise, Mrs. Hopewell in her ignorance commenting on "that nice dull young man." Looking back, we see the clever meticulousness of Pointer's con — the feigned heaviness of his satchel, his feigned simplicity (as in mistaking the name of the house for its owner), the rube suit. It turns out that this specimen of "good country people" reads people better than the highly educated Hulga or the self-aggrandizing Mrs. Hopewell.

The experience of losing her artificial limb to the perverted Manley Pointer is the loss of a certain kind of virginity for Hulga, and however harrowing the experience, we sense that it will be a valuable one. Prior to her victimization, we feel mainly revulsion for Joy/Hulga. We sympathize with her hunting accident, but O'Connor highlights the unpleasant abrasiveness of her personality; clearly Hulga's psyche, as well as her body, has been damaged. Hulga's low self-esteem is exacerbated by her mother's implications of Hulga's abnormality, which focus on her intellectualism as much as on her disfigurement. For all Mrs. Hopewell's assertions that "it takes all kinds to make the world go 'round," she resents her daughter's interest in philosophy (female education is for a "good time") as well as Hulga's individuation: "It seemed to Mrs. Hopewell that every year she grew less like other people and more like herself."

In this multifaceted story of moral blindness, Hulga experiences a physical intimacy with Pointer that forces her into a new mode of reacting and out of her customary detached intellectualism: "Without the leg she felt entirely dependent on him. Her brain seemed to have stopped thinking altogether and to be about some other function that it was not very good at." However dastardly Pointer's actions, he forces Hulga to feel and acknowledge her emotions for the first time. We go away from the story feeling that Hulga will be a changed — and humbled — person less presumptuous and closer to psychic wholeness.

Questions for Discussion

1. What does Mrs. Hopewell mean by "good country people"?
2. Why does Joy change her name to Hulga?
3. In what ways do you expect Joy/Hulga will change after her experience in the barn with Manley Pointer?
4. Discuss O'Connor's choice of names for the characters in this story.
5. Is Manley Pointer a believable character? Have you in your own experience encountered people who are entirely other than they seem? What is Pointer really interested in? Why does he carry off Hulga's leg?
6. Discuss the dramatic function of Mrs. Freeman and her two daughters.
7. Discuss the effects on characterization of O'Connor's choosing to give Joy a Ph.D. in philosophy and an artificial leg. How do these details predispose our expectations?

Topics for Writing

1. Discuss the function of Christianity in "Good Country People."
2. **CONNECTIONS** Compare "Good Country People" with "Everything That Rises Must Converge." What similarities and differences do you find among mother, son or daughter, and stranger in these stories? What can you infer from this comparison about Flannery O'Connor's attraction to certain types of characters?

Related Commentaries

Robert H. Brinkmeyer Jr., Flannery O'Connor and Her Readers, p. 1625.
Dorothy Tuck McFarland, On "Good Country People," p. 1630.
Flannery O'Connor, From Letters, 1954–55, p. 1613.
Flannery O'Connor, Writing Short Stories, p. 1616.

Suggested Readings

See page 196.

FLANNERY O'CONNOR

A Good Man Is Hard to Find (p. 1106)

O'Connor's comments (included in Part Three, p. 1621) direct attention to the climax of her story and suggest how she intended the central characters to be viewed and what she meant the story to imply. Students may benefit, however, from struggling at first to interpret the text unassisted by authorial explanation. The effort should reveal dimensions of O'Connor's art that might otherwise be overlooked.

The grandmother's reawakening to reality, which leads to her gesture of grace as she reaches out to The Misfit as one of her own children, may be triggered by the violence of the murders going on just offstage and the extremity of her own case, but her conversion has been carefully prepared for. Throughout the story this old woman longs in various ways to go back *home* — to Tennessee, to the days of her youth, to the mansion with the imaginary secret panel, which is as much in heaven as it is down a hilly back road in Georgia. Death is seldom far from her thoughts, though for a long time she does not apprehend its reality. Her initial worries about The Misfit are disingenuous, but encountering him or returning to east Tennessee come to the same thing in the end. On the road, the grandmother dresses up in nice clothes so that "anyone seeing her dead on the highway would know at once that she was a lady," observes a graveyard, and remembers her mansion at a town named Toombsboro. The Misfit and his men approach in a "hearse-like automobile"; the family awaits them in front of the woods that "gaped like a dark open mouth." The grandmother is at odds with present times. She squabbles with the children (whose behavior even the reader may find unusually improper), easily upstages the cabbage-headed, slacks-wearing woman who is their mother, joins Red Sammy in deploring the state of world affairs, and disastrously deludes Bailey by smuggling the cat into the car. But she loves the world as well, in a selfish, childish way. She *will* have the cat along; she admires the scenery (including a picturesque "pickaninny" for whose poverty she is not yet ready to feel compassion); she wishes she had married Mr. E. A. Teagarden, who courted her with watermelon and would have supplied all her worldly needs from the proceeds of his Coca-Cola stock; and she even makes a play for Red Sammy, the only tycoon in sight.

These desires may be misdirected, but just as it takes very little to upset the valise, release the cat, flip the car off the road, and carry the story into an entirely new set of circumstances, so, under the intensifying presence of death, it takes only a moment for the grandmother's selfish love for and alienation from the world to flip over into the selfless love that leads her to open her heart to The Misfit. After all, she at least rationalizes bringing the cat to protect it; she supportively asserts that Red Sammy is "a good man" in face of his own cynicism and despair; and she offers the same praise to The Misfit from the moment she recognizes him. Without a doubt the grandmother's motive in insisting that The Misfit is "a good man" and in urging him to pray is to divert him from his evident intention and so to save her skin. But as the bullets ring out in the background and the grandmother's maternal instincts burst forth in her repeated cries of "Bailey Boy!" she begins to act charitably in spite of herself. She offers The Misfit one of Bailey's shirts, listens to his confession (although she is the one who is about to die), and when he *is* wearing Bailey's shirt, she reaches out to him in his anguish. A good man *is* hard to find; Jesus may have been the only one who was intrinsically good. But when she loves and pities the radically fallen Misfit, the grandmother becomes for the moment a *good woman* through her Christlike action, as The Misfit himself acerbically recognizes.

As O'Connor mentions in her commentary, The Misfit has evoked widely differing responses from readers and critics, who have associated him with the devil, the modern agnostic existentialist, or "the prophet he was meant to become," in O'Connor's own phrase. Perhaps The Misfit's daddy provides the best way of distinguishing him from the rest of the characters with his remark "It's some that can live their whole life out without asking about it and it's others has to know why it is, and this boy is one of the latters." Unlike O'Connor, whose vision of the world was grounded in *belief*, The Misfit wants to *know*. With Faustian presumption, he seeks to comprehend the divine mysteries in terms of his own intellect and demands a kind of justice in life that he can understand. When he cannot find the answers to his questions, but only the implication of inexplicable guilt (like Original Sin) in the punishment he receives, The Misfit sees the world not as the charming place it has appeared to the grandmother but as a prison whose empty sky resembles the blank walls of his cell in the penitentiary. In his own calculus of guilt, The Misfit feels he has been excessively punished, and he seems to be going about the world committing crimes in order to right the balance. His most perverse principle, "No pleasure but meanness," is sustained surprisingly well by the world O'Connor portrays. (Is *this* the reason for the story's lack of anything or anyone to admire and its unremittingly ironic tone?) But it gives way after he has been touched by the grandmother to his first true prophecy: "It's no real pleasure in life" — no *real* pleasure in *this* life, though true goodness sometimes appears in those made conscious of death.

WILLIAM E. SHEIDLEY

Questions for Discussion

1.   What is the grandmother's reason for bringing up The Misfit at the beginning of the story?
2.   Describe "the children's mother." Why does O'Connor make her such a nonentity?
3.   What about John Wesley and June Star? What would have been the result had O'Connor characterized them as something other than totally obnoxious?
4.   Discuss the grandmother's reasons for her fatal decision to bring Pitty Sing on the trip.
5.   Why does the grandmother dress so nicely for the trip?
6.   Compare the grandmother's response to the scenery and the trip with that of the children. What does O'Connor accomplish by means of this distinction?
7.   Just before the stop at The Tower, the grandmother reminisces about her old suitor, Edgar Atkins Teagarden. Specify the connections between the two episodes.
8.   What tower might O'Connor have had in mind in choosing the name for Red Sammy's establishment? Why is there a monkey in a chinaberry tree feasting on fleas posted outside The Tower? What do we learn about the world at Red Sammy's?
9.   Contrast The Tower with the mansion the grandmother awakens to remember "outside of Toombsboro."
10. What factors cause the accident? Consider its meaning as a consequence of the grandmother's choices and desires.
11. Describe the manner in which The Misfit arrives on the scene. What effect does his appearance have on the reader?
12. The grandmother's response to The Misfit's remark "it would have been better for all of you, lady, if you hadn't of reckernized me," is "You wouldn't shoot a lady, would you?" Evaluate her question.
13. To what extent is the grandmother correct in her praise of The Misfit? In what ways is he a gentleman?
14. Describe the grandmother's reaction to Bailey's departure. Is her response consistent with her previous behavior?
15. Define The Misfit's experience of the world. To what extent can his criminality be blamed on the conditions of his life? Does The Misfit feel any more free outside the penitentiary than in it?
16. How can the logic of The Misfit's position that "the crime don't matter. . . . because sooner or later you're going to forget what it was you done and just be punished for it" be attacked? To what extent does The Misfit's description of himself apply to everyone? Bear in mind that the whole family is being punished with death for no ascertainable crime.
17. Explain how, to The Misfit, "Jesus thown everything off balance."
18. What is the effect of O'Connor's comparing the grandmother to "a parched old turkey hen crying for water"?
19. Does The Misfit do or say anything to deserve the grandmother's gesture of concern?
20. Explain The Misfit's final evaluation of the grandmother: "She would of been a good woman . . . if it had been somebody there to shoot her every minute of her life."

21. Contrast The Misfit's remark "No pleasure but meanness" with his last words in the story.

Topics for Writing

1. What is the function of tone in O'Connor's story?
2. Describe techniques of characterization in "A Good Man Is Hard to Find."
3. Write a parable or short tale designed to illustrate a religious or philosophical truth. Following O'Connor's example, portray your characters ruthlessly as embodiments of what you want them to represent.
4. **CONNECTIONS** Compare and contrast O'Connor's "A Good Man Is Hard to Find" and Tolstoy's "The Death of Ivan Ilych."
5. **CONNECTIONS** Comment upon the relationship between the grandmother and The Misfit in "A Good Man Is Hard to Find" and the relationship between Connie and Arnold Friend in Oates's "Where Are You Going, Where Have You Been?"

Related Commentaries

Robert H. Brinkmeyer Jr., Flannery O'Connor and Her Readers, p. 1625.
Flannery O'Connor, A Reasonable Use of the Unreasonable, p. 1621.
Flannery O'Connor, From Letters, 1954–55, p. 1613.
Flannery O'Connor, Writing Short Stories, p. 1616.

Suggested Readings

Asals, Frederick. *Flannery O'Connor: The Imagination of Extremity.* Athens: U of Georgia P, 1982. 142–54.

Brinkmeyer, Robert H., Jr. *The Art and Vision of Flannery O'Connor.* Baton Rouge: Louisiana State UP, 1989.

Browning, Preston M., Jr. *Flannery O'Connor.* Crosscurrents/Modern Critiques. Carbondale: Southern Illinois UP, 1974. 54–59.

Burke, John J. "Convergence of Flannery O'Connor and Chardin." *Renascence* 19 (1966): 41–47, 52.

Church, Joseph. "An Abuse of the Imagination in Flannery O'Connor's 'A Good Man Is Hard to Find.'" *Notes on Contemporary Literature* 20.3 (May 1990): 8–10.

Clark, Beverly Lyon, and Melville J. Friedman. *Critical Essays on Flannery O'Connor.* Boston: G. K. Hall, 1985.

Esch, Robert M. "O'Connor's 'Everything That Rises Must Converge.' " *Explicator* 27 (1969): Item 58.

Feeley, Sister Kathleen. *Flannery O'Connor: Voice of the Peacock.* New Brunswick, NJ: Rutgers UP, 1972.

Gatta, John. "*The Scarlet Letter* as Pre-Text for Flannery O'Connor's 'Good Country People.'" *The Nathaniel Hawthorne Review* 16.2 (Fall 1990): 6–9.

Giannone, Richard. *Flannery O'Connor: A Study of the Short Fiction.* Boston: Twayne, 1988.

Grimshaw, James A. *The Flannery O'Connor Companion.* Westport, CT: Greenwood, 1981.

Hendin, Josephine. *The World of Flannery O'Connor.* Ann Arbor, MI: Books Demand UMI, 1986.

Kane, Patricia. "Flannery O'Connor's 'Everything That Rises Must Converge.' " *Critique: Studies in Short Fiction* 8 (1965): 85–91.

Maida, Patricia Dinneen. "Convergence in Flannery O'Connor's 'Everything That Rises Must Converge.' " *Studies in Short Fiction* 7 (1970): 549–55.

Martin, W. R. "The Apostate in Flannery O'Connor's 'Everything That Rises Must Converge.'" *American Notes and Queries* 23 (1985): 113–14.

McDermott, John V. "Julian's Journey into Hell: Flannery O'Connor's Allegory of Pride." *Mississippi Quarterly* 28 (1975): 171–79.

Nisly, P. W. "Prison of the Self: Isolation in Flannery O'Connor's Fiction." *Studies in Short Fiction* 17 (1980): 49–54.

Ochshorn, Kathleen G. "A Cloak of Grace: Contradictions in 'A Good Man Is Hard to Find.'" *Studies in American Fiction* 18.1 (Spring 1990): 113–17.

O'Connor, Flannery. *The Habit of Being.* Letters edited and with an introduction by Sally Fitzgerald. New York: Farrar, 1979.

———. *Mystery and Manners.* New York: Farrar, 1969.

Orvell, Miles. *Invisible Parade: The Fiction of Flannery O'Connor.* Philadelphia: Temple UP, 1972.

Paulson, Suzanne. *Flannery O'Connor.* Boston: G. K. Hall, 1988.

Petry, Alice Hall. "Miss O'Connor and Mrs. Mitchell: The Example of 'Everything That Rises.'" *The Southern Quarterly: A Journal of the Arts in the South* 27.4 (Summer 1989): 5–15.

Pyron, V. "'Strange Country': The Landscape of Flannery O'Connor's Short Stories." *Mississippi Quarterly* 36 (1983): 557–68.

FRANK O'CONNOR

Guests of the Nation (p. 1118)

O'Connor's story draws exceptional power from its concern with a betrayal of the most primitive basis of human society, the host-guest relationship. The English prisoners, billeted with their guards in a cottage so thoroughly rooted in the land that its occupant still bears traces of indigenous paganism, earn the status of guests and come to feel at home. Belcher's contributions to the household chores call attention to the simple satisfactions of the peaceful, cooperative labor that is disrupted by the war, and Hawkins's learning Irish dances implies the underlying brotherhood of men, in contrast to which the scruples of "our lads" who "at that time did not dance foreign dances on principle" seem absurd — and ominous. The futility of Hawkins's debates with Noble on theology calls further into question the reality of the issues that divide the English from the Irish, and his international socialist politics provide a hint that there are issues of at least equal importance that would not polarize the two pairs of men but unite them against a common enemy.

The inhumanity of the conflict that orders Belcher and Hawkins to be executed by their "chums," their brothers, appears clearer for O'Connor's skillful portrayal of the prisoners as distinct from each other, individualized and consistent in their personalities. Further, by opening the story with a plunge into what seems an ongoing state of affairs, O'Connor shows that it is the war that interrupts the natural friendly interaction among the men rather than their fellowship interrupting a "normal" condition of bitter hostility between the English and the Irish. Even Jeremiah Donovan, who eventually brings down the cruel warrant and carries it out, forms part of the circle around the card table and scolds Hawkins for poor play "as if he were one of our own."

Bonaparte, the narrator, embraces the Englishmen as comrades and chafes at his official duties as their guard. With Noble, he imagines that the brigade officers, who also "knew the Englishmen well," will treat them as men rather than as enemies. But when the moment of decision arrives, Noble's resistance only extends to accepting the secondary role of gravedigger, and Bonaparte, though he hopes the prisoners will run away, finds himself powerless to aid them. Belcher and Hawkins are most fully themselves at the moment of their deaths, Hawkins talking on about his larger cause, Belcher finally revealing the fullness of his loving and generous nature. To Bonaparte and Noble the execution conveys a shock of revelation that changes the world for them. As Noble prays with the old woman in the doorway of the cottage — now become a shrine to the communion that took place within it, the only holy place in a world that seems to Noble composed entirely of the grave of his friends — Bonaparte, made profane in the literal etymological sense ("outside the shrine") and figuratively as well by his participation in the killing, feels himself cast out, alone, cut off from all atonement.

WILLIAM E. SHEIDLEY

Questions for Discussion

1. Describe and explain the pacing of the story. Contrast the movement of sections II and III with that of section IV.
2. What is the effect of the abrupt beginning of the story? Why does O'Connor introduce the characters before specifying that they are prisoners and guards in a war?
3. Why does O'Connor trouble to introduce the message from Mary Brigid O'Connell about her brother's socks?
4. Distinguish between the two Englishmen. Are they more different from the Irishmen or from each other?
5. Explore the significance of the old woman's superstitions about Jupiter Pluvius and "the hidden powers." Compare her interest in religion with that of Noble and Hawkins.
6. Why is Bonaparte so shocked when he learns what may happen to the hostages?
7. What is the relevance to the story of Hawkins's political beliefs? Do we think less of him when he volunteers to become a traitor and join the Irish cause?
8. What is the effect of Belcher's last-minute confidences? of his apparently sincere repetition of the word *chum* throughout his ordeal?
9. Discuss Bonaparte's role in the execution. Is he culpable? Does he feel guilty?
10. Define the symbolic implications of the final scene. Why do Noble and Bonaparte have contrasting visions? Do their visions have anything in common? Why does Bonaparte burst out of the cottage where Noble and the old woman are praying?

Topics for Writing

1. What is the meaning of the old woman and her cottage in "Guests of the Nation"?
2. Summarize the conflict and the action of this story on personal, public (national, historical, political), and eternal (philosophical, religious, mythical) levels. Could these levels be reconciled so that the polarities of value would be parallel?
3. **CONNECTIONS**   Compare and contrast O'Connor's "Guests of the Nation" and Babel's "My First Goose" — introductions to war.
4. **CONNECTIONS**   Compare and contrast executions in O'Connor's "Guests of the Nation" and Borowski's "This Way for the Gas, Ladies and Gentlemen."

Related Commentaries

Frank O'Connor, The Nearest Thing to Lyric Poetry Is the Short Story, p. 1523.
Frank O'Connor, Style and Form in Joyce's "The Dead," p. 1524.

Suggested Readings

Bordewyk, Gordon. "Quest for Meaning: The Stories of Frank O'Connor." *Illinois Quarterly* 41 (1978): 37–47, esp. 38–39.
Matthews, James. *Voices: A Life of Frank O'Connor*. New York: Atheneum, 1983.
O'Connor, Frank. *The Lonely Voice: A Study of the Short Story*. Cleveland: World, 1963.
Prosky, Murray. "The Pattern of Diminishing Certitude in the Stories of Frank O'Connor." *Colby Library Quarterly* 9 (1971): 311–21, esp. 311–14.
Steinman, Michael. *Frank O'Connor at Work*. Syracuse, NY: Syracuse UP, 1990.
Tomory, William. *Frank O'Connor*. Boston: Twayne, 1980.

TILLIE OLSEN

I Stand Here Ironing (p. 1129)

One way to begin discussing this story is to look at the ending. "I will never total it all," the narrator affirms and then pronounces the summary whose inadequacy she has already proclaimed. The summarizing passage clarifies and organizes the impressions the reader may have gleaned from the preceding monologue. It is so clear that if it stood alone or came first in the story the validity of its interpretation of Emily could hardly be doubted. But since it follows her mother's "tormented" meditations, the summary seems incomplete in its clinical precision and must give way to a final paragraph of comparatively obscure and paradoxical requests focused in the startling but brilliantly adept image of the "dress on the ironing board, helpless before the iron," which links the story's end to its beginning and directs attention to the true central character.

What is mainly missing from the summary is the love and understanding that Emily's mother feels for her daughter as a result of living through the experiences bracketed by the orderly generalizations. Just as much as Emily, her mother has been the victim "of depression, of war, of fear." By virtue of having had to cope with those circumstances, she can respect Emily's response to them. Doing so enables her to counter the suggestion that "she's a youngster who needs help" with "Let her be." A good deal of the help Emily and her mother have received so far has put them in separate prisons — as when Emily was incarcerated at the convalescent home — and cut them off from love. To let Emily alone is at least to allow her some freedom to grow at her own slow pace.

Her mother is tempted to blame herself for the deficiencies in Emily's childhood, since she learned things about being a mother with her second family that she did not know with Emily. But her consideration of a characteristic incident early in the narrative suggests a crucial qualifying factor: When she parked Emily at nursery school at the age of two, she did not know what she was subjecting her daughter to, "except that it would have made no difference if I had known. . . . It was the only way we could be together, the only way I could hold a job." As much a victim of rigid and unfavorable economic and historic circumstances as her daughter, Emily's mother can speak her concluding line with feeling. In pleading that Emily somehow be made to know "that she is more than this dress on the ironing board, helpless before the iron," Emily's mother asks that her daughter be spared a condition to which she herself has been subjected. But Emily's mother, unlike Whistler's, does not sit for her portrait passively in a rocking chair; she stands there wielding the iron, controlling the very symbol of the circumstances that have not yet flattened her, painting her own self-portrait, and calling for help not in adjusting Emily to the world but in making the world a place in which Emily can thrive.

WILLIAM E. SHEIDLEY

Questions for Discussion

1. Who is "you" in the first sentence? What is the mother's first response to the request to unlock the mystery of Emily? Does her position change?
2. Does Emily's mother feel guilty about how she has cared for Emily? Why? What factors have affected her dealings with her daughter?
3. Why is the passage in which Emily throws the clock so effective?
4. Discuss the "help" Emily gets at the convalescent home. How does it compare with the help her mother calls for at the end?
5. Emily has suffered from the absence of her father, the exhaustion of her mother, poverty, asthma and other diseases, sibling rivalry, and unpopularity, among other complaints. What is the effect of these hardships on the young woman she has become? What is the effect of her discovery of a talent?
6. What has her mother learned from Emily?
7. Does Emily's mother love her daughter? How can we tell?

Topics for Writing

1. Compare and contrast Emily's talent and her mother's.
2. Discuss the function of the interruptions in "I Stand Here Ironing."
3. Consider "I will never total it all" — the importance of indeterminacy in Olsen's analysis of Emily.
4. Analyze the politics of "I Stand Here Ironing."
5. Write a summary statement in general terms about the personality of a sibling, relative, or friend you have known closely for a long time. Put it aside and cast your memory back to three or four specific incidents involving your subject. Narrate them briefly but in specific and concrete terms. Read over your sketches and compare the personality of your subject as it emerges with what you wrote in your generalized summary. Do you still think your summary is accurate? What are its limitations?

Related Commentary

Robert Coles, Tillie Olsen: The Iron and the Riddle, p. 1449.

Suggested Readings

Frye, Joanne S. "'I Stand Here Ironing': Motherhood as Experience and Metaphor." *Studies in Short Fiction* 18 (1981): 287–92.

O'Connor, William Van. "The Short Stories of Tillie Olsen." *Studies in Short Fiction* 1 (1963): 21–25, esp. 21–22.

CYNTHIA OZICK

The Shawl (p. 1136)

The yellow Star of David sewn into Rosa's coat identifies the people on the march as Jews whose destination is a Nazi concentration camp. The prosaic details of Ozick's story are horrible. Rosa's inability to save her baby, Magda, when the prison guard throws her against the electric fence is the grim conclusion to a hopeless situation. Ozick's poetic language and skillful pacing of her narrative transform the nightmarish details of her fiction into art.

The title of the story suggests its blend of fact and poetry. "The Shawl" is on the one hand a prosaic linen shawl that Rosa uses to wrap her baby and carry her under her coat during the forced march to the camp. On the other hand, Ozick tells us that "it was a magic shawl." It nourishes Magda after Rosa's breast milk dries up. It hides the baby in the women's barracks in the camp for many months. It smothers Rosa's scream after she sees Magda thrown against the fence. The shawl appears to have a life of its own, drying like Rosa's breasts; yet before drying it nourishes Rosa: "Rosa drank Magda's shawl until it dried." That is, perhaps, until the memory of her baby's death is bearable.

The narrative develops through two conflicts, the Jewish-Aryan conflict dramatized through the camp setting and the personal conflict between the two sisters, the baby Magda and the fourteen-year-old Stella. The resolution of Stella's jealousy toward the baby — when Stella takes the shawl to cover herself against the cold and Magda totters outside the women's barracks looking for it — precipitates the climax of the story. There is no resolution to the larger Jewish-Aryan conflict, except that Rosa's will endures. She smothers her screams and survives the death of her baby.

The blend of fact and poetry is reinforced by Ozick's use of sound and silence in "The Shawl." Most of the time, the events described are unvoiced, evoking the eerie echo of silence in the black-and-white documentary films shot by the Allies liberating the concentration camps. Many students will have seen these films on TV programs about the Holocaust and will remember the images of the prison barracks, the hundreds of emaciated prisoners, the mounds of skeleton corpses.

Ozick suggests these familiar images by her use of poetic language to describe the malnutrition of her characters in "The Shawl." Stella's knees are "tumors on sticks, her elbows chicken bones." For the baby, death is a kind of deliverance. She makes a noise for the first time since her scream on the road. But the noises of the baby's scream and her cry "Maaaa" are subhuman, like the chicken-bone elbows. They reinforce the terror of the situation, people degraded into subhuman forms. In a way, silence is a relief. Rosa swallows the shawl to smother her howl so the prison guard won't shoot her. Silence is a means of survival in this story. Ironically, the silence of Ozick's words on the printed page is a testimony to the endurance of her people.

Questions for Discussion

1. How does Ozick use details to allude to the plot situation without naming it specifically? What mood does she create by her method of introducing details?
2. What two conflicts are evident throughout the story? How is the shawl central to these oppositions?
3. In what ways is the shawl "magic"? Whom does it nourish? How?
4. Discuss Ozick's use of poetic language to present the images of the story. Give examples of this use.
5. Who is the protagonist of the story? the antagonist? Is there more than one possible answer to these questions? Explain.
6. Sound and silence are integral to the total effect of the story. Discuss.
7. What is the climax of the story? Are any of the conflicts resolved? What is Ozick protesting? What human qualities does the story commemorate?

Topics for Writing

1. Discuss Ozick's use of sensory images and their contribution to the overall story.
2. Rewrite the story from the point of view of Stella.
3. **CONNECTIONS** Compare and contrast the quality of endurance in O'Brien's "The Things They Carried" and Ozick's "The Shawl."

4. **CONNECTIONS** Compare and discuss the theme of quiet desperation in Ozick's "The Shawl," Gilman's "The Yellow Wallpaper," and Steinbeck's "The Chrysanthemums."

Suggested Readings

Berg, Stephen, ed. "Cynthia Ozick: Lesson of the Master." *In Praise of What Persists.* New York: Harper, 1983. 181–87.
Epstein, J. "Fiction: Cynthia Ozick, Jewish Writer." *Commentary* 77 (1984): 64–69.
Ottenberg, E. "Rich Visions of Cynthia Ozick." *New York Times Magazine* 10 (Apr. 1983): 46–47.
Rosenberg, R. "Covenanted to the Law: Cynthia Ozick." *MELUS* 9 (1982): 39–44.
Strandberg, V. "Art of Cynthia Ozick." *Texas Studies in Language and Literature* 25 (1983): 266–312.

GRACE PALEY

A Conversation with My Father (p. 1141)

The story the narrator writes in response to her father's request is so interesting that it is easy to forget for a while that it is only an element within the larger story Paley has to tell. Confronted with the inescapable fact of the father's imminent death, the narrator and her father respond in differing ways because of their differing needs. Both use gallows humor to make the situation less intolerable, as when the father remarks, "It so happens I'm not going out this evening"; but the narrator seeks that refuge much more often, and her father chides her repeatedly for doing so. Things *matter* to a dying man, and it is not surprising that he should prefer the straight line of tragedy — in which failure and defeat are compensated for by a perception of the real value of what has been lost — to the idea of "the open destiny of life," which, by holding out hope of recovery from any disaster, implies that there is nothing indispensable, no absolute loss. A man on his deathbed knows better.

The narrator's first attempt to write a story that suits her father's taste reflects her discomfort with the assignment. Her "unadorned and miserable tale" remains so sketchy that it lacks verisimilitude and conviction, like meaningless statistics on highway deaths or counterinsurgency body counts. Challenged to try again, she partly confirms her father's complaint that "with you, it's all a joke" by writing a brilliantly comic and incontrovertibly realistic version of the story, whose merits even her father has to recognize: "Number One: You have a nice sense of humor." In a few deft strokes, Paley renders an incisive satiric portrait of two contemporary "life-styles," their hypocrisy, and their destructiveness, focused neatly in the competing periodical titles, *Oh! Golden Horse!* (heroin) and *Man Does Live by Bread Alone.* The narrator knows as well as her father how thorough a perversion of true spiritual values is embodied in each of these titles, and she dramatizes her understanding in the destruction of the mother in her story. But she cannot quite "look it in the face," and she ends her tale with one last grim joke: "terrible, face-scarring, time-consuming tears." Her father spies her desperate evasion: "Number Two: I see you can't tell a plain story. So don't waste time."

Ironically, the clarity of his disillusioned vision enables the dying man to feel a purer sympathy for the mother in the story than does the narrator herself, although she claims to care so much about her characters that she wants to give them all a second chance. "Poor woman," he says. "Poor girl, born in a time of fools, to live among fools. The end. The end. You were right to put that down. The end." Not necessarily, the narrator argues, and goes on to invent the kind of future for her character that we always imagine for the dying, in the probably misguided effort to ease their anxiety. But her father, as usual, knows better: " 'How long will it be?' he asked. 'Tragedy! You too. When will you look it in the face?' "

WILLIAM E. SHEIDLEY

Questions for Discussion

1. Describe the medical condition of the narrator's father. How important is it to understanding his position in the conversation?
2. Explain the phrase "despite my metaphors" in the first paragraph. What other writerly tactics of the narrator does her father ignore?
3. The narrator says she *would* like to tell a story with the kind of plot she has always despised. Analyze her conflict.
4. What is the point of the first version of the story? What is wrong with it as a piece of fiction?
5. When her father asks for details, the narrator comes up with things he calls jokes. Are they? What makes them jokes rather than facts?
6. Why does the narrator's father consider that "it is of great consequence" whether the woman in the story is married? Is he simply old-fashioned?
7. What does the narrator add to her story in the second version? Does the point of the story remain the same? Does her father get the point?
8. The woman in the story "would rather be with the young." Consider that motivation and its results from the point of view of the narrator and of her father.
9. What techniques does Paley use to satirize the woman's son and his girlfriend?
10. Explain the term "time-consuming" at the end of the inset story.
11. The narrator's father makes three separate responses to the story. Account for each of them. Do they cohere?
12. What does the narrator's father mean by the statement he makes in various forms culminating in his final question?

Topics for Writing

1. Analyze "A Conversation with My Father" as a story about writing.
2. Evaluate the qualities of tragedy versus satire in "A Conversation with My Father."
3. Write your own version of the narrator's story. Start from her first version and elaborate on it as you choose, without necessarily using the material the narrator includes in her second version and subsequent commentary.
4. **CONNECTIONS** Compare and contrast attitudes toward death and life in Paley's "A Conversation with My Father" and Tolstoy's "The Death of Ivan Ilych."

Related Commentary

Grace Paley, A Conversation with Ann Charters, p. 1526.

Suggested Readings

Aarons, Victoria. "Talking Lives: Storytelling and Renewal in Grace Paley's Short Fiction." *Studies in Jewish Literature* 9.1 (Spring 1990): 20–35.

Arcana, Judith. "Grace Paley: Life and Stories." *Dissertation Abstracts International* 50.7 (Jan. 1990): 2271A.

Baba, Minako. "Faith Darwin as Writer, Heroine: A Study of Grace Paley's Short Stories." *Studies in American Jewish Literature* 7.1 (Spring 1988): 40–54.

Halfman, Ulrich, and Philipp Gerlach. "Grace Paley: A Bibliography." *Tulsa Studies in Women's Literature* 8.2 (Fall 1989): 339–54.

Isaccs, Neil David. *Grace Paley: A Study of the Short Fiction.* Boston: Twayne, 1990.

Logsdon, Loren, and Charles W. Mayer, ed. *Since Flannery O'Connor: Essays on the Contemporary American Short Story.* Macomb: Western Illinois U, 1987. 93–100.

Lyons, Bonnie. "Grace Paley's Jewish Miniatures." *Studies in American Jewish Literature* 8.1 (Spring 1989): 26–33.

Paley, Grace. *Long Walks and Intimate Talks: Stories and Poems by Grace Paley.* New York: Feminist Press and the City U of New York, 1991.

Taylor, Jacqueline. *Grace Paley: Illuminating the Dark Lives.* Austin: U of Texas P, 1990.

———. "Grace Paley on Storytelling and Story Hearing." *Literature in Performance: A Journal of Literature and Performing Art* 7.2 (April 1987): 46–58.

Wilde, Alan. "Grace Paley's World, Investing Words." Wilde, *Middle Grounds.* Philadelphia: U of Pennsylvania P, 1987.

EDGAR ALLAN POE

The Cask of Amontillado (p. 1146)

Poe is the great master of the contrived suspense story, and "The Cask of Amontillado" is a model of narrative compression toward a single effect. Students should understand that Poe had a theory on the short story; its essential points are suggested in his review of Hawthorne's tales in Part Two (p. 1531).

Despite Poe's rational explanation of how a writer should compose a story, his own fiction is directed toward eliciting irrational emotions. Poe's literary style aims at using as many extravagances of character, setting, and plot as he could invent, exploiting the reader's emotional vulnerability to disturbing images of darkness and chaos. The hectic unpredictability of the carnival season, the creepy subterranean wine cellar, and the ancient family crypt with its molding skeletons all challenge us emotionally and make us want to read further.

In the reading, our own fears become the true subject matter. As in a nightmare, Fortunato finds himself being buried alive, one of the most basic human fears. On a more conscious level, we rely on a social contract to bind us together as a human family, and Montresor's lawlessness plays on our fear that any person can take the law into his or her own hands without being checked by conscience. Poe doesn't have to give us a great number of details about his characters; our imagination draws from the depths of the common human psyche to supply all that we need.

This story is a good example to use in stressing the importance of the students' close reading of a text. It's easy for readers to miss, in the last paragraph, the sentence "My heart grew sick — on account of the dampness of the catacombs." Yet upon this sentence rests the interpretation of Montresor's character: Can we excuse his action on grounds of insanity? Was he insane at the time he buried Fortunato alive, or did he go insane in the half century during which, he tells us, his crime has remained undetected? If the reader has not paid careful attention to that sentence, he or she will have missed an essential detail in understanding the story.

The book *Mysterious New England,* edited by A. N. Stevens (1971), suggests that Poe first heard the anecdote upon which he might have based this story when he was a private in the army in 1827. Supposedly, only ten years before, a popular young lieutenant named Robert F. Massie had also been stationed at Fort Independence in Boston Harbor; when Poe was serving there, he saw a gravestone erected to the memory of one Lieutenant Massie, who had been unfairly killed in a duel by a bully named Captain Green.

Feeling against Captain Green ran high for many weeks, and then suddenly he vanished. Years went by without a sign of him, and Green was written off the army records as a deserter.

According to the story that Poe finally gathered together, Captain Green had been so detested by his fellow officers that they decided to take a terrible revenge on him for Massie's death.

Visiting Captain Green one moonless night, they pretended to be friendly and plied him with wine until he was helplessly intoxicated. Then, carrying the captain down to one of the ancient dungeons, the officers forced his body through a tiny opening that led into the subterranean casemate. His captors began to shackle him to the floor, using the heavy iron handcuffs and footcuffs fastened into the stone. Then they sealed the captain up alive inside the windowless casemate, using bricks and mortar that they had hidden close at hand.

Captain Green shrieked in terror and begged for mercy, but his cries fell on deaf ears. The last brick was finally inserted, mortar applied, and the room closed off, the officers believed, forever. Captain Green undoubtedly died a horrible death within a few days.

WILLIAM E. SHEIDLEY

Questions for Discussion

1. How does Poe motivate the behavior of Montresor? Does the story provide any hints as to the "thousand injuries" he has suffered? Are any hints necessary?
2. Why is the setting of the story appropriate?

3. What does Montresor's treatment of his house servants tell us about his knowledge of human psychology, and how does it prepare us for his treatment of Fortunato?
4. How does Poe increase the elements of suspense as Fortunato is gradually walled into the catacombs?

Topics for Writing

(Remind the class that there is a student paper in "Writing about Short Stories," p. 1696 in the anthology, comparing and contrasting this story with Hawthorne's "Young Goodman Brown.")

1. Montresor doesn't tell his story until a half century after the actual event. Analyze how Poe adapts the flashback technique to affect the reader of "The Cask of Amontillado."
2. Explicate the passage in the story in which Montresor entices Fortunato into the crypt.

Related Commentaries

D. H. Lawrence, The Lust of Hate in Poe's "The Cask of Amontillado," p. 1494.
Edgar Allan Poe, The Importance of the Single Effect in a Prose Tale, p. 1531.

Suggested Readings

See page 208.

EDGAR ALLAN POE

The Tell-Tale Heart (p. 1151)

"The Tell-Tale Heart" is a story about what has been called "the demonic self" — a person who feels a compulsion to commit a gratuitous act of evil. Poe wrote explicitly about what he calls this "spirit of perverseness" in his story "The Black Cat," published in 1843, two years before "The Tell-Tale Heart":

> Of this spirit [of perverseness] philosophy takes no account. Yet I am not more sure that my soul lives, than I am that perverseness is one of the primitive impulses of the human heart — one of the indivisible primary faculties, or sentiments, which give direction to the character of Man. Who has not, a hundred times, found himself committing a vile or a silly action, for no other reason than because he knows he should *not*? Have we not a perpetual inclination, in the teeth of our best judgment, to violate that which is *Law*, merely because we understand it to be such?

According to the critic Eric W. Carlson, "The Tell-Tale Heart" was one of Poe's favorite stories. In addition to dramatizing the "spirit of perverseness" in his narrative, Poe combines other elements of the gothic tale (the evil eye, the curse), the psychorealistic (the narrator's paranoia), the dramatic (concentrated intensity of tone, gradually heightened series of dramatic events), and the moral (the compulsion to confess).

Questions for Discussion

1. How would you describe the narrator of the story? How does your description compare or contrast with what he would like to have you believe about him?
2. What disease is the narrator referring to in the first paragraph?
3. What caused the narrator to murder the old man? Was his reason valid?
4. What narrative devices does Poe use to heighten the suspense of the tale? Give examples.
5. Poe believed in the existence of the "spirit of perverseness" within every man. How is this revealed in the story?
6. Do you feel the confession at the end of the tale is necessary? Why? What is Poe's purpose in presenting this confession?

Topics for Writing

1. Discuss the significance of the light and dark imagery in "The Tell-Tale Heart."
2. Consider the effect of premeditation in "The Tell-Tale Heart."
3. Discuss the use of sight and sound as dramatic devices in "The Tell-Tale Heart."
4. Write an essay analyzing the dichotomy between the narrator's view of himself and our view of him in "The Tell-Tale Heart."
5. Explore reality versus illusion in "The Tell-Tale Heart."
6. Rewrite the story from the point of view of the police officers or from the point of view of the old man.
7. Consider the events that might result from the action of this story, and write a sequel presenting these developments.

Related Commentary

Edgar Allan Poe, The Importance of the Single Effect in a Prose Tale, p. 1531.

Suggested Readings

Adler, Jacob H. "Are There Flaws in 'The Cask of Amontillado'?" *Notes and Queries* 199 (1954): 32–34.
Buranelli, Vincent. *Edgar Allan Poe.* 2nd Ed. Boston: G. K. Hall, 1977.
Baudelaire, Charles P. *Baudelaire on Poe: Critical Papers.* University Park: Pennsylvania State UP, 1952.
Carlson, Eric W., ed. *Critical Essays on Edgar Allan Poe.* Boston: G. K. Hall, 1987.
Carlson, Eric W. *Introduction to Poe: A Thematic Reader.* Glenville, IL: Scott, 1967.
Dillon, John M. *Edgar Allan Poe.* Brooklyn, NY: Haskell, 1974.

Fletcher, Richard M. *The Stylistic Development of Edgar Allan Poe*. New York: Mouton, 1974.

Gargano, J. W. "'The Cask of Amontillado': A Masquerade of Motive and Identity." *Studies in Short Fiction* 4 (1967): 119–26.

———. *The Masquerade Vision in Poe's Short Stories*. Baltimore: Enoch Pratt, 1977.

Hammond, J. R. *An Edgar Allan Poe Companion: A Guide to Short Stories, Romances, and Essays*. Savage: B and N Imports, 1981.

Knapp, Bettina L. *Edgar Allan Poe*. New York: Ungar, 1984.

Levin, Harry. *The Power of Blackness: Hawthorne, Poe, Melville*. Columbus: Ohio UP, 1980.

Mabbott, Thomas Olivle, ed. *Collected Works of Edgar Allan Poe*. Cambridge, MA: Harvard UP, 1978.

May, Charles E., ed. *Edgar Allan Poe: A Study of Short Fiction*. Boston: Twayne, 1990.

Muller, John P., and William J. Richardson, eds. *The Purloined Poe: Lacan, Derrida, and Psychoanalytic Reading*. Baltimore: Johns Hopkins UP, 1988.

Pitcher, E. W. "Physiognomical Meaning of Poe's 'The Tell-Tale Heart.' " *Studies in Short Fiction* 16 (1979): 231–33.

Robinson, E. A. "Poe's 'The Tell-Tale Heart.' " *Nineteenth Century Fiction* 19 (1965): 369–78.

Symons, Julian, ed. *Selected Tales*. New York: Oxford UP, 1980.

Tucker, B. D. "Tell-Tale Heart and the Evil Eye." *Southern Literary Journal* 13 (1981): 92–98.

KATHERINE ANNE PORTER

The Jilting of Granny Weatherall (p. 1156)

Porter's title suggests the following interpretation of the theme of her story: Regardless of our chronological age and the circumstances of our life, we always remain young at heart. Granny Weatherall, nearly eighty, is physically worn out after a lifetime of serving her family — bedridden, just hours away from her fatal stroke and heart attack — yet emotionally she is still twenty and still betrothed to the bridegroom who will jilt her on her wedding day. As a young woman, then, she lost her innocence. Some time later she entered into a successful marriage with another man, John, and had four children with him, but as an old woman on her deathbed, she stubbornly fantasizes the return of a bridegroom — Jesus (although he is not named in the story) — who will take her to heaven. The playwright and screenwriter Corinne Jacker understood that since Granny is a Catholic, in this she exhibits a "sin of pride — if not sacrilege. It's an enormous act of hubris, to assume that God is going to send you a sign that you'll be received by Christ. Or that you're immortal."

Porter's conflation of two kinds of bridegroom — the secular and the divine — is the central drama of her story. Porter narrates it in the third-person from the perspective of the dying woman, brilliantly joining Granny Weatherall's stream-of-consciousness with descriptions of her physical sensations as she lies in her bed amid the growing crowd of people who attend her in her last hours — Doctor Harry, her loving daughter Cornelia, Father Connolly, and her other grown children, Jimmy and Lydia.

"The Jilting of Granny Weatherall" was included in Porter's first collection of stories, *Flowering Judas*. In an introduction to a Modern Library edition of the book ten years after its original appearance, she stated that she had "no notion of what [the stories'] meaning might be to such readers as they would find." She believed "that all our lives we are preparing to be somebody or something, even if we don't do it consciously." This element of preparation is evident in Granny Weatherall's actions in the story. The irony is that after being jilted the first time she has lived an active life as wife and mother for more than half a century, yet on her deathbed she feels the emotions she felt as a young girl, waiting for a sign that she has been especially chosen by her bridegroom. This time death itself is the disappointment.

Questions for Discussion

1. What is the setting of the story? Why has Granny Weatherall moved to her daughter's house?
2. What are her feelings toward Cornelia? What are Cornelia's feelings toward her mother?
3. How does Porter establish the failing health of her protagonist?
4. Does Granny Weatherall develop as a character during the narrative?
5. What is the climax of the story?
6. How does Porter use light in the story as a symbol of the protagonist's state of mind?
7. What is the plot of the story? How much of the action relates to this plot?
8. Do you think Porter is making a statement about religious belief in the ending of her story?

Topics for Writing

1. Does the sequence of flashbacks in Granny Weatherall's stream-of-consciousness dramatize her valiant attempts to live her life fully, or do the flashbacks suggest her inability to get over the shock of being jilted as a young woman? Support your argument with references to specific details in the story.
2. Compare and contrast Porter's story and the film version by Corinne Jacker.
3. **CONNECTIONS** Compare and contrast the value of a life lived serving others in Porter's story with Tolstoy's "The Death of Ivan Ilych."
4. **CONNECTIONS** Compare and contrast the dramatizations of a woman's life in Porter's story and in Chekhov's "The Darling."

Related Commentaries

Carolyn G. Heilbrun, A Feminist Perspective on Katherine Anne Porter and "The Jilting of Granny Weatherall," p. 1471.
Corinne Jacker, On Writing the Screenplay for Katherine Anne Porter's "The Jilting of Granny Weatherall," p. 1660.
Corinne Jacker, Scene from the Screenplay of *The Jilting of Granny Weatherall*, p. 1663.

Suggested Readings

Bayley, Isabel. *Letters of Katherine Anne Porter.* New York: Atlantic Monthly P, 1990.

Bruccoli, Matthew J., ed. *Understanding Katherine Anne Porter.* Columbia: U of South Carolina P, 1988.

Demouy, Jane Krause. *Katherine Anne Porter's Women: The Eye of Her Fiction.* Austin: U of Texas P, 1983.

Hendrick, Willene, and George Hendrick. *Katherine Anne Porter.* Boston: Twayne, 1988.

Mooney, Harry J. *The Fiction and Criticism of Katherine Anne Porter.* Rev. ed. Pittsburgh: U of Pittsburgh P, 1990.

Nance, William L. *Katherine Anne Porter and the Art of Rejection.* Chapel Hill: U of North Carolina P, 1964.

Plimpton, George, ed. *Women Writers at Work: The* Paris Review *Interviews.* New York: Penguin, 1989.

Porter, Katherine Anne. *The Collected Essays and Occasional Writings.* New York: Harcourt Brace, 1970.

———. *Flowering Judas.* New York: Harcourt Brace, 1930, 1958.

Stout, Janis P. *Strategies of Reticence: Silence and Meaning in the Works of Jane Austen, Willa Cather, Katherine Anne Porter, and Joan Didion.* Charlottesville: UP of Virginia, 1990.

Tanner, James T. F. *The Texas Legacy of Katherine Anne Porter.* Denton: U of North Texas P, 1990.

Unrue, Darlene H. *Truth and Vision in Katherine Anne Porter's Fiction.* Athens: U of Georgia P, 1985.

WILLIAM SYDNEY PORTER (O. HENRY)

The Gift of the Magi (p. 1164)

Many students will have read this story before or encountered it in one of its many television versions. The story is so well known that it has almost a mythic quality, and the fact that it was first written as a "snappy" popular magazine story has been forgotten. The outline of the story is often parodied, and some in the class may have seen a version on the television program "Saturday Night Live" a few years ago, in which the couple were the multimillionaire Donald Trump and his wife. It may be a surprise to people who think they know the story to go back to the original and find that it has a cocky, optimistic tone, and it doesn't slide into hopeless sentimentality. Sentimentality certainly hangs over the small apartment, but it's leavened with a sense of the irony and the humor of the situation. Jimmy may not get his watch back, but hair grows back at the rate of a half inch a month, so Della will have her hair down to her knees again in eight years.

The students will probably find the story a little closer to their own experience if they make some adjustments for the sums of money involved. Jimmy is being paid $20 for working a six-day week, so the $1.87 Della has managed to save is more than half a day's wages. The salary for the same amount of work for a modern office worker would be about $50, so what Della has in mind is a special present, something that will show him her happiness with their marriage. With her money, she can find something ordinary for him, but what she dreams of is something extraordinary. Jimmy, of course, has the same dream. It's as if a struggling young couple in New York today secretly decide that they'll find presents for each other at Tiffany's.

It would be a different kind of story if each of them managed to find a present that wasn't dependent on Della's having her long hair and Jimmy's having his watch, but the point of the story is that they are ready to sacrifice everything for love. They are not crushed when they find out what the other has done. They are so deeply in love that the misplaced choice of gifts only strengthens their feelings for each other. When everything is revealed, Jimmy simply sits down, smiles, and tells his wife she should go ahead and get dinner.

There are places in the story that will present difficulties for the modern reader. For example, Della is described as being aware of "the honour of being owned by Jim," and her husband is referred to as "the lord of the flat," which are certainly not phrases a couple today would use to characterize their relationship. But the story is still too tender to leave strong marks on our consciousness. Many people forget that the reference in the title is to the young married couple. Because they brought priceless gifts, Jimmy and Della themselves are the magi.

Questions for Discussion

1. We are told that Jimmy goes off to his job every day, and it is taken for granted that we know how Della passes the time. What is a young wife like her expected to do with her day? Why is she shopping from the grocer and the vegetable man and the butcher?
2. What is the author telling us when he makes "the moral reflection that life is made up of sobs, sniffles, and smiles, with sniffles predominating"?
3. What do we learn about Mme. Sofronie when we read how she answers Della?
4. Why does the author refer to "tripped by on rosy wings" as a "hashed metaphor"? How could we fix it?
5. Is there any chance that the young husband will walk in the door and think his wife is no longer pretty?
6. Is the author being serious when he suggests that the gifts the Magi brought to Jesus in the cradle were "no doubt wise ones, possibly bearing the privilege of exchange in case of duplication"?

Topic for Writing

1. Using the details in the story, write a paper discussing marriage roles at the time the story was written and compare them with these roles today.

Suggested Reading

Henry, O. *The Complete Works.* Garden City, NY: Doubleday, 1953.

PHILIP ROTH

"I Always Wanted You to Admire My Fasting"; or, Looking at Kafka (p. 1169)

When this story was included in Rust Hill's anthology *Writer's Choice* (New York: David McKay, 1974), Roth explained in a headnote that his experience as a college professor had taught him that "sometimes serious students of literature tend to read Kafka as though he had written his stories on Mars, or in graduate school, instead of Prague." Roth revealed that his tragicomic Kafka story "came largely out of trying to get my students at the University of Pennsylvania to read Kafka's fiction without becoming Biblical exegists in the process."

In "Looking at Kafka," Roth brilliantly explores the premise of what might have happened if Kafka had lived on into the middle of the twentieth century instead of dying young of tuberculosis in Prague. Roth imagines Kafka as an immigrant in the United States during World War II, fleeing Hitler's army to make a new life for himself in New Jersey. Unknown as a writer, he begins again as a Hebrew teacher preparing boys like Philip Roth for their bar mitzvah (Kafka studied Hebrew in Prague and spoke Yiddish with his parents at home). Invited to the Roth home for Friday dinner, Doctor Franz "Kishka" (the nickname created for him by his impudent students — *kishka* means "intestines" in Yiddish) becomes the victim of a plan contrived by Philip's manipulative father, who hopes to marry off his forty-year-old sister-in-law, Philip's Aunt Rhoda. The plot of the story is the stuff of comic opera, until Kafka proves impotent on a prenuptial visit to Atlantic City and Aunt Rhoda breaks off their engagement. Years later Kafka dies without publishing any books, all of his literary work destroyed except for the four letters he had written to Aunt Rhoda.

Roth tells us his theme at the end of the story: His intent was to dramatize the miracle of Kafka's masterpieces having been written and published at all, given the haphazard operation of chance in all human events. In the process, Roth reveals Kafka's intrinsic humanity by casting him as a normal-sized person deserving of our sympathy. Roth may also be suggesting that more than one potential artist has lived and died in obscurity. An additional irony in the story is that Kafka travels thousands of miles from Prague only to find himself embroiled once more in a family drama instigated by a domineering father, well-intentioned but obstinately insisting on having his own way, somewhat reminiscent of the one Kafka described in "The Metamorphosis."

Questions for Discussion

1. Why is Philip surprised and upset when Dr. Kafka agrees to come to dinner?
2. How is Philip's father both like and unlike Kafka's father?
3. What is the role of Philip's mother? Does it reflect the typical view of women's role in the American family in the 1940s, or is it a particular reflection of the view of the mother's role in a Jewish family?
4. Why does Philip rebel against his father at the end of the story?

Topics for Writing

1. Imagine the contents of Kafka's four *meshugeneh* (crazy) letters to Aunt Rhoda and recreate any one of them.
2. Explicate the meaning of Kafka's "The Metamorphosis" as if you were the young Hebrew student, Philip Roth, in this story.

Related Story

Franz Kafka, The Metamorphosis, p. 794.

Suggested Reading

Roth, Philip. *Beyond Despair: Three Lectures* [on the Holocaust] *and a Conversation.* New York: Fromm International, 1994.

GABRIELLE ROY

The Well of Dunrea (p. 1184)

This wrenching, painful narrative is also a story with many mysteries. We hear the story only second hand, as the narrator relates what she has heard from her younger sister. Perhaps because of the way it is told, many elements of the story hang unresolved until the final sentences, and even then we are left still uncertain that we have learned everything. In the beginning of the story, we are even uncertain about the father's job. What does he do? We are never told directly, but it becomes clear through the plot that he is a land agent for the Canadian government and is responsible for helping immigrant groups settle in the country's new western lands. It is not until the end of the story that we learn why he has told the story only to his younger daughter, Agnes. When he was near death in the well, as the fire swept over the immigrant village, he saw her in a vision, waiting for him at the end of the tram line with her dog, calling to him after he had fainted from the heat and lack of air.

We are told that the father suffers because of the dishonesty of both the railroad company and the government in luring settlers to the raw wastelands of the prairie by displaying posters depicting the small village he has successfully established with the White Russians. We are not told why he doesn't do anything about it. We are also told that he suffers from the agony of what he witnessed as the fire destroyed the village. The resolution of that mystery brings us to a complex involvement in his own sense of guilt. He shouted to the villagers, who were devout Christians, that the fire was a sign of God's wrath. He knew that the fire was only a manifestation of the natural life cycle of the prairie, but he was unable to think of any other way to convince them to flee for their lives. The leader of the group, a man he has worked with during all his years of managing the settlement, acts on his words and walks into the fire, holding a cross before him in a vain attempt to appease God by immolating himself.

Roy's story describes a time in the settlement of the western lands of both the United States and Canada that is still with us. The lands have never been rich enough or watered enough for permanent settlement and extensive planting, and the settlers who tried to stay have been driven away time and time again by drought, dust storms, fire, and floods. In the United States, many of these areas have almost become deserts through overgrazing, repeated plowing, and long periods of drought. Roy shows us how different groups in Canada — from the religious groups such as the Dukhobors, whose fanaticism led them to the edge of starvation, to more fortunate groups such as the White Russians, who for a time found a way to keep the prairie from striking at them — struggled to survive the conditions. This brilliantly conceived and skillfully handled story holds the reader's attention until the final paragraphs.

Questions for Discussion

1. The students may not be familiar with this area of Canada. Where is Saskatchewan, and how is it related to the American prairies?
2. The story is translated from the French language. What does this tell us about Canada?
3. What does the father mean when he says that if settlers planted flowers "it was a sure sign of success"?
4. What are some of the signs of religious fanaticism that are presented in the story?
5. Why would the people in Dunrea have not the "least expectation that God's gentle hand would ever weigh heavily upon them"?
6. Discuss the point of view of the story, and identify the moment of resolution when we find ourselves at the story's climax. Is it where we expect it to be?
7. Why is it significant that their father cannot tell his story himself?
8. Why did the people of the settlement refuse, at the moment of crisis, to accept what her father was telling them?

Topics for Writing

1. Analyze what we learn about the father from his actions, and describe how his character is dramatically revealed to us as the story develops.
2. **CONNECTIONS** Compare the father in this story with the grandfather in Margaret Laurence's "The Mask of the Bear."

Suggested Readings

Clemente, Linda M., and William A. Clemente. *Gabrielle Roy: Creation and Memory.* Toronto: ECW, 1997.
Hesse, M. G. *Gabrielle Roy.* Boston: Twayne, 1984.
Raban, Jonathan. *Bad Land: An American Romance.* New York: Random, 1996.

SALMAN RUSHDIE

The Firebird's Nest (p. 1195)

Many students will be familiar with the threats made to Rushdie's life by the religious authorities in Iran, who have offered millions of dollars in rewards for anyone who succeeds in killing him. The cause was a chapter in his novel *The Satanic Verses* that was considered to be disrespectful to the memory of the prophet Mohammed and to the Muslim religion. In English cities such as Doncaster, the large populations of immigrants from India and Pakistan were not only forbidden to read the book by their religious leaders but also were urged to destroy copies wherever they could be found and to attack any bookstores where copies were available. The threats intimidated American publishers, who waited several years to release a paperback edition, fearing danger to bookstore employees. The threat to Rushdie is thought to have lessened in recent years, but he still lives under constant guard and is moved often to prevent an assassin from finding him.

Through all the furor, it is clear that Rushdie is a major writer, and each book that has appeared since he has gone into hiding has been a major addition to contemporary world literature. At the same time, it is just as clear that Rushdie is a difficult individual, and his work continues to arouse strong emotions. He has often been called "prickly," and the word is a useful description of some aspects of his writing. Students who are aware of any of the problems of today's India will recognize that Rushdie's thinly disguised portrait of a corrupt, dying society in a dead land would not give much pleasure to Indian readers.

It has been suggested by some critics that the story "The Firebird's Nest" has a connection to the story of Bluebeard, the serial wife killer of legend, but it can also be related to one of the problems that has plagued modern India: wife burning. It is not until the last pages that we become conscious that there is more than symbolism behind the calm assumption of the people in the village that "women catch fire, and burn." In traditional Indian families, it is customary to find a husband for a daughter by the promise of large dowries, or bride payments. Months are spent on negotiations between the families if the prospective son-in-law is considered a desirable husband. Often, after the marriage, the husband, or the husband's family, decides that the dowry was too small, or, in some instances, the husband simply decides to put himself on the market again, to be able to claim a new dowry. Since the bride, by tradition, has come into her husband's home, she is at the mercy of his family. The long, flowing robes worn by women in traditional homes are easily set on fire, and the women usually die before help arrives. The Indian government has made a determined effort to end the killings, but the practice has been sanctioned by a long tradition, and it will be generations before it is rooted out. As Mr. Maharaj tells his American fiancée, when she asks about the old man they pass on his way to be married, "In a long life there may be more than a single dowry. These things add up."

Rushdie at first presents the practice of bride burning as a magic event. Women simply burn up. He is often described as a fabulist, a writer who works in myth and legend, so it seems that much of what happens in the story is the result of magic. The reality of what he is describing is there beneath the surface, however, even if he allows us only tantalizing glances. The complete corruption of the man whom the American woman is going to marry is only revealed in stages, as Rushdie strips away his various facades. Mr. Maharaj is a symbol for everything that is weak, dishonest, self-serving, and corrupt in the older India. The American woman, whose financial acumen leads the Indian to think of her as a "rainmaker," symbolizes that faint hope that someone from a new land will come to save India. Rushdie certainly makes it clear in his story that he doesn't think India can do anything to help itself. He is a prickly writer, but his voice is necessary in view of the catastrophic overpopulation and increasing social unrest in India today.

Questions for Discussion

1. Rushdie describes a religious leader who every year was paid his weight in jewels by his followers and subjects. Is this a description of a real event?
2. Wildly conflicting rumors about the new bride-to-be circulate through the village before her arrival. Why are the villagers dependent on rumor and gossip? Would there be this same trust in gossip in a similar situation in our society?
3. Why did Mr. Maharaj tell the American woman that India and the United States were similar?
4. Discuss Mr. Maharaj's characterization of the American woman as a "rainmaker."
5. What is Rushdie telling us about the society when he tells us that Mr. Maharaj's sister believes that "Here there are no old wives' tales. Alas, there are no old wives."
6. Describe the relationship between the American woman and Mr. Maharaj's sister. Would we describe it as a supportive relationship?
7. What is the Indian woman telling the American woman when she says, "Do not mistake the abnormal for the untrue"?
8. Why are none of the dancers married?
9. Does the reader ever know for certain whether Mr. Maharaj has been married before?
10. The final scene, in which the Indian brother and sister confront each other and she is destroyed, has been told on a level of magic symbolism. Describe some possible "real" interpretations of the scene that Rushie describes.

Topics for Writing

1. As Rushdie describes the American woman trying to sleep on her first night in the palace, he writes about the United States, "Amid that surplus of structures, of content, it is not easy for the phantasmagoric to gain the upper hand." Discuss his meaning, and show examples from the story that amplify his statement.
2. Rushdie writes of the Indian man in America, "He has learned to talk like a modern man, but in truth is helpless in the face of the present." Clarify Rushdie's meaning with examples from the story.

Related Commentaries

Salman Rushdie, On Angela Carter's *The Bloody Chamber*, p. 1537.
Salman Rushdie, On Italo Calvino's "If on a winter's night a traveler," p. 1539.

Suggested Reading

Rushdie, Salman. *Imaginary Homelands*. New York: Granta/Viking, 1991.

CAROL SHIELDS

Mirrors (p. 1207)

This story may be discussed as a classic modern story. In stories today there is no longer a need for a complex plot or setting. "Mirrors" is complete with two people, their lightly sketched summer lake house, a mention of two children and their families, and a description of the one thing about the married couple that sets them apart: They have no mirrors in their summer house. A consideration of this small anomaly and a quiet presentation of the couple's history at the lake is the extent of the story. Shields is simply presenting the reader with the background necessary to understand the small epiphany that ends the narrative. The husband looks at his wife one night when she has stayed up to read in bed, and he thinks for a moment that he has lived with her all these years and he doesn't know who she is. "Who was this person?" he asked himself. The moment of self-discovery comes a moment later, when he looks into her eyes and each of them realizes that they have become the other, that each of them is the mirror that they have excluded from the house. And that is the story. In this little anecdote, Shields has described two lives for us, described them so well that we would probably recognize the couple if we were at their lake and saw them pass by.

One way for a class to interpret the story might be to develop this idea of the two people as mirrors of each other — but only at the lake, where they have left so much else of their lives behind. They couldn't shake off their separate identities in the city where they presumably have jobs, and certainly they have children who have lives of their own. In the summer they can slip away from these demands, and it helps them to do so without a mirror, which would bring them back to themselves. What began as a simple series of coincidences — there was no mirror left with the other furniture when they bought the house and they didn't find a mirror they liked at a country auction — became a definition of their lives. Without a mirror she can avoid seeing that she is growing heavy, without a mirror he doesn't have to face the guilt he felt after he had an affair with another woman. The simple exceptional thing about them — that they don't have a mirror — describes them, and it also defines them. When they turn to each other they see themselves, and at that moment that is the only mirror they need.

Questions for Discussion

1. Do we learn anything about the background of the couple that might lead us to expect that they would decide to do without mirrors?
2. What is the author telling us about the couple when she says that in the theater they want to see plays about "men and women who resemble themselves"?
3. The author tells us that when we walked away from the summer house we would be unable to describe what its furniture looked like. From the things she has told us about the couple, how much can we tell about what they look like?
4. Why are we told so little about the couple's children?
5. How can we interpret the woman's ideas about the physical nature of mirrors?
6. How can we interpret the man's idea that "every hour contains at least a moment of bewilderment or worse"?

Topics for Writing

1. Discuss this story in relation to the elements of a short story.
2. **CONNECTIONS** Compare this story, in which almost nothing "happens," to a story such as Alice Munro's more traditional "Meneseteung," in which the reader is presented with a complex narrative, in order to analyze what we have gained or lost with the new mode of storytelling.

Suggested Reading

Shields, Carol. *Coming to Canada*. Ottawa: Carleton UP, 1995.

LESLIE MARMON SILKO

Yellow Woman (p. 1214)

This story is told in the first person and presented episodically in several sections. It takes place over two days, beginning the morning Yellow Woman wakes up beside the river with Silva, the stranger she has spent the night with. The story ends at sundown the next day, when she returns to her family in the Pueblo village.

"Yellow Woman" is built on different traditions from those in the cultural background of most American students. Silko writes fiction that preserves her cultural heritage by re-creating its customs and values in stories that dramatize emotional conflicts of interest to modern readers.

As Yellow Woman narrates the story of her abduction and return to her family, the reader comes to share her mood and her interpretation of what has happened. As a girl she was fascinated by the stories her grandfather told her about Silva, the mysterious kachina spirit who kidnaps married women from the tribe, then returns them after he has kept them as his wives. These stories were probably similar to the imaginary tales passed down in an oral tradition whose origins are lost to contemporary American folklorists. Silko has created their modern equivalent, her version of how they might be reenacted in today's world. The overweight, white Arizona rancher is familiar to us, as is the Jell-O being prepared for supper, and we have no difficulty imagining the gunnysacks full of freshly slaughtered meat bouncing on the back of Yellow Woman's horse.

The dreamlike atmosphere Silko creates in "Yellow Woman" makes such realistic details protrude sharply from the soft-focus narrative. Yellow Woman doesn't think clearly. She seems bewitched by the myths her grandfather told her, and her adventure following the man she calls Silva holds her enthralled. At the end she says, "I thought about Silva, and I felt sad at leaving him; still, there was something strange about him, and I tried to figure it out all the way back home." We are not told what — if anything — she does figure out.

Instead, action takes the place of thought in the story. Yellow Woman looks at the place on the riverbank where she met Silva and tells herself that "he will come back sometime and be waiting again by the river." Action moves so swiftly that we follow Yellow Woman as obediently as she follows her abductor, mesmerized by the audacity of what is happening. There is no menace in Silva, no danger or malice in his rape of Yellow Woman. The bullets in his rifle are for the white rancher who realizes he has been killing other men's cattle, not for Yellow Woman — or for us.

Questions for Discussion

1. Why is Yellow Woman so eager to believe that she and Silva are acting out the stories her grandfather told her?
2. How does Silko structure the opening paragraphs of the story to help the reader suspend disbelief and enter the dreamlike atmosphere of Yellow Woman's perceptions?
3. Why does Silko tell the story through the woman's point of view? Describe the Pueblo Indian woman we know as Yellow Woman. Is she happy at home with her mother, grandmother, husband, and baby? Why is Yellow Woman's father absent from the story?
4. Are there any limitations to Silko's choice to tell the story through Yellow Woman's point of view? Explain.
5. Why doesn't the narrator escape from Silva when she discovers him asleep by the river as the story opens? What makes her decide to return home the next day?

Topics for Writing

1. Tell the story through a third-person omniscient narration.
2. Compare "Yellow Woman" with an Indian folktale about the kachina spirit who kidnaped married women.
3. **CONNECTIONS** Compare Silko's "Yellow Woman" and Oates's "Where Are You Going, Where Have You Been?" as rape narratives.

Related Commentaries

Paula Gunn Allen, Whirlwind Man Steals Yellow Woman, p. 1416.
Leslie Marmon Silko, Language and Literature from a Pueblo Indian Perspective, p. 1544.

Suggested Readings

Allen, Paula Gunn. *The Sacred Hoop: Recovering the Feminine in American Indian Traditions.* Boston: Beacon, 1986.

———, ed. *Spider Woman's Granddaughters: Traditional Tales and Contemporary Writing by Native American Women.* Boston: Beacon, 1989.

Graulich, Melody, ed. *"Yellow Woman."* Women, Text and Contexts Series. New Brunswick, NJ: Rutgers UP, 1993.

Hoilman, Dennis. "The Ethnic Imagination: A Case History." *Canadian Journal of Native Studies* 5.2 (1985): 167–75.

Nelson, Robert M. *Place and Vision: The Function of Landscape in Native American Fiction.* New York: P. Lang, 1993.

Sands, Kathleen Mullen. "Indian Women's Personal Narrative: Voices Past and Present." *American Women's Autobiography: Fea(s)ts of Memory.* Ed. Margo Culley. Madison: U of Wisconsin P, 1992.

Silko, Leslie Marmon. *Almanac of the Dead.* New York: Simon, 1991.

Isaac Bashevis Singer

Gimpel the Fool (p. 1224)

Gimpel's life as a fool seems to encompass three stages. In the first, he is a boy in school, teased unmercifully by the other students and the townspeople. When he goes to the village rabbi for advice, the rabbi tells him to accept the situation, because it is "better to be a fool all your days than for one hour to be evil. You are not a fool. They are the fools. For he who causes his neighbor to feel shame loses Paradise himself." Comforting spiritual advice, yet a minute later Gimpel is made a fool of by the rabbi's daughter.

In the next stage of Gimpel's life as a fool he is a successful baker, employing an assistant. But his wife, Elka, sleeps with his assistant. Gimpel loves the children she produces, and again the rabbi is no help, advising Gimpel to divorce his unfaithful wife but making him wait nine months when Gimpel changes his mind about divorce. Gimpel weeps when he thinks he has misjudged his wife's behavior: "What's the good of *not* believing? Today it's your wife you don't believe; tomorrow it's God Himself you won't take stock in."

After his wife's death Gimpel is in despair, since with her dying breath she confessed that she had deceived him. In his anger he urinates into the bread dough, but the spirit of his wife reproaches him: "Because I was false is everything false too?" Gimpel buries the bread he has spoiled, leaves his money with his children, gives up his business, and becomes a wanderer.

The final page of the story is the third stage of Gimpel's life, when — free from his wife and his business — he becomes the wise fool, resigned to his fate. He dreams constantly of his wife, who has become a saint to him. He prays for death and carries his shroud in his beggar's sack: "When the time comes I will go joyfully. Whatever may be there, it will be real, without complication, without ridicule, without deception." In God's heaven, Gimpel tells us, he "cannot be deceived," so he will finally be free from his role as a fool.

Questions for Discussion

1. "Gimpel the Fool" is told by a first-person narrator. What does Singer gain from this point of view? Does it have any limitations?
2. Singer is saying that the world we live in is difficult to understand; we may all be fools if we are "deceived" or taken in by what people tell us. Agree or disagree with this interpretation.
3. In what ways is Gimpel a "holy fool"? What definitions of a fool or foolish characterize him?
4. Who else might be called fools in this story?

Topics for Writing

1. Analyze the details in the story that create the atmosphere of the Jewish villages of Poland before World War II.
2. **CONNECTIONS** Compare the forms of persecution in Singer's "Gimpel the Fool" and Jackson's "The Lottery."
3. **CONNECTIONS** Compare the treatment of the theme of "the little man" in Singer's "Gimpel the Fool" and Gogol's "The Overcoat."

Suggested Readings

Alexander, Edward. *Isaac Bashevis Singer.* World Authors Series. Boston: Twayne, 1980.
Singer, Isaac Bashevis. *Collected Stories.* New York: Farrar, 1981.

SUSAN SONTAG

The Way We Live Now (p. 1235)

Most stories by contemporary authors in this anthology are told from a limited-omniscient point of view. Leslie Marmon Silko narrates her story through the perceptions of Yellow Woman; James Baldwin uses first-person narration in "Sonny's Blues." Susan Sontag does something very different in "The Way We Live Now." The story chronicles the last months of a man dying of AIDS, but we never learn directly what he sees or feels. Instead, we hear what he is suffering through the comments of his many friends. The end result is a work that deliberately treats its subject the way most people treat AIDS itself — at a distance, through hearsay, with mingled fascination and horror, as something terrible that can only happen to other people.

We never learn the name, occupation, or physical description of the AIDS victim in Sontag's story. Instead, we are told the responses of his friends, like a roll call of potential victims of the virus. These friends — more than twenty-five of them — are also not described, only presented by name as they talk to one another about the sick man. Their names follow one another so rapidly we are not given any explanation of their relationships: Max, Ellen, Greg, Tanya, Orson, Stephen, Frank, Jan, Quentin, Paolo, Kate, Aileen, Donny, Ursula, Ira, Hilda, Nora, Wesley, Victor, Xavier, Lewis, Robert, Betsy, Yvonne, Zack, and Clarice. The first-name basis is fitting, since the majority of the people know one another and inhabit the same world. We are never told what city they all live in, but we assume from the way they talk and their large numbers that they live in New York and are part of its cliques of people active in the arts, literature, and cultural journalism.

The first-name basis of the conversations is also aesthetically appropriate, because for the most part the characters are using the telephone. They repeat the latest gossip they have learned from one another; for all their sophistication, they pass along news of the stages of their friend's illness like the voices of tribal drums alerting the inhabitants of villages in Africa. The reader has the same sense of a closely knit community joined by common interests and means of livelihood. Because the community is left unspecified, the setting and the characters become mythologized into "Anyplace" and "Everyone." Sontag's implication is that we are all participants in this human tragedy. AIDS can happen to anyone.

As we read "The Way We Live Now," our rational impulses function despite the lack of specificity about the central character. The short conversational exchanges function as a literary code that we try to unlock. We attempt to trace relationships (Quentin, Lewis, Paolo, and Tanya have all been lovers of the AIDS victim); we categorize important information about lives outside the main story (Max gets AIDS too, as does Hilda's seventy-five-year-old aunt); we highlight generalizations that suggest a broader social and moral significance to this individual tragedy (the age of "debauchery" is over).

Close readers may even be able to interpret the fragments of conversations to gain psychological insights of use in other contexts. For example, Kate tells Aileen that the sick man is "not judging people or wondering about their motives" (when they come to see him in the hospital); rather, "he's just happy to see his friends." By presenting the numbers of people linked to a specific AIDS victim who appears to be well known and highly regarded in his community, Sontag is making an ironic comment about the isolation of all AIDS victims. Her story is an attempt to write about a taboo subject and encourage compassion toward those suffering from the disease.

Questions for Discussion

1. The story is developed chronologically, from the news of the patient's illness, through his first hospitalization, to his return home and rehospitalization. How does this progression give coherence to the story?
2. How do the relationships suggested among the twenty-five characters in the story give you a sense of the occupation and lifestyle of the central character?

3. Hilda says that the death of the pianist in Paris "who specialized in twentieth-century Czech and Polish music" is important because "he's such a valuable person . . . and it's such a loss to the culture." Do you think Sontag shares Hilda's opinion? Do you? Why or why not?
4. Agree or disagree with Ursula's idea at the end of the story.

Topics for Writing

1. Write a review of Sontag's nonfiction work *AIDS and Its Metaphors*.
2. Choose any five characters in "The Way We Live Now" and invent backgrounds for them.
3. Rewrite the story from the point of view of the AIDS patient, perhaps in the form of his diary.

Suggested Reading

Sontag, Susan. *AIDS and Its Metaphors*. New York: Farrar, 1989.

GERTRUDE STEIN

Miss Furr and Miss Skeene (p. 1249)

If Samuel Beckett's "Dante and the Lobster" is an example of a modernist story weighted with symbolism and allusion, then Gertrude Stein's "Miss Furr and Miss Skeene" is an example of a modernist story set free of heavy meaning. Stein has given us a pencil sketch of the lives of two women whose names are perhaps the most suggestive things about them. Helen Furr's first name suggests her femininity and sexual allure — the Helen whose beauty caused the Trojan War. Her last name suggests animality and sensuality; the name "Furr" rhymes with *purr* if you think about it. Georgine Skeene's first name hints of masculinity; perhaps her parents hoped she would be born a little boy instead of a girl? "Skeene" suggests "skin," of course, stroked silkily under the warmth of an admiring hand. Actually the word seems like a combination of the sounds of both "skin" and "sheen." No doubt students will have other associations with these words.

The physicality of these two women is unmistakable, and yet we know nothing about their appearances — height, weight, hair, eyes, mouth, or chin. Their physicality is less important to the author of the story than the word she uses to characterize the essence of what they are looking for in life — they want to be "gay." Students will assume that this means lesbian. Stein isn't denying this assumption, but she is also careful to define the way she is using "gay" in the opening paragraph. She tells us that Helen Furr comes from a pleasant home and has pleasant parents, who support her desire to cultivate her voice, but that "she did not find it gay living in the same place where she had always been living." Here "gay" implies happiness, *joie de vivre*.

Stein's sketch is one of her most shimmering, transparent narratives. In telling the story about Miss Furr and Miss Skeene, she creates what amounts to a series of short pencil sketches suggesting the outline of their meeting as students, their life together, their study of music ("both cultivating their voices"), their eventual separation, and Miss Furr's "living well" into old age with happy memories of a fulfilled lifetime, *telling* "over and over" the "little ways one could be learning to use in being gay," after *living* them as a younger woman.

Questions for Discussion

1. What associations do you have with the names of the two women characters in the story?
2. How would you define the meaning of the word *gay* as Stein uses it here?
3. How does Stein's sketch echo the format of a fairy tale, which begins with the words "Once upon a time" and ends with "they lived happily ever after"?
4. Why does Stein introduce "some dark and heavy men" into the story?

Topics for Writing

1. Stein was interested in the use of words for their own sake, emphasizing the oral dimension of storytelling in "Miss Furr and Miss Skeene." Analyze how the *sound* of the words in her story is as important as the *sense* of the words.
2. **CONNECTIONS** Stein and Beckett are both experimental writers. How do their stories differ from the traditional stories you have read this semester?

Suggested Reading

Haas, Robert, ed. *A Primer for the Gradual Understanding of Gertrude Stein.* Los Angeles: Black Sparrow, 1971.

JOHN STEINBECK

The Chrysanthemums (p. 1255)

The instinctive life that Elisa Allen loves as she tends her chrysanthemum plants lies dormant under her fingers. She is good with flowers, like her mother before her. Elisa says, "She could stick anything in the ground and make it grow." But it is December, and Steinbeck tells us it is "a time of quiet and of waiting." The Salinas landscape lies peacefully, but Elisa is vaguely unfulfilled. She begins to transplant her little chrysanthemum shoots, working without haste, conscious of her "hard-swept" house and her well-ordered garden, protected with its fence of chicken wire. Everything in her little world is under control. The tension in the scene is in herself, something she vaguely senses but refuses to face: the difference between her little world and the larger one encompassing it. Elisa is strong and mature, at the height of her physical strength. Why should she lie dormant? She has no fit scope for her powers. Steinbeck suggests the contradiction between her strength and her passivity in his description of the landscape: "The yellow stubble fields seemed to be bathed in pale cold sunshine, but there was no sunshine in the valley now in December." Like Hemingway, Steinbeck uses physical and geographical details to suggest the *absence* of positive qualities in his fictional characters. There is no sunshine in the valley, and the chrysanthemum plants aren't flowering, but what is natural in the annual vegetation cycle is out of kilter in Elisa. She experiences the world as a state of frustration.

Steinbeck has written an understated Chekhovian story in which ostensibly nothing much happens. It is a slice of life as Elisa lives it, sheltered and comfortable, yet — in Henry David Thoreau's words — life lived in a state of "quiet desperation."

The two male characters feel none of Elisa's lack of fulfillment. They live in a male world and take their opportunities for granted. Her husband, Henry Allen, is having a fine day. He's sold his thirty head of steer for a good price, and he's celebrating this Saturday night by taking his wife out to dinner and the movies in town. The traveling man is a trifle down on his luck, but it's nothing serious. He's found no customers this day so he lacks the money for his supper, but he knows a mark when he sees one. He flatters Elisa by agreeing with her and handing her a line about bringing some of her chrysanthemums to a lady he knows "down the road a piece." Elisa springs into action, delighted to be needed. Her tender shoots need her too, but she is not sufficiently absorbed by her gardening. The men do the real work of the world in this story. Gardening is a hobby she's proud of, and her husband encourages her to take pride in it, but she needs to feel of use in a larger dimension. Elisa mistakes this need for the freedom she imagines the transient knows on the road. Steinbeck gives her a clue as to the man's real condition in the state of his horse and mule, which she as a good gardener shouldn't have missed: "The horse and donkey drooped like unwatered flowers."

Instead, Elisa is caught up in her romantic fantasy of his nomadic life. Her sexual tension reduces her to a "fawning dog" as she envisions his life, but finally she realizes the man doesn't have the money for his dinner. "She stood up then, very straight, and her face was ashamed." Ashamed for what reason? Her lack of sensitivity to his poverty? Her sexual excitement? Her sense of captivity in a masculine world, where apparently only motherhood would bring opportunities for real work? Elisa brings the man two battered pots to fix and resumes talking, unable to leave him or her fantasy about the freedom she thinks he enjoys. He tells her outright that "it ain't the right kind of a life for a woman." Again she misreads the situation, taking his comment as a challenge. Her response is understandable, since she's never had his opportunity to choose a life on the road. She defends her ability to be his rival at sharpening scissors and banging out dents in pots and pans.

When the man leaves, Elisa is suddenly aware of her loneliness. She scrubs her body as rigorously as she's swept her house, punishing her skin with a pumice stone instead of pampering it with bubble bath. Then she puts on "the dress which was the symbol of her prettiness." An odd choice of words. Without understanding her instinctive rebellion against male expectations, Elisa refuses to be a sex symbol. Again she loses, denying herself pleasure in soft fabrics and beautiful colors. When Henry returns, he is bewildered by her mood and unable to reach her. She sees the chrysanthemums dying on the road, but she still can't face the truth about her sense of the repression and futility of her life. Wine at dinner and the idea of going to see a prize fight briefly bring her closer to the flesh and the instinctive life she has shunned outside her contact with her flowers, but they don't lift her mood. She feels as fragile and undervalued as her chrysanthemums. She begins to cry weakly, "like an old woman," as Henry drives her down the road.

Like Lawrence's heroine in "Odour of Chrysanthemums," Elisa is frustrated, cut off from the fullness of life by her physical destiny as a woman in a man's world. Does Steinbeck understand the sexual bias that undermines Elisa's sense of herself? He makes Henry as considerate a husband as a woman could wish for — he takes Elisa to the movies instead of going off to the prize fight himself. Like Hemingway, Steinbeck was sensitive to women's frustration, depicting it often in his fiction, even if he didn't look too closely at its probable causes in the society of his time.

Questions for Discussion

1. Based on Steinbeck's description in the first three paragraphs, how would you characterize the initial tone of the story? What do you associate with Steinbeck's image of the valley as "a closed pot"? In what way does this initial description foreshadow the events of the story?
2. What kind of character is Elisa Allen? What are the physical boundaries of her world? What is Elisa's psychological state at the beginning of the story?
3. Characterize the two men who are part of Elisa's world. In what ways are they similar and different? How does their way of life compare and contrast with the life Elisa leads?
4. What is the role of the chrysanthemums in Elisa's life? What do they symbolize?
5. How does Elisa delude herself about the life of the tinker? What other fantasies does this lead her to indulge in?
6. In what way does the tinker manipulate Elisa to accomplish his goals?
7. When the tinker leaves, a change comes over Elisa. What has she suddenly realized, and what course of action does she adopt?
8. As Elisa, both realistically and symbolically, goes out into the world, has she achieved any resolution of her problem? Why does she end the story "crying weakly — like an old woman"?

Topics for Writing

1. Discuss Steinbeck's use of setting to establish theme in "The Chrysanthemums."
2. Consider the isolation of Elisa Allen.
3. Analyze Elisa's illusions about the tinker and his interest in her as contrasted with reality.
4. Recall a time when you felt threatened and frustrated by events that isolated you. Write a narrative recounting this experience from a third-person point of view.
5. **CONNECTIONS** Compare male versus female societal and sexual roles in Lawrence's "Odour of Chrysanthemums" and Steinbeck's "The Chrysanthemums."

6. **CONNECTIONS** Discuss woman in a man's world: Steinbeck's Elisa and Silko's Yellow Woman.

Related Commentary

Jay Parini, Lawrence's and Steinbeck's "Chrysanthemums," p. 1530.

Related Story

D. H. Lawrence, Odour of Chrysanthemums, p. 859.

Suggested Readings

Marcus, Mordecai. "The Lost Dream of Sex and Children in 'The Chrysanthemums.'" *Modern Fiction Studies* 11 (1965): 54–58.
McMahan, Elizabeth. "'The Chrysanthemums': Study of a Woman's Sexuality." *Modern Fiction Studies* 14 (1968–69): 453–58.
Miller, William V. "Sexual and Spiritual Ambiguity in 'The Chrysanthemums.'" *Steinbeck Quarterly* 5 (1972): 68–75.
Renner, S. "The Real Woman behind the Fence in 'The Chrysanthemums.'" *Modern Fiction Studies* 31 (1985): 305–17.
Sweet, Charles A. "Ms. Elisa Allen and Steinbeck's 'The Chrysanthemums.'" *Modern Fiction Studies* 20 (1974): 210–14.

AMY TAN

Two Kinds (p. 1264)

"Two Kinds," which was first published in the February 1989 issue of *The Atlantic Monthly*, is an excerpt from Amy Tan's best-selling book *The Joy Luck Club*. It is a skillfully written story that will probably pose no difficulty for most students; plot, characters, setting, and theme are immediately clear. The narrator states what she's "learned" from her experience in her final paragraph: She has come to realize that "Pleading Child" and "Perfectly Contented" are "two halves of the same song."

Looking back to her childhood, the narrator appears to be "perfectly contented" with her memories. Her interpretation of her relationship with her mother is presented in a calm, even self-satisfied way. After her mother's death, she tunes the piano left to her in her parents' apartment. "I played a few bars [of the piano piece by Robert Schumann], surprised at how easily the notes came back to me." The painful memory of her fiasco as a piano student has dissipated. Now she is her own audience, and she is pleased with what she hears. There is no real emotional stress in "Two Kinds"; the girl has had a comfortable life. She has survived her mother and can dispose of her possessions as she likes. She is at peace with her past, fulfilling her mother's prophecy that "you can be best anything."

The mother earned her right to look on the bright side of life by surviving tremendous losses when she left China. Her desire to turn her daughter into a "Chinese Shirley Temple" is understandable but unfortunate, since it places a tremendous psychological burden on the child. A discussion about this story might center on parents' supporting children versus "pushing" them to succeed in tasks beyond their abilities or ambitions.

Still, the narrator doesn't appear to have suffered unduly from her mother's ambitions for her. By her own account she was more than a match for her mother in the contest of wills on the piano bench. After her wretched performance at the recital, the daughter refuses to practice anymore. Her mother shouts, "Only two kinds of daughters. . . . Those who are obedient and those who follow their own mind! Only one kind of daughter can live in this house. Obedient daughter!" The girl answers by saying the unspeakable: "I wish I'd never been born! I wish I were dead! Like [the mother's twin baby girls lost in China]." This ends the conflict, but the narrator goes on to tell us that she was unrelenting in victory: "In the years that followed, I failed her many times, each time asserting my will, my right to fall short of expectations. I didn't get straight *A*s. I didn't become class president. I didn't get into Stanford. I dropped out of college." She tells us that only after her mother's death can she begin to see things in perspective, when she is free to create her version of the past.

Since most students in class will be of the age when they are also asserting their will against parents in a struggle to take control of their lives, they will probably sympathize with Tan's narrator and accept her judgments uncritically. Will any reader take the mother's side?

Questions for Discussion

1. Why is the setting of this story important? What do you learn from it about the experience of Asian immigrants in their first years in the United States?
2. What advantages are offered to the child? What disadvantages?
3. How typical is Tan's story of the mother-daughter conflict? Explain.
4. Explain the meaning of the last paragraph of the story.

Topics for Writing

1. CONNECTIONS   Compare and contrast the theme of initiation in Ellison's "Battle Royal" and Tan's "Two Kinds."
2. CONNECTIONS   Analyze the use of dialect in Wright's "The Man Who Was Almost a Man" and Tan's "Two Kinds."
3. CONNECTIONS   Compare and contrast the mother in Tan's "Two Kinds" with Olenka, the protagonist of Chekhov's "The Darling."

Related Commentary

Amy Tan, In the Canon, For All the Wrong Reasons, p. 1552.

Suggested Readings

Tan, Amy. *The Joy Luck Club*. New York: Ballantine, 1989.
———. "The Language of Discretion." *The State of the Language.* Ed. Christopher Ricks. Berkeley: U of California P, 1990.

JAMES THURBER

The Secret Life of Walter Mitty (p. 1274)

Like a good joke, a successful comic story may be easy to enjoy but hard to explain. Thurber has rendered his hero so convincingly that "Walter Mitty" has long since entered the popular vocabulary as a shorthand term for a certain personality type. The triumph of the story does not come, however, at the expense of the henpecked and bullied daydreamer. Stephen A. Black rightly points out that Mitty's escapism risks a denial of the self in its retreat from reality, but it is important to note that Mitty's fantasy life, despite its dependence on pulp fiction clichés, is just as real on the page as his (equally stereotypical) impatient and condescending wife, the officious policeman, and the insolent parking-lot attendant. Thus the reader may respond with admiration to Mitty's imaginary competence, courage, and grace under pressure.

Throughout the story Thurber uses things from the real environment to trigger Mitty's fantasies, but he also shows that the fantasies can have an impact on his actual life. The phrase "You miserable cur" reminds Mitty of the forgotten puppy biscuit. Near the end, after the sergeant tells "Captain Mitty" that "It's forty kilometers through hell, sir," Mitty has his life in Connecticut in mind when he musingly replies, "After all, . . . what isn't?" In his fantasy, "the box barrage is closing in," but Mitty is just as courageous in standing up to the salvo of questions and criticism launched moments later by his wife, which elicits his vague remark, "Things close in." As he stands against the drugstore wall in the Waterbury rain to face the imaginary firing squad, the reader can agree that he *is* "Walter Mitty the Undefeated" — because his inner life remains, for his banal tormentors, "inscrutable to the last."

WILLIAM E. SHEIDLEY

Questions for Discussion

1. What is Walter Mitty actually doing in the first paragraph of the story?
2. Explain Mitty's attitude toward his wife. Why does she insist that he wear gloves and overshoes?
3. How familiar is Walter Mitty with medical terminology? What is the purpose for Mitty of his medical fantasy?
4. Do Mitty's fantasies help or hinder him in dealing with reality?
5. Explain Mitty's statement that "things close in."
6. Where do you think Walter Mitty gets his ideas of heroism? Is there any sense in which his real life can be called heroic?

Topics for Writing

1. Describe Walter Mitty's final wish.
2. Discuss the romantic and the banal: the basis of Thurber's humor in "The Secret Life of Walter Mitty."
3. Find as many connections as possible between Mitty's actual experiences and his fantasies. How are they related? What do you think will be the consequence, if any, of Mitty's imaginary execution?

Suggested Readings

Black, Stephen A. *James Thurber — His Masquerades: A Critical Study.* The Hague: Mouton, 1970. 15, 18–19, 32, 42–43, 49–50, 54, 56, 119.
Morseburger, Robert E. *James Thurber.* Twayne's United States Authors Series 62. New York: Twayne, 1964. 18–19, 44–48, 123, 151–52.

LEO TOLSTOY

The Death of Ivan Ilych (p. 1279)

No one who comes to "The Death of Ivan Ilych" from a direction other than that of *War and Peace* and *Anna Karenina* is likely to share the opinion of some Tolstoy scholars that it is parable-thin in its evocation of life, providing only a transparent surface of detail through which Tolstoy's allegorical intentions are exposed. The story is studded with brilliantly realistic representations of experiences that the reader encounters with a twinge of sometimes embarrassed recognition — Peter Ivanovich's struggle with the pouffe, for example. But it is nonetheless a product of the period following Tolstoy's religious crisis and a story written by one whose explicit theory of art rested on a utilitarian moral didacticism.

The story's effectiveness depends on Tolstoy's avoiding, until the last possible moment, preaching the sermon that, as the headnote suggests, he eventually means to preach. The opening section places us in the shoes of Peter Ivanovich, causing us to sympathize with the desire to look away from death, at the same time that it subjects that desire to a devastating satiric attack. Then, by returning to a long chronological survey of Ivan Ilych's life, Tolstoy forces us to do exactly the opposite of what Peter Ivanovich does: to confront death and its meaning in an extended and excruciatingly matter-of-fact account. What we see is not a life, but a death — or a life viewed as death. For Ivan Ilych's life, as he eventually comes to realize, is a slow but accelerating process of dying. The narration, however, decelerates, so that the reader may expect it to be nearly over around section VI, whereas in fact there are six more (albeit shorter) sections to come, containing a series of painful revelations that burst through the screen Ivan Ilych has built up to hide himself from reality.

Tolstoy tortures the reader just as Ivan Ilych is tortured, so that the precept finally advanced by the story arrives as the answer to the reader's fervent need. Ivan Ilych is not a particularly bad man; and — bad or good — all men, as Gerasim remarks, come to the same spot. Tolstoy makes this recognition virtually intolerable by his vivid rendering of Ivan Ilych's suffering. Then he offers a way out by proposing that one simple motion of the soul toward charity can release the sufferer from his mortal anguish. Tolstoy prepares us for this revelation by stressing the relief Ivan Ilych finds in the kindness of Gerasim, whose health, strength, and repose are bound up with his simple acceptance of sickness and death as necessary parts of life. Some critics have claimed that Tolstoy's art fails to encompass the illumination Ivan Ilych receives at the end, which rests on doctrines extrinsic to the text; but at least it can be said that he avoids sentimental piety by providing for an ironic interpretation when he caps Ivan Ilych's triumphant assertion "Death is finished. . . . It is no more!" with the paradoxical conclusion "He drew in a breath, stopped in the midst of a sigh, stretched out, and died."

The preoccupations and activities of Ivan Ilych and his peers during Ilych's lifetime in the society portrayed by Tolstoy contrast sharply with those of the unselfish peasant Gerasim. They are directed to no constructive end, serving only to gratify the ego with a sense of power and to hide the fear of death under a surface awareness of pleasure and propriety. Ivan Ilych is never more content than when manipulating the inert objects which are so plentiful in the story — as when decorating his new house — and he does his best to relate to people as he relates to things, insulating himself from true human contact. After he has received his death blow from the quite inert knob of a window frame, however, Ivan Ilych experiences a similar dehumanizing treatment by the doctors, his wife, and his friends, none of whom can bear to face the implications of his evident mortality. As his sickness steadily reduces him to a state of infantile dependency, Ilych comes to recognize first his own powerlessness and then the error in his strategy of living. Finally, as the coffin-womb he has built for himself falls away and he is reborn into the light of spiritual understanding, he sees the fundamental truth he has worked so hard to deny: The feelings of others are as real as his own. At this moment, moved by pity for his wife and son, he at last finds something worthwhile to do; and, in doing it, he attains the sense of ease and "rightness" that has previously eluded him. That the single positive act of Ivan Ilych's life is to die may be seen as either a grim irony or an exciting revelation, depending on the perspective from which the reader views it. But either way the conclusion of the story embodies the kernel of Tolstoy's social theme. As Edward Wasiolek puts it, "Death for Tolstoy now, as the supremely shared experience, is the model of all solidarity, and only the profound consciousness of its significance can bring one to the communion of true brotherhood."

WILLIAM E. SHEIDLEY

Questions for Discussion

1. How does the authorial voice qualify our view of Ivan Ilych's survivors' reactions to his death in section I?
2. Evaluate Peter Ivanovich's view of Ivan Ilych's son when he meets him near the end of section I.
3. Comment on the implications of Ivan Ilych's hanging a medallion bearing the motto *respice finem* (consider your end) on his watch chain.
4. What is wrong with Ivan Ilych's marriage? with his work? with his ambitions?

5. By examining the authorial comments in sections III and IV, define the attitude toward Ivan Ilych that Tolstoy asks the reader to share. Does this attitude change?
6. Consider the opening sentence of section VI. Is this section a low point in the story? If so, what kind of rise ensues?
7. Why does Ivan Ilych find relief in having his legs supported by Gerasim?
8. What is the effect of the shift to the present tense about one-third of the way through section VIII?
9. In section IX, Ivan Ilych complains to God in language similar to that of Job. Compare and contrast their plights.
10. What is the meaning of Ivan Ilych's reversion to childhood shortly before his death?
11. How might Ivan Ilych's dream of the black sack be interpreted?

Topics for Writing

1. Stop after reading section I and write a paragraph or two on the theme and tone of the story as you understand them so far. After reading the rest of the story, write a paragraph evaluating your original response. Write an essay examining the opening section as a story in itself, but one fully understood only after reading sections II–XII.
2. Consider bridge as an epitome of the life Ivan Ilych and his friends try to live.
3. Discuss Tolstoy's use of symbolic, descriptive details in "The Death of Ivan Ilych."
4. Using "The Death of Ivan Ilych" as the basis of your knowledge of society, write a manifesto calling for revolution or reform.
5. Write a sermon, using the demise of Ivan Ilych Golovin as your occasion.

Related Commentaries

Peter Rudy, Tolstoy's Revisions in "The Death of Ivan Ilych," p. 1534.
Leo Tolstoy, Chekhov's Intent in "The Darling," p. 1556.

Related Story

Donald Barthelme, At the Tolstoy Museum, p. 129.

Suggested Readings

Christian, R. F. *Tolstoy: A Critical Introduction*. Cambridge: Cambridge UP, 1969. 236–38.
Greenwood, E. B. *Tolstoy: The Comprehensive Vision*. New York: St. Martin's, 1975. 118–23.
Simmons, Ernest J. *Introduction to Tolstoy's Writings*. Chicago: U of Chicago P, 1968. Esp. 148–50.
Wasiolek, Edward. *Tolstoy's Major Fiction*. Chicago: U of Chicago P, 1978. Esp. 165–79.

John Updike

A & P (p. 1321)

Although Updike was a precociously successful writer who spent his apprenticeship living in New York City and writing for *The New Yorker* magazine, much of the strength of his writing stems from his ability to take the reader back to the atmosphere of the small town where he grew up. "A & P" showcases this ability. This story about a nineteen-year-old at a checkout counter in an A & P supermarket skillfully sustains the point of view of a teenage boy from a small-town working-class family.

The incident the story describes is slight. What gives "A & P" its substance is the voice of the narrator. He is obviously what the author thinks of as an ordinary teenager, impatient with old people, not interested in his job, and deeply aroused by girls. The longest descriptive passage — almost a third of the story itself — dwells on the body of one of the girls; as the story's slight action unfolds, the bodies of that girl and one of her friends are mentioned several times again. The narrator's adolescent desire and adoration are amusingly played off his clumsy bravado and the idiom of sexist stereotypes he is trying to master. "You never know for sure how girls' minds work (do you really think it's a mind in there or just a little buzz like a bee in a glass jar?)." His view of adult women is no less callow: "We're right in the middle of town, and the women generally put on a shirt or shorts or something before they get out of the car into the street. And anyway these are usually women with six children and varicose veins mapping their legs and nobody, including them, could care less."

It is probably true that when the story was written, in the late 1950s, its attitudes were not considered unusual. Today we have to ask ourselves whether the deplorable sexism is redeemed by the artfulness of the story, the technique Updike brings to constructing his narrator's voice.

Questions for Discussion

1. What does the language of the story tell us about the narrator's social background?
2. Are there any details in the story that place it in a specific part of the United States, or could it be happening anywhere within a few miles of a beach? Explain.
3. Is the boy's discomfort with older people limited to women, or is he also uncomfortable with men? Is there anyone in the store he *is* comfortable with? Explain.
4. Do you think Updike shares the narrator's attitudes?

Topics for Writing

1. Analyze the strengths and the limitations of the first-person narrative in "A & P."
2. **CONNECTIONS** Consider "acting like a man": the bag boy in Updike's "A & P" and Dave in Wright's "The Man Who Was Almost a Man."

3.   **CONNECTIONS**   Compare and contrast adolescent narrators in Updike's "A & P" and Joyce's "Araby."

Related Commentary

John Updike, Kafka and "The Metamorphosis," p. 1561.

Suggested Readings

Cantor, Jay. "On Giving Birth to One's Own Mother." *TriQuarterly* 75 (Spring–Summer 1989): 78–91.

Detweiler, Robert. *John Updike*. Rev. ed. Boston: G. K. Hall, 1987.

Fleischauer, John F. "John Updike's Prose Style: Definition at the Periphery of Meaning." *Critique: Studies in Contemporary Fiction* 30.4 (Summer 1989): 277–90.

Greiner, Donald J. *The Other Updike: Poems, Short Stories, Prose, Play.* Columbus: Ohio UP, 1981.

Luscher, Robert M. "John Updike's Olinger Stories: New Light among the Shadows." *Journal of the Short Story in English* 11 (Autumn 1988): 99–117.

Lyons, E. "John Updike: The Beginning and the End." *Critique* 14.2 (1972): 44–59.

Newman, Judie. *John Updike*. New York: St. Martin's, 1988.

Samuels, C. T. "Art of Fiction: John Updike." *Paris Review* 12 (1968): 84–117.

Seib, P. "Lovely Way through Life: An Interview with John Updike." *Southwest Review* 66 (1981): 341–50.

Taylor, Charles C. *John Updike: A Bibliography*. Ann Arbor, MI: Books Demand UMI, 1989.

Thorburn, David, and Howard Eiland. *John Updike: A Collection of Critical Essays.* New York: Prentice-Hall, 1979.

Updike, John. *Hugging the Shore*. New York: Random House, 1983.

———. *Picked-Up Pieces*. New York: Knopf, 1976.

———. *Too Far to Go*. New York: Ballantine, 1979.

Wilhelm, Albert E. "Rebecca Cune: Updike's Wedge Between the Maples." *Notes on Modern American Literature* 7.2 (Fall 1983): Item 9.

———. "The Trail-of-Bread-Crumbs Motif in Updike's Maples Stories." *Studies in Short Fiction* 25.1 (Winter 1988): 71–73.

HELENA MARÍA VIRAMONTES

The Moths (p. 1327)

Although Viramontes has written in many styles, this story shows the influence of one of her teachers, Nobel Prize–winner Gabriel García Márquez. It has close affinities to the subject matter and the characters of a typical García Márquez story, and the literary style reflects García Márquez's commitment to magic realism. Viramontes's magic realism, however, is more rooted in the everyday than that of many other writers using this idiom, and her story about a girl's difficult relationship with her mother and her sisters reflects Viramontes's American upbringing. Students will likely have a strong response to the story's imagery and to the unyielding tale the girl tells of her grandmother's death. The image of small gray moths that come from her grandmother's soul and flutter out of her mouth at the moment of her death is unforgettable, and like so much of the metaphor and symbolism that is at the root of magic realist technique, it is never adequately explained. It is up to Viramontes's readers to make what they can of it.

Students will find it helpful in studying the story to follow one image through various points in the narrative. An image we can follow is the girl's hands. For Viramontes, the girl's hands become a symbol of her emotional difficulties with her family. Already in the second paragraph we are told that one reason the girl didn't fit in with her sisters was that her hands "were too big to handle the fineries of crocheting or embroidery." Her sisters have given her the cruel nickname "bull hands." The girl tells us casually that because she had doubted her grandmother's cure for her fever, her hands "grow like a liar's nose." Her grandmother cures her swollen hands with "a balm [made] out of dried moth wings and Vicks." When the girl tries to talk to her mother about the seriousness of her grandmother's illness, she feels her hands "hanging helplessly" by her side. She falls asleep and is awakened when her hands fall from her lap. As she crushes the chili peppers for her grandmother's tripe stew, she describes herself as doing it with her "bull hand."

Viramontes is not afraid to take chances, and her language is as startling as her imagery. The girl speaks of her grandmother's "pasty gray eye" beaming at her and "burning holes" in her suspicions about the old woman's folk medicines. She talks of a sunset as a moment when "the sun is finally defeated, finally sinks into the realization that it cannot with all its power to heal or burn, exist forever." Beneath the verbal fireworks, however, Viramontes has a simple story to tell. The girl is hardened by the verbal abuse and the whippings she has received at the hands of her family. Only her grandmother has let her escape from them into something like an ordinary life. When the grandmother dies the girl is alone, and she carefully cleans the old woman's body, taking her grandmother into the bathtub with her, holding her in her arms. Sitting in the water with the body, she is finally able to cry. Students will respond to the story's literary qualities — to its language and poetic imagery — but they will first be moved by the immediacy and the poignancy of the girl's experience.

Questions for Discussion

1. Discuss the image of the girl's hands and how the obsession with her hands follows her through the story.
2. One of the girl's difficulties with her family is her refusal to attend church. What does she experience the one time in the story she does visit a chapel?
3. Much of the girl's protest against her family sounds like a typical American teenager's complaints. What is different, or not different, about her complaints about her Latino family?
4. The story jumps from one time frame to another as the girl remembers her life with her *abuelita*. At what moment is the story occurring? How do we know it from the text?
5. How does the author relate the moment of the old woman's death to the eternal rhythms of life and our experience?

6. What is the contrast the author intends when she describes the water running into the bath as filled with "vitality and steam"?
7. Discuss what the author is telling us when she says that the girl, after her grandmother's death, "wanted to go to where the moths were"?
8. Discuss the symbolism of the moths.

Topics for Writing

1. In the same sentence in which Viramontes tells us that the protagonist's sisters have nicknamed her "bull hands," Viramontes describes her sisters' "waterlike voices," using a strong simile. Find other strong similes and metaphors in the text and discuss their importance to the story.
2. When the girl challenges her family's belief in the grandmother's folk medicine, she is challenging their adherence to old-fashioned traditions the way that many young people do. Analyze how this challenge is developed and resolved in the narrative.

Suggested Reading

Viramontes, Helena María, and Maria Herrera-Sobek, eds. *Chicana Creativity and Criticism: New Frontiers in American Literature.* Albuquerque: U of New Mexico P, 1996.

KURT VONNEGUT JR.

Harrison Bergeron (p. 1332)

This humorous fantasy story deserves to become a classic in American literature, like James Thurber's "The Secret Life of Walter Mitty." Vonnegut has stretched the basic premise of American democracy — that all men (and women) are created equal — to its literal limit. In his opening paragraph he explains how this admirable social ideal was realized in the year 2081, and then he shows the consequences of the idea as experienced in the family life of George and Hazel Bergeron and their fourteen-year-old son Harrison.

As a storyteller, Vonnegut makes good use of the traditional elements of fiction in structuring a conventional plot, but you could point out to students that the most dramatic events of the plot (ironically enough) occur in a television program that George and Hazel are watching together in their living room, parodying the "normal" activities of the average twenty-first-century family. On the screen, they see their son shot and killed by the U.S. Handicapper General in a television studio after he has defied the law of the land by freeing himself, a beautiful ballerina, and several musicians of their handicaps.

The most memorable aspect of Vonnegut's story is his description of the effect of the handicap on George Bergeron — the various noises of buzzers, ball peen hammers, and riveting guns transmitted by his "ear radio" are guaranteed to keep him from thinking about anything for too long. Their effect is terribly painful, as it is meant to be. By destroying individual human thought, the government has created a nation of sheep, content in their passivity to accept whatever they see on television, including the murder of their only son.

Questions for Discussion

1. How does the "ear radio" worn by everyone possessing above-normal intelligence in Vonnegut's story anticipate the earphones worn now by people listening to tapes and CDs?
2. How do the noises transmitted by George Bergeron's earphones suggest the effect of the frequent television advertisements infiltrating programs broadcast by the media today?
3. In what way does "Harrison Bergeron" contradict the idea of human equality at the basis of democracy in the United States? How can you defend the idea, despite what happens in the story?
4. Why doesn't Hazel wear a handicap? How does George deal with his handicap?
5. Why isn't Harrison content with the status quo? Does his age alone (fourteen) adequately explain his rebellion against the laws of his society?

Topic for Writing

1. Analyze Vonnegut's use of simile and metaphor in "Harrison Bergeron" to suggest the emotional effect of the handicap radio on George Bergeron.

Suggested Reading

Vonnegut, Kurt, Jr. *Welcome to the Monkey House.* New York: Dell, 1968.

ALICE WALKER

Roselily (p. 1337)

This is the story of a black woman, Roselily, on her wedding day. Contrary to what we might expect, however, the tone is not joyful, but tense and apprehensive. Roselily is full of doubts, about herself and the man who will soon be her husband. Her motivation to marry this man is not love of him as an individual. In fact, she admits she "does not even know if she loves him." What she does love are some of his qualities and properties, "his sobriety," "his pride," "his blackness," "his gray car," "his understanding of her *condition*," and, most important, his ability to "free her" from her current life. And what of his love for her? Roselily is realistic enough to know that he loves her, but again, she admits, he does not love her because of who she is. She acknowledges that "he will make [an effort] to redo her into what he truly wants." We are left with a picture of a woman trying to escape her past by marrying a man who will "free her" to "be respectable and respected and free" and a man marrying out of an apparent desire to reform.

"Roselily" has as its seminal concept the number *two*. It presents two oppo-site individuals at a crucial moment in their lives. Yet, as they symbolically fuse their lives into a single relationship, each brings very different experiences and backgrounds to the marriage. Roselily knows only the southern, small town, coun-try way of life, complete with its provincial religious beliefs and its sense of con-nectedness with family and community. Her husband is "against this." A northerner from Chicago, his ways are city ways, his religious beliefs are alien and restrictive. Rather than a feeling of community, he knows independence and anonymity.

Roselily wants freedom: "She wants to live for once. But doesn't know quite what that means. Wonders if she has ever done it. If she ever will." She spends the entire ceremony rationalizing that this marriage is the right thing to do, despite the fact that she "feels shut away from" this man. By the last paragraph she is finally able to formulate her feelings: "She feels ignorant, *wrong*, backward." By then, however, it is too late. The ceremony is complete, and "her husband's hand is like the clasp of an iron gate."

The structural framework for "Roselily" is the Christian marriage ceremony. It provides form as well as forward movement for a story that is essentially a stream-of-consciousness remembrance and narrative of the lead character, Roselily, from a third-person point of view. Contrast is the subject of the story. Conflict is the theme.

The title, "Roselily," does more than introduce the heroine. It also foreshad-ows the scope of the story. The rose becomes a lily. By means of the marriage vows, Roselily changes from a woman who is passionate, natural, and, in the eyes of society, impure and immoral to one who is resurrected and reborn, but pas-sionless and dead. For a price, she gains respectability. Now she must decide whether or not the cost is equal to the value. The conflict has not been resolved; it has only been postponed.

Questions for Discussion

1. Walker uses the marriage service to break up Roselily's reflections. What does this particular structure emphasize? What effect does it create?
2. Roselily's first passage opens with her dreaming of "dragging herself across the world. A small girl in her mother's white robe and veil, knee raised waist high through a bowl of quicksand soup." What subjects in these sen-tences persist throughout this story? Describe the qualities of this girl that reflect Roselily's own representation of herself in this story. Is she helpless, vulnerable, childish, struggling, or playacting?
3. Why does Roselily spend so much time thinking about her fourth child's father? Do we know as much about the man she is marrying as we do about her ex-lover? What do Roselily's reflections on his character tell us about hers?
4. What does Roselily's fourth child, the one she gave to his father, represent? What kind of a connection does she feel to the child? Can she imagine his future?
5. Part of Roselily's reflections are devoted to wondering "what one does with memories in a brand-new life." What alternatives are open to her? Can she just shut her memories away, or break them off and start again? Consider

the question of memory and the burden of the past against her sudden dream of having no children. Roselily's own mother is dead, yet Roselily still feels a connection to her. What are the "ghosts" that Roselily believes in?

6. Much of this story depends on oppositions. "Her husband's hand," Roselily thinks, "is like the clasp of an iron gate." What are the positive and negative qualities of an iron gate? Roselily thinks of "ropes, chains, handcuffs, his religion." What other images does she associate with this man she is marrying? He's going to "free her." How do you reconcile the images of bondage and freedom? Consider the diction in this passage: "A romantic hush. Proposal. Promises. A new life! Respectable, reclaimed, renewed. Free! In robe and veil." Yet suddenly, Walker presents "a rat trapped, concerned, scurrying to and fro in her head, peering through the windows of her eyes." What is the difference in the language in both examples? Is one kind of diction stronger than the other? Why?

7. What do you infer about Roselily's feelings from these sentences: "The rest she does not hear. She feels a kiss, passionate, rousing, within the general pandemonium. Cars drive up blowing their horns. Firecrackers go off. Dogs come from under the house and begin to yelp and bark." Look first at the syntax of these sentences. Why do you think they are all short and unconnected to one another? What effect does that create? What is the subject of each sentence? Why might Roselily only be able to receive certain kinds of impressions?

8. How do you interpret the final paragraph of this story? Does this paragraph control your understanding of the story retrospectively? How did you weigh the oppositions until this paragraph? Were Roselily's hopes and fears in equilibrium? Which words carry the heaviest burden of meaning for you? Would the paragraph — and your judgment — be very different without them?

Topics for Writing

1. Contrast Roselily's culture and environment and those of her husband-to-be.
2. Discuss the disparity between Roselily's dreams and her situation.
3. Describe the point of view in "Roselily."
4. Think back in your own life to a time when your thoughts received stimulation from an outside event but were not totally controlled by that event. Try to re-create your thought patterns and structure them into an interesting narrative account.
5. **CONNECTIONS** Compare and contrast the concept of marriage in Walker's "Roselily" and Lawrence's "Odour of Chrysanthemums."

Related Commentary

Alice Walker, Zora Neale Hurston: A Cautionary Tale and a Partisan View, p. 1564.

Suggested Readings

Banks, Erma Davis, and Keith Byerman. *Alice Walker: An Annotated Bibliography 1968–1986.* New York: Garland, 1989.

Bell, Roseann P., Bettye J. Parker, and Beverly Guy-Sheftall, eds. *Sturdy Black Bridges: Visions of Black Women in Literature.* New York: Anchor, 1979.

Bloom, Harold. *Alice Walker.* New York: Chelsea House, 1990.

Byerman, Keith, and Erma Banks. "Alice Walker: A Selected Bibliography, 1968–1988." *Callaloo: An Afro-American and African Journal of Arts and Letters* 12.2 (Spring 1989): 343–45.

Byrne, Mary Ellen. "Welty's 'A Worn Path' and Walker's 'Everyday Use': Companion Pieces." *Teaching English in a Two-Year College* 16.2 (May 1989): 129–33.

Cooke, Michael. *Afro-American Literature in the Twentieth Century: The Achievement of Intimacy.* New Haven: Yale UP, 1984.

Davis, T. M. "Alice Walker's Celebration of Self in Southern Generations." *Women Writers of the Contemporary South.* Ed. Peggy Whitman Prenshaw. Jackson: UP of Mississippi, 1984. 83–94.

Erickson, P. "Cast Out Alone/To Heal/and Re-create/Ourselves: Family Based Identity in the Work of Alice Walker." *College Language Association Journal* 23 (1979): 71–94.

Evans, Mari, ed. *Black Women Writers (1950–1980): A Critical Evaluation.* New York: Anchor, 1984. 453–95.

Mariani, Philomena, ed. *Critical Fictions: The Politics of Imaginative Writing.* Seattle: Bay, 1991.

Petry, Alice Hall. "Alice Walker: The Achievement of the Short Fiction." *Modern Language Studies* 19.1 (Winter 1989): 12–27.

Stade, G. "Womanist Fiction and Male Characters." *Partisan Review* 52 (1985): 265–70.

Winchell, Donna Haisty. *Alice Walker.* Boston: Twayne, 1990.

EUDORA WELTY

Why I Live at the P.O. (p. 1342)

This story may be troublesome to some readers, especially if they have been sensitized to racial issues in short fiction through a discussion of Achebe's criticism of Conrad's "Heart of Darkness." The word "nigger" used as a racial slur occurs three times in Welty's story. The narrator who uses the word is clearly an uneducated bigot, but her contempt for people of color living in her community is underscored by her assumption that they are fit only for the lowest kind of work. Here are the passages concerned:

> So I merely slammed the door behind me and went down and made some green-tomato pickle. Somebody had to do it. Of course Mama had turned both the niggers loose; she always said no earthly power could hold one anyway on the Fourth of July, so she wouldn't even try. It turned out that Jaypan fell in the lake and came within a very narrow limit of drowning.

> There was a nigger girl going along on a little wagon right in front. "Nigger girl," I says, "come help me haul these things down the hill, I'm going to live in the post office." Took her nine trips in her express wagon. Uncle Rondo came out on the porch and threw her a nickel.

In both cases, African Americans are assumed to be stupid workhorses, barely tolerated as human beings and undeserving of respect. In the first instance the two house servants are "turned loose" (like animals?) on the Fourth of July, but they are so immature and irresponsible that they go wild on their chance to celebrate Independence Day (irony?); they get drunk, and one of them, Jaypan, nearly drowns. In the second case, African Americans are presumed to be so stupid that a black child won't mind stopping her play with a wagon to help move a white woman; the child will also be satisfied being paid a pittance for working so hard. Welty is writing a humorous story, of course, told from the point of view of a Mississippi cracker, but humor doesn't negate the racism, any more than Marlowe's naiveté condones his judgments about Africans in "Heart of Darkness." Racist jokes aren't any more tolerable because they are meant to be "funny."

Insensitive literary critics discussing "Why I Live at the P.O." usually comment on "the exasperation and frustration, loneliness and near-madness" of the narrator, trapped in a provincial Mississippi town. Or they view her as "a solid and practical person struggling to keep her self-possession and balance in the midst of a childish, neurotic, and bizarre family." In Welty's commentary on the story, she stresses the normalcy of characters like Sister (the narrator) and her family in the South. Thrown against one another with limited social resources, they bicker and feud but usually reconcile their differences, because family solidarity is important to them. At the end of the story we learn that Sister's outburst has been provoked after five days of living by herself in the post office; Welty has said that once the character's anger has cooled, she'd move back home. She writes, "I was trying to show how, in these tiny little places such as where they come from, the only entertainment people have is dramatizing the family situation, which they do fully knowing what they are doing. They're having a good time. They're not caught up; it's not pathological. It's a Southern kind of exaggeration."

Questions for Discussion

1. Can we equate Sister's voice with Welty's opinions? Explain.
2. Does the humor in the story soften or increase the tension between the members of the family? Why or why not?
3. Why do the two sisters fight so much?

Topics for Writing

1. Retell the story through the eyes of the house servant Jaypan or the little girl with the express wagon.
2. **CONNECTIONS** Compare Mississippi small towns as backgrounds for Welty's "Why I Live at the P.O." and Faulkner's "A Rose for Emily."

Suggested Readings

See page 244.

EUDORA WELTY

A Worn Path (p. 1351)

Try not to force the Christian or mythological schemes of allegory the story supports until you encourage students to savor the beauty of the literal narration. Phoenix Jackson is an embodiment of love, faith, sacrifice, charity, self-renunciation, and triumph over death in herself, quite apart from the typological implications of her name or the allusions to the stations of the cross in her journey. Phoenix transcends her merely archetypal significance just as she transcends the stereotype of old black mammies on which she is built. Welty accomplishes this act of creation by entering fully into the consciousness of her character. There she discovers the little child that still lives within the old woman and causes her to dream of chocolate cake, dance with a scarecrow, and delight in a Christmas toy. Phoenix is right when she says, "I wasn't as old as I thought," but she does not merit the condescension of the hunter's exclamation, "I know you old colored people! Wouldn't miss going to town to see Santa Claus!" Even in her greatest discomfort, lying in the weeds, losing her memory, getting her shoes tied, "stealing" a nickel, or taking one as a handout, Phoenix retains her invincible dignity, an essential component of the single glimpse we receive of her triumphant homeward march, bearing aloft the bright symbol of life she has retrieved through her exertions.

In her comments on the story (included in Part Two, p. 1566), Welty implies that the meaning of Phoenix's journey is that of any human exertion carried out in good faith despite the uncertainty of the outcome: "The path is the thing that matters." In keeping with this theme, Welty repeatedly shows Phoenix asserting life in the face of death. Her name itself, taken from the mythical bird that periodically immolates itself and rises reborn from its ashes, embodies the idea. (She even makes a noise like "a solitary little bird" in the first paragraph.) Phoenix makes her journey at the time of the death and rebirth of the year; her own skin color is like the sun bursting through darkness; she overcomes discouragement as she tops the hill; she extricates herself from a thorn bush (of which much may be made in a Christian allegorical interpretation); she passes "big dead trees" and a buzzard; she traverses a field of dead corn; she sees a "ghost" that turns out to be a dancing scarecrow; she is overcome by a "black dog" but rescued by a death-dealing hunter whose gun she faces down and whom she beats out of a shiny nickel; and she emerges from a deathlike trance in the doctor's office to return with the medicine her grandson needs to stay alive. Phoenix's strength lies in the purpose of her journey, and her spirit is contagious. The hunter, the woman who ties her shoes, and the doctor's attendant all perform acts of charity toward her, and lest the reader overlook the one word that lies at the heart of Welty's vision, the nurse says "Charity" while "making a check mark in a book."

Questions for Discussion

1. Notice Phoenix's identification with "a solitary little bird." What other birds does she encounter on her journey? Explain their implications.
2. What techniques does Welty use to suggest the laboriousness of Phoenix's trip?

3. Before she crosses the creek, Phoenix says, "Now comes the trial." Does she pass it? How? To what extent is this event a microcosm of the whole story? Are there other microcosmic episodes?

4. What effect do Phoenix's sequential reactions to the scarecrow, the abandoned cabins, and the spring have on the reader's view of her?

5. What is your opinion of the hunter? What conclusion might be drawn from the fact that even though he kills birds and patronizes Phoenix, he helps her in a way he does not know?

6. Interpret the passage that begins with Phoenix bending for the nickel and ends with her parting from the hunter.

7. Describe Natchez as Phoenix perceives it. Is it a worthy culmination for her journey?

8. In her comments reprinted in Part Two (p. 1566), Welty remarks that Phoenix's victory comes when she sees the doctor's diploma "nailed up on the wall." In what sense is this moment the climax of the story? What is different about the ensuing action from the action that leads up to this moment? Are there any similarities?

9. How does Phoenix describe her grandson? What is Welty's reason for using these terms?

10. Explain the irony in the way the nurse records Phoenix's visit.

Topics for Writing

1. Explain why many readers think that Phoenix Jackson's grandson is dead.

2. Discuss the symbolism of birds in "A Worn Path."

3. After your first reading of "A Worn Path," write a paragraph giving your opinion of Phoenix Jackson. Then study some symbolic interpretations of the story (such as those by Ardelino, Isaacs, and Keys, cited in Suggested Readings). Reread the story and write another assessment of the central character. Does she bear up under the freight of symbolic meaning the critics ask her to carry? Does her relation to these archetypes help to account for your original response?

4. Read Welty's account of how she came to write "A Worn Path" (Part Two, p. 1566). Following her example, write an account of what you imagine to be the day's experience of someone you catch a glimpse of who strikes your fancy. Use the intimate interior third-person limited-omniscient point of view that Welty employs for Phoenix Jackson.

Related Commentaries

Eudora Welty, Is Phoenix Jackson's Grandson Really Dead?, p. 1566.
Eudora Welty, Plot and Character in Chekhov's "The Darling," p. 1568.

Suggested Readings

Ardelino, Frank. "Life out of Death: Ancient Myth and Ritual in Welty's 'A Worn Path.' " *Notes on Mississippi Writers* 9 (1976): 1–9.
Bloom, Harold. *Eudora Welty.* New York: Chelsea House, 1986.

Desmond, John F. *A Still Moment: Essay on the Art of Eudora Welty.* Metuchen, NJ: Scarecrow, 1978.

Isaacs, Neil D. "Life for Phoenix." *Sewanee Review* 71 (1963): 75–81.

Keys, Marilynn. " 'A Worn Path': The Way of Dispossession." *Studies in Short Fiction* 16 (1979): 354–56.

Kieft, Ruth M. *Eudora Welty.* Rev. ed. Boston: G. K. Hall, 1987.

MacNeil, Robert. *Eudora Welty: Seeing Black and White.* Westport, CT: Greenwood, 1990.

Phillips, Robert L., Jr. "A Structural Approach to Myth in the Fiction of Eudora Welty." *Eudora Welty: Critical Essays.* Ed. Peggy Whitman Prenshaw. Jackson: UP of Mississippi, 1979. 56–67, esp. 60.

Preenshaw, Peggy W., ed. *Eudora Welty: Thirteen Essays.* Jackson: UP of Mississippi, 1983.

Schmidt, Peter. *The Heart of the Story: Eudora Welty's Short Fiction.* Jackson: UP of Mississippi, 1991.

Turner, W. Craig, and Lee Harding, eds. *Critical Essays on Eudora Welty.* Boston: G. K. Hall, 1989.

Welty, Eudora. *The Eye of the Story.* New York: Vintage, 1990.

———. *One Writer's Beginnings.* New York: Warner, 1984.

EDITH WHARTON

Roman Fever (p. 1359)

Nearly every detail of this seemingly meandering narration that leads up to the final sequence of three dramatic revelations has a function in preparing for the climax. Wharton knits better than Grace Ansley, and her story does not fully unravel until the last words are spoken. When the secret is finally out, the reader experiences a flash of ironic insight that Wharton has been preparing from the beginning through her masterful delineation of the characters and their situation.

Face to face with "the great accumulated wreckage of passion and splendor" that spreads before them, and deserted in their advancing age by the pair of daughters who are now their sole concerns, the two widows may evoke the reader's condescending pity. They seem as small and pale as the images of one another each sees, in Wharton's metaphor, "through the wrong end of her little telescope." But as the two characters become differentiated, Alida Slade takes on depth and coloration. As the story of her flashy but parasitic life and of the jealousy and guilty resentment she has harbored toward her friend gradually emerges, the reader can no longer pity her but can hardly admire her either. Her revelation that it was she, not Delphin Slade, who wrote the letter inviting Grace to a tryst in the Colosseum may be unexpected, but it follows perfectly from her character as Wharton has established it. Its blow to Mrs. Ansley is severe, and it seems the more cruel to the reader, who has no reason as yet to revise the original estimate of her as merely pitiable. Mrs. Ansley staggers, but to the reader's surprise and gratification she gradually recovers herself. Impelled by the shock for once to assert herself, she caps Mrs. Slade's revelation with an even more dramatic one of her own.

Grace Ansley's reticence, and the quietness of her life in contrast to Alida Slade's, expresses neither emotional pallor nor weakness of character. She had the spunk to take what she wanted from Delphin Slade twenty-five years before, and she has been content with her memory ever since, not needing, as Alida Slade would have (and indeed *has*) needed, to get reassurance by parading her conquest in public. Thus, it is Mrs. Ansley who manifests greater independence and vitality. Mrs. Slade, by contrast, has been conventional and dependent. Widowhood is such an uncomfortable lot for her because she can no longer shine with the reflected brilliance of her husband. Barbara may be unlike Horace Ansley because Delphin Slade was really her father, but her differences from Jenny derive from the fact that Grace Ansley, not Alida Slade, is her mother.

Wharton has constructed her plot with a precision O. Henry would have admired, but she has based it less on contrivances of circumstance than on an understanding of her characters. By placing them in a setting that spans millennia — from ancient Rome to the airplane — she implies the universality of the passions, triumphs, and defeats that make up the lives of even these New York society ladies, whose wealth and status do not protect them from the human condition after all.

WILLIAM E. SHEIDLEY

Questions for Discussion

1. What do Barbara and Jenny think of their mothers? How accurate is their estimate?
2. Why does Grace Ansley place an "undefinable stress" on "me" and "I" in replying to Alida Slade's questions about her reaction to their view of the Roman ruins?
3. Why does Alida Slade consider Grace and Horace Ansley "two nullities"?
4. Compare and contrast the two ladies' responses to widowhood and advancing age. Who takes them harder? Why?
5. Alida Slade remembers that "Mrs. Horace Ansley, twenty-five years ago, had been exquisitely lovely." Explain the importance of this fact to Mrs. Slade, to Mrs. Ansley, and to the structure of the plot.
6. What is Roman fever — literally and figuratively?
7. Why has Alida Slade "always gone on hating" Grace Ansley?
8. What reaction does Alida Slade seem to have expected from Grace Ansley in response to her confession that she forged the letter? Why?
9. Alida Slade remarks, "Well, girls are ferocious sometimes." What about ladies?
10. Near the end of the story, why does Grace Ansley pity Alida Slade? Why does Mrs. Slade at first reject that pity?
11. Comment on the meaning of the way the ladies walk offstage.

Topics for Writing

1. Analyze the importance of setting in "Roman Fever."
2. Show how Wharton manipulates point of view in "Roman Fever."
3. Explain how "Roman Fever" conforms to Wharton's principles of the short story as stated in the excerpt from her book *The Writing of Fiction* (included in Part Two, p. 1570).

4. On your first reading of the story, mark passages whose significance is not entirely clear — such as Grace Ansley's peculiar intonations when acknowledging her memory of a former visit to Rome. After reading the story to the end, return to the marked passages and write explanations of them.
5. Which of the two ladies is more guilty of reprehensible behavior? Consider arguments on both sides, or organize a debate.
6. Write a story of your own about a secret that comes out or a misunderstanding that is resolved. Try to make both the perpetuation of the error or deception and the emergence of the truth dependent on character rather than circumstance.

Related Commentary

Edith Wharton, Every Subject Must Contain within Itself Its Own Dimensions, p. 1570.

Suggested Readings

Flynn, Dale Bachman. "Salamanders in the Fire: The Short Stories of Edith Wharton." *Dissertation Abstracts International* 45.12 (June 1985): 3638A.
Hollbrook, David. *Edith Wharton*. New York: St. Martin's, 1991.
Howe, Irving, ed. *Edith Wharton: A Collection of Critical Essays.* New York: Prentice-Hall, 1962.
Lewis, R. W. B. *Edith Wharton: A Biography.* New York: Harper, 1985.
McDowell, Margaret B. *Edith Wharton.* Boston: Twayne, 1991.
Petry, Alice Hall. "A Twist of Crimson Silk: Edith Wharton's 'Roman Fever.'" *Studies in Short Fiction* 24.2 (Spring 1987): 163–66.
Vita-Finzi, Penelope. *Edith Wharton and the Art of Fiction.* New York: St. Martin's, 1990.
Wharton, Edith. *The Collected Letters of Edith Wharton.* New York: Macmillan, 1987.
White, Barbara A. "Neglected Areas: Wharton's Short Stories and Incest, Part II." *Edith Wharton Review* 8.2 (Fall 1991): 3–10, 32.

John Edgar Wideman

All Stories Are True (p. 1369)

Wideman is one of the major figures of the the new renaissance of African American writing. His themes are drawn from everyday black experience, which he describes in a complex literary language. His view of black life is at once much harder and much more nuanced than the glimpse of black life in the story "Thank You, M'am," by Langston Hughes, which students might be asked to read for comparison. Already in the second sentence of his story, Wideman tells us that there is a problem with the life he is going to describe. The street "is quiet now, as peaceful as it gets here, as peaceful as it always stays in other neighborhoods." His story is an unrelenting and uncompromising presentation of the violence and hopelessness of the lives he has known too well. We are told first that the protagonist's mother has been undergoing chemotherapy, which means that she has been seriously ill with cancer, then the protagonist goes to visit his brother in prison, where his brother tells him that he has again been denied parole.

Despite everything that he is being forced to deal with, the protagonist doesn't take an easy way out. He could blame the white society for what is happening to his family, and there are places in the story where a character does flare up in anger at the racism that has been a factor in creating the society around them. But the protagonist's mother is suffering from cancer, the thief who stole the plants in the neighborhood was a drug addict, and the protagonist makes no effort to hide the fact that his brother is violent. The tragedy is that the prison system gives no help or support to the inmates. If the brother finally is released, he will return to the life he led before, without any new knowledge or training. The only thing he will have learned during his prison years is how to endure prison life.

The story ends with the unforgettable image of the prisoners and their visitors watching a leaf blown in the breeze as it swirls higher and higher, finally escaping beyond the wall. There is a burst of applause. Then the protagonist's brother adds a last detail: "The dumb thing blew back in here again." The implication of the leaf's failed flight is that the brother himself has some responsibility for what is happening to him. The story is richly conceived and thought-provoking. A phrase from the first paragraph perhaps best describes it: "A skein of life dragged bead by bead through a soft needle's eye."

Questions for Discussion

1. Do the students have the same response to the names of city streets as the story's protagonist?
2. The language used by the author and the manner of speech of the people in the story are very different. Is the author telling the reader that he has grown away from his own background? Does he disparage these people for their colloquial speech?
3. Discuss his metaphor of the giant tree as "a dark fist exploding through the asphalt, thrusting to the sky."
4. What does the protagonist mean when he says, "Bible people never were white to me"?
5. Discuss the importance of religion in the society the author is describing.
6. Why hasn't religion helped the protagonist's brother? What are some of the other factors that have destroyed his life?
7. Discuss the image of the leaf in the breeze.

Topics for Writing

1. The author uses language very freely in the story, often writing in incomplete sentences and using elliptical phrases and language. Discuss whether this use of language is an effective way for Wideman to present his story.
2. **CONNECTIONS** Compare this story with Langston Hughes's "Thank You, M'am" or Richard Wright's "The Man Who Was Almost a Man." Discuss the differences in their literary styles and their presentation of black life, using examples from the stories.

Suggested Readings

Wideman, John Edgar. *All Stories Are True.* New York: Random House, 1992.
———. *The Collected Stories of John Edgar Wideman.* New York: Pantheon, 1992.

WILLIAM CARLOS WILLIAMS

The Use of Force (p. 1381)

Although William Carlos Williams is best known as a poet, he also wrote a number of short stories, a successful play, and three novels chronicling the life of his wife's Norwegian immigrant family in the United States. Most of his short stories were written in the 1930s, during the Depression, and many of them were published in small magazines that were committed to the struggle for equality and social justice that dominated American intellectual life in those years. In the 1920s, when Williams was still thinking of himself as an experimental poet, he had written avant-garde prose, but the new stories, because of their political commitment, were written in a more direct style, and their subject matter was the ordinary life of the people who came to him as patients. The term for writing like this in the 1930s was "hard-hitting." Certainly Williams's new spare, unsentimental style was influenced by the stories of Ernest Hemingway, published several years earlier, but the setting in the poor neighborhoods of Rutherford, New Jersey, and the depressed, anxious people of the stories are his own.

The stubbornness of the girl in "The Use of Force" will remind some readers of the refusal of Melville's Bartleby to give in to authority in "Bartleby, the Scrivener," but Williams takes his story a step further. He reveals to the reader that the girl has a reason for her refusal to be examined. She is sick, and she is afraid of treatment. He also has the honesty to admit that he became so angry in the struggle with the girl that he felt pleasure in forcing her to give in.

The story certainly may suggest submerged sexual overtones to some readers in the fact that the patient is a girl and the doctor is trying to force a wooden instrument into her mouth, but there is nothing in the text to suggest that Williams intends to describe anything more than a professional visit to help a sick girl and her worried parents. Today we are more casual about infections like the one the girl is suffering from, but in Williams's time there were no antibiotics. He takes it for granted that his readers understand the necessity for him to get the girl's mouth open. To leave her as she is would probably be to leave her to die. As Williams writes, "I have seen at least two children lying dead in bed of neglect in such cases." He has to try to save her.

Questions for Discussion

1. Today, would a doctor try to examine a child's throat during a house call, or would the patient come to a medical office to have the preliminary examination performed by a nurse?
2. Williams tells us almost nothing about the kitchen where the girl is waiting or about the appearance of her parents. Why? (Students might suggest several possible answers.)

3. When Williams writes that the girl's parents "weren't telling me more than they had to," what is he saying about the relationship between a doctor and his patients?

4. The spare language of the story gives it some of the feeling of a medical report. Do students feel this is helpful or unhelpful in creating the mood of the story?

5. Is it stubbornness or terror that is driving the girl to act the way she is?

6. Why does the girl feel defeated when Williams finally is able to examine her throat? Does she comprehend that she is dangerously ill?

Topic for Writing

1. There have been many changes in the relationship between doctors and patients in the United States since Williams wrote the story. Discuss whether or not you feel that Williams would have been happy with the changes, using examples from the story.

Suggested Reading

Coles, Robert, ed. *William Carlos Williams: The Doctor Stories.* New York: New Directions, 1984.

TOBIAS WOLFF

Say Yes (p. 1384)

Tobias Wolff narrows the scope of "Say Yes" to zoom in on a seemingly ordinary evening in the life of a long-married couple. The unremarkable sequence of events nevertheless leads to the erotically charged atmosphere of the final paragraph. Through the routine domestic gestures of washing and drying dishes, attending to a cut finger, taking out garbage, mopping the floor, and magazine reading, Wolff manages to reveal much about the inner lives of these people. Their namelessness emphasizes their ordinariness.

A conversation about interracial marriage sets the story in motion. Early in the dialogue, after suggesting that interracial marriage is a bad idea (without being able to fully articulate his reasons), the husband, observing his wife's expression, realizes he should back off from the subject but instead presses forward. These two know each other intimately — know how to needle, cajole, hurt, and apologize in subtle and not-so-subtle ways. In fact, this very intimacy — as with most marriages — carries negative as well as positive meanings. The husband's insistence that "a person from their culture and a person from our culture could never really know each other" reflects back on the couple's own relationship, leading the reader to question the extent to which *any* two people can know each other. Taking out the garbage and observing the night stars, the husband reflects on his marriage. Ashamed of fighting, he realizes the depth of the intimacy he shares with his wife as well as the transitoriness of their relationship with an intensity that affects him physically. This epiphany transforms at least his short-term behavior. Where normally he would "heave rocks" at the two dogs that topple his garbage, in this instance he lets them go unharmed.

Back in the house, he apologizes in the terms of the earlier discussion of interracial marriage, which now becomes a fantasy when he affirms that he'd marry her even if she were black. This openness to unexplored possibilities recharges the erotic life of the couple. When his wife enters the room in the darkness, "his heart pound[s] the way it had on their first night together," as if they were strangers.

Questions for Discussion

1. Why doesn't the husband "keep his mouth shut" when he knows he should?
2. What do you think the husband means when he says, "A person from their culture and a person from our culture could never really know each other"? Do you agree? What are some advantages and disadvantages of intracultural versus intercultural romantic relationships?
3. Why does the husband not "heave rocks" at the dogs that topple his garbage on this occasion, as he normally would?
4. In the final paragraph, why is the husband so excited? Does he experience a positive, erotic excitement, or does he realize that he doesn't know his wife as well as he thought he did?
5. Why is the question "Would you have loved me if I had been black?" so important to the wife?
6. To whom does the title apply? Who is expected to say yes?

Topic for Writing

1. Discuss the role of domestic details in advancing characterization in "Say Yes." What do these details reveal about this couple and their marriage?

Suggested Readings

Wolff, Tobias. *Back in the World: Stories*. Boston: Houghton, 1985.
———. *The Barracks Thief and Other Stories*. New York: Bantam, 1984.
———. *In the Garden of the North American Martyrs: A Collection of Short Stories*. New York: Ecco, 1981.
Woodruff, Jay, ed. "In the Garden of the North American Martyrs." *A Piece of Work: Five Writers Discuss Their Revisions*. Iowa City: U of Iowa P, 1993.

Virginia Woolf

Kew Gardens (p. 1390)

This sketch might puzzle some students, since its point of view (clearly dictated by Woolf) seems so unusual. No particular person is having his or her story told. Rather, Woolf seems to be telling the story of a snail in a plot of flowers in

Kew Gardens. "Cosmic" rather than "omniscient" might be the best word to describe Woolf's perspective, which blends blue sky and green earth so closely as to exclude the people strolling the garden paths between the two elements.

Woolf's story is experimental, and her concentration as she attempts to record "the essential life" of the creatures in the garden is almost palpable. According to the critic Susan Dick, in 1919 Woolf learned from studying Chekhov that "inconclusive stories are legitimate." Dick goes on to say that the narrator in a typical story by Woolf functions "as a perceptive observer of the external scene. . . . [or] the narrator dramatizes from within the minds of the characters . . . their perceptions of themselves and their world." In "Kew Gardens," Woolf moves seamlessly in and out of her characters' minds, recording their thoughts and feelings more substantially than the actual words they exchange.

The thoughts and words of the first couple, a married pair with two children, shape the reader's expectations for the rest of the story. Simon, the husband, thinks of Lily, an earlier love, to whom he'd proposed marriage in Kew Gardens when he was young. He remembers the shoe she wore, "with the square silver buckle at the toe," which symbolized her attractiveness and her lack of interest in his proposal. His wife, Eleanor, when he asks her if she ever thinks of the past, answers him bluntly, perhaps jealous that he is thinking of the beautiful Lily. Eleanor's memory of past love in Kew Gardens is the kiss given to her by "an old grey-haired woman with a wart on her nose, the mother of all my kisses all my life." We hear no more of this old woman (Eleanor's art teacher?), and we are not told why the kiss was so unsettling that Eleanor's "hand shook all the afternoon so that I couldn't paint." The married couple leave with their children, as much strangers to us as when they appeared.

The snail is the next character, and his conflict is a physical problem: How should he get around a dead leaf? This shift to the nonhuman prepares the reader for Woolf's shift to a cosmic view. The couples on the garden paths are reduced to colors as she lets the descriptive elements of the scene dissolve "like drops of water in the yellow and green atmosphere." The heat of the summer afternoon overcomes everything, reducing the "gross and heavy bodies" to a drowsy torpidity, but their voices continue as a manifestation of their spiritual essence, "as if they were flames lolling from the thick waxen bodies of candles." The silence is found to be composed of pure sound, the sound of buses, people, and the petals of flowers, whose colors seem to Woolf to be heard in the air.

Questions for Discussion

1. How does Woolf organize her sketch so that her description seems continuous and coherent?
2. Describe the people in the scene. What other living elements in the garden are treated as characters?
3. What is Woolf's tone? To which social class does she belong? Comment on her treatment of the two "elderly women of the lower middle class." How are they described? What can you tell about Woolf's attitude toward them from the words they exchange?
4. What is Woolf's attitude toward romantic love? old age? Do these two elements serve as the extremes of dramatic human conflicts in her sketch? Explain.

Topics for Writing

1. Rewrite "Kew Gardens" as it might be the following afternoon, when it's raining.
2. Analyze Woolf's range of vocabulary in this sketch. How does she suggest a poetic atmosphere in her descriptions of the garden and its inhabitants and visitors?

Related Commentary

Katherine Mansfield, Review of Woolf's "Kew Gardens," p. 1500.

Suggested Readings

Baldwin, Dean. *Virginia Woolf: A Study of the Short Fiction*. Boston: Twayne, 1986.

Beja, Morris, ed. *Critical Essays on Virginia Woolf*. Boston: G. K. Hall, 1985.

Bishop, Edward L. "Pursuing 'It' Through 'Kew Gardens.'" *Studies in Short Fiction* 19.3 (Summer 1982): 269–75.

Homans, Margaret. *Virginia Woolf: A Collection of Critical Essays*. Englewood Cliffs, NJ: Prentice-Hall, 1993.

Marcus, Jane, ed. *New Feminist Essays on Virginia Woolf*. Lincoln: U of Nebraska P, 1981.

Oakland, John. "Virginia Woolf's *Kew Gardens*." *English Studies: A Journal of English Language and Literature* 68.3 (June 1987): 264–73.

Woolf, Virginia. *The Complete Shorter Fiction of Virginia Woolf*. San Diego: Harcourt, 1985.

———. *The Essays of Virginia Woolf*. San Diego: Harcourt, 1988.

RICHARD WRIGHT

The Man Who Was Almost a Man (p. 1396)

Dave Saunders dislikes being laughed at, and his discomfort at becoming an object of amusement for accidentally shooting old Jenny, the mule, precipitates his final step into manhood. Although the anecdote around which Wright builds the story is comical enough, the reader probably should accede to Dave's wish to be taken seriously, for the fate that lies ahead of this young man as he rolls toward his unknown destination atop a boxcar with nothing in his pocket but an unloaded gun is likely to be grim.

At the same time, however, Dave's self-esteem and independence deserve respect. At the beginning of the story he dissociates himself from the field hands and fixes on his ambition to declare his manhood by owning a gun. Throughout the story the idea that *boys* do not have guns recurs, and Dave not only wants a gun but also chafes at being call "boy" by his parents and at being treated as a child. Just before he goes out to master the gun and hop a freight, Dave grumbles, "They treat me like a mule, n then they beat me." His resolution to escape his inferior status will involve not only leaving home but taking potshots at the facade of white society just as he wants to shoot at "Jim Hawkins' big white house" in order "to let him know Dave Saunders is a man." The question Wright leaves hanging for the reader as his story trails off into ellipses is whether Dave has killed the mule in himself or whether he himself, like Jenny, may become the victim of his own wild shots.

WILLIAM E. SHEIDLEY

Questions for Discussion

1. Explain the pun in the last sentence of the first paragraph.
2. Define our first impression of Dave. What reasons do we have to admire him? to laugh at him? to pity him?
3. What does it take to be a man in the world of the story? Is a gun enough? How does one get a gun?
4. What is ironic about the way Dave gets the money to buy his gun?
5. How is Dave treated by his father? Why does Ma say of the gun, "It be fer Pa"?
6. With the gun under his pillow, Dave feels "a sense of power. Could kill a man with a gun like this. Kill anybody, black or white." What does Dave still have to learn before he can be called a man? How does the story bring it home to him?
7. Explain what happens the first time Dave fires the gun. What does he do differently the next time?
8. Why does Wright describe the death of the mule in such detail?
9. Explain why being laughed at is so painful for Dave. What might enable him to join in and laugh at himself?
10. Comment on the possible implications of Dave's remark "They treat me like a mule, n then they beat me," both within the story and in a broader social and historical context. Does Dave's killing the mule have a symbolic significance?
11. Where might Dave be headed as he hops on the Illinois Central? What might he find at the end of his journey?
12. Why is the title not "The Boy Who Was Almost a Man"?

Topics for Writing

1. Examine the tone of Wright's story.
2. Discuss the treatment of Wright's social themes in "The Man Who Was Almost a Man." (See the story's headnote.)
3. Write a sequel to Wright's story, another episode in the life of Dave Saunders — something that happens on the train ride or when he arrives in New Orleans or Chicago or wherever. Try to sustain and develop as many themes and motives already present in Wright's story as you can, but make the material your own by imagining what you think happens, not necessarily what you guess Wright would have written. Decide whether to adopt Wright's style and point of view or employ a different mode of narration. Remember that the story is set during the Great Depression.

Related Commentaries

Leslie Lee, Scene from the Screenplay of *Almos' a Man*, p. 1666.
Richard Wright, Reading Fiction, p. 1572.

Suggested Readings

Felgar, Robert. *Richard Wright*. Boston: Twayne, 1980.
Hakutani, Yoshinobu, ed. *Critical Essays on Richard Wright*. Boston: G. K. Hall, 1982.
Margolies, Edward. *The Art of Richard Wright*. Carbondale: Southern Illinois UP, 1969.
McCall, Dan. *The Example of Richard Wright*. New York: Harcourt, 1969.
Reilly, John M. *Richard Wright: The Critical Reception*. New York: Burt Franklin, 1978.
Wright, Richard. *Uncle Tom's Children*. New York: Harper, 1989.

CHRONOLOGICAL LISTING OF AUTHORS AND STORIES

Margaret Laurence (1926–1987)
The Mask of the Bear (1970)

Gabriel García Márquez (b. 1928)
A Very Old Man with Enormous Wings (1955)

Cynthia Ozick (b. 1928)
The Shawl (1980)

Ursula K. Le Guin (b. 1929)
The Ones Who Walk Away from Omelas (1976)

Chinua Achebe (b. 1930)
Civil Peace (1971)

John Barth (b. 1930)
On with the Story (1996)

Donald Barthelme (1931–1989)
At the Tolstoy Museum (1987)

Alice Munro (b. 1931)
Meneseteung (1990)

John Updike (b. 1932)
A & P (1961)

Philip Roth (b. 1933)
"I Always Wanted You to Admire My Fasting"; or, Looking at Kafka (1975)

Susan Sontag (b. 1933)
The Way We Live Now (1986)

Abe Akira (b. 1934)
Peaches (1972?)

Woody Allen (b. 1935)
The Kugelmass Episode (1977)

W. P. Kinsella (b. 1935)
Shoeless Joe Jackson Comes to Iowa (1979)

Don DeLillo (b. 1936)
Videotape (1996)

Carol Shields (b. 1936)
Mirrors (1995?)

Bessie Head (1937–1986)
Life (1977)

Raymond Carver (1938–1988)
Cathedral (1981)
Errand (1987)
What We Talk About When We Talk About Love (1981)

Joyce Carol Oates (b. 1938)
Where Are You Going, Where Have You Been? (1970)

Toni Cade Bambara (1939–1995)
The Lesson (1972)

Margaret Atwood (b. 1939)
Happy Endings (1983)
Death by Landscape (1991)

Angela Carter (1940–1992)
The Company of Wolves (1977)

Bharati Mukherjee (b. 1940)
The Management of Grief (1988)

John Edgar Wideman (b. 1941)
All Stories Are True (1993)

Bobbie Ann Mason (b. 1942)
Shiloh (1982)

Tess Gallagher (b. 1943)
Rain Flooding Your Campfire (1997)

Alice Walker (b. 1944)
Roselily (1973)

Tobias Wolff (b. 1945)
Say Yes (1985)

Tim O'Brien (b. 1946)
The Things They Carried (1986)

Ann Beattie (b. 1947)
The Burning House (1979)

Salman Rushdie (b. 1947)
The Firebird's Nest (1997)

Charles Johnson (b. 1948)
Menagerie, A Child's Fable (1984)

Leslie Marmon Silko (b. 1948)
Yellow Woman (1974)

Dorothy Allison (b. 1949)
River of Names (1994)

Jamaica Kincaid (b. 1949)
Girl (1984)

Amy Hempel (b. 1951)
In the Cemetery Where Al Jolson Is Buried (1985)

Amy Tan (b. 1952)
Two Kinds (1989)

THEMATIC INDEX

Story Pairs

On Writing

Fantasy and the Supernatural

Childhood

Adolescence and Initiation

Identity and Renewal

Love, Marriage, and Infidelity

Parents and Children

War and Revolution

Looking at the Wall